Getting Started With KPIs

Getting Started With KPIs

Step-by-Step KPI Guide for Ambitious Businesses

Bernie Smith

Metric Press
Sheffield, England

Published by Metric Press
60 Bromwich Road
Sheffield S8 0GG

Email: bernie@madetomeasureKPIs.com
Website: https://madetomeasureKPIs.com

First published in Great Britain in 2018

ISBN: 978-1-910047-02-6
British Library Cataloguing-in-Publication Data
A catalogue record for this book is available from the British Library

Library of Congress Cataloguing-in-Publication Data
A catalogue record for this book is available from the Library of Congress

Printed and bound in Great Britain

190318ING-S

Warning!

Big book alert!

You will have noticed there are lots of pages in this book. You will not have to read them **all**. **Ever**. The entire back half of the book (Section Two) is made up of ready-made KPI definitions for reference. As you follow each of the ROKS™ approach steps you will use just a **handful** of relevant definitions from Section Two, but you will barely touch most of that section.

Tip

Planning to read this 'on the road'?

This book is intended as a **practical manual** for picking KPIs for your organisation. If you are going to be reading it while travelling it's a good idea to download the free templates pack right now, so you have the templates when you need them. Here's the link...

Free templates registration link
https://goo.gl/DFrRyt
No Spam! Email registration required, but your details are **never** shared

Section One: Contents

Step 4: Tune KPI Definitions

Step 5: Dashboard and Report Build

Step 6: Go Live   **223**

Appendix: Cognitive Bias   **275**

Section Two: KPI Definitions

Warning!

This section is for **reference only**. It will make much more sense when you have worked your way through Section One of this book.

Financials

Health & Safety

Staff & Payroll

Recruitment

Equipment Investment

Property Investment

Efficiency - Widget Production

Efficiency - Hours

Efficiency - Per Word Billing

Efficiency - Contract Services

Efficiency - Service Delivery

Procurement & Supply

Fulfilment - Product & Services

Call, Email & Webchat Handling

Equipment Maintenance

Complaints & Incident Handling

Professional Qualification & Membership

Service Quality

Product Quality

Guarantee & Warranty

Acknowledgements

Thanks to Liz, my wife, for her patience and unending support. Thanks also to Karen Wood for her eagle-eyed-accountant feedback on the Finance KPIs, Jenny Emby for her incisive editing, Simon Snow for his expert review of the Contact Centre KPIs and to Dave Bishop, Matt Atkin and James Lawther for feedback. Special thanks to Simon Pearsall for his cartoons and wit.

Who this book is for

This book is for people who:

- Have the task of creating new KPIs for their organisation.
- Have been asked to improve or enhance existing KPIs.
- Need help with the practicalities of implementing a measurement system.

If you follow the steps laid out in this book you should end up with a measurement system that meets your needs. Crucially, you will have a structured and documented record showing how and why the system was developed in that way. You will also be clear on the limitations and assumptions that were made along the way - invaluable for future improvement.

About the author

Bernie Smith coaches businesses to develop meaningful KPIs and present their management information in the clearest possible way to support good decision-making.

As owner of Made to Measure KPIs he has worked with major organisations including HSBC, Airbus, UBS, Lloyd's Register, Credit Suisse, Sainsbury's Bank, Scottish Widows, Tesco Bank, Yorkshire Building Society and many others.

Previously, Bernie led teams delivering operational improvement in FTSE 100 companies using Lean and Six Sigma approaches. This work took him to the US to help paper manufacturers, to Finland to make olefins and to Wrexham to package cheese.

Bernie lives in Sheffield, UK, with his wife Liz, two children and some underused exercise equipment.

Introduction

Introduction

Why this book was written: a confession

I founded Made to Measure KPIs in 2007. It is a business focused entirely on coming up with meaningful performance measures for all kinds of organisations, from global banks and food manufacturers through to churches. I have spoken at international conferences and written books on KPIs, but for a long, long time *I didn't measure anything in my own business*: nothing at all. I was like the cobbler whose children went barefoot. I worked with a wide range of brand-name businesses, helping them put the right performance measures in place, but had almost nothing written down about how *my* own business was performing, or even what its objectives were.

What I *did* have was a long list of things that I felt I *should* be doing swirling around my head. My days were filled with the simple goals of making money and growing the business. All the time there was one nagging, guilty thought… 'I really should *measure* more things in my business'.

Eventually I realised this situation was stupid and embarrassing and it was time to sort out my own KPIs. This book and the ROKS Express™ approach are the products of that journey.

What this book will, and won't, do for you…

The approach used in this book does not assume any prior KPI experience, but it has been tested in a wide range of businesses around the globe and is based on 'what works'.

This guide is a 'getting started' guide. To keep it simple, I have made some reasonable assumptions about the typical types of objectives for small and medium-sized businesses. If you have highly unusual objectives or processes, then this book may not give you *all* the KPIs you need: you will also need the ROKS Express Advanced™ method to cover *everything*. Once you have worked your way through this book, head over to madetomeasureKPIs.com and take a look at ROKS Express Advanced™. The ROKS Express Advanced™ method is designed to help in unusual cases and to fine tune and build on the KPIs you first developed using the basic ROKS Express™ method.

This book will help you select a handful of powerful and effective performance measures as quickly as possible. It's designed to get you started with a tailored selection of the best KPIs for *your* type of business.

To make things as painless as possible, it includes a library of over four hundred fundamental, pre-defined, KPIs to choose from. Example calculations are also shown using case-study example businesses. Included with this book is exclusive access to free Excel dashboards, and many other goodies, to get you up and running as quickly as possible…

To get the most out of this book, you need to be:

1. Open to the idea that performance measurement and KPIs can help you.

2. Prepared to think carefully about what you *really* want from your business.

Why you shouldn't search Google for KPIs (just yet)

Here's the challenge. There's a bit of a tug-of-war when it comes to KPIs. Most business owners want a meaningful set of performance measures that are relevant to their business but they also want to think *as little as possible* about choosing those measures. That's not an insult, it's just you have plenty of other urgent-and-important things to do that may be keeping you awake at night.

Most people, including me, want someone else to give them a list of things they should be measuring. Often this will involve a Google search looking for 'KPIs for [insert whatever business you're in here]'.

There are a few issues with playing 'Google bingo' when selecting your new KPIs....

Reason 1: If you are going to copy someone's homework…

I was given sound advice as a schoolboy: 'If you're going to copy someone's homework make sure they are *better* than you'. The problem with much material on the internet is that it hasn't been through any kind of quality validation and - even worse - some of the KPI definitions offered are wrong.

But there's a bigger problem…

I use an exercise in my training workshops where I ask the group to do a simple 'mind experiment'. I ask them to imagine that they are standing at the entrance of their preferred DIY store. I then challenge them to run and find the 'Most useful tool in the store' in the shortest time possible. We then have an interesting debate about which is the most useful tool in the store. After some discussion, the conclusion is normally 'it depends on the application that the tool is intended for'. After a bit more discussion we normally all agree that my challenge was pretty stupid, as you can't choose a 'best tool' - there is simply the best tool *for the job*. If you need to hammer a nail into some wood, then a hammer is the best tool. If you need to put up wallpaper then a wallpaper paste brush is probably the best tool. It seems blindingly obvious when you're talking about tools, and yet KPIs are exactly the same.

KPIs exist **only** to serve your objectives and strategy.

If you choose them in a ragtag way from the internet without thinking about what strategic outcomes you want, you risk picking them just because they *sound* useful, rather than choosing them because they *are* useful. You also risk copying someone else's strategic objectives, without even realising it or stopping to think if those objectives match your own.

Key Idea

Key point: KPIs are simply tools to enable you to achieve your goals or deliver your strategy. You must be clear on your objectives and strategy before you choose your KPIs. If a KPI doesn't help you achieve your objective or meet a legal or regulatory requirement you have to ask yourself *'Why the heck are we measuring this?'*.

Reason 2: It's like building a car from junkyard parts

The basic components of modern cars are generally pretty similar. However if you decided to build a new car through a broad selection of components from multiple brands and models you found sitting about in a scrap yard you *might* come up with something that works, but the chances are that you will run into all kinds of problems of compatibility and fit. The one thing I can be really confident about is that it will take you longer to build a car this way than if you have a pile of parts from a single manufacturer, and the same is true of setting up KPIs.

Another issue with KPIs from multiple sources is *consistency*. When you choose your KPIs from multiple different sources on the internet those KPIs don't usually come with any kind of consistent definition, so you are left to figure out the details all on your own.

Reason 3: You don't know what you don't know

When you search for KPI inspiration on Google you normally come up with 'families' of KPIs. You'll see articles like '10 must-have HR KPIs' and 'Five killer operational measures every manager must know'. So, if we assume that the people who wrote these blogs actually know what they're talking about, you will have a list of some useful HR and operational KPIs, but what about all the other aspects of your business you haven't even considered: Finance, Customer Service, Call Handling, Web

Marketing... (the list goes on)?

Smaller businesses are in some ways the most challenging type of business to create performance measures for because you have many of the same functions as a much larger business, but in all honesty you're only going to measure a fraction of the things you *could* measure. What you must avoid is ending up with a really narrow set of measures based on a couple of blog templates for 'HR' or 'Operational measures', missing out whole swathes of other aspects of your business performance.

Key Idea

Key point: If you choose your KPIs off the internet, you can be left with a nagging feeling that you may be missing something. You have no logical framework to slot your chosen KPIs into. A logical framework enables you to see whether you're getting the *whole* picture or if there are gaps that still need filling. We also need a structured method for trimming a very long list of KPIs down to something realistic, manageable and practical.

Tip

So, use Google, just not yet...

So, do use Google, but please, please, please do not do it right at the start of your KPI selection process. I strongly encourage you to follow the ROKS Express™ method, *then* have a look at KPIs on Google. The time to use Google is when you have **Shortlisted** your KPIs and you are looking for gaps, oversights and omissions. It may help you spot a complete set of 'traits' (more on these later) that you have overlooked or some extra outcomes or individual KPIs that might be relevant to your business.

Introducing your secret KPI selection weapon... ROKS Express™

ROKS™ stands for **Results-Orientated KPI System**. ROKS™ is a system I've developed over the last ten years to help any organisation clarify its objectives and turn those into a handful of well-designed, meaningful performance measures that will help steer them towards their strategy, goals or objectives.

The ROKS™ method

The original ROKS™ method (ROKS Enterprise™) is a powerful system that works really well, but can be tricky to use without specialist support and some experience. It can also be time consuming for smaller organisations - it includes steps that have been successfully used in global organisations with as many as two hundred thousand employees. With that power and flexibility comes complexity. Seeing a need for quicker and easier-to-use system I came up with the ROKS Express™ and ROKS Express Advanced™ approaches.

The ROKS Express™ system has much of the power and flexibility of the original ROKS Enterprise™ method, but comes with a large library of pre-defined KPI Trees™. The ROKS Express™ system reduces the time, complexity and effort to get up and running quickly with well-chosen KPIs.

Advantages of the ROKS Express™ approach

The ROKS Express™ approach has a number of major advantages over other KPI selection systems out there. The KPIs you choose are specifically relevant to your business or organisation. They are chosen based on what you are trying to achieve - so they are tailored to your needs. The KPIs you select are part of an *integrated package*, so they are defined *consistently* and will work well together. The system is designed to allow your KPI selection to extend and evolve with your business. The foundations it is built on (KPI Trees™) were designed to support customisation. When you use the ROKS Express™ method to choose your KPIs, you can be sure that you will be using your time efficiently, focusing on the things that count and will make a difference.

Here's an overview of the ROKS Express™ method steps. Each of the next six chapters focuses on a single step of the process.

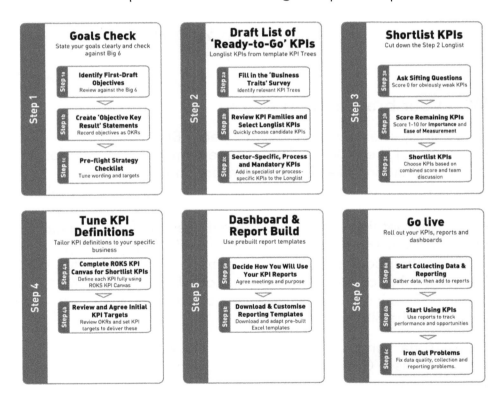

Figure: 1

Key Idea

Why your brain is lying to you

I like cheesy science fiction. Being a geeky British male of a certain age, I like Dr Who. There's a memorable episode called 'Silence', featuring alien creatures called 'The Silence'. These guys have an interesting ability: they can only be perceived when you are looking straight at them. As soon as you look away, you instantly forget they even exist. The only way the feeble human mind can beat The Silence is by writing stuff down, keeping tallies on their bodies using marker pens, and then trying to figure out what on earth is going on. Sounds pretty unlikely, doesn't it? I can say with confidence: you are living your own version of The Silence.

The personal version of The Silence we live with is called 'cognitive bias'. Cognitive bias is a psychological effect identified by research psychologist Daniel Kahneman. His research on the subject won him the Nobel Prize for Economics.

In a nutshell, cognitive bias is the effect where we are unconsciously influenced when we make judgements or decisions. Cognitive bias has a huge impact on our willingness to use KPIs.

Symptoms of acute cognitive bias include...

- Reluctance to collect or use objective data for decision-making
- Individual or team decision-making ignoring or contradicting factual evidence
- Poor outcomes from historic strategic decisions

It's a really important topic, but a bit of a diversion from our main objectives, so I have written a special section for the Appendix of this book with more detail on how cognitive biases can affect you, some practical examples, and suggested behaviours to help you overcome them. If you identify with some, or all, of the symptoms listed above I suggest you take a look.

Key Idea

The ideas behind ROKS Express™

Most businesses are focused on surprisingly similar core objectives. Generally business owners and managers are looking to achieve the following objectives:

1. A profitable and solvent business

2. A growing business

3. A balanced quality of life

4. A legal and compliant business

5. An innovative business

6. Managed risk (legal, health and safety, environmental and so on)

Do these apply to you? Typically, I would expect *at least* four of them to align with what you're trying to achieve.

Key Idea

Business traits - The key to the ROKS Express™ approach

Here's some more good news: many aspects of your business are **predictable and similar to other businesses**. These similarities are grouped into what I call the 'traits' of a business. The 'traits' of a business are things that naturally spring from the nature of your business and some physical characteristics, attributes, or features of that business. The 'traits' we use in this book have been designed as a *complete package*, so they will work together, avoid duplication and are defined consistently.

Let me give you a few example business traits...

Finance - business trait

For all commercial businesses (and even voluntary enterprises) you will need some basic financial measures. So this is one trait that will apply to almost any business or organisation.

Customers present and waiting for service - business trait

A coffee shop deals with customers that *queue* for service. We know that there are certain measures you might be interested in for a business that has queues. For example: How long does a customer have to queue? How many customers got fed up with queuing and gave up?

Selling our time - business trait

Advice-based businesses, like consulting firms, sell their staff's time. These businesses want to focus on KPIs like consultant utilisation and hourly billing rate. These measures would be pretty meaningless to a shop or manufacturing business. So, for the 'traits' of Sales, Efficiency and Quality, we have broken out each one into a *separate* trio of traits; for **service**-based businesses, **word**-based businesses and **production**-based businesses.

Contact handling - business trait

Some businesses need to deal with substantial volumes of inbound contacts - phone calls, emails and web chats. If your business has these, then there's a whole set of KPIs that are worth considering. If you aren't involved in inbound contact work then you can just skip this whole section.

Your own KPI library, ready-built

This book provides you with over fifty ready-built 'Business Trait KPI Families' and more than four hundred pre-defined KPIs to give you a flying start (that's why this book is so large). All you need to do is run through the survey on page 77 (or the template in the download pack), to identify which sets of business traits you need to consider for your business, then use the results of the survey to pick from the pre-built KPIs on offer.

 Free templates registration link
https://goo.gl/DFrRyt
No Spam! Email registration required, but your details are **never** shared

Tricky KPIs - Rare and unusual KPIs just for your business

Many businesses have very specific characteristics that don't appear in a generalised model. These unusual measures normally spring up from specific characteristics of the processes that the business is running. Here are a few examples…

Dairy farming…

- Stocking capacity
- On-farm forage production
- Forage quality

Running a church…

- Donations
- Salvations
- Attendance

Online hotel booking service…

- Total listings
- Total instant bookable listings
- Guests per night

The good news about these types of measures is that *you* are usually in a fantastic position to define them, once you are familiar with the ROKS Express™ approach, as they tend to be more process-technical aspects of a particular business - the sort of thing that people running a business often already have a good knowledge of.

The case studies in this book: Chaos Coffee and others…

Now life is messy and most of my clients want to keep their KPI secrets to themselves, so I've created ten **completely** fictional organisations that cover all of the available ROKS business traits that we will be talking about. I use Chaos Coffee for the examples in Section One - the explanation of the ROKS™

approach. The other nine fictional businesses are used for the KPI definitions in Section 2.

Let me introduce you to the (*totally* fictitious) companies:

Chaos Coffee Shop

Charlie runs a small high street coffee shop. Most of his sales are small, cash and straight to the consumer. He's had some quality issues recently and is also trying to boost customer numbers with a local radio campaign.

Dangerous Developers

Daniella runs 'Dangerous Developers', developing small apps and websites for local clients. Her sales are invoiced weekly and are to local businesses. Daniella has one full-time employee, Dave.

Woeful Widget Warehouse

Will runs 'Woeful Widgets', selling wholesale novelty items, like comedy mouse mats, to shops and party organisers. Woeful Widgets is a business-to-business setup with a strong focus on warehouse management.

Roughshod Repairs

Ruby runs a business that specialises in managing warranties and recalls for electronics manufacturers. She has three major clients and deals with members of the public as well as various repair and parts suppliers. She has a team of 15 call-handling agents, dealing with the public. They spend a lot of time dealing with inbound and outbound contacts, repair scheduling and angry customers. They have also had some tricky problems with warranty fraud.

Mayhem Manufacturing

Mohammed manufactures and sells fantasy-themed office furniture for role-play fans who have grown up and have office jobs now. They make a range of Hobbit-themed chairs, mini-volcano pen holders and desks supported by model turtles. He has two production sites and sells to consumers online and also supplies wholesalers around the world.

Pointless Prose

Patricia is a freelance writer. She helps bloggers with their copy, writes emotional stories for coffee-break magazines, is paid by the number of words she produces, and also writes niche material for tortoise-horror magazines. She also does day-rate work for a small specialist website devoted to tortoises.

Ambiguous Associates

Ambiguous Associates are a small consulting firm, run by Austin Ambiguous, that specialises in advising large corporate clients on making effective data-driven decisions. They typically operate on a consulting day-rate and may, or may not, charge expenses back to the client, depending on the contract agreement. Austin also runs open-access training workshops.

Car Crevice Cleaners

Car Crevice Cleaners is run by Colin Crevice. He is an inventor who is constantly looking for new and patentable cleaning widgets for cars. His inventions include a tiny fluffy magnetic wiper for rear view mirrors and a special device for picking dirt out of the joints between interior plastic panels.

Cracking Chiropractors

Cracking Chiropractors is a small chiropractic clinic, run by Christine. Most of their sessions are pre-booked appointments, but with some emergency slots held back each day. Christine is keen to manage her appointment slots as well as possible, to maximise the number of patients she can help and to keep revenues healthy too.

The Cat Herding Society

The Cat Herding Society is a small charity devoted to the welfare of cats and the cat herders who tend them. The charity is supported mainly by donations, but also grants and a government training contract for re-skilling retired cat herders. Maximising donations and other forms of income is a high priority for the Cat Herding Society.

Why *ten* examples?

As you have probably noticed, each of these businesses has different 'traits' - for example Woeful Widget Warehouse has stock to manage, Roughshod Repairs have a small contact centre and Cracking Chiropractors have bookings and services to manage. This means that we will have a case-study for every type of trait for which we need examples and definitions.

I'm a little nervous in case there are coffee shop owners, software developers and writers reading this book, but I hope that you will forgive any simplifications I make in the examples in exchange for a more friendly and easy-to-read book.

'Your ROKS Express™ method sounds OK, but my business is waaaay more complicated than your examples!'

I've worked with enough businesses now to know that everyone thinks their business is way more complicated than a simple business such as …[insert example that isn't your business here]. The truth is, when you get really close to any business, there's always lots of complexity in there. This is why it is so important to keep a constant eye on your end-objective. If you have that sense of direction then it is easy to see when you are being blown off course. If you don't have that clarity then you drown in the detail, as everything seems potentially relevant and important.

Don't get me wrong, even with a clear set of objectives and key results, you can still get overwhelmed by the detail, but clear objectives and desired results give you a chance to pull yourself out of the mud when you get stuck.

So, if you find yourself becoming overwhelmed by the complexity of your business, take a couple of steps backwards, double-check the tips in this book and if you're still feeling overwhelmed drop me an email (bernie@madetomeasurekpis.com) and I'll see if I can help.

Getting ready to start

Having helped lots of people develop their KPIs over the past ten years, and struggled with setting up my own company KPIs, I have identified three underlying 'golden rules' for creating performance measures for small businesses.

Tip

The three golden rules for small business performance measurement...

1. **Get started right now.** Partial measures are normally better than no measures at all. Testing your measures will quickly tell you whether they are useful or not.

2. **Don't worry about perfection.** You will never be completely happy with your KPIs first-off. It's much easier to fix measures that are being used, than to try and get everything right straight away.

3. **Don't get carried away.** Limit how many KPIs you get started with. The practicalities of measurement are harder than they first look. Don't try and measure too many things to start with. When you are up and running you will start to get a good idea of what's working and what's not, making it easier to ditch irrelevant measures and develop more important ones.

Using your team's brains and getting their buy-in

The most common reason for KPIs not being fully adopted in an organisation is lack of buy-in. This almost always happens because the right people were not involved early enough in the process. When you don't involve people properly you will typically see two very painful symptoms:

get buyin

46

- You launch your newfangled KPIs, dashboards and reports and get huge amounts of negative push-back, cynicism and a lack of any kind of meaningful cooperation.

- Involving people later on in the process results in lots of comments like 'that's not the right measure. We should be measuring such and such…'. This usually means **restarting** the whole KPI selection process.

Fortunately the solution is simple, at least for smaller businesses. All you need to do is ask yourself 'Who is going to be involved in data collection, performance management or decision-making based on these KPIs?'. For most small businesses this will be very straightforward, and if you are a one-man band you get a pass on this step (unless you're putting measures on suppliers or subcontractors, of course).

The other advantage of engaging the right people early on means you will almost always get better KPIs.

Who: collects the data } from
manages performance } to
makes decisions } involve

Introduction

Step I: Goals Check

Step 1: Goals Check

Summary
Step 1: Goals Check

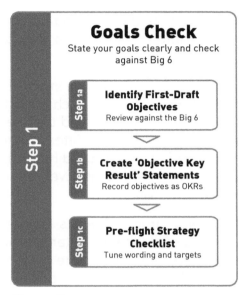

Figure: 2

In this step you will...

- Think hard about what you want from your business and from life. Create your 'First-Draft Objectives' and identify your 'Key Results'.

- State what result achieving each of the objectives will deliver and record as an 'Objective Key Result' - OKR.

- Double-check that your objectives and high-level targets are ready-to-go using the 'Pre-flight objectives checklist'.

What is it you really WANT?

For any business, there is always the burning need to make a profit, manage cash flow and keep your customers happy. If you do all these things you should have a long and glorious business career ahead of you. As you are reading this book, then you may have a suspicion that there are also some things that can help you achieve your objectives.

Everyone is likely to be familiar with the story of King Midas. Poor old Midas wished that 'Everything I touch turns to gold'. After his wish was granted, he quickly realised that he had asked for the almost-but-not-quite-right thing. After accidentally turning his daughter, and all of his food, to gold he probably realised that what he should have asked for is 'Everything I *wish* to turn to gold, turns to gold when I touch it'.

KPIs are used along with targets. Targets are used to drive behaviour. *Rewards* are often linked to targets and can be very powerful tools to achieve objectives. The problem is a small mistake in targeting behaviour can lead to terrible end results.

KPIs exist to deliver your *goals*. If you work hard to achieve a goal, or objective, you need to be absolutely sure it's the right one.

Step 1a) Exercise: Identify your business objectives

Time to do some thinking.

Action

Action: First-draft your objectives

Quickly make a list of your first-draft business objectives. Use the First-Draft Objectives Template (from the free templates download pack) or just jot them down in a list and keep them for later.

Free templates registration link

https://goo.gl/DFrRyt

No Spam! Email registration required, but your details are **never** shared

You should have between two and seven objectives. If you only have one, it's probably too high level, if you have more than seven then you may be heading into sub-objectives and getting too detailed at this stage. Just have another go if you have too many or too few.

Don't worry about getting it exactly right, we will be asking some questions as we go through this section which may make you want to tweak these objectives anyway.

Example

Chaos Coffee: First-Draft Objectives

So, at Chaos Coffee, Charlie has defined his goals. In fact, here it is...

Table: 1 Completed First-Draft Objectives Template for Chaos Coffee

First-Draft Objectives: Chaos Coffee
Make a healthy profit.

It's clear that Charlie is *completely* focused on the financial side of the business. That's not uncommon and is completely understandable. We all need to eat. The interesting thing is that the profit result is an **outcome** of a number of other things. By focusing on the end result rather than the enablers Charlie isn't using the power of measurement to actually improve his situation, just to measure it after it has happened.

Charlie probably needs a bit of a nudge to think about some other objectives that may be useful to him and Chaos Coffee.

Fortunately we have some common ones that may be useful to him. We call them the 'Big 6 Objectives'.

Key Idea

Step 1a) Introducing the 'Big 6'

The 'RO' part of ROKS Express™ stands for 'Results-Orientated'. Results-Orientated means that we start by identifying what it is we want to achieve, then work down from those objectives to identify each specific set of **'outcomes'** or **'results'** that will support those objectives. To do this we need a clear set of initial objectives.

The ROKS Express™ method helps you to do this through the 'core' objectives that have been identified as being common to many businesses. These core objectives are:

- ☑ **ST1:** Run a profitable and solvent business
- ☑ **ST2:** A growing business
- ☑ **ST3:** A balanced quality of life
- ☑ **ST4:** A legal and compliant business
- ☑ **ST5:** An innovative business
- ☑ **ST6:** Manage risk (legal, health and safety, environmental etc.)

The 'ST' is a cross-reference to the KPI Trees™ that are included in the appendix of this book, and is short for 'STrategic objective'.

Now, using the Big 6 above, review/revise your First-Draft Objectives adding in any relevant details. A 'Detailed Objectives Template' is in the download pack, if you want to use it...

 Free templates registration link

https://goo.gl/DFrRyt

No Spam! Email registration required, but your details are **never** shared

Key Idea

The Detailed Objectives Template

Table: 2 The Detailed Objectives Template

Standard Objective	Detailed objectives (Developed from your 'First-Draft: Objectives Template')	Key Result (We cover this on 'Action: Identify your Key Results' on page 61)
ST1: Run a profitable and solvent business		
ST2: A growing business		
ST3: A balanced quality of life		
ST4: A legal and compliant business		
ST5: An innovative business		
ST6: Manage risk		

Strictly speaking, we don't need the First-Draft Objectives to select our KPIs, but they are useful to help focus the mind during the selection steps (Steps 2 and 3) and are essential for Step 4, where we start to set *targets* for our newly-selected KPIs.

What if your objectives don't entirely match with the Big 6 standard objectives?

If the Big 6 don't fully cover your objectives, keep a note of the 'custom objective' you would like to cover, but complete the ROKS Express™ approach with any of your objectives that

are covered by the Big 6. Later, when you have successfully implemented that first batch of KPIs, you should then take a look at the ROKS Express Advanced™ method (link: https://madetomeasurekpis.com/complex-organisation-kpis/).

There are a few good reasons for using these six 'standard' common business objectives:

- The ROKS Express™ method is the *simpler* method to follow first time around.

- Your experience with running through the ROKS Express™ method end-to-end will massively help you if decide to use the ROKS Express Advanced™ approach as your business grows. The Advanced approach is based on the basic method, but with two more steps added.

- Using the ROKS Express™ method is the fastest way to get up and running with *most* of the KPIs you will need, to start getting some benefit.

Example

Step 1a) 'Big 6' review: Chaos Coffee

Following the ROKS Express™ method, Charlie reviews the Big 6 to see which apply to Chaos Coffee. Here are his thoughts…

ST1) Run a profitable and solvent business

Yep, this is top of Charlie's list of business objectives. In fact it's the only objective currently on his list.

ST2) A growing business

Charlie does want to grow, but he doesn't want to become the next Starbucks. His best estimate shows that three or four profitable coffee shops should help meet all of his personal financial objectives.

ST3) A balanced quality of life

This is important to Charlie. Whilst Charlie enjoys testing new business ideas, he is keen not to spend his whole life working *in* Chaos Coffee.

ST4) A legal and compliant business

Check! Charlie has no intention of being fined or going to jail for neglecting his duties as an employer or provider of services to the public. He seen some of his other entrepreneurial friends gloss over health and safety only to pay the price through fines, legal fees and sleepless nights. For Charlie, being 'a legal and compliant business' is non-negotiable.

ST5) An innovative business

Charlie is a bright and imaginative guy and he wants to offer something fresh and new in the world of coffee, so being 'An innovative business' is one of his objectives.

ST6) Manage risk (health and safety, environmental, financial and so on)

Just as for objective ST4 ('A legal and compliant business'), Charlie wants to make sure that he stays out of trouble and can sleep at night. He wants to put checks and systems in place that will make sure that he doesn't miss something that may sink him or his business.

Charlie then goes on to refine and add details to his First-Draft Objectives worksheet. You can see his second attempt shortly, on page 60.

Key Idea

Step 1b) Introducing Objective Key Results (OKRs)

When we write down an objective, it's almost always with an outcome or result in mind. If we don't have a *result* in mind when we create an objective, how do we know when we have *achieved* it?

There's a very simple way of stating this, it's called an 'Objective Key Result', or OKR. It is simply a case of writing down:

1. *What* you want to achieve: the '**objective**'

2. The result, *how* you *know* when you get there: the '**key result**'

Here are some examples of OKRs...

- Objective: Run a profitable and solvent business.
- Key result: A pre-tax profit of £210k.

- Objective: A growing business.
- Key result: Increased sales of 4,000 units per month.

- Objective: A balanced quality of life.
- Key result: Zero (unpaid) overtime needed by the end of the year.

- Objective: A safe food-preparation business.
- Key result: Five star food hygiene audit for next year.

- Objective: An innovative business.
- Key result: 25% of our income from products we don't yet make by the end of next year.

- Objective: Manage risk (health and safety, environmental, financial etc.).
- Key result: Every team member a qualified first-aider by the end of the year.

Example

Detailed Objectives Template - Chaos Coffee example

Here's an example showing Charlie's completed Detailed Objectives...

Table: 3

Standard Objective	Detailed objectives (from your 'First Draft: Objectives Template')	Key Result	
ST1: Run a profitable and solvent business	Make a healthy profit.	£100k per year pre-tax profits.	
ST2: A growing business	Expand the number of shops we have.	Four Chaos Coffee branches within 4 years. – We can charge a 20 percent premium over local average. – >20 percent of customers return at least twice in a week.	
ST3: A balanced quality of life	Charlie has time to travel and develop new business ideas and work **on** the business.	Charlie to spend less than 8 hours per week *in* the business and no more than 20 hours a week *on* the business.	
ST4: A legal and compliant business	We maintain our five star food hygiene rating and continue to have zero prosecutions or compensation claims.	Zero prosecutions or warnings. Five star food hygiene rating from local authority, every year.	
ST5: An innovative business	Our coffee tastes better than the competition.	Our coffee is **measurably** preferred by a typical coffee drinker.	
ST6: Manage risk	We remain open whenever planned.	No unplanned closures.	

Notice that Charlie's 5th objective is quite specialised. Coffee taste testing is beyond the scope of this method. Charlie decides that is something he'll put to one side whilst he runs through the full ROKS Express™ approach, then come back to when he is up and running with the basic KPIs.

Action

Action: Identify your Key Results

Now have a go at identifying your key results for each of your detailed objectives. Use the **Detailed Objectives Template** from the free templates download pack (nearest link on page 53).

Don't worry about getting it *exactly* right. We will be asking some questions as we go through this section which may make you want to tweak these objectives anyway.

Trap

Watching out for 'Woolly Words'

Woolly words are words which sound great, but are hard to pin down. They often have no clear meaning, and may make a phrase *harder* to understand and break down. They pop up all over the place, but are particularly common in mission statements, corporate brochures and advertisements. Woolly words are words and phrases like…

- Excellence
- Aspire
- Fantastic
- Best in breed
- World class
- Boost
- Great
- Support

I once ran a workshop with one organisation which had the words 'brilliant service' in their strategic statement. We were using that statement as the start point for building their KPIs. After an hour of debating what 'brilliant service' actually meant, we were still no closer to an agreed answer. It sounded good, but was impossible to conclusively nail down without some more detailed supporting information.

A quick test for woolly words is as follows...

How would you know if you have *achieved* 'it'? For example, how do you know when you are 'best in breed', 'world class' or 'bleeding edge'?

If it's not clear, then you should substitute the woolly word or phrase with something more precise - often the answers to the question we just used as our 'Woolly words test'. Instead of 'world class', you might have several specific statements, such as 'Have a customer retention rate in the top 25% of our sector', for example.

Checklist

Step 1c) Pre-flight Objectives Checklist

Before we move onto Step 2, we need to check the following to make sure you are in good shape to progress...

☑ Have you reviewed the Big 6 objectives and identified which apply to your business and listed out the key results you are looking to achieve?

☑ Have you checked that none of your key results are completely opposed to each other?

☑ Are the objective descriptions free from woolly words and buzzwords?

☑ Is there broad team consensus that the objectives are the right ones?

☑ Do your stated objectives make sense to an intelligent, but non-specialist, reader?

Recap
Step 1: Goals Check

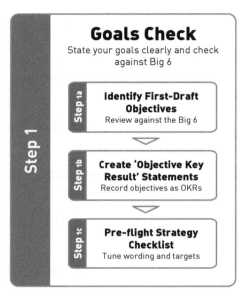

Figure: 3

At the end of Step 1 you will have…

- An identified set of objectives, chosen from the Big 6 standard objectives, with your specific 'First-Draft Objectives' alongside each one.

- A clear set of key results that will help you identify how you are progressing towards your stated objectives.

- Confidence that your objectives and key results are defined clearly and concisely.

Step 2: Draft List of 'Ready-to-go' KPIs

Summary
Step 2: Draft List of 'Ready-to-go' KPIs

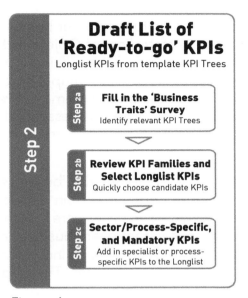

Figure: 4

In this step you will...

- Identify the 'business traits' that apply to *your* business, using a simple survey tool.

- Use the survey to select the KPI Families you need to review.

- Review the relevant KPI Families to select your KPI **Longlist**, ready for trimming down to the essentials in Step 3.

Core measures for YOUR type of business

The core concept behind ROKS Express™ is that we need **two things** to determine the right KPIs for your business. The first thing we need is a clearly stated set of **Objective Key Results (OKRs)**, which we spent some time identifying in Step 1. Many of these objectives are common across multiple organisations and that was how we arrived at the **Big 6** common core objectives: being profitable, having a growing business, a balanced quality of life, staying out of legal and regulatory trouble, innovating and managing risk.

The next thing we need is to identify the **'business traits'** specific to *your* business. Each business has certain realities about the things that need to be managed. There are 'essentials', most of which are financial measures, that every business needs to cover, but as you look into the specifics of each individual business you realise that there are obvious *differences*. The good news is that there are patterns to the differences, if that doesn't sound too weird.

Key Idea

The Business Traits Survey

If you are a food services business then shelf life, stock levels and stock turnover are characteristics of your business and are likely to be critical to your profitability. If you're running a contact centre then there's a family of measures around the characteristics of response speed, quality of response and resource levels that are applicable to you.

In the ROKS Express™ method we call these families of characteristics 'business traits'. There are about fifty of these traits. Each business trait comes with its own KPI Family (see page 80 for a quick explanation of how these KPI Families were designed using KPI Trees™).

So, here's a summary of the steps you will be using in a few pages to identify and use business traits to come up with your KPI Shortlist…

1. Fill in the Business Traits Survey (template in the download pack).

     Free templates registration link
    https://goo.gl/DFrRyt
    No Spam! Email registration required, but your details are never shared

    –   **Don't go too overboard.** It's OK to skip over KPI Families or KPIs that *technically* apply to your business, but measuring them may be overkill at this stage in your company growth. If you aren't sure, have a quick look at the KPI Family in question (see Section 2) and review the Gold (i.e. highly recommended) KPIs in that family to see if they look applicable to your business.

- **Don't worry about choosing to leave certain KPIs out:** the KPI Police aren't going to come and tell you off for not measuring things. There may be a few legally required KPIs for your business, so those are the exception.

2. Once you complete the Business Traits Survey use the page reference next to each trait you have ticked and review the KPI Family for each trait.

   - Gold KPIs are the most common useful measures for each trait.

   - Silver KPIs may be useful for your particular business or if you have a specific issue that you want to focus on.

3. Use the 'KPI Shortlisting Template' spreadsheet in the downloads pack (see box below) to record the KPIs you decide to Longlist, and also note the relevant KPI Definition page reference. If you prefer not to use the download pack, you could just use Post-its on the relevant pages to flag the KPI Families and KPIs that you think are relevant.

 Free templates registration link
https://goo.gl/DFrRyt
No Spam! Email registration required, but your details are never shared

   - You can be fairly relaxed about how many KPIs you pick at this stage. We are going to have a cull in the next step of the ROKS Express™ process, so this is just the **Longlist**.

All the KPIs in Section 2 have full definitions and case-study examples to give you the best possible start.

A bit about 'F1 Financial' measures

Typically, within most businesses, the financial measures are the best (sometimes only) KPIs already in place. This is probably because of the legal requirements to submit accounts, pay tax and the fact that if you lose the plot on financial measures you will quickly go out of business - leaving only businesses with some kind of a grip on their finances.

If you are happy with your financial measures, that's great. If you aren't, then take a close look at 'Financials' KPI Family (tip: all the KPIs with a 'Ref' starting 'F1' are part of this family) . Within the Financials KPI Family should be most of the financial figures you need to keep an eye on. To keep it sensible I've just put the essential financial KPIs in there.

One thing to point out: the KPIs here are probably not going to help you with your legal accounting and reporting requirements (make sure you discuss those with your accountant), but they **are** definitely going to help you run your business. Keeping a close eye on things like 'Cash in the bank' , 'Working Capital Ratio' and 'Net Profit' is the key to a successful business and being able to sleep at night.

Chaos Coffee OKR template

So let's just take a look at the OKRs (Objective Key Results) that Charlie defined earlier on using the Detailed Objectives Template...

Step 2: Draft List of 'Ready-to-Go' KPIs

Table: 4 Charlie's Detailed Objectives Template from earlier on

Standard Objective	Detailed objectives (from your 'First Draft: Objectives Template')	Key Result	
ST1: Run a profitable and solvent business	Make a healthy profit.	£100k per year pre tax profits.	
ST2: A growing business	Expand the number of shops we have.	Four Chaos Coffee branches within 4 years. – We can charge a 20 percent premium over local average. – >20 percent of customers return at least twice in a week.	
ST3: A balanced quality of life	Charlie has time to travel and develop new business ideas and work **on** the business.	Charlie to spend less than 8 hours per week **in** the business and no more than 20 hours a week **on** the business.	
ST4: A legal and compliant business	We maintain our five star food hygiene rating and continue to have zero prosecutions or compensation claims.	Zero prosecutions or warnings. Five star food hygiene rating from local authority, every year.	
ST5: An innovative business	Our coffee tastes better than the competition.	Our coffee is **measurably** preferred by a typical coffee drinker.	
ST6: Manage risk	We remain open whenever planned.	No unplanned closures.	

Chaos Coffee: 'Business Traits Survey'

Here's how Charlie filled in the Business Traits Survey for Chaos Coffee....

Table: 5 Charlie's completed Business Traits Survey for Chaos Coffee

Quick Ref.	Name	Description	Applicable to your business?	KPI Family page number
A1	Admin Effort, Time and Cost	Significant amount of internal administrative activity		page 293
C1	Present Customers Waiting for Service	Live queues for service or 'service on demand'	Yes	page 295
C2	Perishable Goods	Wastage, discounting and product condition for businesses selling or using perishable products	Yes	page 301
C3	Customer Goods Stored	Safe and accurate management of customer goods and storage capacity on business premises		page 305
C4	Sensitive Customer Data Stored	Security and compliance when storing customer data on business systems		page 311
C5	Bookings & Appointments	Effectiveness of booking process, resource utilisation and management		page 315
C6	Attendance and Ticket Sales	Management of ticket sales, management of event utilisation and optimising event income		page 319
C7	Donations	Request and management of charitable donations		page 327
F1	Financials	Financial management of business or organisation	Yes	page 337
H1	Health and Safety	Compliance with Health and Safety regulations and good practice	Yes	page 351
HR1	Staff and Payroll	Managing payment and benefits of employees	Yes	page 359
HR2	Recruitment	Managing advertising, selection and recruitment of human resources		page 365
I1	Equipment Investment	Investment and equipment performance where business equipment is purchased and leased		page 371
I2	Property Investment	Property investment performance - e.g. private rental property		page 375

I3	Time Investment - New Product Development and Skills	Time invested in new product development or skills development and the outcomes from that investment		page 381
I4	Business Vehicles	Performance of investment in business vehicle(s)		page 385
L1	Service Improvement Activity	Improving operational performance of service organisations		page 389
L2	Production Improvement Activity	Improving operational performance of production organisations		page 395
L3	Contact Centre Improvement Activity	Improving operational performance of contact centres		page 407
M1	Public Reviews	Customers reviewing the businesses publicly, e.g. online, in papers	Yes	page 409
M2	Footfall	Passing trade to create customers and generate sales	Yes	page 413
M3	Web Marketing	Generating sales leads or awareness through online media (web, social media, email marketing)	Yes	page 417
O1	Efficiency - Widget Production	Manufacturing 'things' and want to understand production performance	Yes, a bit	page 427
O2	Efficiency - Hours	Delivering services by time, and want to understand their performance		page 437
O3	Efficiency - Per Word Billing	Deliver services by the paid word, and want to understand performance		page 441
O4	Efficiency - Contract Services	Understand your performance, where you deliver services for a contract.		page 445
O5	Efficiency - Service Delivery	Service businesses who want to understand their operational performance	Yes	page 449
O6	Procurement and Supply	Purchase of significant amounts of goods or services and need to manage the process	Yes, a bit	page 451
O7	Fulfilment - Product and Services	Supply of significant amounts of goods or services and need to manage the process		page 457
O8	Call, Email and Webchat Handling	Inbound telephony, email or web chat and need to manage costs, quality and performance		page 461
O9	Equipment Maintenance	Maintaining equipment and manage the cost, risk and reliability delivered by that maintenance	Yes, a bit	page 479
O10	Complaints and Incident (Ticket) Handling	Managing complaints resolution and complaint handling costs		page 485

P1	Professional Qualification and Membership	Professional membership, qualification or membership requirements and/or coverage.		page 489
Q1	Service Quality	Managing quality for service organisations	Yes	page 491
Q2	Product Quality	Managing quality for manufacturing businesses		page 501
Q3	Guarantee and Warranty	Product or service guarantee/warranty measures		page 505
R1	Creative Effort	Tracking of effectiveness and quantity of creative effort		page 511
R2	Technical Research and Development	Tracking of quality and quantity of technical research and development		page 513
R3	Service Research and Development	Tracking of quality and quantity of services research and development	Yes	page 519
R4	Intellectual Property Protection (Patents and Copyright)	Management and enforcement of copyright, royalties income, infringement and ideas-related sales		page 523
S1	Sales Value, Activity and Results	Selling 'things' (as opposed to selling services or words)	Yes	page 527
S2	Sales - Hourly Billing	Selling hours of service		page 535
S3	Sales - Words	Selling product where paid by the written word		page 539
S4	Sales - Contract Services	Selling contract services (not hourly)		page 543
S5	Sales - Pricing	Pricing any goods or service	Yes	page 545
S6	Sales - Advertising, Pay Per Click & Organic Traffic	Advertising through radio, TV, organic web hits and pay-per-click	Yes, a bit	page 549
S7	Sales Referrals	Sales referrals, both to us and us to others		page 563
S8	Sales - Proposals & Contracts	Creating successful sales proposals and contracts		page 569
T1	Business Premises	Maintenance, safety and management of business property	Yes	page 575
T2	Stock	Stock availability, management, retrieval performance and wastage	Yes	page 581
U1	Fraud & Theft	Tracking and managing fraud, theft and recovery		page 587

Notice how some of the categories apply to things that he *does* deal with, like Recruitment and Complaints, but Charlie feels that the scale and frequency of these activities just doesn't justify KPIs, at this stage anyway. For some of the other categories, like Procurement and Efficiency, he's put 'Yes, a bit' next to them and will have a quick look to see if one or two of the KPIs in the KPI Families might be useful.

If you need to know how the KPI Families were designed, so you can make sense of what you are doing now, skip ahead and read page 80 to page 87 . If you are happy following the flow, just keep reading…

Action

Action: Choose your Ready-to-go KPIs

Run through the Business Traits Survey below, or printed-out version from the downloads pack, and record which KPI Families may apply to your business…

Table: 6 Business Traits Survey for completion

Quick Ref.	Name	Description	Applicable to your business?	KPI Family page number
A1	Admin Effort, Time and Cost	Significant amount of internal administrative activity		page 293
C1	Present Customers Waiting for Service	Live queues for service or 'service on demand'		page 295
C2	Perishable Goods	Wastage, discounting and product condition for businesses selling or using perishable products		page 301
C3	Customer Goods Stored	Safe and accurate management of customer goods and storage capacity on business premises		page 305
C4	Sensitive Customer Data Stored	Security and compliance when storing customer data on business systems		page 311
C5	Bookings & Appointments	Effectiveness of booking process, resource utilisation and management		page 315
C6	Attendance and Ticket Sales	Management of ticket sales, management of event utilisation and optimising event income		page 319
C7	Donations	Request and management of charitable donations		page 327
F1	Financials	Financial management of business or organisation		page 337
H1	Health and Safety	Compliance with Health and Safety regulations and good practice		page 351
HR1	Staff and Payroll	Managing payment and benefits of employees		page 359
HR2	Recruitment	Managing advertising, selection and recruitment of human resources		page 365
I1	Equipment Investment	Investment and equipment performance where business equipment is purchased and leased		page 371
I2	Property Investment	Property investment performance - e.g. private rental property		page 375

I3	Time Investment - New Product Development and Skills	Time invested in new product development or skills development and the outcomes from that investment		page 381
I4	Business Vehicles	Performance of investment in business vehicle(s)		page 385
L1	Service Improvement Activity	Improving operational performance of service organisations		page 389
L2	Production Improvement Activity	Improving operational performance of production organisations		page 395
L3	Contact Centre Improvement Activity	Improving operational performance of contact centres		page 407
M1	Public Reviews	Customers reviewing the businesses publicly, e.g. online, in papers		page 409
M2	Footfall	Passing trade to create customers and generate sales		page 413
M3	Web Marketing	Generating sales leads or awareness through online media (web, social media, email marketing)		page 417
O1	Efficiency - Widget Production	Manufacturing 'things' and want to understand production performance		page 427
O2	Efficiency - Hours	Delivering services by time, and want to understand their performance		page 437
O3	Efficiency - Per Word Billing	Deliver services by the paid word, and want to understand performance		page 441
O4	Efficiency - Contract Services	Understand your performance, where you deliver services for a contract.		page 445
O5	Efficiency - Service Delivery	Service businesses who want to understand their operational performance		page 449
O6	Procurement and Supply	Purchase of significant amounts of goods or services and need to manage the process		page 451
O7	Fulfilment - Product and Services	Supply of significant amounts of goods or services and need to manage the process		page 457
O8	Call, Email and Webchat Handling	Inbound telephony, email or web chat and need to manage costs, quality and performance		page 461
O9	Equipment Maintenance	Maintaining equipment and manage the cost, risk and reliability delivered by that maintenance		page 479
O10	Complaints and Incident (Ticket) Handling	Managing complaints resolution and complaint handling costs		page 485

P1	Professional Qualification and Membership	Professional membership, qualification or membership requirements and/or coverage.		page 489
Q1	Service Quality	Managing quality for service organisations		page 491
Q2	Product Quality	Managing quality for manufacturing businesses		page 501
Q3	Guarantee and Warranty	Product or service guarantee/warranty measures		page 505
R1	Creative Effort	Tracking of effectiveness and quantity of creative effort		page 511
R2	Technical Research and Development	Tracking of quality and quantity of technical research and development		page 513
R3	Service Research and Development	Tracking of quality and quantity of services research and development		page 519
R4	Intellectual Property Protection (Patents and Copyright)	Management and enforcement of copyright, royalties income, infringement and ideas-related sales		page 523
S1	Sales Value, Activity and Results	Selling 'things' (as opposed to selling services or words)		page 527
S2	Sales - Hourly Billing	Selling hours of service		page 535
S3	Sales - Words	Selling product where paid by the written word		page 539
S4	Sales - Contract Services	Selling contract services (not hourly)		page 543
S5	Sales - Pricing	Pricing any goods or service		page 545
S6	Sales - Advertising, Pay Per Click & Organic Traffic	Advertising through radio, TV, organic web hits and pay-per-click		page 549
S7	Sales Referrals	Sales referrals, both to us and us to others		page 563
S8	Sales - Proposals & Contracts	Creating successful sales proposals and contracts		page 569
T1	Business Premises	Maintenance, safety and management of business property		page 575
T2	Stock	Stock availability, management, retrieval performance and wastage		page 581
U1	Fraud & Theft	Tracking and managing fraud, theft and recovery		page 587

Optional section: How the KPI Families were designed....

Introducing KPI Trees™

The ROKS Express™ approach is based on **KPI Families**. These families of KPIs weren't just pulled out of thin air, they were developed using a tool from the ROKS Enterprise™ approach. That approach is called KPI Trees™.

KPI Trees™ are a structured, visual, way of breaking down high-level strategic objectives into measurable results. KPI Trees™ can take a bit of time and experience to create confidently. That's why in the ROKS Express™ approach we use 51 pre-built KPI Trees™ to generate the KPI Families for you. This pre-built approach gets you started as quickly as possible. Although you may never have to build a KPI Tree™ from scratch, it can still be useful to understand what they are and how they are built.

How a KPI Tree™ works...

The best way of coming up with your KPIs involves starting with your objectives and breaking that main objective down into smaller objectives or outcomes.

Let's imagine you are an ambitious actor who decides your objective is to win an Oscar. Now, winning an Oscar is a perfectly measurable outcome, but for most actors is going to be a very rare event that happens at the **end** of the sequence of outcomes that lead up to the Oscar. Here's how you would break down that high-level outcome. Each level shown goes one level lower (normally shorter-term and more into-the-detail) than the one above. We give those levels names. The level names are: Strategic, Theme, Tactical then KPI. (Don't worry too much about the naming, it will become clear as you read through this section).

Strategic Objective: Win an Oscar

To win an Oscar, it *really* helps to be in a film that has been *nominated* for one, or more, major cinema awards…

Theme: Be nominated for major awards

Being in well-reviewed films is going to dramatically *increase your chances* of being nominated for major awards…

Tactical: Appear in well-reviewed films

As an actor, you are only going to appear in well-reviewed films if you go to *auditions*. So one of our critical KPIs for winning an Oscar…

KPI: Number of auditions

Here's what this branch of the KPI Tree™ would look like….

Figure: 5

Clearly there are more branches to this tree than I've just shown here, but this example should give you the general idea.

Hey, but you don't know what *my* business objectives are!

Each of the 'business traits' that you have identified has been turned into a KPI Tree™.

KPI Trees™ give us a structure

The idea behind a KPI Tree™ is that each trait has a set of *relevant Big 6* objectives that goes along with it. It's probably easiest to give you an example…

Let's say we chose the Pricing KPI Tree™ - a really commonly used KPI Tree™.

Pricing is something that directly affects the **growth** of our business - **profitability and solvency** too. So the KPI Tree™ is based on two of our Big 6 core objectives…

ST1) Run a profitable and solvent business

ST2) A growing business

So these form the 'top' of our KPI Tree™….

Figure: 6

The next level of our tree (called the 'Theme' level) shows the high-level pricing objectives we need to be successful…

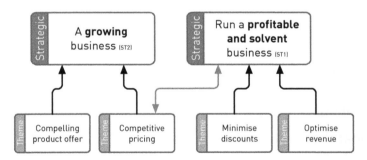

Figure: 7

We then break this down further, for 'We offer price and service that are competitive', this looks like...

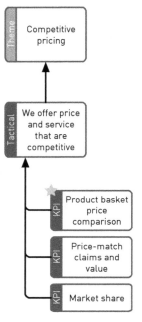

Figure: 8

Following this process, we build up a family of potential KPIs that are grouped in logical ways to deliver the high-level outcomes we are looking for.

Here's what the finished Pricing KPI Tree™ looks like....

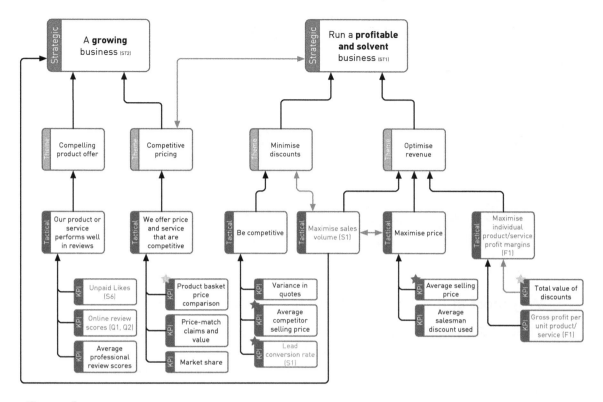

Figure: 9

How do Business Traits, KPI Trees™ and KPI Families fit together?

When the ROKS Express™ approach was developed, over fifty **Business Traits** were identified that would cover most small-to-medium sized organisations.

A **KPI Tree™** was built for each of these **Business Traits**.

The *most useful* KPIs from each **KPI Tree™** were then selected and fully defined, giving us our **KPI Families**. Here's a picture showing the relationship...

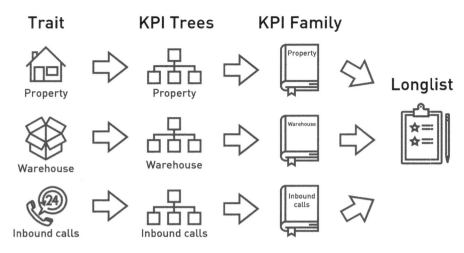

Figure: 10

Why most of the KPI Trees™ are *not* shown in this book

These KPI Trees™ can get big and complicated and need a lot of space to show them properly, so I haven't included them in this book. What I *have* included are the most widely applicable and useful KPIs resulting from each KPI Tree™. The fruits of our KPI Trees™, if you like!

What do the red (lighter grey) arrows mean?

Sometimes there are things that work together, for example a 'Compelling product offer' will cause 'A growing business'. These relationships are shown as a black arrows. Sometimes things fight each other. 'Competitive pricing' may reduce 'Run a profitable and solvent business' if it's taken to extremes. These conflicting relationships are shown as red arrows (lighter grey in this book).

What does greyed-out text in the KPI boxes mean?

Some of the text in the KPI boxes is *greyed out*. This indicates that the KPI is relevant, but covered by another KPI Tree, with the reference shown in brackets after the KPI name - for example (S6). Doing this prevents multiple definitions of the same KPI.

What do those stars mean?

Not all KPIs pack the same punch. Some KPIs are used almost universally by businesses of a certain type (cash in bank, efficiency (OEE), call abandon rate, to give three examples), whereas others are much less commonly used.

Gold Star (darker star in diagram)

These are the most useful, or widely applicable, KPIs. They are generally focused on things that have the most impact on a business. The star colour is listed in each definition (just below the KPI Name) in Section 2 (page 289 onwards). Start by reviewing these, then move onto the Silver Star KPIs.

Silver Star (lighter star in diagram)

These are slightly more niche or specific KPIs. They may not be as widely applicable as the Gold Star KPIs, may have some duplication in coverage with others, or only apply in certain situations. They are still worth looking at, so review these after you have chosen from the Gold Star KPIs.

Action

Action: Choose your Longlist KPIs

Now, having been through the Business Traits Survey, you have a selection of KPI Families that reflect the type of business you are in. You can now choose your 'Longlist' of KPIs. You don't have to be too fussy at this stage as we will be shortening the list in the next step.

Review the KPIs in each KPI Family in Section 2 (page 289 onwards) listed against each Business Trait you have ticked in the survey. There is a KPI index on page xiii. Choose the KPIs that you think will be useful and relevant for achieving your Detailed Objectives identified in Step 1.

Longlisting steps...

1. Download the template pack and open the Excel file called 'KPI Shortlisting Template'...

 Free templates registration link
https://goo.gl/DFrRyt
No Spam! Email registration required, but your details are never shared

   Have the **Business Traits Survey** that you completed earlier in front of you. Use the page reference next to each trait you selected to guide you through the KPI Families to review (Section 2).

2. Scan through the relevant KPI Family pages. Record the names of the KPIs that look interesting - you can enter them straight into the KPI Shortlisting Template if you like. Read the KPI description on the referenced definition page if the intent of the KPI isn't clear from the name.

3. Finally, fill in the first two columns on the **KPI Shortlisting Template - KPI Family Name** and **KPI Name**. Click the **KPI Family Name** column on the spreadsheet. Scroll down the list and select the relevant one, doing this will load the correct KPIs into the KPI name cell next along. Click on the cell and select your chosen KPI. **At this stage we are only going to manually complete the first two columns.** We will come back to the other columns in Step 3. (Note: the grey columns will automatically populate, so don't fill them in at all).

If you prefer, you can do the Longlisting on paper using the Manual Longlist Form in the download pack, but it will mean more work for you.

How long is long?

The list of candidate KPIs you have just produced is called the 'Longlist'. The trick here is to make sure the list isn't *too* long, as you will have a harder time in Step 3 if you have too many entries. I'd suggest keeping the list under one hundred KPIs, ideally closer to fifty. If you do find you have been too brutal, you can come back and add some more onto the list later.

Example

Chaos Coffee: Longlisting example

Here were the KPI Families that Charlie chose using his Business Traits Survey...

Table: 7

Quick Ref.	Name	Description	
F1	Financials	Financial management of business or organisation	
S1	Sales Value, Activity and Results	Selling 'things' (as opposed to selling services or words)	
S5	Sales - Pricing	Pricing any goods or service	
S6	Sales - Advertising and PPC Effectiveness	Advertising through radio, TV, organic web traffic and pay-per-click	
Q1	Service Quality	Managing quality for service organisations	
R3	Service R&D	Tracking of quality quantity of services research and development	
T1	Business Premises	Maintenance, safety and management of business property	
T2	Stock	Stock availability, management, retrieval performance and wastage	
C1	Present Customers Waiting for Service	Live queues for service or 'service on demand'	
C2	Perishable Goods	Wastage, discounting and product condition for businesses selling or using perishable products	
M1	Public Reviews	Customers reviewing the businesses publicly, e.g. online, in papers	
M2	Footfall	Passing trade to create customers and generate sales	
M3	Web Marketing	Generating sales leads or awareness through online media (web, social media, email marketing)	
H1	Health and Safety	Compliance with Health and Safety regulations and good practice	
O1	Efficiency - Widget Production	Manufacturing 'things' and want to understand production performance	
O5	Efficiency - Service Delivery	Service businesses who want to understand their operational performance	
O6	Procurement	Purchase of significant amounts of goods or services and need to manage the process	
O9	Equipment Maintenance	Maintaining equipment and manage the cost, risk and reliability delivered by that maintenance	
HR1	Staff and Payroll	Managing payment and benefits of employees	

Here are the KPIs he Longlisted, after reading through the KPI Families. The sheet reference and description are shown to help you make sense of the list.

F1: Financials - Financial management of business or organisation

- Cash receipts in period
- Total costs
- Total non-controllable (fixed) costs
- Total controllable costs
- Net profit
- Gross profit per unit product
- Cash in bank
- Total accounts payable
- Tax owed
- Cash forecast

S1: Sales Value, Activity and Results - Selling 'things' (as opposed to selling services or words)

- Average order value by customer
- Total lifetime spend by customer
- Segmented value of sales
- Total value of sales
- Average value per sale

S5: Sales - Pricing - Pricing any goods or service

- Average competitor selling price
- Average selling price

S6: Sales - Advertising and PPC Effectiveness - Advertising through radio, TV, organic web and pay-per-click

- Confirmed newsletter signups
- Facebook follower growth
- Twitter followers
- Before-and-after traffic and sales
- Marketing Return on Investment (ROI)
- Revenue generated per ad
- Total advertising spend
- Promotion generated leads volume, by channel

Q1: Service Quality - Managing quality for service organisations

- Percentage of orders with customer-reported problems
- Volume of new complaints
- Customer survey scores
- Customer retention rate

O1: Efficiency - Widget Production - Manufacturing 'things' and want to understand production performance

- Staff utilisation

O6: Procurement - Purchase of significant amounts of goods or services and need to manage the process

- Market price comparator, by product - percentage deviation
- Total cost of supplier quality issues

O9: Equipment Maintenance - Maintaining equipment and manage the cost, risk and reliability delivered by that maintenance

- Unplanned equipment downtime due to failure
- Total cost of maintenance

R3: Service R&D - Tracking of quality and quantity of services research and development

- Number of new service improvement ideas
- Number of new improved service ideas tested
- Number of new service ideas tested

T1: Business Premises - Maintenance, safety and management of business property

- Maintenance spend - premises
- Number of outstanding safety-related actions

T2: Stock - Stock availability, management, retrieval performance and wastage

- Stock-outs
- Total stock value

C1: Present Customers Waiting for Service - Live queues for service or 'service on demand'

- Walkout rate
- Median customer wait

C2: Perishable Goods - Wastage, discounting and product condition for businesses selling or using perishable products

- Value of waste due to expiry
- Storage temperature record

M1: Public Reviews - Customers reviewing the businesses publicly, e.g. online, in papers

- Customers leaving feedback
- Online review site scores - average
- Existing customer survey scores
- Unpaid 'Likes', '+1's etc.

M2: Footfall - Passing trade to create customers and generate sales

- Number of unique visitors per day
- Timing of visits
- Forecast number of sales

M3: Web Marketing - Generating sales leads or awareness through online media (web, social media, email marketing)

- Number of unique website visitors per day
- Total subscriber signups
- Total number of shares by social platform
- Email newsletter open rate

H1: Health and Safety - Compliance with Health and Safety regulations and good practice

- Number of accidents
- Number of near misses

HR1: Staff and Payroll - Managing payment and benefits of employees

- Staff sickness & absence rate
- Hours worked by each team member

He has selected 60 candidate KPIs from Section 2. Next he thinks about KPIs that may be specific to coffee making, his process or are legally required...

Key Idea

Identify sector-specific, process-specific and mandatory KPIs

There are two sets of measures that cannot be fully covered 'off the shelf' or by picking from a pre-defined selection.

These types of KPIs fall under...

Sector-specific KPIs

These are measures that are specific to a particular sector. Often they will be very close to more 'common' measures, but will have a special name. In paper manufacturing there's a term for one important production variable called 'calliper'. In normal language it just means 'thickness'. In paper-making everyone uses the term 'calliper', so that's the term you have to use. There are hundreds of thousands of terms like this, and they often vary within the same industry depending on where you are in the world - for example 'shrinkage' in paper making means 'how much the paper gets narrower when you dry it' but in paper conversion (cutting paper to narrower strips and putting paper onto rolls) it refers to 'how much is left on either side of the original reel when you cut the paper to the roll widths you want'.

Now I could attempt to list every sector-specific KPI somewhere, but it's definitely the road to madness. There's good news though. YOU almost certainly know most of the relevant sector-specific terms already. If you know your field, you have almost certainly come across the language used every day in your sector. Many of the terms and calculations used in specific industries are a variation on core terms covered in our KPI Trees™. Concepts like material yield, capacity utilisation or efficiency come up time after time, in multiple industries, just hiding under the cover of different names.

So use the KPI Families as the start point to identify the fundamental aspects of your business that you need to measure, then tweak the names and definitions to match the conventions and language in your particular sector.

Process-specific KPIs

There are more processes in the world than the human mind can comprehend. From crossing the road, to booking a dentist appointment through to ordering a new computer, there are both visible and invisible processes everywhere you look. Each process is different, but all processes have common features. We could never cover the measures for even a tiny fraction of specific processes, but what we *can* do is outline the steps you need to follow to figure out the KPIs for your process.

Because processes have multiple steps, and are very varied, we need a slightly adapted approach to choosing these KPIs - one which includes some understanding of *what* the process steps are and what we are trying to *achieve* in the process.

Here are those steps:

How-to

1. **Assemble process experts**, along with any process maps (if they exist), in a meeting or workshop. This step applies to medium-to-large organisations. If yours is a one-person business then skip to the next step.

    Having the right people in the room helps in multiple ways…

    *   They see many of the underlying process issues (think 'improvement opportunities') on a daily basis.
    *   The process experts understand the process flow (often the reality is different from the documented process - 9 times out of 10 the process expert is right).
    *   Their buy-in will be crucial when the measures roll-out, so get them involved early to maximise their support for the new process measures.
    *   The high-level process maps will be needed in step 4 and provide an essential focus for discussion. If you have machine/process-step speeds (or cycle times) shown by product variant and resource levels on them, even better.

2. **Agree on the operational questions you need to answer**

    Process KPIs vary greatly in the detail, but will generally aim to answer the following questions…

Table: 8

Question	KPI
How efficiently did we use our materials?	Yield (percentage)
How efficiently did we use our equipment?	OEE / OPE (percentage) - common efficiency measures.
How efficiently did we use our people?	Labour Efficiency / OLE (percentage)
How much product did we make/process?	Output
What proportion of products were in spec?	Quality rate (% or count)
How many went wrong?	Waste (kg or units or percentage)
How many did we have to fix?	Rework (% or count)
How many customer complaints did we have?	Complaints (number or percentage)
How long did our customers have to wait?	- Order lead time (average time) - Customer demand (volume/hour)
Did we meet orders in full?	Order fulfilment (percentage)
How much more could we make?	Plant/process capacity or utilisation
How much does it cost to make/process an item?	Activity based costing (£/$)
How many of our customers gave up in frustration?	Call abandon rate / Order cancellation rate

In some cases, several questions will be answered by one 'core' measure, like OEE, yield and so on.

There are often process-specific and product-specific measures for a given industry. These normally fall under 'yield' and 'efficiency', but are helpful to break out separately. Examples might include 'giveaway' in the packaging industry (putting more than legally required in a packet) or 'call-abandon' rate in a call centre environment. Both affect yield and are a specific type of (avoidable) loss.

Map the KPIs to measurement points on each process

This step determines *where* in the process the measurement will take place (e.g. which bottleneck speed dictates the process potential for the OEE calculation).

You may need to do some hands-on process measurement to do this, for example physically measuring cycle times or maximum output rates.

Tip

Tip: With measures like OEE, getting the right equipment identified as the bottleneck is critical. Getting this wrong can throw the accuracy of your efficiency off by an order of magnitude.

Agree on the specific definition of each process KPI

Many of your more common measures will be 'off the shelf' measures, like OEE and Yield. Even these will require some clarification. In some processes there are unavoidable losses (shrinkage in paper making, for example), and there needs to be a discussion about what is, and is not, included. I tend towards 'brutal' measurement - leaving things 'in' even if they are seen as 'part of the process'. This is because some of my most successful manufacturing consulting results came from reducing the 'but that's just part of the process' losses that could have been hidden if they were excluded from the yield or efficiency measures.

Note: Many of the slightly more 'exotic' process KPIs are variants on the answers to these questions. For example - Capacity planning is simply the combination of a forecast with a fine-grain capacity/utilisation answer.

The journey of a thousand miles starts with a single step

As with all KPIs, it can be easy to plan them but much harder to implement them. If process KPIs are a fairly new idea for your organisation, start with something fundamental. For those completely new to process measurement, just measuring daily output can deliver a lot of insight and value. For more advanced operations, OEE and Yield are early 'must-have' KPIs. Focus on getting the implementation right, rather than rushing into too many different measures.

Mandatory KPIs

Some sectors require you to measure certain things. This is normally for legal or regulatory purposes. These will vary by country and over time, but as a business owner it's your responsibility to be aware of them and to record them in line with the rules/law.

Example

Chaos Coffee: Sector-specific and process-specific KPIs

Charlie is a bit of a coffee geek and is very interested in how much good-tasting coffee he gets from each sack of beans he buys.

He knows that getting the right amount of 'dissolved solids' in the customer's cup is a critical part of delivering the right taste along with efficient use of the expensive coffee beans.

After some thinking and research, he decides that he is potentially interested in…

Coffee strength

Also known as 'solubles concentration', as measured by Total Dissolved Solids (TDS) – how concentrated or watery the coffee is.

Extraction yield %

The percentage by mass of coffee grounds that ends up dissolved in the brewed coffee.

Extraction yield % = Brewed Coffee [g] x TDS [%] /Coffee Grounds [g]

E.g. (espresso) 36g brewed coffee x 10% TDS / 18g ground coffee = *Extraction yield of 20%*

Updating the Longlist

So Charlie adds these two extra KPIs to his Longlist, ready for next step. His candidate list - the Longlist - now stands at 62 KPIs.

Action

Action: Identify your sector-specific, process-specific or mandatory KPIs

Follow the steps on page 97 and record any additional KPIs that are sector-specific, process-specific or mandatory. Add these extra KPIs to the KPI Shortlisting Template.

If you are using paper, printable versions of the simple forms for recording process-specific, sector-specific and mandatory KPIs are in the downloads pack.

Once you have done this, you will have built your completed KPI Longlist. You are now ready to review and shorten that list to something a bit more manageable for implementation. Our next step is Step 3, Shortlisting KPIs.

Recap
Step 2: Draft list of 'Ready-to-Go' KPIs

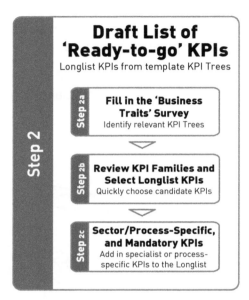

Figure: 11

In this step you will have...

- Identified which 'business traits' apply to your business.

- Reviewed the relevant KPI Families, based on your selected business traits, and selected useful-looking KPIs.

- Identified sector-specific, process-specific and mandatory KPIs.

- Added selected KPI Family selections, sector-specific, process-specific and mandatory KPIs to the KPI Shortlisting Template.

Step 3: Shortlist KPIs

Summary
Step 3: Shortlist KPIs

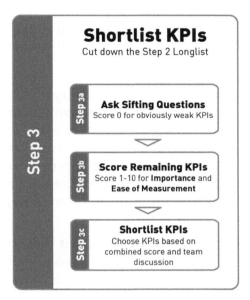

Figure: 12

In this section you will...

- Rapidly reduce the KPI Longlist by asking the 'Sifting questions'.

- Use the KPI Shortlisting Template to score each candidate KPI for **Importance** and **Ease of Measurement**.

- Shortlist your KPIs by scoring rank, deciding on your cut-off threshold and any exceptions that you may want to make.

Key Idea

Shortlisting: Why you need it and how it works

The single most common problem I've come across over the years isn't *coming up with KPIs,* it's coming up with a *small selection* of the **right** KPIs. The approach that most businesses instinctively take is either:

- **A debate in a meeting.** The group try to reach a consensus, often after lots of argument, about which are the most important things to measure. Potentially useful KPIs are often thrown overboard as they are 'too hard' and there are 'already too many KPIs'. The shortlist is typically decided based on current 'hot problems' and 'gut feel'. The selection is often contentious and may well be changed frequently after 'agreement'.

- **Not making a proper decision to cut the list of KPIs down at all.** This results in huge load on the people producing the KPI reports and dashboards and mental overload for the poor souls who have to use them.

The good news is, there's a simple, structured, approach we can use that takes a lot of the heat and stress out of the Shortlisting process. This approach is the Shortlist KPIs step of the ROKS Express™ approach, Step 3. The Shortlist step is broken into two parts, Sifting and Scoring.

Why the two-step approach of Sifting questions *and* KPI scoring?

Depending on the level of debate, it can take 2-3 mins to score each Longlisted KPI using the Importance/Ease of Measurement scoring approach. If you have 200 Longlisted KPIs (not uncommon), we are looking at 6-10 hours of Shortlisting - not much fun! This is where the Sifting questions come into play and can potentially save you hours of review time.

Key Idea

Introducing the Sifting questions

The first part of the Shortlist step is to quickly reduce the Longlist by eliminating the weakest KPIs without lots of time-consuming discussion. We do this using the Sifting questions. Once we have done this we will then concentrate on scoring the remaining KPIs to identify the 'winners'.

Here are the Sifting questions...

- **Should** we really try to improve that thing being measured?
  - Is it worth the time, effort and resources to improve it?
  - Don't care? - Then just eliminate it.
- **Can** we improve it? Do we have the influence to improve it?
  - No? Just eliminate it (unless having knowledge of it might affect your decision-making).
- **Will** we want to measure it in the *future* (perhaps when we have grown) but not now?
  - If it's one for the **future**, eliminate it, but perhaps keep a separate note of it for future reference.

What to do with KPIs rejected using the Sifting questions?

All the KPIs in your original Longlist will eventually be given a final score in the KPI Shortlisting Template spreadsheet. We can also use this score to push our eliminated KPIs to the bottom of the list, by setting the **Importance** or **Ease of Measurement** scores to zero. We don't want to *lose* the weakest ones altogether and this way they're still there (with a *reason* for the zero next to each) and can be easily retrieved if you change your mind.

To set scores you will need to use the KPI Shortlisting Template (see 'Scoring Longlist KPIs for 'Importance' and 'Ease of Measurement'' on page 112).

Example

Chaos Coffee: Using the Sifting questions

Charlie looks at the KPI Longlist and counts the candidate KPIs. There are 62. He would like to shorten the list a bit more before we get to the proper Shortlisting stage.

He applies our three **Sifting questions** from 'Introducing the Sifting questions' on page 109. Charlie eliminates the following KPIs, recording his reasons on the KPI Shortlisting Template as he does so…

Table: 9 Charlie's eliminated KPIs, with reason for elimination

Eliminated KPI	Reason for removing from Longlist...
Total lifetime spend by customer	Chaos Coffee doesn't have a trackable loyalty card in place yet.
Average selling price	Charlie will do like-for-like price comparisons with competitors, rather than comparisons of averages.
Promotion generated leads volume, by channel	The number and complexity of promotions being run don't justify this yet.
Customer survey scores	Charlie wants to run surveys, but doesn't have the time or energy to do this in the short term.
Staff utilisation	Just not high on the priority list at the moment.
Total cost of supplier quality issues	Would like to do this, but not yet.
Unplanned equipment downtime due to failure	Not a big enough issue at the moment to justify a KPI.
Total cost of maintenance	Will be rolled up into the total business costs.
Maintenance spend (premises)	Will be rolled up into the total business costs.
Forecast number of sales	This is one for the future: it's overkill right now.

Charlie adds these reasons in the Reason for Choice box and sets the **Importance** score to 0 (see Scoring section, page 112), so those KPIs will always come at the bottom of the ranking list, but they remain on the template for reference.

Using the Sifting Questions, Charlie has managed to trim the list down to 52 candidate KPIs.

Action

Action: Apply the Sifting questions to trim down *your* Longlist

Apply the three Sifting questions to each candidate KPI in your KPI Shortlisting Template spreadsheet (questions shown on page 109).

On the KPI Shortlisting template, set the Importance score to 0 for any KPIs that you discard during the sift. That keeps a copy of the discarded KPI but makes sure it will be at the bottom of the ranking, saving you time.

Key Idea

Scoring Longlist KPIs for 'Importance' and 'Ease of Measurement'

We now move on to the second part of the Shortlist step, scoring. You are going to score each of the **Longlisted** KPIs for **Importance** and **Ease of Measurement** on a scale of 1-10. You will then multiply those scores together, for each KPI, to produce the KPI Ranking Score. Sorting the Longlist KPIs by KPI Ranking Score will then give you a way of identifying your priority KPIs. Crucially, this approach also gives you a *really good reason* for **NOT** measuring some things. Deciding *not* to measure certain

KPIs can be the hardest thing to do in practice and is the key to KPI success.

Here's what we mean by 'Importance'

The easiest way to quantify **Importance** is to ask 'If this 'thing' is within our 'sphere of control' and goes out-of-control, what happens to the business?'.

Examples of Importance score = 10

A **10** indicates that a lack of control of this KPI may permanently and irreversibly destroy your business. Examples might include…

- If we are an online business and we get zero website hits, what happens? We don't sell anything and go bust - that's a **10** for Importance.

- We run out of 'cash in the bank'. We can no longer trade, so monitoring 'Cash in the bank' scores a 10 for Importance.

- We are a business that lets members of the public do potentially high-risk activities (e.g. Sky-diving) and we have a fatality as a result of poor process or procedure - that's a tragedy and the end of your business. Robust safety processes and KPIs are a must and some will be a 10.

Examples of Importance score = 5

An Importance score of **5** shows something that has significant impact on the business in the short-to-medium term but that impact is unlikely to profoundly change the future of the business in isolation. Put another way, these are things that, if neglected, would cause our business some harm but probably won't sink us.

- Junk email complaints about marketing emails going through the roof.

- Itemised controllable costs running out of control (as opposed to total costs).
- High staff attrition - although serious, it's visible without KPIs, so this might be a 5 in terms of KPI Importance.

Examples of Importance score = 1

There are a vast number of things you could count or measure that are trivial or are completely outside of your control, and so would score a **1** on the Importance scale. These are all flawed or irrelevant measures that have little or no impact on meaningful strategic goals. Examples might include…

- Lines of code written per day by a developer. It's an almost meaningless productivity measure for coding as volume of code has almost no positive relation to code performance.
- Quality problems fixed. Is being busy fixing problems good, or better to have no problems in the first place?
- Gross Domestic Product for country of operation. If you are a small business this is vastly beyond your sphere of influence, so, although it may affect you, we give it a 1 for Importance in this situation.

Typically, if a reported KPI makes no difference to the business decisions then you should give it a minimal score for Importance.

Note: we do give a score of 0 sometimes, but this is to effectively eliminate the KPI during the sifting process.

Next…

Here's what we mean by 'Ease of Measurement'

The 'Ease of Measurement' score should show how easy it is to record, collate and calculate a KPI.

You should also consider if the work required to be able to collect a KPI is a 'one-off' (e.g. Write a query for a database, installing a data logger etc.) or sustained (e.g. Manual data collection standing in a shop recording queue lengths on a regular basis). Generally, valuable KPIs with high 'one-off' effort are good candidates to put on our 'to-do list' (or 'Aspire' list) - KPIs we want to implement in the future - as they don't suck up too much resource *once* they have been implemented.

Examples of Ease of Measurement Score = 10

- If we already had an automated display showing live data for 'Average call queue time' - that would be a 10 for 'Ease of Measurement'.

- Our online banking app displays our current business cash balance at the touch of a button on our mobile phone.

- Takings for our shop today - automatically generated by our EPOS/till system.

Examples of Ease of Measurement Score = 5

- Average market hourly pay rate. Some internet research and collation required, but nothing too challenging, followed by some light arithmetic.

- Queue time for [physical] queues of people - requires simple manual sampling and data collection, but may be automated (with some effort).

- Contact interaction audit score - requires manual scoring and collation.

Examples of Ease of Measurement score = 1

- Percentage of shopper's food budget spent in our store versus competitors.

- Measuring baby enjoyment of baby-gym business.
- Value of royalties infringed - a potentially unknowable figure.

Key Idea

Calibrating your KPI scores

The only tricky part of the Shortlist KPIs step is getting the scoring *right*. You should aim to have your candidate KPIs spread fairly widely across both the Importance and Ease of Measurement 1-10 scales. If all your KPIs are clustered in one part of the scoring range you will need to revise your scoring to give a wider spread. There's a simple solution to this.

How to do calibration

Have a quick read through the Longlist of KPIs you produced in Step 2. As you skim through the list, ask…

- Which is the *most* Important KPI on the list - this becomes your '10' on Importance
- Which is the *least* Important KPI on the list - this becomes your '1' on Importance

Now we do just the same for Ease of Measurement…

- Which is the *most* Easy to Measure KPI on the list - this becomes your '10' on Ease of Measurement
- Which is the *least* Easy to Measure KPI on the list - this becomes your '1' on Ease of Measurement

If you are struggling to find a 10-10 then 'Cash in bank' is a maximum score on both measures for many businesses.

The important thing to understand is that we are giving these scores to spread out the values and establish a priority order, so the precise values of Importance and Ease of Measurement aren't critical in themselves, but having a good spread of scores within our Longlist *is* important.

Calibration KPI column - KPI Shortlisting Template

There is a column on the KPI Shortlisting template download called 'Calibration KPI'. These flags are designed to help you to easily pick out your calibration KPIs and review them as needed.

Example

Chaos Coffee: Calibration example

Looking through the Longlist, Charlie makes a note of calibration KPIs - KPIs that will score very high or low on **Importance** and **Ease of Measurement**. Charlie identifies...

Table: 10

KPI	Importance Score	Reasoning	Ease of Measurement Score	Reasoning
Cash receipts in period	10	Life and death critical for business survival	9	Easy, but need to log in to accounts system and run report.
Median customer wait	6	Fairly important, but will dent sales rather than kill business if out of control.	3	Requires manual observation and recording throughout day, without tech solution.
Percentage of orders with customer-reported problems	3	Problems are fairly rare, easily fixed and normally minor.	5	Would require a manual tally sheet and entering into a spreadsheet.

So, as he goes through and scores each of the remaining KPIs he will use these three sets of scores for comparison.

Action

Action: Calibrate your KPIs...

Run through *your* Longlist of KPIs on your KPI Shortlisting Template, identify and assign a score to...

- The **most important** KPI on the list
- The **least important** KPI on the list
- The **easiest** KPI to measure
- The **hardest** KPI to measure

These high and low scores will give you a reference point for scoring your other KPIs in the next step.

Example

Chaos Coffee: KPI scoring example

Charlie has his Longlisted measures from Step 3. He has run through the Sifting questions and trimmed the original 62 KPIs down to 52. Having calibrated his list, he then goes through each of the remaining KPIs and scores each for Importance and Ease of Measurement. He decided to use a score of 50 (Importance x Ease of Measurement) as the cut-off threshold.

Doing this cut out just over half the KPIs, leaving 24 KPIs - 9 Finance KPIs and 15 Non-finance KPIs. Here's his final list, sorted by ranking score...

Table: 11

Tree Name	KPI Name	Ranking Score
F1: Financials	Cash receipts in period	90
F1: Financials	Cash in bank	90
M2: Footfall	Number of unique visitors per day	81
F1: Financials	Total accounts payable	72
M1: Public Reviews	Online review scores - average	72
T1: Business Premises	Number of outstanding safety-related actions	72
F1: Financials	Net profit	70
C2: Perishable Goods	Storage temperature record	70
H1: Health and Safety	Number of accidents	70
F1: Financials	Gross profit per unit product	64
R3: Service R&D	Number of new service-improvement ideas	64
R3: Service R&D	Number of new service ideas tested	64
M1: Public Reviews	Unpaid 'Likes', '+1's etc.	64
F1: Financials	Total costs	63
C1: Present Customers Waiting for Service	Walkout rate	63
F1: Financials	Cash forecast	60
F1: Financials	Total non-controllable (fixed) costs	56
F1: Financials	Total controllable costs	56
S1: Sales Value, Activity and Results	Average value per sale	56
Q1: Service Quality	Volume of new complaints	56
S6: Sales - Advertising and PPC Effectiveness	Facebook follower growth	54

T2: Stock	Total stock value	54
C2: Perishable Goods	Value of waste due to expiry	54
H1: Health and Safety	Number of near misses	54

Action

Action: Score your KPIs and select your Shortlist

1. Open your downloaded KPI Shortlisting Template. You should have your Longlist of KPIs from Step 2 already in there, with some already scored as 0 during the Sifting stage.

2. If you are entering calibration KPIs ('Calibrating your KPI scores' on page 116) enter the calibration scores in the Importance and Ease of Measurement columns. Flag those calibration KPIs using the 'Calibration KPI?' column.

3. Rate each KPI for **Importance** and **Ease of Measurement** in the next two columns on a scale of 1 (low) to 10 (high). The **Ranking Score** will then be displayed in the next column.

4. Make a note of the reasoning behind your scores in the **Scoring reasons** column.

5. Sort the table based on **Ranking Score**, in descending order.

6. Get together with anyone else that you are involving in the KPI selection process to review the list.

7. Start at the top of the list and, for each KPI, discuss and decide whether it is one that you want to measure on a regular basis. The top few KPIs should be a clear and emphatic 'yes' in the **'Shortlisted'** column. As you work

down the column you will come to a point where the answers are mostly 'No' for **'Shortlisted'**. Carry on until you are deep in 'No' territory, then stop. If you want to play it safe, you can go right down to the end of the list, but most people realise after a while that there are no more useful KPIs past a certain point.

You now have your 'Shortlist KPIs'. The Shortlist KPIs are the ones you are going to define, turn into reports and start recording in Steps 4-6.

Warning!

Don't discard all your low scoring KPIs

Many of your lower-scoring KPIs will be things you will never *want*, or be *able*, to measure. It's absolutely fine to make a note of the reason and reject them. However, there is a category of rejects that you **shouldn't** just dismiss. I call this category the 'Aspire' KPI list. These are things you would *love* to measure, but doing so seems difficult or impossible at the moment: these KPIs have a low Ranking Score because they have a *low* Ease of Measurement Score, but are *high* Importance. This type of KPI can be a **secret weapon** for your business *if* you can work out how to measure them (think Google and 'Page Rank' - the measure of how important a web page is).

The Aspire list is where you focus your KPI development effort. These KPIs may need some (maybe lots of) work to make them reasonably measurable. Don't give up on them though. If you can measure something that others find hard to measure, then it can be a 'gold bar' for your business. Commit to moving one or two into use in the future. I would recommend setting up each measure as a 'mini project'. This gives you some structure and stops you potentially sleepwalking into something nasty.

Example

Chaos Coffee: Aspire list

There are some KPIs that Charlie would like to measure in future, but didn't make the cut because they are too hard to collect at the moment. These are his **Aspire** list of KPIs. Here's that list...

Table: 12

Tree Name	KPI Name	Importance Score	Ease of Measurement Score	Ranking Score
M1: Public Reviews	Number of negative feedback comments	7	7	49
O5: Efficiency - Service	Hours worked by each team member	8	6	48
O5: Efficiency - Service	Staff sickness & absence rate	7	6	42
S5: Sales - Pricing	Average competitor selling price	9	3	27
S6: Sales - Advertising and PPC Effectiveness	Before-and-after traffic and sales	9	3	27
S6: Sales - Advertising and PPC Effectiveness	Marketing Return on Investment (ROI)	9	3	27
O6: Procurement	Market price comparator, by product - percentage deviation	9	2	18
Sector specific:	Extraction %	9	2	18
Sector specific:	Coffee strength	9	2	18
M1: Public Reviews	Existing customer survey scores	8	2	16
Q1: Service Quality	Customer retention rate	9	1	9

Action

Action: Identify your Aspire KPIs

- Add any of these potential KPIs, that are valuable but need more work on ease of collection, to your **To-do list** or mark the **Shortlisted** field next to those KPIs as **Future**.

These KPIs are often the 'magic pixie dust' that will make your business thrive in the long term. Think about saving the Aspire List KPIs as a reminder in your diary for a year or so down the line, so you get a gentle trigger to do something with them.

How many KPIs should I have?

I'm afraid there is no simple answer to this question. If you have *no* measures currently then the answer is 'At least one'. What I would strongly advise *against* is overloading yourself. Choosing too many KPIs initially means you run the risk of giving up part way through and feeling like you failed. If you aren't sure, the best approach is to choose a very small number of KPIs (two or three) that you are in no doubt are super important to your business. Get started with those. Once you have started to develop the 'KPI habit', it's a good idea to go back and run through your KPI Shortlisting Template and review some of the 'narrowly rejected' KPIs you 'parked' the first time.

Key Idea

Leading and lagging indicators: What's the difference and why should I care?

You may have heard people talking about leading and lagging indicators.

It is worth considering whether a measure is leading or lagging when you score your Longlist for **Importance** in our Shortlisting process.

If you're not familiar with these terms, here's a quick summary of the difference between leading and lagging KPIs, and why you should care about the difference:

A **lagging indicator** is something that tells you how you performed in the *past*.

Here are some examples of lagging indicators:

- Sales income
- Profit
- Workplace accidents

A **leading indicator** is a measure that tells you how you will perform in the *future*. Here are some leading indicators, and why they are useful...

- Quality of sales advice - good advice has been shown to lead to increased long-term sales.
- Customer satisfaction - happy customers lead to repeat business and referral sales.
- Near misses - near misses are a strong leading indicator of accidents and even fatalities.

The lagging indicators are still very important. The issue with them is that by the time you find out your business has made a loss, your sales have collapsed or if you have had serious workplace accidents it may well be *too late* to fix the root causes. It is crucially important to have lagging measures, so you know objectively how your business has performed, but you must also have some **leading** KPIs that you use to *actively manage* your business.

You may notice that many classic financial measures are lagging, and it's very common for businesses to be skewed towards lagging measures. Lagging measures aren't *bad*, but trying to run a business solely on lagging measures is exactly like trying to drive a car solely by using the rear view mirror.

It's easy to nod and agree that leading indicators are a useful idea, but I think a true (anonymised) story best shows the power of well-chosen leading indicators...

True Story

Leading indicators: Looking forward to unhappy customers

Selling private pensions is a serious business. They are high-value, long-term financial products. Selling pensions is complex, expensive and heavily regulated. Profitability of these providers depends on scale - having as much money as possible in the 'pot' to invest. So, like most commercial businesses, pension firms want as many people signed up to their products as possible. There are two main ways to do this. The first route to customer growth is to *sell* as many (appropriate) pensions as possible. The second 'growth lever' is to **retain** those customers once they have signed up with your firm.

'Policy retention' is the obvious measure here. For one of my financial services clients, 'policy retention' was their primary 'retention' KPI and was the focus of regular executive meetings. The retention figures made for grim reading. Each month they watched as customers took their pension pots elsewhere. In fact it had got dramatically worse six months previously and continued to be terrible.

The unasked question was 'How can we tell if a customer intends to leave *before* they leave?'.

The local improvement team did some fantastic investigative work, exploring the journey that dissatisfied customers made, *before* they transferred their policy to a rival. Their work showed that the last interaction that unhappy customers had with our financial services firm was to call for a 'valuation' of their pension investment. Once the customer had the policy valuation, they would explore the market for 'better' policies and transfer their policy to a rival if they found something more attractive. The improvement team made a startling discovery. The process of a customer obtaining a policy valuation by phone had recently been *automated*. The process had been automated at the exact point in time that retention took a nose-dive. Previously, customers would call in and deal with a contact centre agent, but the new process handled the entire valuation process with *no* human interaction. In a quest to reduce costs they had **automated the process of leaving**, giving up their best chance of retaining those customer.

Once the team understood the customer journey for leaving, the process changes and KPIs they should focus on became clear. They re-routed those valuation-request calls to call agents. Realising how important a proportion of those calls were to the business, they made sure the calls were handled by agents well trained in retention. Agents would politely probe customers to see if they were happy with their products. If the customer showed signs of dissatisfaction, the agents were trained to explore ways of retaining that customer.

Now the process was properly understood, the new management KPI focus was on 'Volume of valuation calls', 'Retention interventions' and the success of those interventions. The business had moved from counting the **cost of policy transfers** (a lagging measure) to **managing the success of retention interventions** (a leading measure).

These new leading measures enabled them to rapidly recover the potentially disastrous situation they had unintentionally created. By moving from just **lagging** to **leading and lagging measures**, they had gone from driving the car just using the **rear view mirrors** to driving using the **front** windscreen as well.

Tip

Shortlisting tips:

1. If you are scoring straight on the spreadsheet and there's only one or two of you, then you can do this on the screen. If there are more people, I'd suggest you use a data projector, so everyone can easily read and comment on the list.

2. The scoring process can be quite intense. I often find that my head starts to hurt after scoring 10-15 of the KPIs. That's quite normal. Just take a break, maybe even sleep on it. It's normally easier when you return with a fresh head.

3. If you are a bit sketchy on exactly what a KPI means, don't forget that all the ROKS Express™ KPIs are defined in Section 2. It's not cheating to skip ahead and read the descriptions.

4. Don't *over-think* the scores. Blast through them, then review them as many times as needed.

5. Adding commentary in the 'Other comments' column can help clear up your own thoughts, making the scoring a bit easier sometimes.

6. If you decide to eliminate a KPI (perhaps because it duplicates another) just set the Importance score to 0 - that way it will be bottom of the sort and eliminated automatically. Just make sure you put something in 'Comments' so you don't think you just overlooked it accidentally.

This Shortlist, is that *it*?

The funny thing is, if you follow the ROKS Express™ process carefully you won't have a big list, or lots of complexity. You will have a dozen, maybe two dozen, carefully chosen and defined KPIs.

It might be tempting to look at your fairly short list of KPIs and think that it's all been a waste of time. Like most things, the answer looks really simple *once you have it*. In the same way that winning lottery numbers look a lot less mysterious and unobtainable *after* they won or, looking back, Apple shares at $7 in 1998 really do look like a *total bargain*, coming up with the right KPIs for your business may feel like a bit of an anticlimax. The KPI selection list you have just produced looks a lot like the one you could have copied off a five minute web search, doesn't it? The difference is that they are carefully chosen secret weapons which will deliver for your business, not someone else's idea of what your business is. Like 'the winning lottery numbers' these are exactly what you need to go out and spend your time and effort in the wisest possible way.

Now, there's little value in having a winning lottery ticket unless you take it back to the shop and claim your prize. So, let's take that winning lottery ticket to the shop in Step 4.

Recap
Step 3: Shortlist KPIs

Figure: 13

In this step you will have...

- Dramatically shortened the list of candidate KPIs down to our final list.
  - You will have also identified another list of important, but currently 'hard to measure', KPIs that you would like to implement at some point in the future, your **to-do** list.

- Where you have rejected KPIs, you will have recorded your reasoning for their lower scores.

- If you decide to expand or contract your Shortlist, you can do this easily, as you have a ranking score for each KPI on the Longlist.

Step 4: Tune KPI Definitions

Step 4: Tune KPI Definitions

Summary
Step 4: Tune KPI Definitions

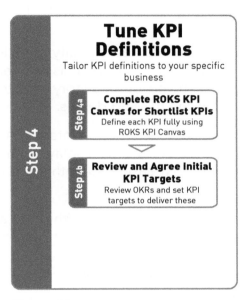

Figure: 14

In this section you will...

- Clearly and simply **tailor** the definitions of the **Shortlisted** KPIs to **your specific organisation** and record other useful information, such as where the data is stored, what the known problems with the KPI are and who the owners of the KPI and definition are.

- Think carefully about the targets you set, the behaviours they might drive and whether you can make your targets more engaging.

- Reach agreement with those the targets will affect.

Trap

The Problem with words

Human language is designed to tell stories. It does this through a rich selection of words. Many of these words overlap. Sometimes the same word can paint completely different pictures in people's minds.

The human mind also has a fantastic ability to fill in gaps and blanks using our imagination. This ability is one reason so many people prefer the written version of a story over the film; their minds seamlessly fill in the missing details.

Now if you are a novelist, this effect is fantastic. A few well-chosen words can set off a fireworks display of imagination in the reader. If you are trying to measure something, it's a potential disaster.

When it comes to describing anything with great accuracy, we have two big problems with words...

Problem 1: One word, several meanings

Our first issue is that words can hold multiple formal definitions (e.g. close, employ, key, match and mean all have more than one definition) and there are often even more informal meanings. Natural language is not designed to pin down definitions to the level that we need to define a KPI precisely.

A good reception...

Problem 2: Our minds gloss over

It's not just the ambiguity of the *words themselves* that is a problem. As humans, we also have a habit of thinking we know what something means, even if it turns out to be wildly different to the rest of the people in the room. Here's a true story, with some of the details blurred out to protect the innocent...

True Story

Executive KPI Russian roulette

A number of years ago I worked with a global engineering organisation. They charged out their engineers by the hour to clients. Like any company that charges for an hourly service, they were intensely interested in making the best economic use of their expensive engineers. A common measure for how 'busy' we keep our resources is a measure called 'utilisation'. In plain English 'utilisation' is the ratio of how much billed work we did vs. how much we could have done (flat out). Sounds simple enough doesn't it?

As a global organisation, they were split into four distinct regions. Each region had a regional 'head of' who had complete profit and loss responsibility for that region. Every month or two the leaders gathered in a room with the CEO and compared notes on performance. One of the regions was consistently reporting utilisation 10 percentage points below that of the other regions. This 'under-performance' of that region, let's call it ESSA (Europe & Sub-Saharan Africa), had dominated the management discussions for the previous few months. A recovery plan had been put in place and little else was talked about in each of the meetings. Looking from the outside it was clear that the head of ESSA was very close to being sacked.

What was not clear at the time was that they were comparing apples with oranges. All four regions reported **utilisation**, but no one had taken the trouble to ensure that they were calculated in the *same way*. After some digging we discovered that **utilisation** was being calculated as follows...

North America, Latin America and AMENA (Asia Middle East and North Africa) measured Utilisation as follows...

Total engineer billed hours / Total actual available engineer hours

So if an engineer was billed for 20 hours in a week, but was paid and available for 35 hours, her utilisation would be...

20/35 = 57%

Our 'problem region', ESSA, had defined **utilisation** slightly *differently*. ESSA had realised that it is possible to offload some of the burden from engineers to admin support staff. Offloading this work to admin support staff increased the number of site visits the engineers could achieve. As they were using existing support staff to boost engineer productivity they had decided to include admin support hours in the available hours part of the calculation. They had opted for a 'harder' measure. Here it is...

Total engineer billed hours / (Total actual available engineer hours + allocated admin support)

Now each engineer had about a fifth of an admin resource to use, so it added about 7 hours to their 'available hours' in the week. So for the engineer billed for 20 hours above, the utilisation would have been...

20/(35+7) = 48%

Now both examples would involve the same amount of paid resource. The first region just didn't include admin support in the calculation, but the second region *looks* much worse than the first.

So for our global business, they had wasted the time of their entire senior global leadership team for several months by being focused on COMPLETELY the wrong thing. When the numbers were re-cut, we discovered that the ESSA slightly outperformed the other areas, **and had always done so**. Worse still, they had almost fired their best performing regional head based on those flawed performance figures.

All that wasted effort and risk just because they had not clearly and consistently defined what should, and should not, be included when calculating a KPI.

So what's the solution to the KPI definition problem?

I could reel off stories of horrors that happened because of poorly defined KPIs, but what's really important is how we *avoid* getting in a mess in the first place. The answer is simple: ask good sensible questions. Lots of them.

It can be quite hard to remember everything we need to ask. Let's take our example of utilisation. Here are some of the questions that you might reasonably ask:

- By available hours do you mean nominal (what they are paid to work) or actual (the hours they actually worked) and do you include overtime?

- What about holidays or sickness absence? Is that zero utilisation?

- Do you include mandatory commitments, such as safety training, in the available hours?

- What about sales? This is clearly a value-add activity but is not billable.

- What happens if you bill at a much reduced hourly rate? Does that utilisation count the same as full-rate work?

- What do you do with staff who have dual roles, only one of which is a billable position?

- By individual do you mean only individuals who are billable, or do you include support staff?

- Exactly what data should I use?

- Where does the data come from?

- What are the known problems?

- Why do we have the targets we have?

- Who uses the data?

The list can get long very quickly. To help you cover most of the questions you need to ask I've come up with the ROKS KPI Canvas™.

Key Idea

Introducing the ROKS KPI Canvas™

The ROKS KPI Canvas™ acts as a **structured memory jogger** to help you navigate through the key questions you need to answer in order to fully define your KPIs. The ROKS KPI Canvas™ helps you describe, design and challenge each KPI on single sheet.

It's a simple but powerful approach that...

- Is the quickest way to cover the *right* questions for a full and accurate KPI definition

- Is quick and easy to use as a reference tool

- Can be a fantastic resource for training new team members on how specific KPIs *really* work

Here is what the blank canvas looks like...

ROKS™ KPI Canvas

madetomeasureKPIs.com

MADE TO MEASURE KPIs

Designed by:	Designed for:	Date	Version

KPI Name

Purpose
Why we should measure this?

Definition or Formula
If there's any calculation, how is the measure worked out?
What **is** and **is not** included in the values used?

Targets
What score do we want to achieve? (If we know at this stage)

Target Outcomes
What will achieving the target deliver?

Customers
Who will **use** this KPI?

Production Resources
What **resources** are needed to produce the KPI and reports?

Production Cost
What is the cost of implementing and producing this KPI?

Data Sources
Where will the KPI data come from?

Problems and Errors
What are the **known issues** with KPI production & accuracy?

DESIGNED BY: Bernie Smith
Turning Strategy into Results
Version 1.4
26th Sept 2017

This work is licensed under the Creative Commons Attribution-ShareAlike 4.0 International License. To view a copy of this license, visit http://creativecommons.org/licenses/by-sa/4.0/ or send a letter to Creative Commons, PO Box 1866, Mountain View, CA 94042, USA.

Figure: 15

You can download the canvas from the free downloads page...

Free templates registration link
https://goo.gl/DFrRyt
No Spam! Email registration required, but your details are **never** shared

Whether you fill it in using the 'forms' capability of Adobe Acrobat Pro, print it out - covering it in Post-its and ink, or recreate it in the software of your choice, it should help you properly define each and every one of your Shortlisted KPIs. Of course, it will only help if you actually *use* it.

Licence for using the ROKS KPI Canvas™

The ROKS KPI Canvas™ is covered under the Creative Commons Attribution-NonCommercial-ShareAlike Licence. This licence lets others remix, tweak, and build upon my work non-commercially, as long as you credit me and license the new creations under the identical terms. Full details live here: https://creativecommons.org/licenses/by-nc-sa/4.0/

About the ROKS KPI Canvas™

The ROKS KPI Canvas™ is designed to be intuitive and self-explanatory. I have given you a little bit of description on each box from the template below. There are also two Chaos Coffee case-study examples included later in this chapter.

Paper form or spreadsheet?

Whilst the ROKS KPI Canvas™ is shown as a sheet, one that's designed to be printed off and scribbled on, it's the questions and headings that are important. An Excel template that uses the box headings as labels is available on the free downloads page...

 Free templates registration link
https://goo.gl/DFrRyt
No Spam! Email registration required, but your details are **never** shared

I prefer to start with a paper sheet, then type the definitions into a spreadsheet once they are worked out. That's just my preference. If you are comfortable going straight to the spreadsheet and entering the definitions - that's fine - it will save you some time.

What the boxes on the ROKS KPI Canvas™ mean...

The header box at the top of the page contains basic information that helps you keep track of who created the Canvas, when it was created and what version you are on.

The header box on the ROKS KPI Canvas™...

Here's a really quick summary of why we have the fields that we do on the header...

Designed by

The person who initially created the KPI. In organisations with more than a handful of people it can be a real time-saver to easily find out who created a KPI. Once you know who to talk to, you can (hopefully) straighten out any questions with the minimum of hassle. In a large organisation it's worth adding the job description/role of the designer, so if they move on and are replaced you can find that new person more easily.

Designed for

Was the KPI requested by a specific person or team? If so, it can be useful to record who requested it. Again, this makes queries much quicker.

Date

This shows the initial creation date. If the ROKS KPI Canvas™ has been updated, you might add a revision date too.

Version

Version control is particularly important as using an out-of-date definition is a particularly frustrating, and unnecessary, self-inflicted wound.

The main definition boxes on the ROKS KPI Canvas™...

 ### KPI Name

This may seem like an obvious field, but it's surprising how often you find multiple measures all of the same name in one organisation. If you have several measures that relate to efficiency, make sure you give them distinctive names. If one relates to a particular process, say Line 7, then call it 'Line 7 Bottling Efficiency', rather than just 'Efficiency'. The key thing here is that there's **only one measure definition** for each name, so there's no chance of getting them mixed up by accident.

 ### Purpose

Why we should measure this?

Sometimes we lose sight of why we are measuring something (this is particularly common in very top-down businesses where the boss may ask for some specific data - but analysts are too scared, or unsure, to ask what it's going to be used for). You should have thought carefully about the purpose of each measure in Step 3, the Shortlist KPIs step, so this should not be too hard.

 ### Customers - [Optional]

Who will use this KPI?

We produce KPI reports to help with decision-making. If you are a one-person business, then this is a very easy question to answer. If there are more people in your business, you need to have a clear understanding of who uses the data. That way, if a question comes up about how we measure or report something we can talk to our KPI customer and discuss it with them, instead of just trying to guess what they want. If there's no clear customer you should seriously think about dropping it.

 ## Data Sources

Where will the KPI data come from?

One of the most common sources of errors comes from holding similar data in multiple places. If you have lots of spreadsheets holding data that is similar, but maybe slightly different in content or scope, then you have a real risk of mistakes creeping in. This risk can be particularly severe if you have more than one person involved in producing KPI reports. This field needs to go down to painful levels of detail.

For example, rather than just saying 'From the production performance spreadsheet', you should specify the name of the server the document lives on, the folder path, the precise sheet name, the tab in the spreadsheet and the column-line range. Your test for whether you have done this properly is whether someone who hasn't used this data before can successfully navigate to exactly the right data by following the instructions shown under Data Sources.

 ## Definition or Formula

If there's a calculation required, how is the measure worked out?

What is and is not included in the values used?

As shown in our example earlier (utilisation, page 136), it's important to be crystal clear about the calculation used, and what is, and is not, included in the figures that are used in the calculation.

 ## Production Resources - [Optional]

What resources are needed to produce the KPI and reports?

Sometimes you will need input from other teams, companies or a particular individual to provide or analyse data. It's not uncommon to need data from a particular system, or piece of software, that only a specific person is able to extract. Knowing what or who you need to produce the data enables you to plan and spot dependencies that may cause problems.

It's fairly obvious who the 'Production resource' is going to be in a one-person-company, which is why this section is marked as 'Optional'.

Targets

What score do you want to achieve? (If you know at this stage)

Targets can get pulled out of thin air and can sometimes change over time. Note what target you are trying to achieve so that you have a record. If it changes, fine, but let's record the new and the old, so you can see how things have changed. One of the problems with targets is that there is a kind of inbuilt assumption that when you reach that target something **good** will happen. It's really important to ask 'Why are we aiming for a '10% reduction' not a 7.3% or 11.7% reduction?' Generally, if you see targets that are nice round figures you should become incredibly suspicious. Ask searching questions about exactly how that target was arrived at. More often than not you find the figure was plucked out of the air because 'Someone thought it sounded good' or it was a 'Stretch target'. This leads us on to our next box…

☺ Target Outcomes

What will achieving the target deliver?

If you have nice round targets (10%, 50% or 100% improvement) ask 'So what, when we hit that target?'. The most powerful and compelling targets are ones that are linked to outcome.

Backing up your targets with reasons like this…

- If we achieve a turnover of £200k we can become a government approved supplier.
- If we undershoot our budget by £11,500 we can invest in a new espresso machine.
- If we cut downtime by 14% we can all have an extra day of vacation this year.

… can make targets much more meaningful. Notice this format is very close to the Objective Key Result (OKR) approach.

 ## Production Cost - [Optional]

What is the cost of implementing and producing this KPI?

KPIs don't come for free. Unless they are a 10 for Ease of Measurement, there's time and effort involved in collecting, collating and calculating KPIs. People tend not to 'suffer in silence' in smaller organisations - the team will moan if something is a pain to collect - but in big organisations I have seen fifty or sixty people toiling to deliver a KPI that a senior exec has requested on a whim. I have also seen the same execs express surprise when they discover the resources that needed to be dedicated to deliver an answer to what they thought was a simple question or 'Something I thought we already reported'.

Recording this 'cost' of reporting helps us when we review what we are measuring and whether it is worth the effort.

 ## Problems and Errors

What are the known issues with KPI production & accuracy?

Pretty much all KPIs have issues. It's one of the most common reasons I hear for not bothering to measure something: 'We could try and measure that, but it's pointless because…'. All KPIs are flawed to some degree. The crunch question is: 'Is the information delivered by the flawed KPI better than no information at all?'. If the answer to that question is 'Yes', then we should still consider using that KPI but be very clear and open about the problems and limitations it has. This section is where we record, as honestly as possible, the known problems and errors with the KPI and its source data. By keeping this record up-to-date we encourage ourselves to put the right level of trust in the KPI and to try and fix the known problems.

Why are some bits of the ROKS Express Canvas™ 'optional'?

As this method is focused on a wide range of business sizes, not all the steps in the method make sense for all sizes of organisation. If you are a sole trader, you really are not going to have to worry too much about who the 'Customer' for the KPI is: it's almost certainly going to be you. Similarly, it's likely that the 'Production resource' is going to be you too.

Chaos Coffee: Example KPI Definitions Using the ROKS KPI Canvas™

Let's pick two of the Shortlisted KPIs for Chaos Coffee and have a go at defining them…

- We will start with a really straightforward KPI: **Number of accidents**
- Then we will have a go at defining: **Online review site scores - average**

First step: Check Section 2, our library of pre-defined KPIs at the back of this book, to see if there's already a definition. There is a KPI index on page xiii.

We already have a couple of definitions in Section 2 - 'Number of accidents' on page 352 and 'Online review site scores - average' on page 411. They may need some extra work, but here they are…

Example 1: Number of accidents

 ### KPI Name

Number of accidents

 ### Purpose

Where there are accidents we will normally need to record these accidents in a log. This KPI is simply the total of recorded accidents in the period. Look at 'Lost days' to get some indication of severity.

Keeping a close eye on this figure is a useful, if lagging, indicator on our safety performance.

 ## Customers - [Optional]

Who will use this KPI?

The whole team. Charlie will monitor it and make sure each accident is investigated properly, with preventative measures put in place where needed.

 ## Data Sources

Where will the KPI data come from?

The safety and accident log book and our KPI tracking spreadsheet.

 ## Definition or Formula

If there's any calculation, how is the measure worked out?

*What **is** and **is not** included in the values used?*

It's a simple 'count' of the number of logged accidents in the week.

It will include any accidents recorded in the 'accident log book'. This will potentially include staff, customers, delivery staff and contractors.

 ## Production Resources - [Optional]

What resources are needed to produce the KPI and reports?

Once a week the accident book needs to be checked and the KPI spreadsheet updated.

Estimated time to complete - 5 mins.

Targets

What score do we want to achieve? (If we know at this stage)

We will not target this at all. Whilst we want to see this figure as low as possible, this must be as a result of a genuinely safe environment. We will not target any specific figure so as to make sure we don't deter staff from reporting accidents.

 Target Outcomes

What will achieving the target deliver?

See comments on Targets (above).

Production Cost - [Optional]

What is the cost of implementing and producing this KPI?

5 mins of team leader's time each week. Cost <£2

Problems and Errors

What are the known issues with KPI production & accuracy?

People must **record** accidents. Sometimes people can be reluctant to record accidents, especially when they weren't following the rules. Need to build a culture of 'it's good to record accidents, whatever the cause'.

A potential engagement issue may occur when there are long periods between accidents. There will be many periods with nothing to report. This a great outcome, but not a very engaging figure to report. It might be better to focus on 'days since last accident' - just be careful this doesn't become a disincentive for people to report accidents.

Example 2: Online review site scores - average

 KPI Name

Online review site scores - average

 Purpose

Many ratings and review sites give a star rating, or score, for overall feedback. Online review scores can be critical for generating a steady stream of new customers for many new businesses. A summary of the scores, particularly when trended, can show us how our business is being perceived by its customers. Drilling down into the reasons given for particular scores can also be very valuable.

 Customers - [Optional]

Who will use this KPI?

Charlie

 Data Sources

Where will the KPI data come from?

Initially: Google and TripAdvisor

 Definition or Formula

If there's any calculation, how is the measure worked out?

*What **is** and **is not** included in the values used?*

The average is a 'weighted average'. For example, we want 400 'five star' reviews on one review site to count more than just a single 'two star' review on another site. Using a weighted average stops lots of good reviews on one site being overwhelmed by just one overly positive/negative review on another review site.

Average score = (Site 1 average score x number of reviews on Site 1) + (Site 2 average score x number of reviews on Site 2) / (Number of reviews on Site 1 + Number of reviews on Site 2)

 Production Resources - [Optional]

What resources are needed to produce the KPI and reports?

Once a week, someone needs to sit down at a computer, with internet access, and note the average review scores. They also need to read the new reviews and record any major issues that are mentioned in those reviews.

These records will be kept in the review log, which can be found on the shared drive in the 'Reviews Tracking Log', on the tab labelled 'Review scores' and 'Review comments'.

Should take 10-15 mins maximum. Checking out the competitor scores will probably take another 20-30 mins.

 Targets

What score do we want to achieve? (If we know at this stage)

An average of 4.8 or better

 Target Outcomes

What will achieving the target deliver?

Achieving this will mean we have an average score of at least 0.2 more than our current local competitors.

 Production Cost - [Optional]

What is the cost of implementing and producing this KPI?

About 15 mins of Charlie's time, about £10 (or £30 including competitor scores).

☹ **Problems and Errors**

What are the known issues with KPI production & accuracy?

Anyone can leave a review, so staff (and family) could leave positive reviews if it affected their pay. Competitors can leave bad reviews to drive customers to them, if they wanted to. We need to develop some methods for identifying rogue reviews if possible (e.g. Reviewers with recent accounts, no other reviews and minimal personal details on their profile).

Fine-tuning your KPIs

Even if all your KPIs are 'off the shelf' ones from Section 2 of this book, there are still some decisions you need to make. Those decisions include…

- How often to measure
- Which way to break down the figures: by individual, team, product or department?

There are also some tweaks that can be made, depending on why you are measuring something. Typical tweaks include…

- Choosing the right type of average
- Using bar charts to enhance understanding of averages
- Choosing whether to use a count, percentage or ratio

The next five sections cover each of these topics.

How-to

Slicing and dicing: How should I break a KPI down?

What I don't want to do with this book is to pack it with thousands of slight variations on the same measures. To avoid this I need you to exercise some judgement when it comes to choosing the **exact** measure breakdown.

Let me give you an example. If we are talking about 'call volume' in a call centre call handling environment, then you may be interested in segmenting those call volumes by:

- The agent who is handling them
- The problem type
- Product offer type
- The time interval - day, week and so on

I'm not suggesting that we have a separate measure for each of those call volumes. What you need to do is think carefully about what you're trying to understand when you look at this measure and fine tune the breakdown of the KPI accordingly.

Here are some memory jogger questions for slicing and dicing:

Ownership?   Individual team, department and so on.

Product type? Product family or product grouping?

Enquiry type? Problem, query, refund, extra service etc.

The key here, is to decide what is **meaningful for your business** and fine tune accordingly.

The next thing to consider is *how often* you should measure that thing…

How often to measure and review? Finding the 'heartbeat' of your business

One of the most common questions I get asked is: 'How often should we measure this?'. There are five things that you need to think about when you decide how often to measure…

How long does it take for us to react or intervene when this number goes in the wrong direction?

I have an Apple watch which recently received updated software. Slightly to my surprise my watch started buzzing me around midday with an interesting message. The message was 'All three of your [progress] rings are usually farther along by now. You've got time to get back on track'. The designers of the software had realised that it's no good waiting until the *end* of the day to miss your target. If you want the user to hit the daily target, tell them *before* they miss it, and whilst they still have time to do something about it. This is the thinking behind our next sensible question…

How quickly does this thing we are measuring change?

Some things naturally change very slowly. For example, measuring the number of **new patents granted** might be something we review every few *months*, perhaps once a year. **Call queue waits** in a call centre environment can build and dissolve in minutes. **Heart rate** and **blood pressure** of a patient in an operating theatre must be measured in real-time.

How often do we need to review this?

For the **patents granted** example above, it really only makes sense to review it on a six or twelve monthly basis. Now of course, the **number of patents granted in period** is a *lagging* measure, this means you are reviewing things *after* they have happened. There's a real risk that if you review something every six or twelve months, and it reveals something terrible, you have missed your opportunity to put it right.

One way to mitigate this is to measure and review something which is a *leading* indicator of the big thing that you are interested in. For example: recorded novel ideas, patent applications or patent searches can all be early indicators of activity that may lead to patents being granted further down the line. So, it might make sense to measure and review these *early warning indicators* on, say, a monthly basis, then review the outcomes (e.g. patents granted) on a low frequency basis.

How many data points do I need to be confident something has changed?

Although it is beyond the scope of this book, there is a branch of statistics that helps us where we have data points that fluctuate naturally. A good introduction to this field is 'Understanding Variation' by Donald Wheeler (details in Recommended Reading at the end of this book). This approach (called control charts) gives us statistically-valid rules for determining whether a process has really changed or is just fluctuating naturally.

If you don't have the time to dig into control charts, a very approximate rule-of-thumb is to work on the assumption that you need at least eight points in a trend to have a reasonable level of confidence in the direction a chart is moving.

How serious is it if this KPI goes in the wrong direction?

Using our surgery heart rate example, it doesn't get much more serious than being unaware that there's a cardiac problem during surgery, so real time monitoring is an obvious requirement. Where a business process *must* remain under control, aim for review frequency that enables you to fix things before they go seriously wrong.

So, here are the five questions you can ask yourself to help you decide…

- How **long** does it take for us to **react or intervene** when this number goes in the wrong direction?
- How **quickly** does this thing we are measuring change?
- How often do we need to **review** it?
- How many data points do I need to be **confident**

something has *changed*?

- How **serious** is it if this KPI goes in the wrong direction?

Rather than slotting your KPIs into daily, weekly or monthly buckets to fit in with your meeting schedule, consider those five questions to find the *real* heartbeat of your KPIs, so your monitoring and review is focused on **outcomes** not management convenience.

Tip

Different types of averages and when to use them

Many of our pre-defined KPIs in Section 2 are 'averages', for example 'Average debtor days'. When you talk about averages, most people think of the most common type of average (called the 'mean'). In fact there are three commonly used averages. Each one has its own strengths and particular set of circumstances where you should use it. This section is a simple guide, or refresher, that shows how they are calculated and when you should use them.

Here's a quick round-up of how they work and when they are helpful (or not).

We will use the following data for the examples.

Days to resolve complaint:

24, 25, 27, 23, 13, 100, 17, 36, 23

Mean

The mean, sometimes called the arithmetic mean, is the most common kind of average in general use and it's most likely the first one you thought of.

It's worked out by adding together all your values, then dividing that total by the count of numbers.

Example

For our sample data, the **mean** is = (24 + 25 + 27 + 23 + 13 + 100 + 17 + 36 + 23) / 9 = 32 days

When it can cause problems…

Very large or very small numbers can distort the answer. In our example the 100 day response has a big impact on the mean, even though that wait was only experienced by one customer.

Median

The median is the *middle* number in the group of the numbers listed in numerical order, so half the numbers will be greater than the median and half will be smaller. Where there are two 'middle' numbers (i.e. there is an *even* count of numbers), it's the mean of those two numbers that we use.

In our example, the sorted data is…

13, 17, 23, 23, **24**, 25, 27, 36, 100

So the **median** value has been highlighted and is 24 days

When to use it…

It can be a useful figure where you have some **very large or very small values** that may distort the mean. In our mean example, the 100 day value distorted our average; using the median avoids this distortion.

Mode

The mode shows the most **frequently occurring** number in our list - the number that is repeated most. It's like taking a vote on which value is most popular.

The mode - the most 'popular' value - in this example is the number 23.

When it can cause problems…

You can have more than one mode, and they don't have to be close to each other. This can cause confusion (say you had 2 results of 27 and 2 results of 13, they would **both** be the mode). The mode may also not give a very representative picture of data that is sparse or does not follow a normal distribution (bell curve).

How to choose the right average type

You need to be clear on *why* you are interested in the average and think about what you are using the data to show when you pick which average type. Here are some points that may help you decide…

- Most situations: use the **mean**.
- You don't want your figure distorted by a few very high or low values: Use the **median**.
- You want to find the 'most popular value': Use the **mode**.

Tip

Should I use counts, percentages or ratios?

There are normally several different ways that you can report a KPI. They each have their pros and cons and each should be used in different situations.

Let's take a common measure: Complaints. There are a few different ways we could report complaints.

Option 1: Count of complaints

We could have a simple **count** of complaints. This is where we simply add up the number of complaints we received in the period (a week, for example) and report that figure.

The upside

The upside of this KPI is that it's really easy to calculate. You just keep a record of when complaints arrive and you can easily figure out how many complaints you received in a period.

The downside

Let's say complaints increased this week. What would be one of the first questions you would ask? I'd be very interested in whether we are getting more complaints simply because we had *more sales*. If the complaints count had doubled, but sales had gone up four times compared with last week, that's actually a pretty good performance. If the complaints count stayed the same as last week, but sales were down 50%, that's a worrying performance.

The **count** is useful where we are interested in the **actual number** of occurrences - for planning resources for dealing with the complaints, for example.

Option 2: *Percentage* of complaints to sales

Looking at the downside in Option 1, it's clear that it is the **number of complaints we receive compared with sales** that should also interest us. One complaint from one sale is terrible but one complaint from a million sales paints a very different picture. This suggests we should be interested in the **percentage of sales which generate complaints**. This is typically calculated as 100 x [Number of complaints] / [Volume of sales].

The upside

The good thing about this measure is that it paints a fairer picture of the *rate* at which complaints are generated. If we see a surge in sales and complaints go up in line with the sales volume, it doesn't look like a catastrophe on your reports, if the **rate** of complaints stays similar.

The downside

Let's say that complaints take a few weeks to surface, but may happen on day 1 of sale or a few months after the sale. Let's say that our sales volume goes up and down quite a bit too. Taking an extreme example, let's say we normally sell one hundred widgets a week but last week sold only one. During that same 'poor sales' week, where we sold only one widget, we received five complaints from previous sales. If we use the complaints from that week and the sales from the same week our complaints percentage would appear to be **500%**.

That's clearly not a fair measure, as those complaints refer back to previous sales. To do the calculation 'correctly' we should tie a complaint back to when the sale was made. The trouble with this is:

- It can often be tedious, sometimes impossible, to link a complaint to a specific sale.
- Your complaints percentage from previous periods can fluctuate as 'new' complaints from a previous reporting period are added to that period. This can lead to historic complaints percentages fluctuating, even after publication, causing confusion and uncertainty.

Option 3: *Ratio* of complaints to sales

Although very similar in upsides and downsides to Option 2, you could express complaints as a ratio. For example: Last week we had a complaints rate on sales of 1 in 50. The upsides and downsides of this are almost identical to showing percentage complaints to sales, but some people find ratios easier to understand and relate to.

How to choose

The best way to decide whether a count or percentage/ratio is the right measure type is to ask yourself:

- What makes sense, based on how I'm going to use the data? In our example…
  - Counts make sense for operational planning (in this case)
  - Complaint percentages make sense for manufacturing, operational and sales performance assessment (in this case)
- Do I need to 'close' the KPI each period or is it acceptable to revise it later (as explained in the Option 2 **downside**

example)

- Do I care specifically about the **number of occurrences** (e.g. Accidents) or the **rate** (e.g. Sales conversions)?
- What happens if I have big fluctuations in the ingredient figures for the KPI - does the KPI still make sense and tell me something useful?

This may look a little complicated, but if it in doubt you might want to start with **counts** *and* **percentages**. It will be extra effort but after a little use it should become clearer which is suitable for your needs.

When just an 'average' isn't enough...

We talked about averages in the last section. There are some situations where an average just does not give you a clear enough picture of what is going on. In that situation you can use a combination of a data table and a bar chart.

Here's an example...

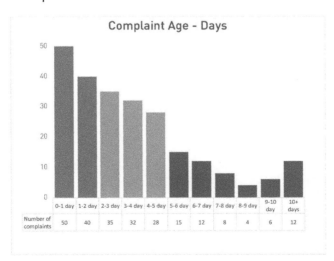

Complaint Age - Days

	0-1 day	1-2 day	2-3 day	3-4 day	4-5 day	5-6 day	6-7 day	7-8 day	8-9 day	9-10 day	10+ days
Number of complaints	50	40	35	32	28	15	12	8	4	6	12

Figure: 16

Adding the 'age' dimension to this data helps us see a 'bulge' in the volumes before they head into 'overdue' territory.

You may also choose to supply the mean, or maybe add it to the chart. This kind of profile can help the reader really 'get to grips' with the shape of the data.

Although bar charts like the one in Figure: 16 are extra work to create, they are a powerful way to share a heap of information quickly and easily.

How-to

Creating and managing your KPI definitions

Why define your KPIs?

It's important to write down your KPI Definitions using the structured approach of the ROKS KPI Canvas™, or something like it. Writing the definition down…

- Highlights gaps in our own knowledge
- Enables us to check back when we forget the specifics of a KPI
- Creates the foundations for a KPI production process
- Enables us to easily train others how they work and are calculated

There are three options for capturing your definitions…

Paper-based definitions

Just printing off several copies of the ROKS KPI Canvas™ template and filling them in with a pen is the simplest and quickest way of getting started. Stick the definitions in a ring binder, label the binder and put it somewhere handy for reference. Fairly cheap, very quick and easy to manage. Perfect if there's one person, or just handful of you, using the definitions and you are all physically located near to each other. Take a photocopy or scan as a backup of your definitions once they are drafted.

Spreadsheet

Download the KPI Definition Management Tool spreadsheet template...

 Free templates registration link
https://goo.gl/DFrRyt
No Spam! Email registration required, but your details are **never** shared

It's not as 'visual' as using the ROKS KPI Canvas™ PDF template, but it's probably easier to manage. You can fill this in and update it as you need. If you want to categorise, filter or sort your KPIs then it's super-simple to do this using a spreadsheet. Just make sure you back up your template.

Database

This kind of task is ideally suited for a database (although, unless you are part of a reasonably large organisation, it is probably overkill). Any database package will have no problem at all coping with a task like this. This approach has the advantage of fine-grained user privilege management too. Just set up a table with fields corresponding to the box names on the template, create any forms you need to enter, edit or view definitions and away you go. There are so many different database tools that I'm not going to attempt to describe the steps involved, but the chances are, if you go down this route, you probably have a favourite database tool and know how to use it, so you should already know what you are doing.

The ROKS Express™ definitions

The pre-built KPI definitions in Section 2 already fit very nicely with the ROKS KPI Canvas™. This isn't an accident and gives you a big head-start when it comes to defining the KPIs for your business.

Trap

Trap: Mixing targets and measures

It's interesting, when I hear people groan and moan about KPIs it is almost always because of the *targets* that come with KPIs, not the KPIs *themselves*. Now this may sound a bit of a fussy distinction, but a KPI is quite different from a target. Let me give you an example: If I weigh myself on some bathroom scales, the figure that is reported is a measure of my weight. Now the scales don't know whether one hundred kilograms is 'good' weight or 'bad' weight for me as an individual - it just reports the *value*. I may decide that I'd rather be 90kg than 100kg, and that is a *target*.

I have often seen excellent potential KPIs discarded during workshop discussions because people have mentioned KPI and the target in the same breath. Typically some of the group have focused immediately on the target and have objected to the target as 'unfair', 'unachievable' or 'unrealistic', and then discarded the KPI and the target without any serious discussion. This is incredibly dangerous and destructive as the discussion about the right thing to **measure** and the discussion about the correct **target** are two entirely separate things.

Complaints about unfair, unachievable or unrealistic targets normally come from a poor approach to target setting (see page 170) or previous failures to deliver improvement. You should **never** stop measuring something just because you don't like the KPI answer it is giving you.

Key Idea

Why you have to be *really careful* with target setting and incentives

Targets are another easy-to-mess-up part a KPI system. When people set targets, the logic normally goes like this...

Our business depends on maximising [important KPI here]. We need to make sure everyone focuses on [important KPI here] so that [important outcome here] happens. We can incentivise people by targeting them on delivering [target for important KPI].

This will work if:

1. The target is genuinely achievable.

2. The people tasked with delivering the target have everything they need to meet that target legitimately.

3. The people tasked with delivering the target are honest.

4. People are strongly motivated by the reward on offer.

Experience tells us that attaching strong rewards to stretching targets often goes horribly, horribly wrong. Here are two examples...

True Story

Scandal: VW Audi group being caught cheating international diesel engine emission tests.

Root-cause: Technologies exist that will legitimately manage harmful emissions in diesel engines. One of the most common emission control methods uses a urea-based fuel additive called AdBlue. AdBlue is commonly used in premium diesel cars and commercial vehicles. There's a snag: adding a system like AdBlue to a car during manufacture adds several hundred pounds to the ticket price of that car. To hit both price and emission targets, without using AdBlue, VW instructed its engine management systems supplier to add cheat codes to the engine management systems of its cars. These cheat codes were designed so the software would identify the exact conditions that indicated an emissions test was being run then dramatically change the engine management rules. During testing, the engines were instructed to behave in a very frugal and low-emission way. However, in the real world, the engines behaved completely differently, giving much higher power output, but also lower fuel efficiency and dramatically higher levels of harmful exhaust emissions. This meant that the engines 'hit the emissions and fuel efficiency targets' in lab conditions but would never achieve this in real-world usage.

Compensation and rectification cost: $23.9 billion and rising.

True Story

Scandal: Financial mis-selling of payment protection policies in the UK.

Root-cause: Bank sales staff were strongly financially incentivised to meet sales targets for 'payment protection insurance' on financial products. They achieved their bonuses by selling insurance to people who were specifically excluded from policies, selling to family members (who often were told to cancel the policies once the salesman had his bonus) and by pressuring vulnerable customers into buying unnecessary, or invalid, policies.

*Cost: £40 billion in compensation and processing costs **so far.***

I can give you countless other examples, including why I have four fillings in my healthy teeth (dentists in the UK, in the 1970s, were paid per-filling. Guess what? They did a lot of fillings!).

The point is, an over-reliance on using targets to drive individual behaviour is extremely dangerous. Employees have a habit of hitting targets by any means possible, if the incentive is strong enough.

Ways to avoid the pitfalls of targets…

1. Focus on targeting processes and outcomes, NOT individual performance.

2. Get buy-in from your team before setting targets.

3. Reverse brainstorm targets (see page 175).

4. Don't put too much reward on any specific goal or target.

The 'cobra effect'

Legend has it that, when Britain ruled India, the thriving local population of [venomous] cobras in Delhi was identified as a problem by the governor. The colonial government decided to offer a reward for every cobra skin brought to the authorities. The bounty scheme appeared to be a great success: payments showed large numbers of cobras being killed, skinned and turned in for the reward. As the wild population began to dwindle, we can assume that anxiety increased amongst those hunting cobras. Being shrewd business people, the new cohort of cobra hunters started breeding cobras in *captivity*. Breeding cobras in captivity gave the cobra hunters a stable income without having to hunt the dwindling supply of wild cobras.

The authorities discovered this deception and decided to rescind the bounty. As cobras were now worthless, the newly created 'cobra farmers' released their cobras into the wild.

So, a well-intended initiative to reduce the cobra population not only cost the government bounty money for the snakes caught, it increased the wild cobra population.

Although this sounds almost comic in its unintended effect, it's remarkably similar to some of the ill-thought-out measures, targets and rewards you will see in use in businesses around the world today.

How do you avoid this? The best approach is to talk to the teams that you will be measuring. Share the measures and ask 'How could you make each measure go the 'right' way whilst *missing the point* of the measure completely?'. As long as there's some trust in the group you will normally get some really good (and surprising) answers. If you dig a little deeper the group will normally come up with a much better set of measures to achieve your goals.

Key Idea

Reverse brainstorming: A tool to help you see into the future

Most theories sound good until you come to apply them. As we saw with the 'cobra effect' (page 173), it is only *after* you use your new KPIs and targets that the unexpected consequences of your new KPIs, targets and incentives may show themselves.

There is a simple, powerful tool we can use that can help us spot these problems *before* we go live. That tool is Reverse Brainstorming.

Reverse brainstorming is perfect when your organisation is *planning* to change KPIs, targets and incentives to deliver a particular improved outcome.

The approach is based on a simple idea: asking the people affected by the new targets and incentives *'How could the 'right' result be achieved in the stupidest possible way?'*

It sounds as though there's no possible way it would work. I can say, from experience, it works very well.

When to use reverse brainstorming

The right time to reverse brainstorm is when you have come up with your 'master plan' for improving something but have not yet implemented it.

How-to

Running a reverse brainstorm workshop

Here's a step-by-step guide to reverse brainstorming that will save you, and your team, from embarrassing unexpected problems with targets and incentives...

1. Identify a handful of people who are closely involved in the day-to-day business of whatever you are interested in improving.

2. Set up a half hour informal workshop in a quiet room with a flip chart.

3. Make sure the person running the session is not seen as having a bias towards the activity you are looking to reverse brainstorm - i.e. It's not the manager trying to implement the 'whatever' that you want to reverse brainstorm.

4. Explain the result that is being worked towards, for example 'Shorter wait times for email banking query responses'.

5. CRITICAL POINT: Make sure the participants in the workshop feel completely safe expressing honest opinions. They must feel that there will be no negative consequences from being completely open and honest. If the group feel they have to be 'on best behaviour' this will not work. If you have concerns about using an internal staff member, think about getting in an external facilitator.

6. Explain the purpose of the workshop and how Reverse Brainstorming works. I sometimes tell the Cobra Effect story to show the point of the workshop.

7. Explain what the proposed improvement plan is - the KPIs, Targets and Incentives that are planned; and what the expected results - or 'right' outcomes - are.

8. Ask the group the question *'How could the 'right' result be achieved in the stupidest possible way?'*

9. Use a flipchart, with a vertical line down the middle, and write the 'Stupid' actions, behaviours or outcomes in the left-hand column.

   Real life examples that have come up in workshops include:

   – Hanging up on live customers during a call to keep the calls short and to hit the target 'Average handling time' in a call centre.

   – Booking £186m of bad debt in the wrong category on a balance sheet because the 'Board don't look at that category'.

   – Masking off multiple customer queries (from the same customer) on a faxed sheet of customer queries, to make handling the query easier and faster (where agents were assessed on a per-customer turnaround, not on the number of queries dealt with).

10. When you have reached a natural end of the 'Stupid' brainstorm, it's time to think about how to prevent the items in the 'Stupid' column from happening.

11. In the right-hand column, write ideas for preventing 'Stupid actions, behaviours or outcomes' next to each of the issues you identified in step 9. Sometimes the solution will involve extra measures.

    – One way to lessen 'Hanging up on live customers during a call to keep the calls short and to hit the target for 'Average handling time in a call centre' is to measure 'First touch resolution' - the proportion of customer issues that are resolved on the first call. You could also look at 'Average number of calls to resolution' and 'Post-call satisfaction scores'.

By the end of your Reverse Brainstorming session you should have a clear, and sometimes shocking, view of behaviours and problems that may make all your hard work wasted effort.

The approach works so well because people are much better at figuring out how things will go **wrong** rather than how they will go **right**. Reverse brainstorming taps into that common human ability to spot 'what is broken' and turns it on its head. It's time to harness your team's 'inner pessimist'.

Action

Action: Define your KPIs using the ROKS KPI Canvas™

- Decide how you are going to store your KPI definitions.
    - Print out a number of copies of the ROKS KPI Canvas™ on A3 (tabloid) paper. Punch and place in ring binder.

    or

    - Download the ROKS KPI Canvas™ Template spreadsheet.

- Decide if the 'Optional' fields on the ROKS KPI Canvas™ are relevant to your business (these are Customers, Production Resources and Production Cost).

- Fill in each field on the ROKS KPI Canvas™ for your Shortlisted KPIs.

- Back up your definitions. The only thing more tedious than defining your KPIs is having to do it twice.

- Keep the definitions somewhere visible, easy to get to but safe.

- Run a **reverse brainstorming** session to identify and fix the gaps and loopholes in your newly defined KPIs and targets.

Recap
Step 4: Tune KPI Definitions

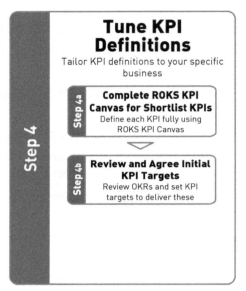

Figure: 17

In this step you will have...

- Created a full definition for each of the KPIs you selected in the Shortlist KPIs step.

- Reviewed any targets set and have discussed and agreed them with those affected by those targets.

  – If you are concerned about unintended outcomes you will have run a reverse brainstorming session.

- Considered *how often* you need to measure your KPIs to intervene effectively when the performance of your organisation goes in the wrong direction.

Step 5: Dashboard and Report Build

Step 5: Dashboard and Report Build

Summary
Step 5: Dashboard and Report Build

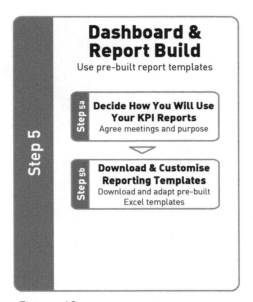

Figure: 18

In this step you will...

- Decide how and when you will review your KPIs.
- Decide how you will present and review your KPIs.
- Get a helping hand with whiteboard and Excel templates.
- Learn the simple rules of clear report and dashboard design.
- Understand how to lay out data in easy-to-read in tables.
- Learn some tips and tricks for designing and customising Excel reports and dashboards.

Key Idea

Why you need a whiteboard, dashboard or KPI report...

Now that you have designed your individual KPIs you need some way of presenting them for review and decision-making. The normal way of presenting KPIs is using a dashboard (quick summary overview of the situation) or through reports (normally a more in-depth view of a situation).

Dashboards and reports come in all sorts of styles and complexities. They range from a simple print-out of some figures on a spreadsheet through to sophisticated 'infographics'. If you have ever tried reading a figures-only spreadsheet, you will have found it usable for the simplest of data but it can quickly become indigestible as the sheet gets bigger and more complicated.

The problem: our short-term memory is terrible.

When we read raw data, we need to hold it in our memory for

long enough for our brains to make sense of it.

To do this our brain relies on **short-term memory**. Short-term memory is the kind of memory that enables you to remember what drinks you're ordering at a bar, which hotel room you're staying in or to recall what was in the TV news. It's a kind of short-term holding area. It is also called 'active memory'. We can use it for comparing a few figures or 'chunks of information'.

Research shows that we can only remember between five and nine **chunks** of information simultaneously. We typically hold items in short-term memory for 20-30 seconds.

Why the term 'chunk' can help us

The memory researchers talk about memory in terms of our ability to retain **'chunks'** of information. The good news is that the term 'chunk' is quite broad. *A chunk can be a number but it can also be a shape or line.* A **chart line** can give a lot more insight than a single number. One of the key aims with dashboard design is to include as much information into a chunk as we can in a meaningful way.

In a nutshell...

- Use charts for all but the simplest data review
- Keep your charts as simple as possible
  - Get rid of gridlines, shading and 3D effects
  - Avoid putting more than one data set on one chart unless essential

This means 'no' to hard-to-understand data tables and 'yes' to simple, streamlined charts.

Tip

Tips for building clear, simple, dashboards and reports

The dashboard template downloads included with this book have been carefully designed to be efficient and readable. They are a *start point* for you to modify to meet your needs. We don't have space in this book to go in-depth on the science and rules behind good dashboard report design, but here are some of my most useful tips on the subject. For a more in-depth look at dashboard and report design, you might find my first book, BlinkReporting, useful. More details here...

https://madetomeasurekpis.com/kpi-books/blinkreporting/

Be clear on the questions your report needs to answer

- Establish the *purpose* of the report or dashboard and the benefits it is there to enable.

Most report/dashboard design difficulties happen because the designers are not clear on the exact *purpose* of the report/ dashboard. Not knowing the true purpose will lead to the inclusion of charts and tables 'just in case', creating complex and hard-to-read outputs.

How will the dashboard be used?

Is it the driver for a specific meeting? Will a group or an individual use the dashboard? Will they have sight of it before the decision-making process, or will they have to make an on-the-spot decision?

Use the simplest possible individual charts

Create extremely *simple* charts

Charts need to work well as part of a pack, show a consistent approach and demonstrate a design 'style' that the user will come to intuitively understand and love. A chart that looks great in isolation may just look like chaos when combined with twenty or so others on a page.

Pick the right chart type for the job

If you are really struggling to fit all your data onto one chart you should be very wary. Your struggle will normally indicate that the reader will **also** struggle to understand the chart. Some charts are not capable of representing the chosen data. If you can't fit everything on to one chart, ask yourself:

- Do I really need all that information to be visible?
- If I really do need all that information, could it be split into several simpler charts?

The golden rule is… 'Do not confuse your end-user. Keep the tables and charts as sparse and simple as humanly possible'.

We must aim to keep things as simple as possible.

Make sure your output is *readable*

Manage the volume and density of information

There are practical limits to the amount of data you can sensibly fit on a page. Make as much of your data as visual as possible, but accept that some people will want to see some numbers as well. There is always pressure to put too much on a dashboard. Be mindful and be prepared to take a different approach if you can't fit what you need on one page.

Eyes not good enough?

If you find yourself using fonts on the lower end of 'readability' (smaller than about 8 point) then you have probably overloaded the dashboard or report page.

Understand where the report will be read

Print-outs, laptop displays, tablets and smartphone screens all have different readability characteristics. You need to think ahead, knowing what the target display tool will be, as this will have a big effect on the readability of your report or dashboard.

Make linking the charts and commentary painless

Use physical 'nearness'

Since people tend to assume that text next to a chart graphic is referring to that chart or object, use physical nearness to show relationships.

Lines and boxes used in a *restrained way* can help show groupings and relationships. This works for text as well. Use lines to separate unrelated topics and **lead lines** to guide the readers' eyes. Example: the horizontal lines on Figure: 19 show that the heading to the left relates to the text on the right. Be careful about using boxes though as they shut down any relationship with surrounding text or objects.

There's an example on the next page. I've used 'lorem ipsum' dummy text so the content isn't distracting...

Executive Complaints Dashboard

Overall Complaints Volume

Lorem ipsum dolor sit amet, consectetur adipiscing elit. Morbi euismod mi et tortor gravida pulvinar sed in erat. Aliquam turpis risus, blandit vitae porttitor non, accumsan quis ligula. Etiam eu tortor a erat iaculis sagittis. Phasellus ornare enim vitae eros lacinia dignissim. Nulla blandit libero in arcu dignissim ornare aliquam tortor elementum. Ut vitae fermentum nulla. Praesent faucibus, velit tempor molestie luctus, nisi augue congue felis, id imperdiet ante ipsum consequat felis. Nam rutrum augue nec turpis eleifend eu interdum felis mollis. Duis semper orci non dolor consectetur vitae euismod turpis sodales. Praesent nec dolor et magna iaculis pharetra ut ac odio. Duis ornare tortor sit amet purus blandit molestie.

Core Complaints Measures

Volume breakdown (by brand)

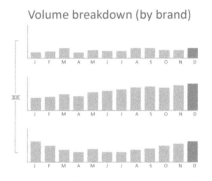

Brand A: Lorem ipsum dolor sit amet, consectetur adipiscing elit. Morbi euismod mi et tortor gravida pulvinar sed in erat.

Brand B: Aliquam turpis risus, blandit vitae porttitor non, accumsan quis ligula. Etiam eu tortor a erat iaculis sagittis.

Brand C: Nulla blandit libero in arcu dignissim ornare aliquam tortor elementum. Ut vitae fermentum nulla. Praesent faucibus.

Lorem ipsum dolor sit amet, consectetur adipiscing elit. Morbi euismod mi et tortor gravida pulvinar sed in erat. Aliquam turpis risus, blandit vitae porttitor non, accumsan quis ligula. Etiam eu tortor a erat iaculis sagittis. Phasellus ornare enim vitae eros lacinia dignissim. Nulla blandit libero in arcu dignissim ornare aliquam tortor elementum. Ut vitae fermentum nulla. Praesent faucibus, velit tempor molestie luctus, nisi augue congue felis, id imperdiet ante ipsum consequat felis. Nulla blandit libero in arcu dignissim ornare aliquam tortor elementum. Ut vitae fermentum nulla. Praesent faucibus, velit tempor molestie luctus, nisi augue congue felis, id imperdiet ante ipsum consequat felis.

Figure: 19 Example of lead lines and proximity to show chart-text relationship.

Use logical hierarchy

It helps the reader make sense of a page if all the text gets more detailed or specific as you read across/down a page in a consistent way. So you might have high-level commentary on the left, business unit commentary in a centre column and product-specific text in the right hand column.

Be consistent

Contradicting the 'unwritten rules' that you define through your first few pages can seriously confuse or mislead the reader.

Be brutal about content

If you are in a larger business and have a few contributors, some will write too much, fail to cover important topics or use complicated language. If this happens, readers can quickly give up on the content.

When you have this problem, the first step should be constructive feedback to the contributors. If that doesn't work then it is probably time to think about a 'style guide' for contributors.

Key Idea

The weird power of physical 'stuff' - my whiteboard shame

Anyone who knows me knows that I'm a real gadget fiend. I love trying out the possibilities of new technology and have apps and gadgets for almost anything. Despite this, I have surprised myself. I have discovered that I am massively more motivated by physically writing things down on a whiteboard and by using magnetic markers than I am by entering data into a spreadsheet and looking at graphs. There are two physical trackers/dashboards that I use on a daily basis. My office action board and effort (**Deep Work**) tracker looks reasonably presentable. Here it is...

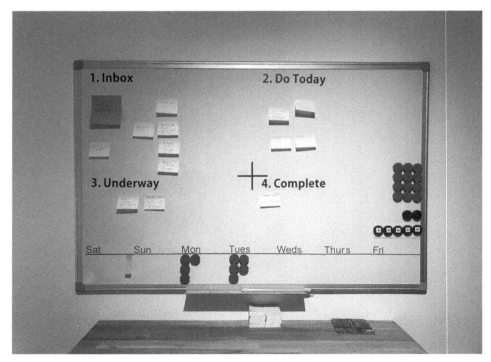

*Figure: 20 **Action board and effort tracker.***

Yes, I really do write actions down on Post-its and move them around a white board. And yes, I really do record my 'deep work' time in 20 minute chunks using little green magnetic markers.

The other board that I use to run my life is the whiteboard in my gym that I use to track my indoor-rowing times. Now I hesitated before sharing a picture of this board, not just because of my very slow rowing times, but because it an absolute disgrace to look at. Here it is…

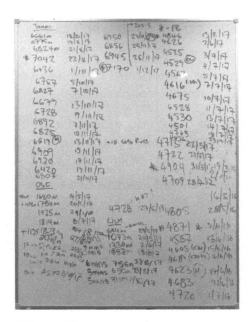

Figure: 21

I have terrible handwriting and pretty shaky hands after an intense session on the rowing machine. The reason I'm sharing this embarrassing mess with you is because I find it really effective at motivating me and encouraging me to record and monitor my exercise performance. At a glance I can see what my recent performance looks like and a simple asterisk shows my 'personal best'. It has also served as a motivational tool for my kids who enjoy using the same machine and have spontaneously taken to recording their times on the same whiteboard.

You may notice this is not in line with my advice from our earlier section, about not using columns of raw figures to review performance. For me, my main motivation comes from seeing how I have performed compared with my 'personal best'. As it's just a two-figure comparison (current performance against PB), even my exercise-addled brain can cope without a chart. I could look at the trend over time, but I haven't got to that level of sophistication yet.

Thinking about why the whiteboard has been so successful has led me to draw a few simple conclusions:

- **Physically writing** things on a board increases engagement – it makes you look at what you're writing down and creates ownership.

- Having things **on display all the time** makes it much more likely *you will look at it*.

- A whiteboard, particularly with little formal structure, gives you (the user) lots of *flexibility* to easily tweak and tune how you lay information out. You can also add notes and markers instantly.

- It doesn't really matter how *tidy or pretty* the data is as long as you are *interested* in the content and the *message is clear*.

One last thought I'd like to share with you is the difference between *hearing* something works and *knowing* that it works. From my background in Lean Six Sigma I spent an awful lot of time working with organisations that used Japanese production improvement techniques. A key part of these techniques centres on shop-floor visual display boards. These boards are normally paper-based or whiteboard-based and are located where things are actually happening. I worked with clients and encouraged them to use these boards but I had never actually applied them to my *own* work. So, although I could talk about the theoretical power of the boards, I hadn't experienced that impact *myself*. Having used them, as you can probably tell, I'm now an evangelist but it took me a number of years to get there. My enthusiasm was only triggered when I *gave them a try*. My suggestion to you, if you have any doubts, is just to **give it a go** and see how physical display boards work for you. I think you may be surprised by how attached you become to your new performance board, however rough it looks, in just a few short days.

Tip

Tips for building your own KPI whiteboard

It's really very simple to get up and running with a performance whiteboard. There are a few tips and tricks I have picked up through creating one many times. Here they are:

Firstly, some really basic, but important things to think about…

Don't guess the size

Make sure you get the right size of whiteboard. I discovered the hard way that it's actually pretty hard to estimate how big a whiteboard will be in real life from the dimensions on the website. I have tended to order whiteboards that are much too big in the past and this can cause all kinds of practical problems with trying to find a home for them.

Does your whiteboard need to be magnetic?

Decide if you need a magnetic whiteboard or just one that can cope with dry wipe markers? Magnetic counters can be great for keeping a tally of things without the board getting messy. Magnetic whiteboards are more expensive and heavier than non-magnetic ones, so make sure you really need one.

Once you have your board(s) in place…

Let the board evolve before you set the design

Marking out a board with dividing tape or even cut vinyl lettering is a great idea, *but don't be tempted to do it too early*. It's far better to let the board evolve using dry-wipe pens (or permanent-but-removable-with-solvent marker pens). After a bit of use you will know what you want, and where, on the board. You can then finalise the layout using vinyl letters and dividing tape if you really need it to look 'tidy'.

Some templates to get you started

Once you have dipped your toe in the 'whiteboard pond' you may decide you want something a little slicker - particularly if your board is visible to customers.

I have created a pair of whiteboard design templates that you are free to download, modify and use in your business. Don't rush in and use them straightaway. Try using a 'freeform' board before you have anything formal made up. You will almost certainly want to create your own variation, but there are a couple of templates you can use as a starting point on the free downloads page.

There are a few ways to use these templates. It is probably

easiest to use a video projector to throw the template image onto the whiteboard and then use gridding tape and permanent marker pen to create the layout. The better-looking option is to give the design to a sign maker to create a board layout for you – this option looks great but will normally cost quite a lot more.

The templates are available on the free downloads page...

 Free templates registration link
https://goo.gl/DFrRyt
No Spam! Email registration required, but your details are **never** shared

Templates licensing

The templates in the download pack are covered under the Creative Commons Attribution-NonCommercial-ShareAlike Licence. This licence lets others remix, tweak, and build upon my work non-commercially, as long as you credit me and license the new creations under the identical terms. Full details live here: https://creativecommons.org/licenses/by-nc-sa/4.0/

If a whiteboard just won't cut it

Interactive performance displays like whiteboards are great, but sometimes there are very good reasons why you need a more powerful and flexible way of storing and presenting data. If you need long-term trend data, have confidential data or just want the data to be portable, you may well want to use a software tool. That's where reporting tools and KPI reports come in.

If you have worked in any sort of corporate environment you

will know that the act of creating KPI reports can quickly spawn monstrous, unreadable and confusing information packs. That's what we are going to **avoid** here.

There are two elements to good KPI reports:

1. Choosing the right tool to store and present your information.

2. Structuring your data and charts in a way that is easy to present, read, understand and maintain.

For many smaller businesses, the reporting tool of choice will be a spreadsheet, often Excel. Included with this book are free downloadable reporting Excel templates which have been designed to help you structure your data and charts in a sensible way. There's practical advice on customising these templates on page 204.

Tip

Choosing the best tool for reporting your KPIs and data...

There are lots of options when it comes to tools for producing dashboards and reports. There is so much choice it can get a bit overwhelming. To simplify things, we can split the options into five broad groupings. Each of these product types has its own 'sweet-spot' for *when* and *where* to use them. Here's a run-down on those options:

Whiteboards

Whiteboards have a fantastic 'immediacy' which is hard to beat. Using them when you need to get a team to record and plot the data themselves builds ownership and engagement.

Verdict: Fairly cheap and quick. Effective for team engagement.

Spreadsheets

Spreadsheets have a poor reputation amongst most data 'pros'. Truth is, every single client I have dealt with over the past twenty years has used spreadsheets in every part of their business for critical data analysis and decision-making. Despite their flaws, (easily messing up the data, formula mistakes and version control challenges) spreadsheets will continue to be the data analysis 'weapon of choice' for most small-medium businesses. I use Excel for my own company dashboard.

Verdict: Spreadsheets are a great general reporting solution for most smaller businesses, despite their well-known problems. Quick, cheap, flexible and reasonably straightforward.

'Business intelligence' tools

There is another group of tools - 'business intelligence' tools. Tools such as Tableau, QlikView and Tibco Spotfire fall into this camp. This type of tool is slightly different from both spreadsheets and online KPI services, in that it doesn't *store* your KPI data in the software. You will still need to record your KPIs in a spreadsheet or database. The business intelligence tool will connect to that data and present it as interactive dashboards and reports.

Verdict: Useful if you need 'drill down' on a dashboard (click on a chart to see the data and charts below). Use these if spreadsheets can't present data the way you need it presenting.

Online KPI services

The key difference between this class of tools and the 'business intelligence' tools, is that these tools also allow you to **record and store your data** in their software/cloud service.

Verdict: Useful if you want zero local maintenance, easy remote access and don't mind living with the constraints and costs of your chosen service.

If you do go with this kind of tool, be sure that you have a way of extracting your data in a structured way in case the service goes bust or you decide to change provider.

Industrial-strength solutions: Oracle, SQL and the other big boys

Sometimes you need a fully-fledged database solution. These solutions are often based on Oracle, Microsoft SQL or MySQL. These bring many technical benefits: data integrity, scalability and performance, but can be expensive, inflexible and complex. Generally, smaller organisations will not go down this route for data analysis and reporting unless it's an 'off the shelf' solution.

Verdict: **Makes the IT pros happy, but usually not easy or flexible enough for most smaller businesses' needs.**

Example

Chaos Coffee: Decide on your reporting tool

Charlie has decided to go with Microsoft Excel, as it is already on all the Chaos Coffee computers and most of the team are familiar with using it. Here's a Data Analysis Tool memory jogger to help him...

- ☑ Buying the software, if required

- ☑ Setting up support and software maintenance contracts and agreements, if required

- ☑ Installation

- ☑ Setting up data backup procedure and ownership

- ☑ Local help and support ownership

- ☑ Setting up access and appropriate permissions

Charlie makes a few notes…

Buying the software, if required

Chaos Coffee already have Excel on their shop PCs, so this is sorted.

Setting up support and software maintenance contracts and agreements, if required

201

Software updates are covered by their subscription to Microsoft.

Charlie feels confident enough with Excel to sort any problems or queries he has through a quick bit of internet research. He also has a small local IT support company to give spreadsheet support if he needs anything more technical setting up or trouble-shooting further down the line, like Visual Basic functionality.

Installation

Already installed on all required machines. Charlie just downloads the Dashboard templates and tweaks them to meet his needs.

 Free templates registration link
https://goo.gl/DFrRyt
No Spam! Email registration required, but your details are **never** shared

Setting up data backup procedure and ownership

The spreadsheet file is located on Charlie's cloud drive, so there's some contingency if a hard drive fails. Charlie also takes a weekly copy on a removable USB drive and stores it in a safe at home.

Local help and support

Again, as for 'Setting up support contracts', Charlie feels confident enough in his Excel abilities to sort out most problems. His intention is to pass most of this responsibility over to the team leader when things are up and running.

Setting up access and appropriate permissions

Charlie goes through and 'protects' the calculation and reporting cells and sheets with a password, to prevent calculations being accidentally over-written or altered. He's aware that it is possible for the team to change the raw data, but he's aiming for a level of trust in the team and decides to live with that risk.

Action

Action: Decide on your reporting tool

Having read through 'Choosing the best tool for reporting your KPIs and data...' you should have made a decision on which type of tool you will be using.

Actions you need to plan, whichever solution you went with, are:

- ☑ Buying the software, if required

- ☑ Setting up support and software maintenance contracts and agreements, if required

- ☑ Installation

- ☑ Setting up data backup procedure and ownership

- ☑ Local help and support ownership

- ☑ Setting up access and appropriate permissions

Action

Action: Tweaking your free Excel dashboard templates

If you decided to go with one of the free templates from the goodies section of the download pack, then you will have a bit of customisation work to do on your copy before you can get up and running.

Here are the basic steps you need to go through:

Download the free template pack...

Free templates registration link
https://goo.gl/DFrRyt
No Spam! Email registration required, but your details are **never** shared

Choosing your free template:

- Decide how sophisticated you want the template to be.
    - If you are happy with switching between tabs and understand the idea behind vlookup, go for the 'Advanced' template.
    - If you just want to keep the spreadsheet as simple as possible (but realise this may mean more cutting and pasting) use the 'Simple' template.
- Look at the templates on offer and decide if you want
    - Just charts
    - Charts and commentary
    - Charts, data tables and commentary
- Save your chosen template and give it a meaningful name. If you are going for the 'Simple' templates, you may want

to save old versions in a backup folder, so you keep the old data for your records.

- Split your Shortlisted KPIs into groups based on how often you will report them. (Typically this will be daily, weekly and monthly). There are tabs for weekly and monthly in the template. Daily and in-day measures are normally best done with a whiteboard.
- Change the KPI name fields to match your chosen KPIs. The default names are in the form 'KPI M1' - you will need to change these to something meaningful.
- Add in the target values in the 'target' fields.
- Advanced template only: if you need to add in calculations to your report do this by:
  - Adding in columns on the Weekly and Monthly 'Analysis' tabs.
  - Re-range the charts to pick up the new columns.
  - Copy and paste those modified charts on to the Dashboard tabs - deleting the previous chart versions on the Dashboard tabs.

How-to

Some useful Excel dashboard how-to guides

This is not a book for learning *how* to use Excel. However, over the years I have found some specific solutions, super-useful functions and time saving ideas specifically for dashboard and report design. These are listed over the next five pages...

Workbook design guide for building reports in Excel

i) Keep your raw data, calculations and charts on separate tabs.

Sometimes I will go one step further, creating an 'analysis sheet' that sits between the 'data-entry sheet' and the 'dashboard sheet'. Doing this may seem like a wasteful and overcomplicated way of laying out your spreadsheet, but it makes finding problems and tweaking your reporting tool much simpler. The free sample reports have been built using this three-sheets approach.

ii) Use clear, plain English, in your descriptions of data and charts.

I've been in this situation many times, where I've written something down that made perfect sense at the time but when I came to it a month or two later I wasn't clear what the description meant. Use more description than you think is necessary. If you find you don't have space on your dashboard or sheet to give a full description, then keep a full description on a separate sheet, as a cell 'comment', or in your journal.

iii) Use a simple colour scheme to mark areas which accept new data and areas which are calculated values.

I mark areas which accept data entry in white and areas which do not accept data entry (for instance calculated cells) in light grey. Doing this naturally draws your eyes towards the areas for data entry. You can also indicate protected areas that aren't intended for data entry. Here's an example of what I mean…

	Books sold Count
Oct-17	426
Nov-17	377
Dec-17	489
Jan-18	550
Feb-18	523
Mar-18	233
Apr-18	669

Figure: 22

iv) Protect cells and sheets that are important calculations.

Protecting cells and sheets can do two things. Firstly, it can stop people tinkering with things that they might have a special interest in changing: attendance records, performance standards and so on. Secondly, locking cells and sheets can prevent accidental damage to the spreadsheet by someone who is not paying attention or perhaps isn't skilled at using an Excel spreadsheet. It is best to couple this with some kind of visual indication of whether a cell is locked (see the tip above) otherwise it can be a bit frustrating for a user trying to figure out which areas are locked and which aren't.

It may sound obvious, but you do need to make sure that any passwords used to protect cells or sheets are in a safe accessible place for anyone who needs to get hold of them.

v) Get rid of gridlines to improve readability.

Just like dashboards, spreadsheets become harder to read as the amount of visual clutter increases. Gridlines are extremely useful when you are building a sheet, but when it comes to reading that sheet they impair our ability to clearly see what's going on. I will often turn off grid lines once I finish the design. This can make the finished dashboard much clearer and more readable. If you struggle to read the sheet without gridlines, consider increasing link height/column width or using alternate row shading.

vi) Use colour coding on tabs.

Using colour coding makes navigating a book of Excel tables much quicker. For instance on my spreadsheets I marked the data entry tabs in yellow and the dashboard tabs in green. Just right-mouse-click on the tab and select 'Tab color'.

vii) Add notes in a worksheet at the back of the workbook.

You can add your KPI definitions on the tab at the back of your book. Here's what the KPI Definitions for Ambiguous Consulting look like…

Monthly KPI Definitions - Ambiguous Consulting

Reporting Period End   Last day of calendar month

Category	Name	Units	Description	Intent
Consulting	Average £ per day (gross before VAT)	£/day	Invoiced days from the current month up to the Reporting Period End	Shows position in market, competition levels and negotiation ability
	Income (gross before VAT)	£	Income earned	Shows income streams and allow trending
	Days		Billed days of delivery	Useful for spotting potential burnout or poor lead development
	Hours		Hours of work making up days of delivery	Shows the real effort involved in delivering a contract and allows a 'per hour' rate calculation
Web Presence	Links to my site	Count	How many links there are to my site	Indicator of site authority
	Average page views per day	Number	Average page views per day for month	Indicator of site popularity
	Number of subscribed MailPoet signups	No. confirmed signups	Number of new opt-in email subscribers to newsletter	Shows attractiveness of free content on offer and is the first step in the online sales funnel
Be Visible	Number of business-interest leads	Number	Number of unique business-related leads/enquiries	A rough indicator of the amount of inbound interest in the business, a results-measure of success in book writing, blogging, speaking and networking combined.

Table: 13

Which figures to use	Reported period	Which month to put the figures under	Where to find the figures	How figures are calculated
Values shown on invoices for relevant month	First to last day of calendar month	Period shown on the 'billing period' on the invoice	Invoices folder	Sum of invoiced delivery / planned working days
Gross £ (no VAT or expenses)	First to last day of calendar month	By day of delivery, delivery £ from 1st to last day of month	Invoices folder	Sum of income
.			Invoices folder	Count of equivalent full days worked
Actual hours (estimated if necessary)	First to last day of calendar month	By day of delivery, delivery days from 1st to last day of month	Invoices folder	Sum of hours worked
Google Webmaster Search Traffic - Links to your site - total Links	Current period	Current Period	Log into Google as Austin. Go to https://www.google.com/webmasters/tools/external-links?hl=en&siteUrl=https://ambiguous-consulting.com/ then choose Search Traffic (left hand tool bar) then 'Links to your site' then note 'Total Links'	Just use the total figure
WordPress 'Site Stats ' - 'Average page views per day'	Required calendar month	Period queried	Safari (on iMac) AC toolbar, AC Admin, Site Stats, Click the 'view all' button, then the small blue 'Summaries' link in the top right hand corner of the graph. Middle table called 'average per day'	Use total figure for month
Total confirmed subscribers shown in filtered 'New subscribers'.	Required calendar month	Period queried	Log into admin page on ambiguous-consulting.com (use 1 password or go to AC favourites bar at top of Safari and follow AC Admin). Choose MailPoet on left-hand menu bar, then Subscribers. In the main panel of the page click Export button and select Format -CSV and then select the Email, Status and Subscription Date radio buttons and click the blue Export button. A yellow bar will appear at the top of the web page with a blue download hyperlink. You will be offered the chance to open it in Excel, do this	Count of opt-in confirmed subscribers in period
Austin to provide	Current period	Current Period	From memory - Austin	Simple count of unique leads

True Story

Why you should sanity check your spreadsheet…

On 4 January 2010, in the Marriott hotel in Atlanta, two giants in the world of economics, Prof Carmen Reinhart and former chief economist of the International Monetary Fund, Ken Rogoff, were presenting their research paper, 'Growth in a Time of Debt'.

Their paper was particularly timely and relevant, coming just after the global economic and financial crisis and at a time when many governments were considering austerity as a solution to the economic problems they faced.

The headline message was clear and head-turning: When the size of the country's debt rises above 90% of Gross Domestic Product, economic growth slows *dramatically*.

This message, and its authors, were getting an awful lot of attention. The 90% debt-to-GDP limit was quoted by people like EU Commissioner Ollie Rehn and prominent US Republican Paul Ryan. The paper was frequently cited during the 2012 US presidential campaign. It strongly influenced economic policy in the UK, under the coalition government, driving an increase in taxes, a cut in spending and the 'No pain, no gain' mantra.

This was heavyweight economic research being taken seriously, and shaping the opinions of politicians around the world.

Only there was a problem.

Thomas Herndon, a 28-year-old graduate student at the University of Massachusetts Amherst, was assigned to pick and replicate the results of an economics paper. He chose 'Growth in a Time of Debt', by Reinhart and Rogoff, and spent a whole semester attempting, and failing, to reproduce the results of the paper.

'I remember I had a meeting with my professor, Michael Ash,

where he basically said, 'Come on, Tom, this isn't too hard - you just gotta go sort this out.'' (Source: BBC News)

After several failed attempts to reproduce the results in the paper, his professor suggested that he contact Reinhart and Rogoff. Reinhart and Rogoff provided their original spreadsheet.

'Everyone says seeing is believing, but I almost didn't believe my eyes,' (source: BBC News). Herndon called his girlfriend to double-check his discovery.

He had unearthed a basic spreadsheet error. Reinhart and Rogoff had **accidentally missed out 5 of the 20 countries** in their calculation of average GDP growth of countries with high public debt (the countries were *listed* but the formula didn't include the *data* for those countries). The countries they had missed were Australia, Austria, Belgium, Canada and Denmark.

Herndon and his academics then found other problems with the calculations underlying Growth in a Time of Debt which had an even greater impact on the result. Reinhart and Rogoff had found that little good quality post-war data was available for Canada, Australia or New Zealand so they simply left it out. Omitting these countries made a substantial difference to the results.

Yet another compounding problem was the way in which Reinhart and Rogoff averaged their data. They did not take into account the size of the country or the duration the debt was held for.

'New Zealand's single year, 1951, at -8% growth is held up with the same weight as Britain's nearly 20 years in the high public debt category at 2.5% growth', Michael Ash says (Source BBC News).

When Thomas Herndon and his professors published their working paper, they showed that high levels of debt did still correlate with lower growth, but the link was much weaker than Reinhart and Rogoff had shown with their flawed data. The relationship is gentler, more progressive and there are many exceptions to the rule.

No-one is immune to the problem of flaws in calculations. In the story of Growth in a Time of Debt, the key to uncovering the problem was independent checking of results, access to the original data and dogged determination by Thomas Herndon.

There is an extremely good chance that problems like this exist somewhere within your data and your organisation. The key questions are:

- Do we have a way of preventing issues like this from happening?
- Do we have a system for uncovering existing issues?
- Is there a structured approach for preventing problems recurring?

And the scariest of all questions:

'How many decisions have we made on the basis of invalid data and results?'.

Let's just hope than any of the existing problems you uncover haven't crippled the global economy.

Tip

Checking your Excel dashboard is correct

Making sure you avoid a mess-up like the one in the Reinhart Rogoff story is really fairly straightforward. It just involves some persistence and a bit of testing. There are a few tools in Excel that make it easier.

Find errors in your formulas

Excel can find errors in your *formulas*. To make sure error checking is switched on go to the 'File' menu, then select 'Formulas > Error Checking > Enable background error checking'.

Trace precedents

This function adds (temporary) arrows as an overlay on your spreadsheet and selected formula, showing which fields feed into your formula. This will help you pick out formula and selection errors.

Figure: 23

Trace dependents

This works much like the 'Trace Precedents' function, but from the other direction. It shows you which other cells use the currently selected cell.

Show formulas

This button changes the sheets view from showing the results of the formula in each cell, to the formula generating the result.

Evaluate formula

Evaluate formula allows you to step through a formula, one calculation at a time.

Data selection errors

- For formulas

Double click on the formula cell. It will then highlight the cells which input to that formula - outlining them in colour.

- For charts

Select the bars/lines/points on your embedded chart and Excel should highlight the data cells used to plot the selected series on the chart.

Change a number to something stupid-huge or stupid-small

Force a big, known, change in one data point, then to make sure the charts and tables show that change as expected. This can be a quick and simple check where you have several linked sheets and a chart as the final output.

Chaos Coffee: Charlie's Excel dashboard

Charlie runs through his Shortlisted KPIs and decides how often he will measure each KPI. He sorts the KPIs based on frequency of measurement...

Table: 14

KPI Family Name	KPI Name	Frequency of measurement
C2: Perishable Goods	Storage temperature record	Hourly
M2: Footfall	Number of unique visitors per day	Daily
C1: Present Customers Waiting for Service	Walkout rate	Daily
S1: Sales Value, Activity and Results	Average value per sale	Daily
C2: Perishable Goods	Value of waste due to expiry	Daily
T2: Stock	Total stock value	Weekly
H1: Health and Safety	Number of near misses	Weekly
F1: Financials	Cash receipts in period	Weekly
F1: Financials	Cash in bank	Weekly
F1: Financials	Total accounts payable	Weekly
Q1: Service Quality	Online review scores	Weekly
T1: Business Premises	Number of outstanding safety related actions	Weekly
F1: Financials	Net profit	Weekly
H1: Health and Safety	Number of accidents	Weekly
F1: Financials	Gross profit per unit product	Weekly
M1: Public Reviews	Unpaid 'Likes', '+1's etc.	Weekly
F1: Financials	Total costs	Weekly
F1: Financials	Cash forecast	Weekly
F1: Financials	Itemised non-controllable costs	Weekly

F1: Financials	Itemised controllable costs	Weekly
Q1: Service Quality	Volume of new complaints	Weekly
S6: Advertising and PPC Effectiveness	Facebook follower growth	Weekly
R3: Service R&D	Number of new service-improvement ideas	Monthly
R3: Service R&D	Number of new service ideas tested	Monthly

He decides that the hourly and daily KPIs will go on a whiteboard - with the data being copied into a spreadsheet at the end of each week. The weekly and monthly data will go straight into a spreadsheet.

 Free templates registration link
https://goo.gl/DFrRyt
No Spam! Email registration required, but your details are **never** shared

Charlie downloads one of the free templates from the goodies download link above and does some cutting and pasting. He has gone for the Simple templates to get started (when he's happy with the content he will probably move to the Advanced templates). He takes care to make sure the charts that he has copied and pasted use the correct data range.

Here are extracts from his weekly and monthly dashboards, with dummy data in them...

Chaos Coffee: Weekly Dashboard

Finance - Cash & Stock   Report to week: 40

	Week:	29	30	31	32	33	34	35	36	37	38	39	40		Commentary
Cash receipts in period	Reciepts	298	311	243	185	97	50	67	84	92	170	389	632		Lorem ipsum dolor sit amet, consectetur adipiscing elit, sed do eiusmod tempor incididunt ut labore et dolore magna aliqua. Ut enim ad minim veniam, quis nostrud exercitation ullamco laboris nisi ut aliquip ex ea commodo consequat.
	Target	400	300	250	250	250	250	250	250	300	300	400	400		
Cash in bank	Cash in bank	298	311	243	185	97	50	67	84	92	170	389	632		Lorem ipsum dolor sit amet, consectetur adipiscing elit, sed do eiusmod tempor incididunt ut labore et dolore magna aliqua. Ut enim ad minim veniam, quis nostrud exercitation ullamco laboris nisi ut aliquip ex ea commodo consequat.
	Target	400	300	250	250	250	250	250	250	300	300	400	400		
Total stock value	Value	298	311	243	185	97	50	67	84	92	170	389	632		Lorem ipsum dolor sit amet, consectetur adipiscing elit, sed do eiusmod tempor incididunt ut labore et dolore magna aliqua. Ut enim ad minim veniam, quis nostrud exercitation ullamco laboris nisi ut aliquip ex ea commodo consequat.
	Target	400	300	250	250	250	250	250	250	300	300	400	400		
	Week number:	40	41	42	43	44	45	46	47	48	49	50	51		
Cash forecast	Cash	298	311	243	185	97	50	67	84	92	170	389	632		Lorem ipsum dolor sit amet, consectetur adipiscing elit, sed do eiusmod tempor incididunt ut labore et dolore magna aliqua. Ut enim ad minim veniam, quis nostrud exercitation ullamco laboris nisi ut aliquip ex ea commodo consequat.
	Target	400	300	250	250	250	250	250	250	300	300	400	400		

Figure: 24

Chaos Coffee: Monthly Dashboard

Service development   Report to Month: October

	Month:	Nov	Dec	Jan	Feb	Mar	Apr	May	Jun	Jul	Aug	Sep	Oct		Commentary
Number of new service-improvement ideas	Ideas	0	0	0	2	1	2	2	2	0	1	1	3		Bernie's shocking donut sales can only be explained by the his wholehearted consumption of the store's product. We need to put some budget in to buy him some elastic waisted trousers and put security cameras on the donut counter.
	Target	2	2	2	2	2	2	2	2	2	2	2	2		
Number of new service ideas tested	Ideas tested	0	0	0	0	1	0	1	0	2	1	1	0		Bernie's shocking donut sales can only be explained by the his wholehearted consumption of the store's product. We need to put some budget in to buy him some elastic waisted trousers and put security cameras on the donut counter.
	Target	1	1	1	1	1	1	1	1	1	1	1	1		

Figure: 25

Although hard to see in this small version, he has given the 'Cash forecast' its own scale (it's a *forecast*, so we are interested in future, not past, weeks). He has also changed the colour of the week markers, to make sure it's not confused with backward-looking measures (obviously, not visible in this monochrome copy!).

219

Key Idea

When to use your reports: Setting up your reporting cycle

Now you have designed your reports, you need to consider how and when you do your reporting. This depends on a number of things, but may include:

- When the raw data becomes available.
- Who does the data entry and report preparation and when they are likely to have some free time.
- How much time and effort the process takes.
- When you plan to review the data.

There aren't too many hard-and-fast rules on this, but I would suggest that you follow these tips:

- Set a regular time and a place to do the data entry and reporting and stick to it. This helps form the 'KPI habit'. If you don't do this, it's very likely that KPIs will rapidly move down the priority list and will soon not be collated or reviewed at all.

- Do your data collection and report production in **one** go, if possible. Of course it depends on how often you are processing your data, but if you are doing it monthly (for example), try and get everything done in one sitting, rather than spreading it across two or more sessions. Multiple sessions wastes time as you need to get set up and get into the right frame of mind each time. Multiple sessions also increases the risk of mistakes.

- Write it down as a procedure. Even if it is just you who does data collection and reporting, write down precise instructions for where to find the data and how to record it.

Doing this has a few benefits:

- It forces you to be absolutely clear about the data collection and processing steps.

- It will be a great memory jogger, if you forget (very useful for monthly or quarterly reporting cycles).

- It puts you in a perfect position to hand over the reporting function to someone else if you are on vacation, grow and need to hand it to someone else, or if you decide to sell your company and retire to a hammock with a large cocktail.

- Have a 'completion' ritual. When I have finished producing my weekly and monthly KPIs, I like to print them out as an A3 (US paper size - Tabloid) sheet, review them and then put them up on my office wall. This 'completion' of the KPI production process makes me review them and gives me a visible end point. Having a set of 'completion' steps encourages you to do the right thing and will also make you a little uncomfortable if you find yourself looking at an out-of-date KPI sheet on the wall.

Action

Action: Decide your reporting schedule

Decide *how often* you plan to collate and analyse your performance data.

Put those reporting dates in your diary (and/or the diary of the person responsible for production) on a repeating alert.

Recap
Step 5: Dashboard and Report Build

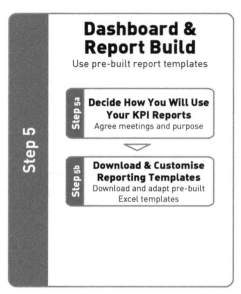

Figure: 26

In this section you will have:

- Decided on what reporting tool you will use.
- Grouped your Shortlisted KPIs by reporting frequency.
- If you decided to use Excel for reporting you will have…
  - Downloaded a sample dashboard template.
  - Customised that template to your needs.
- Set up your regular reporting cycle, with documented procedures.

Step 6: Go Live

Summary
Step 6: Go Live

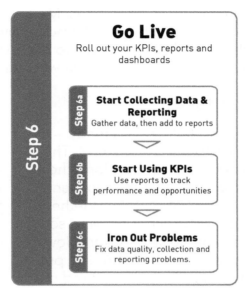

Figure: 27

This section covers…

- Planning your KPI rollout
- Collecting data
- Putting your KPIs into action
- Dealing with common KPI problems

There's also a special section on forming, and maintaining, KPI habits.

Key Idea

Building a KPI rollout plan

Why you need a plan

KPIs are like New Year fitness resolutions. Many of us start off with strong resolve, but quickly get sidetracked by everyday life. Breaking down the KPI rollout process into basic steps can help you stay on track and stop you being overwhelmed.

How long will it take?

The steps you need to follow are already laid out in the ROKS Express™ method. The main challenge is working out how long they will take you, who you need in the room and when you can get the right people together to work on it. What we have not covered so far is how long each of the steps takes. Now these timings can vary massively, but I've put some very rough guidelines below, based on personal experience, to help you…

Assumptions: These timings are based on a small team of around six people, all working in the same business but covering all functions of the business. The assumption is that the team know their roles well and timings are on the basis that they are fully focused on the task in hand (no answering emails or phone calls during workshop sessions).

226

Table: 15

Activity	Activity description	Who should be involved	Estimated time needed
Setting Up Team Expectations	Letting the whole team know *why* we are setting up KPIs, how it will affect them and making sure everyone is fired up to get involved.	The whole team.	Typically it takes one or two **informal session(s) of 15-30 min.** May require one-to-ones if there are any particular sensitivities the team might have with the idea of implementing KPIs.
Goals Check	Step 1 of ROKS Express™ approach.	Founders/Owners/Senior managers.	It usually takes between **one hour** and a full day, depending on the number of senior stakeholders and their clarity of thought on the purpose of the business. If you are comfortable with the 'Big 6' objectives it should be much nearer one hour.
Draft List of Ready-to-go KPIs	Step 2 of ROKS Express™ approach.	The senior team and specialists as required for specific KPIs. For example: Company accountant, serving staff, call agents and so on.	Expect it to take **2-3 hours** for a smaller business. This step can be split over two sessions if required.
Shortlist KPIs	Step 3 of ROKS Express™ approach.	The senior team and specialists as required for specific KPIs. For example: Company accountant, serving staff, call agents and so on.	It depends on the number of KPIs generated in Step 2 and the decisiveness of the review team. Typically it takes **2-3 hours to review 100 candidate KPIs**, if done briskly. Best done in one sitting but I'd suggest a few coffee breaks as it can be quite intense.
Tune KPI Definitions	Step 4 of ROKS Express™ approach.	The senior team and specialists as required for specific KPIs. For Example: Company accountant, serving staff, call agents and so on. **The individuals do not normally need to be assembled as a group to do this.** It can really help to have a designated 'owner' of the definitions.	Plan for about **30 mins per KPI**, including review of the definition by others in the team. These definitions can easily be spread over time - they don't have to be done in one sitting. Setting targets typically takes one to two hours of discussion, depending on the number of targets involved, the number of team members in the discussion and how controversial the targets are. Allow 1-2 hours longer if you want to run a reverse brainstorming session too.

Continued...

Dashboard and Report Build	Step 5 of ROKS Express™ approach.	One 'Dashboard design' owner, plus input from users.	The duration of this step is very dependent on the complexity of the dashboard you want. If you are using one of the free Excel download templates and it requires little modification, you will probably have what you need in **2 hours.** A more complicated dashboard, with lots of customisation will typically take a day of building, tweaking and testing, for someone confident in Excel.
Go Live	Step 6 of ROKS Express™ approach.	Everyone.	Expect to spend **15 mins every day** ironing out problems and discussing KPIs and data collection with the team for the first 2-4 weeks.
Snagging	Identifying and fixing practical KPI collection, processing and reporting problems.	In a small business it's usually the owner of the KPI initiative that does this (often the founder or general manager) plus the person or group experiencing the problem.	You will find there are several things you need to tweak and improve, particularly on the dashboard. **Expect to spend up to 5 hours a week for the first few weeks sorting things out.** This timing is highly variable, and depends on how well you have covered the earlier steps.

The plan does not have to be anything too fancy. It may just be an action list in your favourite to-do app or a series of diary entries with alerts. The important thing is that you make some sort of commitment to getting up and running with KPIs. Without that, 'implementing effective KPIs' will most likely stay on the 'good intentions' list. Remember you can start with a **very short** list of KPIs and revisit your **Shortlist** after your first batch of KPIs is up and running smoothly.

Action: Building your KPI plan

Use the table on the next page to identify:

- Who you need to involve
- When you will do each activity
- How much time you expect things to take

Step 6: Go Live

Table: 16

Activity	Planned session dates	Who should be involved	Estimated amount of time needed
Setting Up Team Expectations			
Goals Check			
Draft List of 'Ready-to-go' KPIs			
Shortlist KPIs			
Tune KPI Definitions			
Dashboard and Report Build			
Go Live			
Snagging			

Collecting good quality data

Good quality real-world data is the raw material from which your reports and KPIs are built. Without good quality data, all other KPI effort is a waste of time.

There are a number of ways the data can be captured. In an ideal world, we would already have computer systems in place which painlessly capture good quality information that we can then view in a clear and insightful way, at the click of a button. If you're running a small business you probably started laughing at this point, as you know the reality is a lot more about Post-its, scraps of paper and 'notes jotted on a whiteboard'.

Tip

Tip: Some (not very surprising) discoveries I have made over the years about manually recording data include…

- The longer the gap between something happening and it being written down, the less likely it is to be written down. Long gaps also mean that, when data is eventually written down, it is much more likely to be wrong.

- The easier it is to record something, the more likely people are to record that data.

- People are much more reluctant to record bad news, particularly when it makes them look bad.

How-to

Common ways of collecting data

To help you decide which data collection method is right for you, here is a run-down of the most common approaches:

Using a whiteboard and marker pen

A white, wipe-clean board that you mount on the wall and write on using 'dry markers'.

Clipboard, paper and pen (including printed forms)

Paper form and a pen to fill it in. Pretty much fool-proof, but you do need to keep fresh forms handy and regularly collect the completed ones.

Capture straight into a spreadsheet

Enter data directly into a spreadsheet. This may be a spreadsheet saved on the local computer or some kind of shared spreadsheet, using Excel or Google Docs.

Using a cloud-based note-keeping tool

There are a large number of free or premium web-based note-taking tools available. To use something like Evernote, simply create a note with an appropriate title and use that document to record data as and when you need it.

Using a portable electronic device linked to a system

This type of solution usually comes ready-built and is often designed to solve a particular problem - such as order-taking or stock-management. It's possible to create a hand-held data collection solution for most data collection challenges, but it normally requires serious thought, time and investment to do it well.

Checklist

Data collection selection checklist

Here are some important questions you can ask that will help you decide which collection method is best for your business:

- ☑ How much data needs recording. Is it a single number every day, hourly recording or multiple tallies throughout the day as an event happens?

- ☑ Is it an environment where hygiene is important?

- ☑ Is there a computer already to hand?

- ☑ Are the team comfortable putting data straight into spreadsheets?

- ☑ Do you have a whiteboard on the wall already?

- ☑ How disciplined are you, or your team, at recording data - will they need a memory jogger?

- ☑ Is there a desk/clipboard that can be used for paper-based forms?

- ☑ How often does the recordable-event happen?

- ☑ Low-frequency events will often need some kind of memory jogger to get staff to remember to record the data. Visible recording - like a whiteboard - can act as that prompt.

Tip

If the measure isn't working for you....

When I first used the ROKS™ method to create KPIs for my business I was quite surprised by the ones I eventually found useful. Some of the KPIs I thought would be useful turned out to be less so than I expected (particularly the ones around website performance, for example *number of inbound links*). Unexpected correlations, like the relationship between quantity of good quality reviews and book sales, also popped up in use.

The lesson I learned was: 'You should always feel free to change and tinker with your measures, but only for the right reasons.'

The **'right reasons'** would include...

- The measure isn't telling you anything that can be acted upon.
- The measure is only giving a partial picture.
- People don't understand the measure (make sure you try a clearly defined ROKS KPI Canvas™ before you give up on explaining it). Be careful about giving up too soon though.
- There's a *better/more practical* measure you can think of.

Bad reasons for changing your KPIs will include......

- Not *liking* the message your KPI is delivering.
- *Being embarrassed* by the message.
- Not having ironed out all *problems* with measurement method.

Remember, the 'KPI Police' are not going to come and challenge you on your decision, it's up to you what you do and don't measure. If you have considered the points above and a measure is still not working for you, **change it**.

How-to

Starting to use your KPIs

There comes a point where you are up and running with your KPIs and start to review the results they deliver. How you review them will depend on the number of people in your business, the type of business and your natural style. There are a few typical review sessions you will need to set up, depending on the reporting rhythm of your business and the number. A lot of KPI activity will be based around daily 'huddles' (daily, brisk, standing-up meetings centred around performance boards) or meetings. Here are a few things you can do to get your meetings off to a good start and to help them stay on track.

If you have a team...

Daily KPI reviews with the rest of your team

This can feel a bit weird and embarrassing, particularly the first time you get together to review them. It is **OK** to feel uncomfortable. Discomfort comes from forming new habits.

You can lessen awkwardness by...

- Preparing the group, right at the start, with the idea that it's going to be a bit awkward for the first few sessions.

- Having a clear (very short) agenda, that you can work through briskly. Getting to the end rapidly gives you permission to close the meeting without awkwardness if there's really not much to talk about.

- Rotate ownership of the meeting, if possible. It helps prevent an 'us and them' forming and gives you a useful backup plan if the usual meeting chair isn't there.

- Keeping the sessions *issues* focused and not using it to pick on individuals' poor performance or failings. If you need to challenge the performance of individuals, it's best done one-to-one.

Checklist

Weekly and monthly KPI reviews with the rest of your team

Weekly and monthly KPI reviews should be a bit more structured and meaty than daily huddles. Here are a few guidelines to follow to make sure the sessions go well..

- ☑ A good clear agenda. You don't need too many points, but you need the right people (based on what they control and their ability to agree to actions), clear inputs (reports, dashboards, previous action log and so on) and clear outputs (agreed actions, spend authorisations). Everyone going to the meeting needs to know the agenda in advance and be held to it.

- ☑ Focus on issues and actions, **not** blame or people's individual failings.

- ☑ Avoid problem solving **in** the meeting. In the absence of any decent quality first-hand evidence, this usually descends into opinion and solution-guessing.

- ☑ Making sure the 'top priority' from the last meeting doesn't disappear from view in the next meeting.

- ☑ Ensure the meetings stay evidence-focused.

- ☑ And, most critically, if the KPIs show that someone needs to *brief* the meeting on a problem and solutions (but not attempting to problem solve *in* the meeting) - **they must prepare properly before the meeting.** If you don't do this, you will normally end up agreeing that someone needs to go and find out more/come up with a solution and you will lose an entire meeting cycle of activity. For this preparation to happen the relevant **reports must be available in good time before the meeting.**

If you are one-person business, performance reviews can be particularly odd and hard to get started. It does depend to a large extent on your personality and preferred way of working, so all these tips come with that caution. Here are some things that I have seen work well for me or others in 'micro-business land'…

If you are a solo business...

How-to

Solo daily KPI reviews

Decide if you *need* a **daily** meeting. If yours is a fast-paced business, then you might find it useful to do this. I look at my online sales on a daily basis, just to check there aren't any obvious problems like sales suddenly cratering, for example. It is easy to settle into a certain set of review habits without really thinking about it. It may be worth consciously deciding what you need to review when you first start a daily review so you don't just slide towards what is easiest and most interesting.

I find it helps me to have a routine and a diary reminder to create and review my KPIs. This gives me a nudge to do it at a *certain time* of the planned reporting day and gives me a little twinge of guilt if I skip it.

Solo weekly and monthly KPI reviews

For me, it's the act of *compiling* my KPI report that also becomes the review process. Just by entering the data, checking it's accurate and making a few notes, it forces me to start thinking about the underlying issues and actions. How you do this is really up to you and depends on your personal style. If you are struggling to hold yourself accountable, you might want to consider teaming up with someone else in the same situation. You probably won't want to do this with a direct competitor, but maybe you know someone in the same situation as you who is prepared to talk through your performance challenges in exchange for you doing the same with them? This is something I do on an informal basis all the time and it helps me hugely.

How to quickly kill data collection stone-dead...

Whichever type of business you are in, broken reports and data collection problems kill motivation stone-dead very, very quickly.

When you find data collection or reporting problems, *permanently fix them as fast as you can*.

Optional section: Habits, compulsion and KPIs

Why is it I check my email inbox several times a day but shy away from weighing myself? What makes social media so irresistible, yet expensive home-gym equipment often sits around, barely used?

The answer to these questions lies in the formation of habits and the way our brain seeks rewards. The addictiveness of social media is not an accident: it's the prized outcome of very careful design.

What have habits got to do with KPIs?

A KPI that is never reviewed or acted upon might as well not exist. Worse than that, an unreviewed KPI is a kind of 'tax' on the organisation, a costly piece of information that was never used.

241

Forming a 'review habit', particularly for short-term KPIs, is an essential behavioural requirement to enable KPIs to have a positive impact on your business performance.

The challenge

To generate positive change, some performance data require **frequent** review and action. Often these are operational measures, like queue length, wait times or stock levels.

If we want to steer team actions and behaviour using short-term KPIs, we need to make looking at those figures as hard to resist as glancing at your phone for new emails, checking your smart watch fitness score for the day or checking your social media feed.

Let's just be clear on what we mean by a 'habit'. The definition I use is...

'Behaviours done with little or no conscious thought'

(Definition from 'Hooked' by Nir Eyal).

Most of the published work in the field of creating habit-forming products looks at software products, so we need a little lateral thinking to understand how those insights apply to KPIs and performance reports. The good news is that one of the most commonly used methodologies is fairly easily adapted to our needs.

Three steps to strengthen your KPI habits

Behavioural research has shown that there are several ways you can nurture or destroy habit formation. Anyone who has raised children may well already have figured out the critical steps through trial and error.

Step 1: Be *precise* about the type of behaviour you want.

*Be as **clear as possible** and don't make people think too hard.*

Break down your strategic objectives into 'bite-sized chunks' - clear and specific behaviours and activities that will help you achieve your objective.

How to apply this...

There's a huge difference between saying...

'I'd like the team to do a regular performance review'

...and...

'I would like you (the team leader) to run a standing-up huddle every two hours, on the hour, following this agenda. It must last no more than 5 mins and cover these performance measures...'.

Which instruction is most likely to lead to a regular routine and ultimately the formation of a habit?

Step 2: Make it easy to do the right thing.

*The **easier** you make it, the more likely it is to **happen**.*

How can you remove obstacles and make the right behaviour *easy* to do?

Making the desired behaviour *easy to do* has a few angles:

- **Time.** The longer something takes, the less likely people are to do it.

- **Money.** If there is some direct cost involved in the behaviour (for example, having to make a call using their own phone) or indirect cost (missing out on overtime) it will act as a strong disincentive to take action and ultimately not form a habit. Ideally they should *gain* financially from doing it, for example hitting a team performance target.

- **Physical effort.** If the action you intend to habitualise involves having to walk up some stairs, get out of a chair or go out in the cold, for example, physical effort or discomfort will discourage habit formation.

- **Brain effort.** Having to think too hard puts people off taking action. This brain-effort deterrent becomes even stronger if people are tired and/or busy.

How this might translate into practice for performance measurement and management…

For manual data gathering: habit formation is critical for good quality manual data capture. Let's say we need the team to regularly record the temperature of the food chiller cabinets in a coffee shop…

Example

Example: Make it easy for Chaos Coffee temperature recording

- Use well laid-out printed sheets (minimise time and brain effort), ready-printed with spare copies stored in a clearly marked place (minimise time and physical effort), near to where the measurement takes place (minimise physical effort).

- Provide clear step-by-step instructions for the measurement at the top of every sheet (minimise brain effort).

- Make sure the user does not have to hunt around for sheets and provide pencils (minimise brain and physical effort).
  - Avoid losing the recording pencil by putting it on a string attached to the clipboard (saves time, brain and physical effort).

- Have the temperature probe already in place, so the user does not have to wait for the probe to 'get up to temperature' (reduces time and brain effort - brain effort saved as the individual does not have to decide when temperature has been achieved).

Step 3: Make sure the behaviour is triggered.

*What will **activate** the desired behaviour?*

All behaviours require a trigger: sometimes it's internal, sometimes external.

Types of triggers

Triggers are the nudge to take action. It may be as simple as a reminder popping up on a screen, an email landing in your inbox or a team leader prompting the team to do something. Our lives are filled with triggers, but we often barely notice them. For many, their day starts with an external trigger (alarm clock goes off) and is followed by a firework display of internal triggers that gets us washed, dressed and packed for the day ahead. The best triggers are ones that are sparked by your own memory or by some minor but reliable environmental factor.

Triggers are the vital final step in our habit-forming method, our cue to take action. Triggers fall into two camps…

☑ **External triggers** tell us what to do next by placing a prompt or information in the user's environment. Alarm clocks, timed texts, smart watch alerts, calendar alerts or Post-its on your PC monitor all fall into this category.

☑ **Internal triggers** prompt the user on what to do next through associations stored in their memory. Going into the bathroom first-thing in the morning will trigger you to remember to clean your teeth. Leaving the house will remind you to check you have your keys, phone and wallet. We rely on thousands of internal triggers every day but, because of their nature, they are almost imperceptible to us.

Quite often we use a mixture of internal and external triggers. I have to remember to look at my 'to-do' task manager on my phone but, once I remember to do this, there is a list of 'External triggers' listed to get me to act on my tasks.

What this might mean in practice for performance measurement and management…

There are a selection of external triggers we can use…

- Calendar reminders
- Meetings
- Agenda items (though there often needs to be a pre-meeting trigger, otherwise this just catches out the unwary)
- Performance boards
- Alarms

Formal performance reviews are fine, and a good start, but KPIs become so much more useful and powerful when they become a seamless part of our view on the world.

Our ultimate goal must be to create **internal** triggers. These are more powerful and do not require sustained effort or vigilance once they are established - just some occasional nurturing and care to make sure we don't accidentally break them.

Visual prompts can be a very good way of sparking internal triggers. A well-placed performance board can really grease the wheels when it comes to forming internal KPI review triggers.

How to tell when 'triggers' have become internal

Our end goal is the whole team actively 'pulling' performance information. When a team member walks in, do they request and show a genuine interest in the performance figures? Do the shop-floor team show a keen interest in how the day's figures are progressing, how they are doing compared with other teams, whether they are close to breaking a record? When performance figures are referred to in every-day work conversation you know that you are well on your way to building 'the KPI habit'.

Habit forming: Chaos Coffee queue busting

Example

So, how would our habit formation method apply to an operational situation, let's say 'queue time', in a coffee shop?

Step 1: Be *precise* about the type of behaviour you want.

*Be as **clear as possible** and don't make people think too hard.*

Aim: For non-customer-serving staff to help with service whenever queues start to build, so that customers never to have to wait more than 5 minutes for their order to be taken.

Translate target outcomes into goals and behaviours:

Behaviour: When the average wait time hits 4 mins or more, pull staff off cleaning, kitchen duties and non-legally-required breaks to 'bust the queue'.

Step 2: Make it easy to do the right thing.

*The **easier** you make it, the more likely it is to **happen**.*

*To make the decision a 'no-brainer' we need to give clear guidelines on **when** the team need to call 'queue busters'.*

The Chaos Coffee team discuss this and decide that they could have markers on the customer side of the serving counter, with each mark showing a typical wait time of +1 minute. When the queue goes past the +4 minute mark the team leader needs to find extra staff if possible.

Step 3: Make sure the behaviour is triggered.

*What will **activate** the desired behaviour?*

The team will probably be at their most busy at the exact time the queue goes past the 4 minute wait mark. The Chaos Coffee team brainstorms ideas for alerting the team when the queue is building, here are some of their ideas….

1. *A bell, with a sign inviting queuing customers to ring it for a free 'loyalty point' if they find themselves standing by it. This could irritate staff and possibly be 'gamed' by the customers (deliberately hanging back to 'ding' the bell), but it is very cheap and simple to try out.*

2. *A ceiling sensor, or floor pressure plate, that can detect when someone is stood directly under/on it for more than*

a few seconds - lighting an indicator in direct view of the team.

3. *A tablet/computer game fixed at the 4-minute-wait marker for the customers to play on. When a bored customer starts to use it, the action of using it (or perhaps the tablet waking from sleep) could alert the serving team that the queue has built back to that point. It should also be possible to automatically record that tablet activity throughout the day, giving a record of the ebb and flow of queues throughout the day. Of course this could backfire, and you may struggle to get customers to move down the queue for service, if the game is too addictive.*

What would **you** do? Can you think of any other ways of gently alerting the overworked team that they need more hands on deck?

Questions to help you focus on KPI habits

Triggering habit actions

- ☑ Who uses the KPIs currently? Are these the people who should use them?

- ☑ What precise actions do you want them to get into the habit of doing?

- ☑ What is the user doing immediately prior to the point you want them to record data or review KPI data?

- ☑ What internal triggers could prompt your KPI user to take the action you want them to?

- ☑ What external triggers might help train the users' internal trigger?

Try and list as many external triggers as possible - including crazy ideas…

Action

Action: Develop KPI habits

Focus your habit formation efforts on a small number of critical KPIs.

- Pick **three really crucial measures** whose use you want to become habitual and run through the three steps of the habit formation method for each one.
- Identify issues/potential issues with habit formation for the three selected KPIs.
- Discuss multiple potential solutions, including the slightly insane ones, with your team.

Common go-live problems and how to fix them

If you are up and running with your new KPIs, 'Well done!'. Unfortunately, going live can also bring *problems*. The good news is that many KPI problems are quite common and have tried-and-tested solutions.

Here is a run-down on nine of the most common KPI problems and sensible solutions...

Problem!

Problem 1: Forgetting to collect or review your KPIs

Symptoms

You realise it is several days, or weeks, since you last looked at your KPIs.

Causes and solutions

1. **You genuinely forgot.**

   – Put it in your diary, with a reminder (or two, if you need to, and use your diary reliably).

2. **You are bored of looking at them.**

   This suggests you are not be measuring the right stuff, or perhaps the right stuff but *too frequently*.

   Revisit your KPIs, using the ROKS Express™ approach, if needed. Ask yourself:

   – Why am I bored of looking at these figures?

   – If I don't care about them, why not? Is there a nagging

suspicion that they are just not the right things to be measuring?

3. **You don't like the message the KPIs are telling you,** so you subconsciously decided not to look at them any more.

   When I put on weight, I tend to weigh myself less often. Looking at KPIs when things are going badly can feel the same. If you find yourself in that situation, don't stop looking at the KPIs that show outcomes. *Do* channel the pain of your poorly performing KPI to..

   - Accept that simply 'doing what you did before' will not lead to the outcome you are looking for. Review your strategy for improving.
   - Focus on the things that you can do to *positively influence* the 'problem' KPI.
     - Break those actions down into activity-based subtasks to make you feel better and give a sense of progress.

Problem!

Problem 2: Talking about the *same stuff* every review

Symptoms

You have your KPI review and find yourself discussing the same problems every time.

Causes and solutions

1. **You do not have robust *problem-solving* taking place after the 'go and investigate it' type actions are agreed.**

   If problem-solving isn't progressing to plan you will need to investigate why. Typical issues will include:

   – Lack of first-hand evidence gathering and observation

   – Lack of a structured, effective, problem-solving approach

   – Jumping to cause (i.e. assuming you understand the root cause of the problem without proper investigation or evidence)

   The solution to these problem-solving issues is beyond the scope of this book, but there's a lot of good material and support available once you recognise your improvement bottleneck is one of problem-solving effectiveness.

2. **Clear, effective, improvement actions are not being put in place to address the problems.**

   Focus on generating clear practical **actions** to address issues identified by your KPI reports. Be careful to follow up previous actions and make sure those assigned the actions have the time, skills, motivation and resources to progress them.

3. **Improvement actions are being delivered as agreed, but they will take time to show as improved performance.**

   If you are repeatedly revisiting improvement actions that are on-track, but have yet to deliver results, create a review-point action and park the review of that measure until that date.

4. **You are focusing on the wrong problems. Solving this type of problem results in little, or no, improvement in the things you care about.**

   Use problem prioritisation based on something **meaningful**, in relation to your strategy. Typically this involves 'valuing' problems in something universal, like 'lost time' or 'lost income'. This will enable you to compare different 'types' of improvement opportunity and rank them. For example, valuing 'lost time' in financial terms can enable you to prioritise efficiency (OEE) losses spanning speed losses, waste and downtime.

Problem!

Problem 3: Meetings go off track and you start talking about stuff you shouldn't

Symptoms

Meetings go on far too long, you don't get through the agenda and people come away frustrated with the lack of progress.

Causes and solutions

1. **Lack of a clearly defined meeting purpose or brief**

    If the scope is too wide/narrow or the wrong people are around the table the meeting is unlikely to deliver. Create a meetings 'terms of reference' to nail down the brief, identify correct participants and define expectations. Download a free template...

     Free templates registration link
    https://goo.gl/DFrRyt
    No Spam! Email registration required, but your details are never shared

2. **Poor meeting chairing**

    Make sure you get someone running the meeting who is up to the job and understands the purpose of the meeting.

3. **Poor meeting accountability**

    What happens if the review doesn't deliver? If there are no consequences, then you need to create consequences and hence motivation.

4. **Poor attendee behaviour**

This links closely to the quality of the meeting chairing. The worse the behaviour, the stronger the chairing skills required. If you see persistent poor behaviour, it might be time to ask if these are really the people you want to entrust the future of your business to…?

Problem 4: KPI mistakes

Symptoms

Whilst looking at the data someone comments on how 'Such-and-such data is clearly wrong'.

Causes

Assuming the data *is* wrong, there can be multiple causes, but they will normally fit into one of these categories

1. The KPI calculation is incorrect

2. Keying errors during data entry

3. Spreadsheet error or corruption

4. Missing/incorrect raw data - data not returned/entered

If this family of issues is not fixed quickly **it will quickly destroy any trust in the KPIs you have created.** You must address this speedily, transparently and correctly to restore trust in your KPI system.

Solutions

Once a problem with KPI accuracy is identified, the approach to permanently solving the issue is similar, whatever the specifics of the KPI mistake identified:

- **Thank** the person who identified it - make sure they come away prepared to stick their neck out and tell you about problems in the future.

- Investigate the problem(s). Why did it happen? Is it likely to happen again?

- Make sure it doesn't happen again - put 'mistake proofing' in place.

- Share your understanding of *why* it happened - particularly with the person who flagged the problem.

- Explain the permanent fix to all affected - and why the mistake will not happen again.

Every system has problems. It's how you *deal* with those problems that makes the difference between success and failure. You must care, and be seen to care. If you don't care about accuracy, why should anyone else?

Problem!

Problem 5: Toxic 'targets' culture

Symptoms

The team become angry and emotional over the use of KPIs. When people react like this it's normally a reaction to management abuse of KPI **targets**. If you are implementing KPIs for the first time and experience this reaction, it can be their previous KPI experiences that are driving emotional conflict.

Cause and solution

Poor managers can sometimes target **individuals** using KPIs and targets. The unsaid logic goes along the lines of 'If I create a target for my team they will do anything they can to reach that target. If they don't hit the target I can get rid of them based on evidence'. Using targets to drive individual behaviour, especially when linked to reward, can work but it often backfires spectacularly.

Appeal to people's natural competitiveness, not their greed. Pay your team properly, without the need to hit targets. Make rewards symbolic, not financial. Encourage hitting targets 'the right way' not by gaming the system. This may seem like a 'soft' approach but it is much more likely to drive successful long-term outcomes.

Problem!

Problem 6: Lots of cutting/pasting to create reports. Reporting takes too long and involves too much effort.

Symptoms

One or more of the team spends lots of time each week/month cutting and pasting figures between spreadsheets. This typically delays report production and can lead to errors creeping in.

Causes and solutions

1. **Data comes from multiple data capture sources**

    If you want to remain with a spreadsheet solution, you can either:

    – **Sensible solution:** Share one sheet and have people enter data directly into the same, shared, sheet.

    – **Risky solution:** Link sheets together across the network. The report sheet automatically downloads the source sheet data on request. I would **strongly advise against this solution**. Links are ridiculously easy to break and hard to follow.

2. **Source data is extracted from *other systems***

    The best solution is to alter the export format of the source system so that exported data is correctly formatted for your needs.

    If you cannot fix the source formatting then your options are:

    – Create a spreadsheet to tidy-up the data automatically. This may involve macros or Visual Basic if the challenge is complex and your team have these skills.

– Some 'business intelligence' tools on the market have much better import abilities than Excel. Often you can use these as a step in your production process, if only to import the data and then send it straight on to Excel.

3.   Badly structured data capture spreadsheets

Most spreadsheet packages have 'data validation'. You can normally set your data entry fields to only accept valid data, for example a valid date. Doing this ensures that you don't get a mixture of data types through user inexperience. You can also use drop-down selections to improve data consistency and make life easier for the user. Locking down non-data entry cells with protection will also eliminate the chance of data ending up in unexpected areas of the spreadsheet.

If all of these solutions sounds a bit 'techy' to you, then it might be time to find the services of an Excel expert.

Problem!

Problem 7: Culture of angry debate, based on opinions, rather than neutral review of the facts

Symptoms

This can happen in high-pressure situations either because:

- There's a lack of good quality information
- Some participants have a dislike for fact and reasoned argument

Causes and solutions

Given this book is on KPIs, it would be easy for us to focus on fixing the quality of the information presented, but in all honesty angry debate is normally a symptom of the second issue. Some people are naturally more fact/reason focused than others. Your main lever here is around how much scope they are given to vent their emotional views and how well the review is managed.

Firstly, double-check that the behaviour you are seeing isn't as a result of individuals being targeted, rather than processes (see page 259) or is happening as a result of a blame culture. If you are confident the people in the meeting are not feeling personally threatened, but are still acting irrationally, the list of improvement options is pretty short. Improving the quality of reports available will only fix the situation if there is at least one fact-focused meeting member present and they also have significant influence in the group. If those conditions are not met, then it's probably time to think about changing some of the faces around the table.

Problem!

Problem 8: Information overload. Massive, hard-to-understand reports that no one really looks at or uses

Symptoms

A hefty ring-bound mishmash of tables and charts is produced on a regular basis to support management meetings. Individuals may refer to the odd chart, table or figure in the report, but no serious attempt is made to review the pack.

Causes and solutions

Though most common in corporate situations, this can be a symptom of several underlying problems:

- The people writing the report are scared to challenge the 'customer' of the report on the real purpose of the report.

- — An open discussion between the people/person producing the report and those using it about what is really needed in the report.
- The 'customers' of the report don't really know what they want, so ask for too much 'just in case'.
  - — A proper meeting 'terms of reference' - a one-page document summarising meeting **purpose**, inputs and outputs.
- The meetings that the report supports has a poorly defined brief and set of inputs, so the 'kitchen sink' is included to try and cover every possibility.
  - — As for the previous problem, the solution is a proper meeting 'terms of reference' - a one-page document summarising meeting **purpose**, inputs and outputs.
- There may be underlying performance problems and 'blanket bombing' with reports is a way of distracting from the lack of progress on the real issues.
  - — An agreement on issue/action focused data - for example problem-impact Paretos, trended problem tracking and so on.

Problem!

Problem 9: The figures are bouncing around all over the place - I can't figure out what is going on.

Symptoms

When you look at a particular KPI, it jumps up and down so much naturally that it is hard to tell whether the variation you are seeing is a result of a genuine change in underlying performance, or not. Similarly, when you put a fix in place you find yourself on an emotional roller-coaster as the figures jump up and down, often leading to debates about whether the 'fix' has actually worked.

Causes and solutions

Almost anything you can measure has natural variation, or 'noise'. It even applies to weighing yourself on scales. Bodyweight can often vary from day-to-day, but a slight dip may or may not indicate meaningful weight loss, as the figure can be skewed by hydration and other factors.

An entire toolset to tackle just this problem has been developed over the past 100 years. That family of tools is called control charts. One of the most useful control chart tools is the XmR chart. Control charts give you a crystal clear set of rules, backed by sound statistics, for figuring out whether variation is fundamental process change or just natural process variation. Control charts are definitely in the **advanced tools** camp and are most commonly used in highly technical situations. A classic text on how XmR charts work, by Donald J Wheeler, is also listed in the bibliography at the back of this book.

Key Idea

Using KPIs to drive improvement

The most common reason for implementing KPIs is to improve a business in some way. Hundreds of books have been written on how to improve businesses. I've read a good selection of them and have recommended a couple that will give you a good overview. They are listed in the Recommended Reading section of this book. I'm not going to try and summarise them here, but there are a couple of ideas from these books which will really help your improvement activity and are quite straightforward.

Understand where KPIs fit in the improvement process

At the heart of it, improvement isn't that complicated. It's about identifying your biggest-impact problems, deciding to fix them, making sure they are fixed and that they stay fixed. You can show this with something called an improvement cycle. It looks like this…

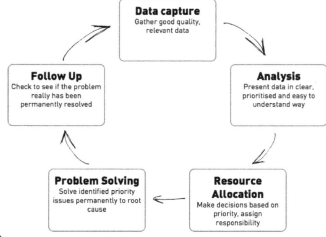

Figure: 28

If any part of the improvement cycle isn't working properly then you will see poor, or non-existent, levels of improvement. For example, you can have fantastic data and analysis but if there are no effective meetings (resource allocation on our diagram above) to review issues and create meaningful actions then the excellent reporting is wasted. Great data and effective meetings become meaningless if problem-solving is weak or non-existent.

The point of an improvement cycle is that all five boxes need to work properly for improvement to be delivered.

For many of my readers, improvement will mainly consist of identifying and dealing with problems. These problems may be causing lost production capacity, mistakes that irritate customers, or costly process waste.

Reporting by problem *type*

It can help to group problems by the type of impact they have, as the actions and solutions will normally be determined by that grouping. Here are some of the more common groupings I use…

Wasted effort - Lost labour time - the team not being used to do what they are paid to do. This may include idle time, time doing things that are not productive or time spent making things (or delivering services) that are out of specification.

Lost process time - Expensive kit, that should be in use, sat idle for whatever reason.

Poor or unsaleable product - We waste time and, (in the case of widget production) materials, producing something that we won't get paid for. I would include quality problems detected before the product gets to the customer in this category.

Quality problems discovered by the customer. This may show as complaints, repairs, returns or warranty claims. There's a lot of reputational damage done by this type of problem too.

Wasted materials. Material waste is where we use more material than we should for the amount of saleable finished product we produced.

Never forget: You don't fatten a pig by *weighing* it

The important point to keep in mind is that *KPIs on their own do not deliver improvement*, it is the decisions you make and the actions you take based on those KPIs that deliver the improvement. Great KPIs get you off to a strong start, but don't forget about the impact of the last three boxes in the improvement cycle.

Tip

Getting over the hump and getting going

A common reason for not using KPIs is wanting to get everything 'right'. When people, especially perfectionists, realise there are problems with their KPI system they often put off go-live until they 'have time' to sort those problems out. The trouble is 'having time' often never happens.

There's a neat solution to this problem…

You may have heard of Matt Mullenweg. He is the genius (and quite wealthy chap) behind WordPress, the software that powers more than 25% of all the world's websites. He was interviewed by Tim Ferris (author of the '4-Hour Work Week' and 'Tools of Titans') and was asked how he managed to exercise everyday, even with his ridiculous workload.

Quoting Ferris's interview with Mullenweg, his secret was…

*He committed to **one** push-up before bed. Yes, just one push-up: 'no matter how late you are running, no matter what's going on in the world, you can't argue against doing one push-up. Come on. There's no excuse. I often find I need get over the initial hump with something that is almost embarrassingly small as a goal, and then can become a habit.*

I have very similar approach to my own KPIs and dashboards. I have a diary reminder in my desktop calendar and all I do is commit to updating my performance tracking spreadsheet on a weekly and monthly basis. I've written instructions for me to follow, so I don't have to stress my brain trying to remember how to find source data, and that's it. What I find, as I type numbers in and look at the dashboard developing, is that I can't help but become engaged in what the spreadsheet is showing. Without any lofty ambitions, I end up reviewing my weekly and monthly performance anyway.

So, my advice would be, if you struggle with starting your KPI reviews and taking action, just make a very modest commitment. For example, try committing to one minute looking at your dashboard. Chances are, if you actually take that small action regularly, something bigger will happen naturally. The one thing I can guarantee is, if you do nothing, 'nothing' will be the result.

Action

What next?

So, you have chosen and implemented your KPIs using the ROKS Express™ approach. You have started to use your insights to improve and develop your business. Where do you go from here?

Improve your brand new KPI system..

If you have followed the steps in this book and are up and running, that's fantastic, but the chances are you will have some rough edges and things that could be better. Think about..

- Identifying measurement problems, weaknesses and pain points and fixing them.
- Gaining more benefit from your data by exploring relationships between the things you are measuring. Once you have a decent-sized dataset think about exploring relationships that may help you develop predictive measures or optimise previously hidden improvement levers in your business processes.

Start measuring the hard stuff…

Once you have your 'core' KPIs running smoothly, it might be time to think about the 'killer KPIs' from the 'Aspire KPIs' list in the Shortlist KPIs step. These are the KPIs that are hard to measure but will give you a business edge, and which your rivals almost certainly can't measure currently. Most businesses never get to this stage, so this would put you way ahead of the crowd if you do.

Go deeper into the ROKS™ approach

ROKS Express Advanced™ approach for tools to help you with...

- Building your own KPI Trees™ and custom KPIs.

- Filtering out 'noise' in your data using XmR charts.

- Creating 'index' measures - like the single-figure exercise scores you get on fitness watches - for easy at-a-glance insight.

To find out more about ROKS Express Advanced™ visit **https://madetomeasurekpis.com/complex-organisation-kpis)**

Hire a ROKS™ specialist

If you want practical help and support for any of step of the ROKS™ approach, drop me an email...

bernie@madetomeasurekpis.com

...and we should be able to put you in touch with a ROKS™ specialist to give you practical support and advice on any aspect of choosing and setting up KPIs.

Whichever option you go with, **action** is the key. You now have all the tools you need to get up and running with KPIs. Getting started will put you on the road to your objectives and the dreams that achieving those objectives will deliver. Now is the time to get on and make it happen. The only question is, 'Are you ready to get started with KPIs'?

Recap
Step 6: Go Live

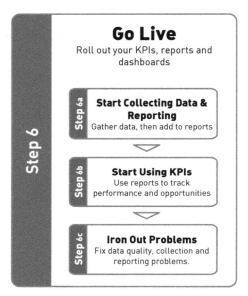

Figure: 29

Appendix: Cognitive Bias

Your brain is lying to you. Here's why you need KPIs, much more than you realise...

Cognitive bias has a huge impact on our willingness to use KPIs. To explain why this is we will need a bit of background on what cognitive bias is, how it works and who it affects.

The first challenge: you probably don't believe you are affected by cognitive bias...

You and I both understand that I don't know your business. So how can I say with absolute conviction that you are affected by cognitive bias and that KPIs will benefit you? Well, I can say with some confidence that all humans show cognitive bias, and we are all unaware of it. The 'unaware' part is what **makes** it a cognitive bias (that blind spot is a cognitive bias in itself called 'Bias blind spot'. The 'Bias blind spot' is one of the one hundred and four different identified biases). What I can do is show you that you are affected by at least some cognitive biases…

Three bias examples you can see for yourself…

There are over one hundred identified cognitive biases, covering social, memory, decision-making and probability.

Many of them need carefully designed experiments to demonstrate them, but some of the biases are visual and are easier to explore on your own. I will show you three examples that should demonstrate that we are all subject to biases. Just note these examples **are not** the biases that will mess with your business judgement (these fall in the decision-making, memory and probability biases and are trickier to demonstrate in this book). What I hope is that, by showing you these, you might just believe some of the other biases do exist and could affect you. By this point your brain is probably shrieking 'I'm far too smart to fall for that nonsense'.

Example 1

Here's the first example of visual cognitive bias…

Task: Decide which horizontal line is the longer…

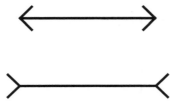

Figure: 30

Answer: Both horizontal lines are exactly the same length.

Measure them to check.

Now, this is a vintage illusion you may well have seen before. What it illustrates is that the brain automatically incorporates context when processing images. In this case, our visual processing is distorted by 'framing'.

Example 2

Here's another example, in case you think the previous one was a fluke…

Figure: 31

Your reading of the middle block is influenced by whether you read top-to-bottom or left-to-right. This is an example of 'Prior expectations bias'.

This second example demonstrates a useful piece of processing that the brain is performing (helping us make sense of the shapes). However, in the wrong situation, this kind of processing can lead to our brains misleading us.

These examples may look like party tricks, but they are a small glimpse of a whole family of cognitive phenomena that have been scientifically proven. If you want to explore cognitive bias in much more depth, then Daniel Kahneman's book 'Thinking Fast and Slow' is your best bet. In the book, Kahneman outlines the work that won him the Nobel prize for Economics in 2002.

Example 3

Here's one more test, from 'Thinking, Fast and Slow…'

A bat and ball cost $1.10.

The bat costs one dollar more than the ball.

How much does the ball cost?

Record your answer

Solution over the page...

If you decided the ball cost 10¢ you are wrong - along with over 50% of Harvard students who took this test.

The correct answer is 5¢.

In this quote from 'Thinking, Fast and Slow' Kahneman explains why most people get this wrong…

> "A number came to your mind. The number, of course, is 10¢. The distinctive mark of this easy puzzle is that it evokes an answer that is intuitive, appealing, and wrong. Do the math, and you will see. If the ball costs 10¢, then the total cost will be $1.20 (10¢ for the ball and $1.10 for the bat), not $1.10. The correct answer is 5¢. It is safe to assume that the intuitive answer also came to the mind of those who ended up with the correct number - they somehow resisted the intuition.
>
> Many thousands of university students have answered the bat-and-ball puzzle, and the results are shocking. Over 50% of students at Harvard, MIT, and Princeton gave the intuitive - incorrect - answer. At less selective universities, the rate of demonstrable failure to check was in excess of 80%. The bat-and-ball problem is our first encounter with an observation that will be a recurrent theme of this book: many people are overconfident, prone to place too much faith in their intuitions. They apparently find cognitive effort at least mildly unpleasant and avoid it as much as possible."

Starting to think that cognitive bias *does* apply to you?

The truth is, in their heart of hearts, most people don't really believe they are biased. They may know that they are biased, but they don't believe it. Hopefully, these three exercises may have started to chip away at that belief. If it makes you feel any better, a study by West, Meserve and Stanovich (Cognitive sophistication does not attenuate the bias blind spot. J Pers Soc Psychol. 2012 Sep;103(3):506-19. doi: 10.1037/a0028857. Epub 2012 Jun 4.), suggests that intelligent people are actually *more* vulnerable to cognitive bias.

Why do we have biases?

Your brain uses some clever processing tricks to make the world easier to understand. Many of these tricks seem to have evolved to make living in social groups manageable, keeping our friends close and staying out of fights by reading a situation very quickly. They also help us think fast enough to avoid getting injured, or worse, in dangerous situations.

There are two major problems with these biases - or shortcuts:

1) They don't give you the best outcomes in all situations.

2) You are completely unaware of them.

So how does cognitive bias explain people not wanting to use KPIs?

The model that Kahneman uses to explain cognitive bias is based on two decision-making modes that we all use:

System One: This is seat of your pants, intuitive, decision-making. The brain uses shortcuts to get to the answer quickly. It's where you use your 'gut feel' to make a rapid decision and then move on. If you a Star Trek fan, I call this the 'Captain Kirk' decision-making mode. Captain Kirk was the emotional, gut-feel, kind of guy - the exact opposite of Mr Spock in most episodes.

System Two: The System Two approach is where you sit down and consider the facts, the situation, and alternative potential actions. You then use logic and reason to decide on the best option. Carrying on the Star Trek theme, I call this the 'Mr Spock' decision-making mode.

I'll call them the Captain Kirk/Mr Spock approaches from now on, as I find it easier to remember.

The heart of this model is that all of us use **both** decision-making approaches on a regular basis. The Captain Kirk approach is quick and easy, but can produce flawed decisions - you can describe it as 'seat of the pants', 'intuition' or 'gut feel' decision-making. The Mr Spock approach requires effort, discipline and hard work but (and this is the important bit) when done with structure and good quality information it can produce *demonstrably better* decisions.

There is a problem with moving from the Captain Kirk to Mr Spock thought process. The problem is that, although experimental research shows you are likely to make better decisions, you feel you will make worse ones, plus it's much harder work. So, the Mr Spock approach feels like it will deliver worse outcomes and takes much more effort. No wonder we are all so reluctant to go down the route of objective measurement and KPIs!

As an added pressure, if you move into Mr Spock thinking, but your team doesn't, you can come under huge pressure to revert to 'seat of your pants' decision-making.

Are Captain Kirk decisions *really* over-optimistic?

Take this simple statistic:

'About half of all new establishments survive five years or more and about one-third survive 10 years or more.'

- Source: U.S. Bureau of Labor Statistics, BED

This information is readily available (although the exact figure seems to vary slightly by source). It means with just 10 seconds of searching on the internet any prospective small business can see the business they are looking to set up has a two-thirds chance of failure within 10 years of starting up. So around one-third of these fledgeling founders are absolutely right when they think to themselves 'No, it's fine I have a good proposition and an excellent business plan', but **two thirds of them are being over-optimistic**, or probably never even looked at the statistics and the realistic possibility of failure. So, a good number of these company founders have flawed business concepts but are firmly in the Captain Kirk mode. Many are relying on a gut feel that the business will succeed, whilst we know from official statistics that the majority are being over-optimistic and will fail in the first ten years.

The U.S. Bureau of Labor Statistics, BED, goes on to say *'Survival rates have changed little over time.'*

So, our inbuilt biases mean that many people in their heart-of-hearts **don't think they need KPIs**, because deep down they believe in the quality of their intuitive decision-making, even when that decision-making is over-optimistic.

Avoiding over-optimism

How do you avoid falling into this kind of over over-optimism trap? You avoid the traps *by looking at the objective data - KPIs*. This doesn't mean that you don't ever take a risk, or that every single decision is data driven, but it does mean that when you do take risks you do so with a proper grasp of the odds involved and the chances of success. Of course, this means sometimes you aren't going to like the message your data is giving you.

Why you may make Captain Kirk decisions more than you would like…

Here's another thing that made me sit up and pay attention: people are more likely to revert to Captain Kirk, seat of the pants decision-making, when they are **tired, stressed or very busy. Tired, stressed and very busy**, remind you of anything… like running a business?

Okay, so you've convinced me I might slip into 'seat of the pants' decision-making too often, how do I avoid that?

Now you are an open-minded person as you are reading a book on KPIs. I've got a strong suspicion you got over the initial road-bump of disbelief, but there's a real risk that some point you can decide this is all 'a bit too hard' and give up. As business people there are three important things we only have a limited amount of:

1. Time: However hard you work, there are only a finite number of hours in the day and days in the week. There is a hard stop of 168 hours in a week. Being under pressure, and working longer weeks, will drive you into fatigue. A tired mind will push you towards Captain Kirk 'intuitive' decision-making, with the increased risk of poor decision-making. One of the side effects of poor decision-making is additional pressure, often leading to working longer hours. It's a vicious cycle.

2. Money: Every business has to manage the pot of available money and to use and invest it as wisely as possible.

Our third finite resource is…

3. Willpower: Research shows willpower is a finite resource - we can exhaust it through overuse or tiredness. Deciding to use Mr Spock decision-making is particularly significant because this form of decision-making requires some willpower to engage. Remember that when you are tired, stressed and distracted, you are most likely revert to 'seat of the pants' Captain Kirk decision-making.

Every day we make conscious, or unconscious, decisions on how we will invest these three things. Sometimes we may make that decision hundreds of times in a day. Most of the time we will use Captain Kirk decision-making, so we don't even notice we are making these decisions. KPIs are there to support us in our Mr Spock decision-making.

With all three resources being limited, you must make sure that any big decisions on how you spend time, money or willpower count. To make the best decisions on 'the big stuff', we should use Mr Spock (System Two) decision-making.

Five key behaviours for better decision-making on 'The Big Stuff'

These are the things you can do to make the most of your time, money and willpower on those big decisions that need Mr Spock, not Captain Kirk…

1. Only focus your time and willpower on deciding things that count

- Decide clearly what you're trying to achieve.
- Choose a handful of KPIs that are directly linked to the things you're trying to achieve.
- Keep your dashboards and reports focused on meaningful timeframes and strictly relevant data. Strip away excess data (e.g. time periods, historic data that aren't really relevant), visual clutter or rubbish. These will deplete your ability to focus and make rational decisions.

- Regularly review how you are performing on those carefully chosen KPIs and targets.

2. Hold yourself accountable on a regular basis

- Put review points in your diary.
- Even better, get others to hold you accountable.
- Hire a coach. Make sure you hire a coach who understands and is bought-into the idea of rational, Mr Spock, decision-making.

3. Review data and make decisions when you are at your most rested, and clearest, state of mind

- Work out if you are a 'morning person' or 'evening person' and time difficult decisions for when you are at your most alert and resolute.

4. Use these tips to force yourself into Mr Spock thinking

- Think twice.
- Take a break, sleep on it or ask someone else for an opinion.
- Use 'reverse brainstorming' (details on page 175)
  - Imagine a future failure and then explain the cause.
- Take the 'Outside view'. Many teams are over-optimistic about the chances of project success. Take a cold hard look at the success rates of similar projects outside your team or organisation.

5. Focus on building the 'Mr Spock habit'

- Behaviour takes time to shape. Sitting down with a formal

agenda and data can be uncomfortable for many, especially when you're used to a freewheeling and informal small business environment. However, over time, it can gradually change to become 'the way we do things now' and lead to better quality 'big decisions'.

- Review the quality of the decisions made in the past and think about successes and failures, and the reasons behind them.

The ROKS Express™ method is built around these principles. So, if you implemented the steps in Section One you should be well set up to apply these five key behaviours.

Section Two: KPI Definitions

Full KPI index on page xiii

Warning!

This section is for **reference only**. It will make much more sense when you have worked your way through Section One of this book.

Anatomy of a KPI definition

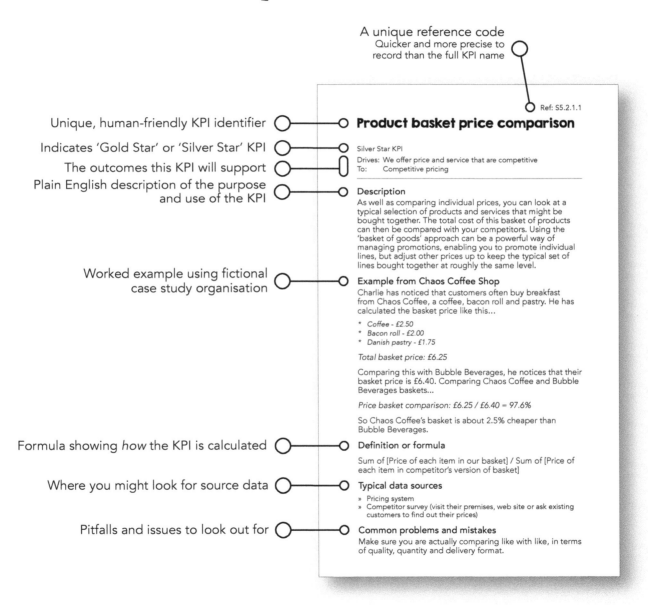

A unique reference code
Quicker and more precise to record than the full KPI name

Ref: S5.2.1.1

Unique, human-friendly KPI identifier → **Product basket price comparison**

Indicates 'Gold Star' or 'Silver Star' KPI → Silver Star KPI

The outcomes this KPI will support → Drives: We offer price and service that are competitive
To: Competitive pricing

Plain English description of the purpose and use of the KPI →

Description

As well as comparing individual prices, you can look at a typical selection of products and services that might be bought together. The total cost of this basket of products can then be compared with your competitors. Using the 'basket of goods' approach can be a powerful way of managing promotions, enabling you to promote individual lines, but adjust other prices up to keep the typical set of lines bought together at roughly the same level.

Worked example using fictional case study organisation →

Example from Chaos Coffee Shop

Charlie has noticed that customers often buy breakfast from Chaos Coffee, a coffee, bacon roll and pastry. He has calculated the basket price like this...

* Coffee - £2.50
* Bacon roll - £2.00
* Danish pastry - £1.75

Total basket price: £6.25

Comparing this with Bubble Beverages, he notices that their basket price is £6.40. Comparing Chaos Coffee and Bubble Beverages baskets...

Price basket comparison: £6.25 / £6.40 = 97.6%

So Chaos Coffee's basket is about 2.5% cheaper than Bubble Beverages.

Formula showing *how* the KPI is calculated →

Definition or formula

Sum of [Price of each item in our basket] / Sum of [Price of each item in competitor's version of basket]

Where you might look for source data →

Typical data sources

» Pricing system
» Competitor survey (visit their premises, web site or ask existing customers to find out their prices)

Pitfalls and issues to look out for →

Common problems and mistakes

Make sure you are actually comparing like with like, in terms of quality, quantity and delivery format.

Administration Effort, Time & Cost

Hours of work on admin

Ref: A1.1.1.2
Silver Star KPI

Drives: We keep track of the time we spend on admin
To: We manage our administrative overheads

Description
Where we have substantial administrative work, we may want to keep a record of that work. The total hours of admin work is an obvious one to record.

Example from Roughshod Repairs
Ruby has two full-time admin staff and an external book-keeper who works half-time for them. Ruby has decided not to track the admin-related time for non-admin staff due to the hassle.

Hours of work (per week) on admin: 75 hours

Definition or formula
Sum of [Time spent on administration tasks]

Typical data sources
» Time and attendance records
» Role descriptions
» Payroll
» Finance system + admin cost code if used

Common problems and mistakes
Decide whether you want to include the time of staff whose role is not primarily administration. Whilst doing this gives a more accurate picture of the true cost of admin, it can be a lot of hassle for not much benefit, so do what makes sense for your organisation.

Total admin cost

Ref: A1.1.2.1
Gold Star KPI

Drives: We track the cost of admin
To: We manage our administrative overheads

Description
The cost associated with administration. Will normally include labour, materials and possibly office building overheads (rent, space etc).

Example from Roughshod Repairs
Ruby has two full-time admin staff and an external book-keeper who works half-time for them. In addition, there are materials costs for things like postage, printers and so on.

Total admin cost (per month): £7k (mostly wages and materials for administration).

Definition or formula
Sum of [Money spent (including wages) on administration tasks]

Typical data sources
» Time and attendance records
» Payroll
» Finance system + admin cost code if used
» Invoices

Common problems and mistakes
Decide whether you want to include the time of staff whose role is not primarily administration. Whilst doing this gives a more accurate picture of the true cost of admin, it can be a lot of hassle for not much benefit, so do what makes sense for your organisation.

Present Customers Waiting for Service

Agent utilisation

Ref: C1.1.1.1
Gold Star KPI

Drives: Optimal number of staff serving
To: We minimise wait times

Description

This is a measure of 'How busy are our staff with [apparently] work related tasks?'. It is the ratio of time spent on work-related tasks to overall available time.

It is fairly easy to get a quick estimate of utilisation. You just need to watch the team for a bit of time and make a note of when they seem busy - engaged in something that is probably work-related, and when they are not. In IT or telephony environments this information is sometimes collected automatically. Just be open and honest with your staff about what you are doing, otherwise you may end up upsetting them.

Example from Chaos Coffee Shop

Charlie's barista is saying that they are too busy at 9am each day (missing sales as customers refuse to queue) and too quiet after 2pm. Charlie agrees to spend a day observing. Noting down the utilisation every 15 mins. Here are some extracts from that full day sample...

* 8:30 100%
* 8:45 100%
* 9:00 100%
* 9:15 100%
* 9:30 95%

and later in the day...

* 13:30 40%
* 13:45 30%
* 14:00 25%
* 14:15 10%
* 14:30 25%

Definition or formula

Sum of [Work related activity time] / Sum of [Time available]

Typical data sources

» Desktop activity recording (PC based environments)
» Telephony activity recording
» Observational studies
» Review of video footage
» EPOS activity

Setting targets

This is a very dangerous KPI to target, as it is mostly determined by resource levels and demand. Targeting utilisation, without giving teams the ability to flex resource or demand, is pretty much inviting them to find new and creative ways to waste time whilst looking busy.

Common problems and mistakes

Although utilisation can give a rough guide to how busy the team is, it does not tell you what they are busy with - is it something that makes a customer happy, makes the business money or is maybe just fixing problems that shouldn't have happened in the first place? To get deeper insight you need to look at efficiency measurement - be warned though - it's much harder to measure well. Start by looking at 'Labour efficiency' (page 429) and 'OEE' (page 433) if you decide to go down the efficiency route.

Whatever you do, put careful thought into how to bring your staff along with you. Many are suspicious of this type of measurement, so think before you jump in.

Customers served per agent

Ref: C1.1.1.4
Silver Star KPI

Drives: Optimal number of staff serving
To: We minimise wait times

Description

Customers served per agent is a simple productivity measure. It can be useful in working out the number of agents required to meet forecast demand.

Depending on the type of business you are in, this can be quite variable. In some situations some problems are much more lengthy to resolve than others. If that's the case for your business, use the average (or median, if you have a few ridiculously time-consuming customers that would skew the mean).

Example from Chaos Coffee Shop

Charlie is interested in the 'flat out' customer serving rate, so he can make sure he never has to turn people away or see long queues. Looking at his 'peak demand' time of day and the EPOS (cash register) data, he sees that the two people behind the counter are serving 38 coffees per hour, which are part of 21 orders per hour (average).

Definition or formula

Count of [Sales or service units] / Unit time

Typical data sources

» Desktop activity recording (PC based environments)
» Telephony activity recording
» Observational studies
» Review of video footage
» EPOS activity

Common problems and mistakes

Be clear what you mean by 'output'. In our coffee shop example do we mean 'making a coffee' or 'one customer's entire order'? It depends on whether you are talking order-taker or barista in this example.

Accuracy

Ref: C1.1.2.1
Gold Star KPI

Drives: Staff perform at expected level
To: We minimise wait times

Description

What proportion of orders were performed completely correctly?

Mistakes cost money, capacity (fixing the issue) and erode customer confidence and goodwill.

Example from Chaos Coffee Shop

In Chaos Coffee they keep a tally of mistakes. Charlie has gone to great lengths to explain that he is interested in knowing about mistakes only to make the job easier and more reliable, not to beat up staff about errors. Mistakes fall into three categories: order taking, order fulfilment and cash handling.

Accuracy problems from last week:

* *Order taking: 12*
* *Order fulfilment: 14*
* *Cash handling: 6*
* *Total accuracy problems: 32*
* *Total customers served last week: 1,625*

Accuracy for last week: (1,625 - 32) / 1,625 = 98%

Definition or formula

(Count of [Transactions] - Count of [Transactions with accuracy problems]) / Count of [Transactions]

Typical data sources

» EPOS / Till records
» Accuracy/mistake logs

Setting targets

Any target set on accuracy will normally be achieved, whether accuracy improves or not, as it's laughably easy to bias these figures.

Common problems and mistakes

Just encourage people to record problems, promising an open and honest approach to 'mistake proofing' as much as possible and getting to the root cause of problems.

Resource-to-plan percentage

Ref: C1.1.3.5
Silver Star KPI

Drives: We anticipate demand levels
To: We minimise wait times

Description

It is one thing to plan the number of agents you need, it is another to actually have those agents at the right time and place. This is a measure of how many people you did have versus those people you planned to have.

Example from Chaos Coffee Shop

Charlie plans to have two staff in the coffee shop, six days a week. Last week his barista was sick for two days and he couldn't find a replacement.

* *Planned resource level: 6 x 2 person days = 12 person days*
* *Actual resource level: 10 person days*

Resource to plan percentage: 10 / 12 = 83%

Definition or formula

(Sum of [Planned resource days/hours] - Sum of [Days/hours deviation from plan]) / Sum of [Planned resource days/ hours]

Typical data sources

» Resource plan
» Time and attendance records
» Payroll

Common problems and mistakes

It's really important to use 'deviation' from the plan - that is count 1 person understaffed as +1 deviation and 1 person overstaffed as +1 too. If you don't do this, overstaffed days could end up 'cancelling out' understaffed days - which doesn't work in reality!

Walkout rate

Ref: C1.1.5.2
Gold Star KPI

Drives: Customer wait better than expectation
To: We minimise wait times

Description

When customers get fed up they vote with their feet. It is commonly measured in call centres (abandon rate) but applies to any environment where there is queuing. Walkouts are a sign of serious customer irritation.

It's probably the worst time for staff to be looking out for this behaviour (as they will be flat-out at the times when this is most likely to happen) but it is a sign that something is seriously wrong and needs attention.

Example from Chaos Coffee Shop

Charlie is concerned about lost custom (and staff burnout) at the peak periods. Watching the security tapes from peak periods last week he sees at least 80 customers join the queue and then give up before they are served. He sees even more look through the window and not even join the queue. Looking at the ones who join, then abandon the queue...

Walkout rate: 80 / (1,625 + 80) = 4.7%

This may not seem a massive figure, but Charlie is deeply worried about the way the customers that stick out the queues are feeling too.

Definition or formula

Count of [Walkouts] / (Count of [Walkouts] + Count of [Customers served])

Typical data sources

» Walkout tally
» Review of security video
» EPOS/cash till transaction count

Median customer wait

Ref: C1.1.5.4
Silver Star KPI

Drives: Customer wait better than expectation
To: We minimise wait times

Description

How long is your typical customer having to wait? A simple question which has a major impact on customer perception of your business. It is often difficult to measure customer waits in physical queues, much easier for contact centres. For physical queues you can take a 'snapshot' at regular intervals - just noting down how long the queue is at certain intervals. From this you can estimate the wait time based on the average time to serve a customer.

Example from Chaos Coffee Shop

Charlie decided to do some 'queue sampling' on a typical morning. Every 10 minutes he wrote down the number of people queueing. He had previously measured the average time to serve a customer, and it's 3 mins. Using these two pieces of information, he built a 'wait table' like this one...

* 0-3 mins: 6
* 3-6 mins: 12
* 6-9 mins: 14
* 9-12 mins: 7
* 12-15 mins: 3
* 15+ mins: 2

Median wait time: 6-9 mins (the 22nd event out of 44 in wait order)

Definition or formula

Median [Customer wait time]

Typical data sources

» Observational study
» Use of electronic or paper 'queuing tickets' with time stamps for issue and order collection

Common problems and mistakes

Measuring wait times can be tricky. Depending on the environment, there may be technology based methods to measure wait times. An example of this would be electronic 'queuing tokens' used in restaurants. Often these systems can produce data on wait times.

Worst customer wait

Ref: C1.1.5.5
Silver Star KPI

Drives: Customer wait better than expectation
To: We minimise wait times

Description

This 'Worst customer wait' will be experienced by just one customer per 'interval' you are measuring over. It shows the very worst waiting experience.

Understanding the reasons behind this long wait can be a crucial part of improving your customer service.

Example from Chaos Coffee Shop

Charlie decided to do some 'queue sampling' on a typical morning. Every 10 minutes he wrote down the number of people queueing. Using an average service time he can come up with an estimated wait for the person at the end of the queue.

Worst wait (observed): 18 mins

Of course there may have been worse waits when he wasn't doing his study, but given that he was there during the busiest part of the day he thinks he probably saw the worst.

Definition or formula

Longest duration [Customer wait time]

Typical data sources

» Observational study
» Use of electronic or paper 'queuing tickets' with time stamps for issue and order collection.

Present Customers Waiting for Service

KPI Family: C2
Perishable Goods

Value of discount due to short shelf life

Ref: C2.1.1.2
Silver Star KPI

Drives: Minimise discounts for short/no shelf life
To: We minimise date-related waste

Description

Where a product is nearly at the end of its shelf life, you may decide to discount it to make sure it sells before it expires.

This figure shows the total value of that discounting.

A low discounting figure, coupled with a low 'Value of waste due to expiry' suggests you are managing your stock shelf life well.

Example from Chaos Coffee Shop

Charlie likes his pastries to be not more than 2 days old when sold. He will discount them 2 hours before the end of their second day.

Last week he sold 100 donuts at a 50% discount to make sure they didn't go over 2 days.

Value of discount = [Full price - discounted price] x [Volume sold at discount]

= (£1.50 - £0.75) x 100

Value of discount due to short shelf life: £75.00

Now it is possible to argue that he's still making a decent profit on these (cost price is £0.35) and the reason he had some left over was the result of over-ordering, so even though he discounted he brought in additional profit Chaos Coffee would not have made otherwise.

Definition or formula

Sum of [Value of discounts due to short/expired shelf life]

Typical data sources

» Stock management system
» Finance records
» Finance system
» Discount records/bar codes

Value of waste due to expiry

Ref: C2.1.2.2
Gold Star KPI

Drives: We minimise the amount of goods we need to throw away
To: We minimise date-related waste

Description

When we have to throw product away because the 'sell by' date has been exceeded or the product is no longer in saleable condition due to deterioration, this is 'waste due to expiry'. This figure puts a financial value to that waste.

If the product would, realistically, have been sold had it not expired, then the value is the sale price. If it would not have realistically been sold, then the lost value is the cost price.

Example from Chaos Coffee Shop

Charlie discounted, then threw away 50 Danish Whirls last week when they didn't sell at the discounted price.

* *Cost price of Danish Whirls: £0.50*
* *Number wasted: 50*

Value of waste due to expiry last week: 50 x £0.50 = £25

Definition or formula

Sum of [Value of scrapped product due to short/expired shelf life]

Typical data sources

» Stock management system
» Finance records
» Finance system
» Waste disposal records

Value of stock at or past 'sell by' date not discounted or discarded yet

Ref: C2.2.1.2
Gold Star KPI

Drives: We minimise stock going past 'sell by' date
To: Our stock does not go 'out of date'

Description

If stock is out of date, or on its expiry date, but has not yet been thrown away, you would record its value under this heading.

If the product would, realistically, have been sold had it not expired, then the value is the sale price. If it would not have realistically been sold, then the lost value is the cost price.

Example from Chaos Coffee Shop

For Chaos Coffee, Charlie has already thrown away the Danish Whirls that went out of date and didn't sell and the donuts that were discounted to half price. Unfortunately he finds two cheesecakes in the fridge on the last day of their shelf life. These cost £12 each.

Value of stock at or below 'sell by' date, not discounted or discarded yet: 2 x £12 = £24

Definition or formula

Sum of [Value of expired-but-not-yet-sold-or-scrapped product due to short/expired shelf life]

Typical data sources

» Stock management system
» Finance records
» Finance system

Age-related quality complaints

Ref: C2.3.2.3
Gold Star KPI

Drives: Customer is happy with the condition of the stock they buy
To: The goods we sell have adequate shelf life

Description

Complaints due to age deterioration or short shelf life are warning signs that you may have a shelf life management issue.

Customers are a good, honest bunch on the whole, but just make sure they haven't got confused and had something on their shelves longer than they realise. We all have some tins at the back of our cupboards 4 years past their sell-by date, don't we?

Example from Chaos Coffee Shop

Charlie had two people complain about stale donuts last week. Charlie is a bit stumped, as he feels he is on top of his stock shelf life. He's wondering if his supplier may be not quite as careful.

* Number of age-related quality complaints: 2
* Number of pastry products sold: 1,200

Percentage of age-related quality complaints: 2 / 1,200 = 0.2%

Definition or formula

Count of [Age-related quality complaints] / Count of [Items sold]

Typical data sources

» Sell-by and Best before dates on product
» Batch code from product
» Receipts

Storage temperature record

Ref: C2.4.1.1
Gold Star KPI

Drives: The goods are kept at the right temperature and humidity
To: We store goods in the correct conditions

Description

Depending on your product, temperature may be something you need to manage. If you do need to manage this, then you will also want to record its value to make sure your product is not damaged by incorrect storage.

For certain food businesses in many countries, temperature records are a legal requirement.

Example from Chaos Coffee Shop

Chaos Coffee is legally required to keep a record of fridge temperatures where it stores fresh salads. Records are kept to make sure the fridge is kept below 5C at all times. The records confirm that this has been the case.

Definition or formula

Varies, but typically

[Value of storage temperature] over time as graph or table.

Typical data sources

» Logging thermometer

Common problems and mistakes

If it's a legal/insurance requirement, make sure you are using properly calibrated and certified recording instruments.

Customer Goods Stored

Number of fraudulent item retrievals

Ref: C3.1.1.2
Silver Star KPI

Drives: We keep the items secure
To: The customer goods are safe and secure

Description

Where we store things that may be of value to others, we may experience fraud. This measure is a simple count of known incidents of fraudulent retrieval.

Example from Roughshod Repairs

For one of their commercial customers, Roughshod Repairs have customers send in or drop off their broken consoles, which are then fixed and returned or collected. To Ruby's horror, some fraudsters have figured out that they can collect fixed consoles that don't belong to them.

Number of fraudulent item retrievals last month: 5

Definition or formula

Count of [Fraudulent retrievals]

Typical data sources

» Storage log book/sheet/system

Number of lost items

Ref: C3.1.2.2
Silver Star KPI

Drives: We keep the items safe
To: The customer goods are safe and secure

Description

Where we store things that may be of value to others, we may lose items. This measure is a simple count of known incidents of items lost whilst under our care.

Example from Roughshod Repairs

For one of their commercial customers, Roughshod Repairs have customers send in or drop off their broken consoles, which are then fixed and returned or collected. They have a pretty good filing system at Roughshod, so after problems last year they haven't lost any at all this year.

Number of lost items last month: 0

Definition or formula

Count of [Lost items]

Typical data sources

» Storage log book/sheet/system

Number of storage-damaged items

Ref: C3.1.2.3
Silver Star KPI

Drives: We keep the items safe
To: The customer goods are safe and secure

Description

The customer experience is mostly determined by the speed at which an item is retrieved and the condition in which it is returned. Keeping count of how many items we damage is an essential part of identifying and eliminating any sources of damage.

Some sources of damage may be very infrequent, but extremely serious - fire and flood being obvious candidates. KPIs won't help you with these. You will need to do risk assessments and take action before these things happen.

Example from Roughshod Repairs

Some late collecting customers have been complaining about scratches on the top of their repaired consoles. Investigating, Ruby finds they have been stacking them for lack of space, leading to scratches.

Number of storage-damaged items last month: 3

Definition or formula

Count of [Storage damaged items]

Typical data sources

» Storage log book/sheet/system

Number of misfiled items

Ref: C3.2.1.1
Silver Star KPI

Drives: We know the location of customer items
To: We keep accurate records of stock movements

Description

Sometimes items are misfiled, making it slow or impossible to retrieve them.

Clearly it is not possible to distinguish between lost, stolen and misfiled items initially. These figures will often be revised some time after initial categorisation as things are discovered (e.g. a misfiled item is retrieved).

Example from Roughshod Repairs

Roughshod had a couple of hairy moments last month where they couldn't initially find two customer consoles (aside from the 5 that were stolen). Turns out they were at the bottom of the wrong pile, but with some extra searching they found them.

Number of misfiled items last month: 2

Definition or formula

Count of [Misfiled items]

Typical data sources

» Storage log book/sheet/system

Average time to retrieve

Ref: C3.2.1.2
Gold Star KPI

Drives: We know the location of customer items
To: We keep accurate records of stock movements

Description
The customer experience is mostly determined by the speed at which an item is retrieved, with the assumption it will be returned in the condition deposited. How fast you get your goods back is a critical measure of the service offered.

Example from Roughshod Repairs
When things are filed correctly, the Roughshod team are pretty quick at retrieving the right console.

Average time to retrieve: 2 mins

Definition or formula
Average of [Retrieval time]

Typical data sources
» System timings (if relevant)
» Timed samples

Common problems and mistakes
You may not want to, or be able to, measure the time taken for every retrieval. If that's the case, just time some typical retrievals and use that figure.

Storage revenue

Ref: C3.3.1.2
Gold Star KPI

Drives: We charge for storage, where appropriate
To: We manage storage

Description
If we are charging for storage, the revenue generated through paid storage is an important measure, along with 'Percentage of capacity used'.

Example from Roughshod Repairs
Roughshod do charge if it takes a customer more than 2 months to collect their console. Last month they collected…

Storage revenue: £50

The fee isn't really to make a profit, rather to nudge people into actually collecting their consoles.

Definition or formula
Sum of [Storage revenue]

Typical data sources
» Finance system
» Finance spreadsheets
» Invoices

Percentage capacity used

Ref: C3.3.3.1
Gold Star KPI

Drives: We manage capacity
To:　　We manage storage

Description

Whether we are selling storage or just storing customer items as part of our service, we need to keep an eye on how much space we have left. 'Percentage capacity used' gives us an indication of how much storage capacity we have left.

Our drivers for 'paid for' storage will be slightly different from 'storage as part of our service'. If we are charging we will want to keep the 'percentage of capacity used' as high as possible (whilst maintaining service). If storage is just part of our overall service, we may be looking to minimise 'Percentage of capacity used'.

Example from Roughshod Repairs

Roughshod have storage capacity for 200 consoles. They currently have 240 in storage. This means they are stacked, leading to damage and the odd misfiled/lost console.

Percentage of capacity used: 240 / 200 = 120%

Definition or formula

Sum of [Capacity used] / [Maximum design capacity]

Typical data sources

» Storage log book/sheet/system
» Physical review of available space

Sensitive Customer Data Stored

Number of information security process breaches

Ref: C4.1.1.1
Gold Star KPI

Drives: We comply with company policies
To: We follow our information security processes

Description

This figure is a simple count of the number of information security breaches.

Where a breach is detected, we also need to record the details of the breach - e.g. information compromised, date compromised, method of penetration, exploits used and so on.

Example from Dangerous Developers

Daniella invited a third party to investigate some strange network behaviours. The security consultant found 120 cases of customer data being sent unencrypted by email and a piece of malware on their DNS server, leading to another 4,000 DDoS attacks - although these did not lead to any customer data being leaked (it still spoiled Daniella's day though).

Information security breaches last month: 120

Definition or formula

Count of [Information security process breaches]

Typical data sources

» Data security logbook

Internal information security risk and data protection audit scores

Ref: C4.1.1.3
Silver Star KPI

Drives: We comply with company policies
To: We follow our information security processes

Description

Our overall audit score gives a snapshot view of information security.

Our best chance of stopping criminals from breaching our systems is to audit and identify weaknesses before they are exploited or detected in external audits.

Example from Dangerous Developers

Daniella finds a data protection and data security self-assessment toolkit on the UK's Information Commissioners Office website. They use this audit tool and discover they are 'red' for both information security and data protection.

Information security internal audit status: Red

Data protection internal audit status: Red

Definition or formula

[Info sec audit score]

[Data security audit score]

Typical data sources

» Information security audit score
» Data security audit score
» Data security logbook/sheet

Number of physical security process breaches

Ref: C4.2.1.1
Gold Star KPI

Drives: We comply with company policies
To: We follow our physical security processes

Description

A major part of security, including information security, is preventing physical security breaches - people entering areas they should not be, having access to paperwork or computers they should not have access to.

This measure involves recording incidents and the details around the incident for future prevention. There's overlap between physical and virtual security, as physical access to computer hardware makes unauthorised access to data much easier.

Example from Dangerous Developers

Dangerous Developers had not really given a lot of thought to physical security until thieves walked into the next door office and walked off with all their laptops, including client data.

Thankfully Dangerous haven't had that kind of issue yet, but they have decided to keep a log of incidents and near misses, so they can monitor if they have a problem (and they have fitted some extra locks!).

Number of physical security process breaches: 0

Definition or formula

Count of [Physical security breaches]

Typical data sources

» Data security logbook/sheet
» Security logbook/sheet
» Intrusion alarm notifications/logs

Average time to remove system access from leavers

Ref: C4.3.1.2
Gold Star KPI

Drives: Our user access list is up-to-date
To: We actively manage IT access privileges

Description

When someone leaves the organisation it is important to remove access to customer data promptly. Where you have more than a handful of employees and a defined leaver process, you may decide to measure the time between intention to leave and withdrawal of systems access.

Many customer data leaks occur when exiting employees take customer details with them. For this reason it is common to remove privilege at the same time as someone gives notice (or is given notice) that they are leaving.

Example from Dangerous Developers

As soon as someone tells the company that they intend to leave, or they are asked to leave, Daniella disables their single-sign-on account, which withdraws all system rights.

Average time to remove system access from leavers: 1 hr or less

Definition or formula

Average of [Time to remove system access from leavers]

Typical data sources

» Leavers checklist

Key return compliance from leavers

Ref: C4.4.1.2
Gold Star KPI

Drives: Our key holder list is up to date
To: We actively manage physical access privileges

Description

When someone leaves the organisation it is important to retrieve keys. Keeping a log of who has keys and monitoring their return is an important part of physical security.

Example from Dangerous Developers

Dangerous Developers use special locks with key-copying restrictions. When an employee finishes with Dangerous they return that key and sign a form to say they have done so, as part of the leaving process. So far, they haven't failed to retrieve any keys from exiting employees.

* *Employees departed in past year: 2*
* *Keys recovered: 2*

Key return compliance from leavers: 2 / 2= 100%

Definition or formula

Count of [Key sets retrieved] / Count of [Leavers]

Typical data sources

» Leavers checklist

Bookings & Appointments

Booking slot utilisation

Ref: C5.1.4.1
Gold Star KPI

Drives: We minimise unused booking slots
To:　　We maximise the use of our service

Description

Where we have a fixed number of slots, most businesses would like to sell as many of those slots as possible. Slot utilisation is a good measure of this. It is the ratio of slots sold to available slots.

Some organisations do not want 100% utilisation, especially where there's an emergency element to their service - for example doctors and dentists - so they will intentionally target a utilisation figure of less than 100%.

Example from Cracking Chiropractors

The practice's week is divided into twelve thirty-minute appointment slots, Monday to Friday. Last week they sold 53 of the 60 available slots.

Booking slot utilisation: 53 / 60 = 88%

Definition or formula

Count of [Sold booking slots] / Count of [Available booking slots]

Typical data sources

» Shopping cart software
» Booking service software

Value of unbooked slots

Ref: C5.1.4.2
Silver Star KPI

Drives: We minimise unused booking slots
To:　　We maximise the use of our service

Description

Where we were not able to sell a service appointment, this figure shows the total value of those unsold slots.

Where you discount to sell available slots, you need to decide whether to include this 'loss' in the 'Value of unbooked slots' figure.

This figure represents the 'opportunity' for the business, in its current configuration, to make more income. If you sell your time it's a really important one to focus on.

Example from Cracking Chiropractors

The practice's week is divided into twelve thirty-minute appointment slots, Monday to Friday. Last week they sold 53 of the 60 available slots. Seven slots were unbooked, with an average price of £35 per 30 minutes slot (it's a little cheaper if you buy an hour, so this is an average figure).

Value of unbooked slots: 7 x £35 = £245

Definition or formula

Count of [Unbooked slots] x [Average slot price]

Typical data sources

» Shopping cart software
» Booking service software

Booking service uptime percentage

Ref: C5.2.1.1
Gold Star KPI

Drives: The booking process works properly
To: The booking process is quick, easy and reliable

Description

If your service relies on an online booking service, it is crucial the booking service is available. This measure shows the proportion of the week that the service was available for the customers to use for booking.

Example from Cracking Chiropractors

Cracking Chiropractors use an online booking service. They offer a guaranteed uptime of more than 99%. Christine has no independent way to verify if this is what is being delivered, but the booking company claim just 30 minutes of outage in the past year.

Booking service uptime: (365 x 24 - 0.5) / (365 x 24)

Booking service uptime percentage: 99.99%

Definition or formula

[Uptime percentage]

or

([Intended system up time] - [Downtime]) / [Intended system up time]

Typical data sources

» Booking service
» Internet service provider (if self-hosted)
» Booking software diagnostics

Booking problems reported

Ref: C5.2.1.2
Gold Star KPI

Drives: The booking process works properly
To: The booking process is quick, easy and reliable

Description

When customers have problems with the booking process, a small number of them might ring, email or Tweet to tell you about it. This is the count of those helpful notifications.

Example from Cracking Chiropractors

Christine has had 5 emails and comments from clients in the past month saying they had problems using the online service. In each case it seems they were using very old website browsers. Christine has put a plug-in on her website that alerts users to potential problems if they are using an old web browser.

Booking problems reported: 5

Definition or formula

Count of [Reported booking problems]

Typical data sources

» Queries log
» Flagged emails
» Social media queries

Percentage abandoned bookings

Ref: C5.2.1.3
Gold Star KPI

Drives: The booking process works properly
To: The booking process is quick, easy and reliable

Description
Customers will sometimes abandon the booking process part way through. This is a percentage figure showing how often that happens.

Customers can abandon for a number of reasons, payment issues, technical problems, distractions and so on. As the booking process is the last step before they become a paying customer, this represents a tremendous loss to your business. Pay close attention to this figure and spend time understanding the root cause behind the problems.

Example from Cracking Chiropractors
Christine's online booking service has an 'Abandoned booking' figure, showing where and when the booking was abandoned. She sees 8 abandoned bookings last week. There were 53 successful bookings last week.

Percentage abandoned bookings: 8 / (8 + 53) = 13%

Definition or formula
Count of [Abandoned bookings] / (Count of [Abandoned bookings] + Count of [Successful bookings])

Typical data sources
» Shopping cart software
» Booking service software

Common problems and mistakes
Note that some of the abandoned bookings may be re-attempted successfully in a separate session, so be careful about assuming all abandoned sessions automatically represent a lost sale.

Average number of queries per booking

Ref: C5.2.2.2
Silver Star KPI

Drives: The booking process is quick and easy
To: The booking process is quick, easy and reliable

Description
When customers contact us with questions during or after a booking, this is a 'booking query'. These are important and must be dealt with, but they take time and money to deal with. An ideal process is one where the customer gets the vast majority of information they need through the materials provided on the website/brochure etc.

Lots of booking queries can be a good thing, but normally it indicates incomplete information or a broken booking process.

Example from Cracking Chiropractors
Christine and her assistant dealt with 23 booking queries last week related to 40 bookings, by email, phone and internet chat.

Average number of queries per booking: 23 / 40 = 0.58 per booking

Christine and her assistant keep a note of queries and review them at the end of the month to see if they can improve the information on their website.

Definition or formula
Count of [Booking queries] / Count of [Bookings]

Typical data sources
» Queries log
» Flagged emails
» Social media queries

Attendance & Ticket Sales

Social media event comments and mentions

Ref: C6.1.1.1
Silver Star KPI

Drives: We see engagement before the event
To: We fill our events profitably

Description

Developing a 'buzz' before an event is an important part of generating interest and ticket sales. Monitoring and counting social media mentions gives you a hard measure of the level of 'buzz'.

This becomes even more useful if you have previous event data to enable you to gauge the 'buzz' of the current event promotion, and how you are doing in comparison.

This is a leading indicator, so the great thing about this kind of feedback is that you still have time to tweak and improve your promotional campaign.

Example from Ambiguous Associates

Austin is running a workshop to train people in 'Aspirational Ambiguity'. He has been plugging the event hard on LinkedIn and Twitter.

He has logged 10 mentions on LinkedIn and 12 on Twitter.

Social media event comments and mentions: 22

Definition or formula

Count of [Agreed social media comments or mentions]

Typical data sources

» Social media stats pages

Common problems and mistakes

Social media platforms vary widely in terms of what stats they report, and this can change with time too. So it's not possible to come up with a universal formula here. For analysis I like to divide social media exposure into 'comment/observation' and 'active promotion/enthusiasm'.

Social media likes

Ref: C6.1.1.2
Gold Star KPI

Drives: We see engagement before the event
To: We fill our events profitably

Description

Media 'likes' are another useful measure of pre-event 'buzz'. Counting them gives you a hard measure of social impact.

Just like 'Social media mentions' this becomes even more useful if you have previous event data to enable you to gauge the 'buzz' of the current event promotion, and how you are doing in comparison.

It's a leading indicator, giving you a chance to tune and improve things as you go along.

Example from Ambiguous Associates

Austin has posted some photos of workshops he's run in the past, along with details of his next workshops. These posts received 50 'likes'.

Social media 'likes': 50

Definition or formula

Count of [Agreed social media 'likes' or positive endorsements]

Typical data sources

» Social media stats pages

Web traffic volumes to landing page

Ref: C6.1.1.4
Silver Star KPI

Drives: We see engagement before the event
To: We fill our events profitably

Description

If you have set up a special landing page, traffic to that page can give you an indication of event visibility and engagement.

Dig into 'what does our page visitor do next' by tracking visit duration, next page visited and so on, if you want more insight.

Example from Ambiguous Associates

Austin has set up a landing page for his 'Aspirational Ambiguity' course. Looking at the administrator stats page for his website, he can see he had 150 hits for that page last week.

Web traffic volumes to landing page last week: 150 unique visitors

Definition or formula

Count of [Unique visitors to landing page(s)]

Typical data sources

» Web site admin page stats

Common problems and mistakes

Be clear exactly what you are measuring. Is it page hits, or unique visitors? Will you include bounces (very short visits)? Whatever you decide, be clear on your logic and be consistent in using the same measure each period.

Number of attendees

Ref: C6.1.2.1
Gold Star KPI

Drives: We sell all of our tickets
To: We fill our events profitably

Description

How many people attended the event? Although a lagging measure, this is one of the primary outcomes we are looking for from our promotion and ticket sales.

Example from Ambiguous Associates

When Austin's workshop took place, he had 28 attendees on the day.

Number of attendees: 28

Definition or formula

Count of [Event attendees]

Typical data sources

» Registration records
» Head count
» Estimate (unticketed events)

Drop-out rate

Ref: C6.1.2.2
Silver Star KPI

Drives: We sell all of our tickets
To:　　We fill our events profitably

Description

People sometimes say they are going to come, buy tickets even, then cancel or don't come - these are 'drop-outs' . Keep a tally of these to see how it's affecting your event.

Drop-out can be a major issue, particularly for free events, where people have little to lose by cancelling (or not showing up).

Example from Ambiguous Associates

Austin originally had 35 people buy tickets to his workshop. Five cancelled in advance and had partial refunds. Two did not turn up on the day - 'no-shows'.

Drop-out rate: 7 / 35 = 20%

Definition or formula

Count of [Drop-outs and no-shows] / Count of tickets sold]

Typical data sources

» Ticket sales system/provider
» Registration records
» Head count

Percentage of tickets sold

Ref: C6.1.2.3
Gold Star KPI

Drives: We sell all of our tickets
To:　　We fill our events profitably

Description

Our primary objective for promoting any event is to sell all the tickets. Percentage of tickets sold tells us how well we have fulfilled that objective.

Tracking this figure before the event date can help you know whether your promotions are on track. It's sometimes hard to know what ticket sales patterns should look like, but once you have some previous events behind you, you can compare the sales pattern to those previous events.

Example from Ambiguous Associates

Austin originally had 35 people buy tickets to his workshop. Of those five cancelled in advance. Although he retained part of the ticket value, he decided not to count those refunds as ticket sales. The two no-shows were counted, as they had paid in full and received no refund. The maximum capacity was 40 seats.

Percentage of tickets sold: 30 / 40 = 75%

Definition or formula

Count of [Paid tickets not refunded] / Count of [Maximum number of tickets to be sold]

Typical data sources

» Ticket sales system/provider
» Registration records
» Venue/workshop capacity limit

Common problems and mistakes

There can be grey areas - e.g. partial refunds for advance cancellations. Do what makes logical sense and be consistent.

Value of unsold tickets

Ref: C6.1.2.4
Silver Star KPI

Drives: We sell all of our tickets
To: We fill our events profitably

Description

Tickets sometimes vary in price, depending on location etc. As well as tracking the percentage of seats sold, it can be sensible to look at value of unsold seats as well, to see whether some types are selling better than others.

Tracking this figure before the event date can help you know whether your pricing strategy is working. If you have previous data to compare your current promotion with, even better.

Example from Ambiguous Associates

Austin had 10 tickets that he could have sold but did not (this includes 5 cancellations for which the customer received a partial refund). The full price for the tickets is £600.

Value of unsold tickets: 10 x £600 = £6,000

Definition or formula

Count of [Unsold tickets] x [Price of unsold tickets]

Where there are multiple price bands, perform this calculation for each price band and add up the products.

Typical data sources

» Ticket sales system/provider
» Registration records
» Ticket pricing records

Value of discounting

Ref: C6.1.2.5
Silver Star KPI

Drives: We sell all of our tickets
To: We fill our events profitably

Description

If we have to discount tickets to increase 'percentage of tickets sold' how much are we discounting by? This figure represents the sum of all discounts used so far.

A discount only represents a real discount (or lost income) when it is actually used.

Example from Ambiguous Associates

Austin offered an 'early bird' discount of 20% to anyone who booked more than 8 weeks in advance. Twenty of the tickets sold had the early bird discount.

Value of discounting: 20% x £600 x 20 Tickets = £2,400

Definition or formula

[Discount percentage] x [Face value of tickets] x [Number of tickets discounted]

Where there are multiple price bands, perform this calculation for each price band and add up the products.

Typical data sources

» Ticket sales system/provider
» Registration records
» Ticket pricing records

Total ticket revenue

Ref: C6.1.3.1
Gold Star KPI

Drives: We optimise income from ticket sales
To: We fill our events profitably

Description

Total ticket revenue shows us the income for an event. For commercial events, revenue is one of the primary drivers for profitability. It's best to track revenue throughout the promotion, as well as at the end, of course.

Example from Ambiguous Associates

Austin sold 20 tickets at a 20% discount and 15 at full price. Of those 15, 5 cancelled and received a 50% refund:

Total ticket revenue: (20 x 80% x £600) + (15 x £600) - (5 x 50% x £600)

Total ticket revenue: £17,100

Definition or formula

Sum of [Ticket revenue]

Typical data sources

» Ticket sales system/provider
» Sales records
» Finance records/system

Total event profit

Ref: C6.1.3.2
Gold Star KPI

Drives: We optimise income from ticket sales
To: We fill our events profitably

Description

For commercial events, event profit is very important.

You may be holding an event to promote your business or to increase exposure, but turning a profit will help even these types of events. Charging for attendance will make it harder to sell tickets but will dramatically reduce your drop out rate - giving you solid attendance figures on the day.

Example from Ambiguous Associates

Austin's costs for the events were:

* *Venue: £2,000*
* *Catering: £800*
* *Equipment hire: £200*
* *Hotel and food for presenter: £200*
* *Promotional costs: £2,000*

The revenue for the event was £17,100

Total event profit: £17,100 - £5,200 = £11,900

Definition or formula

Sum of [Event revenue] - Sum of [Event costs]

Typical data sources

» Ticket sales system/provider
» Sales records
» Finance records/system

Repeat visits

Ref: C6.2.1.1
Gold Star KPI

Drives: We have repeat visits
To: People come back

Description

If you are running the type of event that occurs regularly (church, slimming club or art classes, for example) your prime targets for ticket sales are likely to be previous attendees. Monitoring how many attendees have been to your previous events will give you a good gauge of how popular your events really are.

For most businesses, encouraging previous attendees to come again should be easier than finding completely new customers. If that's not the case you need to understand the reason why - is there a quality problem with your event? Or is something else deterring people from coming back?

Example from Ambiguous Associates

Austin added the thirty attendee names to his sales system as people bought tickets. He noticed five names of people who had been on his previous events.

Percentage of repeat visits: 5 / 30 = 17%

Definition or formula

Count of [Previous customers] / Count of [Customers attending event]

Typical data sources

» Customer relationship management (CRM) system
» Ticket sales system/provider
» Sales records
» Finance records/system

Common problems and mistakes

Be clear on whether you include someone who has been before, bought a ticket but was a no-show. Generally best not to, unless you think there's a valid reason to do so.

Repeat bookings triggered by special offers

Ref: C6.2.1.2
Silver Star KPI

Drives: We have repeat visits
To: People come back

Description

If you decide to promote your event using some kind of offer, it's worth tracking how effective that offer was. You can do this with this 'Repeat visits triggered by special offers' measure.

Typically you would track this using a discount voucher or code. If you can use personalised codes, that's even better, as you can build up a profile of individual customers and figure out what does, or does not, get them to buy tickets.

Example from Ambiguous Associates

Austin noticed that all five of his 'repeat customers' used their unique early-bird code, sent to them in one of his promotional emails.

Repeat bookings triggered by special offers: 5

Definition or formula

Count of [Bookings involving special offer identifier]

Typical data sources

» Booking record 'discount code' field
» Customer relationship management (CRM) system
» Ticket sales system/provider
» Sales records

Feedback rating by section

Ref: C6.3.1.1
Gold Star KPI

Drives: We know what people enjoyed
To: People enjoy our events

Description

Feedback ratings systems will vary, depending on the complexity of your event, type of event and audience. Typically this KPI is an overall score, then broken down into sections such as 'Quality of content', 'Quality of delivery' and so on.

Honest feedback is what will enable you to improve your offer next time. Gathering good quality feedback, broken into sensible levels of detail, will enable you to make things better.

Example from Ambiguous Associates

Austin asks all his course delegates to fill in an anonymous feedback questionnaire. This gives him quite detailed feedback on each element of each workshop. He tracks the headline 'overall score'. It's a percentage…

Feedback rating: 92%

Definition or formula

Average of [Feedback score]

Broken down into sections if appropriate.

Typical data sources

» Feedback sheets
» Online feedback survey
» Feedback email responses

Number of reported event issues by issue type

Ref: C6.4.2.1
Gold Star KPI

Drives: We discover what need improving
To: We seek honest feedback

Description

If there are problems, you need to know about them and try to fix them as quickly as possible. As well as a simple 'count' of problems, make sure you capture plenty of details in a log somewhere.

Reported issues are normally the tip of the 'dissatisfaction iceberg', so listen, take them seriously and sort them if you can.

Example from Ambiguous Associates

During the course, a couple of people commented that the room was quite cold and two people said they found the projector too dim. Austin sorted those problems out as quickly as possible and made a note of them, so he could double-check the temperature and projector at the beginning of the next workshop.

Reported issues by type:

* *Comfort: 2*
* *Audio visual kit: 2*

Number of reported issues: 4

Definition or formula

Sum of [Issues reported]

Also broken down by issue type.

Typical data sources

» Requests and complaints during event
» Feedback sheets
» Online feedback survey
» Feedback email responses

KPI Family: C7
Donations

Value of pledges promised

Ref: C7.1.1.2
Gold Star KPI

Drives: Pledges are converted into donations
To: We maximise gifts

Description

A pledge is a promise to give. It's not always possible to get a donation on the spot, but a promise of a donation is the first step towards a donation.

Pledges only become useful to a non-profit when they are converted into donations. We do this by measuring the 'Pledge fulfilment percentage'. To calculate the 'Pledge fulfilment percentage' we must have the 'Value of pledges promised'.

Example from The Cat Herding Society

The Cat Herding Society received £1,200k worth of pledges in the previous year.

Value of pledges promised = £1,200k

Definition or formula

Sum of [Value of pledges promised]

Typical data sources

» Donation records

Value of pledges received

Ref: C7.1.1.3
Silver Star KPI

Drives: Pledges are converted into donations
To: We maximise gifts

Description

This is the total value where pledges have been made then followed up with actual donations.

This measure, along with 'Value of pledges promised', is the other KPI required to calculate 'Pledge fulfilment percentage'.

Example from The Cat Herding Society

The Cat Herding Society collected £700k of fulfilled pledges in the previous year.

Value of pledges received £700k

Definition or formula

Sum of [Value of pledges received]

Typical data sources

» Donation records

Pledge Fulfilment

Ref: C7.1.1.4
Gold Star KPI

Drives: Pledges are converted into donations
To: We maximise gifts

Description
This measure shows what percentage of pledged donations were actually donated.

Example from The Cat Herding Society
With £1,200k of pledges and £700k of that received…

Pledge Fulfilment Percentage: £700k / £1,200k = 58%

Definition or formula
Sum of [Value of pledges received] / Sum of [Value of pledges promised]

Typical data sources

» Donation records

Common problems and mistakes
There will often be a time lag between a pledge and a donation. Some donations may come in a long time after pledges, so we may have to accept 'old' values trending upwards or have a cut off age and accept we may be missing some of our conversions.

Average number of donations per donor

Ref: C7.1.2.1
Gold Star KPI

Drives: We attract repeat donations
To: We maximise gifts

Description
Recurring donors are critical to the fundraising of non-profits. Typically more than 80% of donations come from 10-15% of donors, with the majority of that 80% made by repeat donors. Retaining relationships is always easier than building new ones, and this is a critical measure of relationship retention.

Every donor you do not retain is a new donor you must acquire.

Example from The Cat Herding Society
Looking at their donation records, for traceable donations…

Average number of donations per donor: 2.4

Definition or formula
Count of [Attributable donations] / Count of [Unique donors]

Typical data sources

» Donation records

Common problems and mistakes
It may not be enough to just look at the average. If the distribution is peculiar (for instance a significant number of very high or very low value donations) it is almost certainly worth looking at the value distribution histogram.

Donors with more than one donation

Ref: C7.1.2.2
Silver Star KPI

Drives: We attract repeat donations
To:　　We maximise gifts

Description

This is another way of looking at donor retention and, along with average number of donations per donor, will help you understand the spread of donations amongst your donors.

Example from The Cat Herding Society

Looking at their donation records, for traceable donations…

Percentage of donors with more than one donation: 83%

Definition or formula

Count of [Unique donors with more than one donation] / Count of [Unique donors]

Typical data sources

» Donation records

Total donation value

Ref: C7.1.3.1
Gold Star KPI

Drives: We maximise donation revenue
To:　　We maximise gifts

Description

A key measure, simply showing the total monetary value of donations.

Example from The Cat Herding Society

* *Actual pledges collected £700k*
* *Donations £800k*
* *Bequests £400k*

Total donation value: £1,900k

Definition or formula

Sum of [Donations]

Typical data sources

» Donation records

Average gift size

Ref: C7.1.3.2
Gold Star KPI

Drives: We maximise donation revenue
To: We maximise gifts

Description
When people give, how much do they give? This figure shows the average figure.

Example from The Cat Herding Society
Total donation value = £1,900k. Number of donations = 85,067

Average gift size = £1,900,000 / 85,067 = £22.34

Definition or formula
Sum of [Gifts] / Count of [Gifts]

Typical data sources

» Donation records

Common problems and mistakes
It may not be enough to just look at the average. If the distribution is peculiar (for instance a significant number of very high or very low value gifts) it is almost certainly worth looking at the value distribution histogram.

Donations with relevant tax relief/ uplift

Ref: C7.1.4.1
Gold Star KPI

Drives: We maximise donation tax advantages
To: We maximise gifts

Description
Depending on your local tax laws, you may be able to recover government taxes on personal donations, if you collect the tax payer details. If you can do this, then collecting 100% of the tax benefits on offer is an important way of maximising donation income.

Note, this figure does not show the weighting. A large bequest with tax details counts the same as a £10 donation with tax details. If there are a wide range of donated amounts, you may want to break this figure down into donation 'bands', of for example, £0-£100, £100-£200 and so on.

Example from The Cat Herding Society
Total number of donations = 85,067 . Donations with valid tax relief details = 66,067.

Percentage of donations with relevant tax relief/uplift = 66,067 / 85,067 = 78%

Definition or formula
Count of [Gifts with valid tax details] / Count of [Gifts]

Typical data sources

» Donation and tax records

Total bequests amount

Ref: C7.1.5.1
Gold Star KPI

Drives: People remember us in their wills
To: We maximise gifts

Description
How much have people left you in bequests? This figure is the total amount of this donation type. For some charities this can be a major income stream.

Example from The Cat Herding Society
From the Cat Herding Society records, they can see for last year…

Total bequest amount = £400k

Definition or formula
Sum of [Bequest value]

Typical data sources

» Donation records

Common problems and mistakes
Be careful on how you interpret this figure, as it is a very 'lagging' figure, it can reflect fundraising efforts from decades ago.

Number of bequests

Ref: C7.1.5.2
Silver Star KPI

Drives: People remember us in their wills
To: We maximise gifts

Description
This is a count of bequests to your charity/non-profit.

A healthy 'Total bequest amount' can mask a narrow base of high value benefactors. Whilst that situation many sound great, having a few high value benefactors means that bequest income may plummet if there's a small dip in the number of [large] donations. A wider spread of smaller gifts suggests lower risk of bequest income fluctuations.

Example from The Cat Herding Society
From the Cat Herding Society records, they can see for last year…

Number of bequests = 67

Definition or formula
Count of [Bequests]

Typical data sources

» Donation records

Common problems and mistakes
Be careful on how you interpret this figure, as it is a very 'lagging' figure, it can reflect fundraising efforts from decades ago.

Fundraising ROI

Ref: C7.3.2.1
Gold Star KPI

Drives: Our fundraising is cost effective
To: Manage costs to maximise revenue & minimise overheads

Description

Fundraising return on investment tells us whether we made money on fundraising, and if we did how many £ we got back for each £ spent on campaigning.

Example from The Cat Herding Society

The Cat Herding Society spent £15k on promotional campaigns last year, leading to £225k in donations.

Fundraising ROI = (£225k - £15k) : £15k = 14 : 1

Definition or formula

(Sum of [Gain on investment] - Sum [Cost of Investment]) / Sum of [Cost of Investment]

Typical data sources

» Donation records
» Campaign financial expense records

Fundraising campaign ROI

Ref: C7.3.2.2
Silver Star KPI

Drives: Our fundraising is cost effective
To: Manage costs to maximise revenue & minimise overheads

Description

Fundraising campaign ROI is just the same as 'Fundraising ROI' but at a campaign level, so you can see which campaigns worked and which didn't.

Example from The Cat Herding Society

On each of the campaigns, the charity has cost and revenue figures. Taking the 'Cuddle a Cat' campaign:

*   *Cost of campaign: £6k*
*   *Revenue from campaign: £100k*

Campaign ROI = (£100k - £6k) : £6k = 16 : 1

Definition or formula

(Sum of [Gain on investment] - Sum [Cost of Investment]) / Sum of [Cost of Investment]

By campaign

Typical data sources

» Donation records
» Campaign financial expense records

Percentage of income as costs and overheads

Ref: C7.3.2.5
Silver Star KPI

Drives: Our fundraising is cost effective
To: Manage costs to maximise revenue & minimise overheads

Description
Closely related to the Fundraising ROI and Cost per £ raised, this is another way of showing what percentage of income gets swallowed up in costs and overheads.

Example from The Cat Herding Society
Cat Herding Society costs and overheads £350,000

Total income £2,070,000

Percentage of income as costs and overheads: £350k/£2,070k = 17%

Definition or formula
Sum of [Costs and overheads] / Sum of [Income]

Typical data sources

» Donation records
» Finance records

Grant funding value

Ref: C7.4.1.1
Gold Star KPI

Drives: We manage costs and results for grants and contracts
To: We benefit from institutional grants and contracts

Description
Where your charity or non-profit receives grants from any source, this figure shows the total value of those grants.

Example from The Cat Herding Society
The society receives £20k in grants from government and other charitable trusts.

Grant funding value = £20k

Definition or formula
Sum of [Grant funding value]

Typical data sources

» Finance records

Contract funding value

Ref: C7.4.1.2
Gold Star KPI

Drives: We manage costs and results for grants and contracts
To: We benefit from institutional grants and contracts

Description

Where your charity or non-profit receives contracts from any source, this figure shows the total value of those contracts.

For contract-related work it may also make sense to measure contract profitability, as there's normally a cost for delivering the contract service. Use the other relevant KPI Families for service profitability and operational performance KPIs.

Example from The Cat Herding Society

The society receives £150k in contract funding to deliver sheltered accommodation care for retired cat herders.

Contract funding value = £150k

Definition or formula

Sum of [Contract funding value]

Typical data sources

» Finance records

Income split by income type

Ref: C7.5.1.1
Silver Star KPI

Drives: No single source of income is essential for survival
To: We manage our income risk actively

Description

A spread of income sources helps manage risk. This set of figures will show how each income stream (donations, bequests, grants and contracts) contribute to the whole, as a percentage.

Example from The Cat Herding Society

The funding sources are…

* Donations	£800,000
* Actual pledges collected	£700,000
* Bequests	£400,000
* Grants	£20,000
* Contracts	£150,000

Shown as percentages…

* Donations	39%
* Actual pledges collected	34%
* Bequests	19%
* Grants	1%
* Contracts	7%

Definition or formula

Sum of [Funding category type] / Sum of [All funding category types]

Typical data sources

» Donation records
» Finance records

335

Donations

KPI Family: FI
Financials

Invoiced amount in period

Ref: F1.1.1.1
Gold Star KPI

Drives: Income
To: Maximise income

Description

To show the total value of sales invoiced in the period. It's a leading indicator of cash income and cash flow. A vital part of 'staying in the black' and not going bust. For a 'cash' business, like a small shop, this may not be a relevant measure.

Example from Dangerous Developers

Each week Daniella invoices her five major clients for development time.

The total value of the invoices for last week is £3,100

Definition or formula

Sum of [Amounts invoiced during the period, less known refunds and cancellations]

Typical data sources

- » Invoice copies
- » Sales system
- » Sales spreadsheet
- » Accounting software

Setting targets

It is simple and important to set targets on this, but beware of driving the wrong behaviour. Some organisations have set targets on this but discovered that sales teams have 'sold' products, only to cancel them after the bonus period is up.

Common problems and mistakes

Be clear on whether you include or exclude sales taxes in this figure. Remember to deduct cancellations and refunds.

Cash receipts in period

Ref: F1.1.1.2
Gold Star KPI

Drives: Income
To: Maximise income

Description

This shows the amount of cash coming into the business in the period. For businesses that invoice, this is about counting the money when it's paid or received, not invoiced. This is a crucial figure, as you can spend cash but you can't spend unpaid invoices!

Example from Chaos Coffee Shop

Charlie sells 2,000 cups of coffee, 1,200 donuts and 300 hot chocolate drinks, taking £5,500 in cash (all his sales are cash).

Cash receipts for the period are £5,500 (Charlie likes to measure things weekly, so that's his 'period').

Definition or formula

Sum of [Cash received in period] - Sum of [Refunds in period]

Typical data sources

- » Bank accounts
- » PayPal accounts
- » Till receipt roll or similar
- » Accounting software

Average days to issue invoice

Ref: F1.1.1.3
Silver Star KPI

Drives: Income
To: Maximise income

Description

One common pitfall, particularly for busy small companies, is that they "forget" to invoice.

It's very unlikely that someone will pay until you invoice them, so the quicker you get the invoice out of the door the faster you get paid and the better your cash flow will be. This is a measure to consider if you know you have a problem issuing invoices on time.

Example from Woeful Widget Warehouse

Will typically works one day a week for each of his clients, invoicing on the following Monday. That means his Monday client gets invoiced 6 days after the work, his Friday client 2 day after the work.

Average days to issue an invoice is 5 days.

Definition or formula

Average of [Number of days from completion of work to issuing of invoice]

Typical data sources

» Invoices
» Accounting system
» Work records
» Accounting software

Common problems and mistakes

You need to be clear whether you count non-working days in this calculation. It's probably worth thinking about what is meaningful. I generally include weekends and bank holidays, as many of your costs and overheads 'keep on costing', even when it's not a working day.

Total costs

Ref: F1.2.0.1
Gold Star KPI

To: Optimise costs

Description

'Total Costs', sometimes described as 'Total Expenses', is the total of all costs associated with running your business over a given period. It will include things like payroll, raw materials, loan repayments and many other things. The total costs figure is needed for our Net Profit calculation.

Example from Woeful Widget Warehouse

Will adds up his expenses for each month. These include warehouse rental, van costs, wages, inventory purchase, postage, energy, rates and many other things. If you spend money on it, and it's for the business, then it's probably a cost.

Total business costs for the month: £8,400.

Definition or formula

Sum of [All costs for period]

Typical data sources

» Receipts
» Bank records (statements or transactions download)
» Supplier invoices

Total cost of goods sold

Ref: F1.2.1.1
Silver Star KPI

Drives: Manage controllable costs
To: Optimise costs

Description

These are the costs directly associated with the production of whatever it is you sell. This would include raw materials, packaging, parts etc.

Example from Chaos Coffee Shop

For Charlie this includes:

- Coffee beans
- Cups
- Milk
- Bought-in food and ingredients

Definition or formula

Sum of [Cost of goods sold]

Typical data sources

» Receipts
» Bank records (statements or transactions download)
» Supplier invoices

Total controllable costs

Ref: F1.2.1.2
Silver Star KPI

Drives: Manage controllable costs
To: Optimise costs

Description

A controllable cost is a cost which is not directly associated with creating the product, but which you still have some (or total) control over.

For example, in a fast food restaurant, controllable costs might include payroll, advertising, promotions, linen, maintenance and repairs, utilities.

Controllable costs are often called 'variable costs'. I like controllable, as it's a bit more self-explanatory. Controllable costs increase for one of two reasons. Either we are making something less efficiently (bad) or we are making more of something (good, so long as we sell them as well). We can spot the first situation by looking at the 'unit costs'. If the unit cost goes up then we might have a problem.

Example from Woeful Widget Warehouse

Of Will's costs, the following are 'controllable':

- Van fuel and repairs
- Wages
- Energy bills
- Uniforms
- Maintenance and repairs on the warehouse

Definition or formula

Sum of [Cost of items classified 'controllable']

Typical data sources

» Receipts
» Bank records (statements or transactions download)
» Supplier invoices

Total non-controllable (fixed) costs

Ref: F1.2.2.1
Silver Star KPI

Drives: Manage non-controllable (fixed) costs
To: Optimise costs

Description

A non-controllable cost or expense is something where you have no control over whether you pay and how much you pay. Tax is a non-controllable cost for every business.

Example from Chaos Coffee Shop

Charlie adds up all of the costs that he would categorise as 'non-controllable'. Some of his non-controllable costs include:

- Loan interest
- Insurance (several types of cover)
- Accounting fees
- Taxes

The sum of these gives his total non-controllable costs.

Definition or formula

Sum of [Cost of items classified as 'non-controllable']

Typical data sources

» Receipts
» Bank records (statements or transactions download)
» Invoices
» Accounting software

Net profit

Ref: F1.3.1.1
Gold Star KPI

Drives: Maximise product/service profit margins
To: Maximise profit

Description

Net profit is the money left once we have covered all our costs. Along with 'Cash in bank', this is the most important measure for any business, from a dog walking firm to a multinational.

Net profit is sometimes called 'the bottom line' or 'net earnings'.

Example from Chaos Coffee Shop

For Charlie, last week breaks down like this...

Sales revenue: £5,500

Costs (both controllable, and non-controllable): £4,600

Net profit for week is £5,500 - £4,600 = £900

Definition or formula

Sum of [Sales revenue] - Sum of [Total costs]

Typical data sources

» Receipts
» Bank records (statements or transactions download)
» Invoices

Common problems and mistakes

Unlike gross profit, net profit includes overheads and interest payments. This makes it a little trickier to apply to *individual* products and services, as you have to 'allocate' overhead costs. 'Allocating overheads' means chopping up the cost of say, rent, and adding a little bit of the rent costs to the 'cost' of each product (or service) sold. This can get complicated pretty quickly, so Gross Margin (or Gross Profit) can be a quicker and easier indicator when you are trying to spot your super-star profitable products and services.

Gross profit & margin

Ref: F1.3.1.2
Gold Star KPI

Drives: Maximise individual product/service profit
To: Maximise profit

Description

Gross profit is the revenue (the money you make selling something) less the cost of making that thing or providing that service. It does not include overheads, so it's not the full picture, but it can be very useful for identifying your 'star' products and services (or the ones you need to drop or re-price). Gross Profit expressed as a percentage is called the Gross Margin (or Gross Profit Margin).

Example from Chaos Coffee Shop

Chaos Coffee took £2,800 in coffee sales, £1,800 in donut sales and £900 in hot chocolate sales - a total of £5,500 for the week, last week. His costs for making those products were £280 for coffee sales, £420 for donut sales and £150 for hot chocolate sales - a total of £850 for the week. The figures are summarised in the table below.

So, the overall Gross Profit is £5,500 - £850 = £4,650

The Gross Profit Margin is £4,650 / £5,500 = 85% (Don't get too excited, this figure doesn't include Charlie's considerable overheads). In the table below, we break that down and go a step further and work out the gross profit per item, by type. To do this, just divide the Gross profit for a category (e.g. Coffee) by the volume sold.

Definition or formula

Gross profit: Sum of [Sales revenue] - Sum of [Cost of sales and other direct costs]

Gross profit per item: (Sum of [Sales revenue] - Sum of [Cost of sales and other direct costs]) / Volume

Typical data sources

» Purchasing records
» Inventory control system
» EPOS system
» Till summary
» Receipts
» Bank records (statements or transactions download)
» Invoices
» Accounting software

	Volume	Sales	Sale price	Unit Cost	Total cost	Gross profit	Gross profit per unit	Gross profit margin
Cups of coffee	1,120	£2,800	£2.50	£0.25	£280	£2,520	£2.25	90%
Donuts	1,200	£1,800	£1.50	£0.35	£420	£1,380	£1.15	77%
Hot chocolate	300	£900	£3.00	£0.50	£150	£750	£2.50	83%
Totals		£5,500			£850	£4,650		85%

Gross profit percentage split

Ref: F1.3.1.3
Silver Star KPI

Drives: Maximise individual product/service profit
To: Maximise profit

Description

This shows which products or services made the 'lions share' of your gross profit. The amount you make for a product or service type is a result of both gross profitability on the sales and volume, so is good for focusing the mind on where the majority of your income comes from.

The Gross Profit Percentage isn't as meaningful a figure as the Net Profit Percentage, but it's a lot quicker and easier to work out for most businesses.

It's a close relative of 'Gross profit per product/service/item type', but this is calculated based on the **total** profit on sales of that item/service type compared with other types. Selling more of an item type (compared with other types) will increase the Gross profit percentage split for that type of product.

Example from Chaos Coffee Shop

Using the Gross profit (£4,650) and the Gross Profits by product from earlier, the Gross Profits percentage split are shown in the table below.

Definition or formula

100 * (Sum of [Gross profit per product type]) / Sum of [Total sales revenue]

Typical data sources

» Purchasing records
» Pricing lists
» Inventory control system
» EPOS system
» Till summary
» Receipts
» Bank records (statements or transactions download)
» Invoices
» Accounting software

Common problems and mistakes

Your percentages should add up to 100%. If they don't, first check your rounding. If they still don't add up then you have made a mistake or missed something out of your calculations.

	Volume	Sales	Sale price	Unit Cost	Total cost	Gross profit	Gross profit per unit	Gross profit margin	Gross profit % split
Cups of coffee	1,120	£2,800.00	£2.50	£0.25	£280.00	£2,520.00	£2.25	90%	54%
Donuts	1,200	£1,800.00	£1.50	£0.35	£420.00	£1,380.00	£1.15	77%	30%
Hot chocolate	300	£900.00	£3.00	£0.50	£150.00	£750.00	£2.50	83%	16%
Totals		£5,500.00			£850.00	£4,650.00		85%	

Gross profit per unit product/service/item

Ref: F1.3.1.4
Gold Star KPI

Drives: Maximise individual product/service profit
To: Maximise profit

Description

Gross profit per product shows the profit made on an individual item (or service) after you deduct the direct costs of making that product (or providing that service). It can be very useful if you need to simplify your business by dropping unprofitable lines or want to focus on the ones that make the most money. You can show this as either the profit made in £/$ or as a percentage.

This figure should be high for most small businesses, particularly where the product is low cost and there are serious overheads. As an example Dunkin' Brands - of Dunkin' Donuts fame - reported an 84% gross profit margin (gross margin is just gross profit as a percentage) in the March quarter of 2017. If you have a low or negative gross profit per product, you should seriously think about why you are selling that product or service.

Example from Chaos Coffee Shop

For donuts, Charlie buys the donuts in at £0.35 each and sell them for £1.50.

This gives a gross profit per donut of £1.15. You can also express this as a percentage if you like - £1.15 / £1.50 = 77%

Definition or formula

[Unit sale price] - [Direct unit costs] for the cash profit per unit

([Unit sale price] - [Direct unit costs]) / [Unit sale price] for % profit per unit

Typical data sources

» Purchasing records
» Pricing lists

Cash forecast

Ref: F1.0.0.1
Gold Star KPI

Drives: Maximise individual product/service profit
To: Maximise profit

Description

A cash forecast is a running total showing cash income and outgoings over a period of time, and the cash balance at any given time.

This measure is about looking ahead, seeing problems and avoiding them, not just dealing with the mess. It's a really key tool that will help you avoid one of the most common causes of business failure - running out of cash.

Example from Dangerous Developers

Daniella has £18,000 in the company bank account. Next month she has to pay £4,000 tax bill, £4,000 in wages and another £1,000 in sundry expenses, but expects to receive £10,000 in invoice payments.

The cash forecast for the end of next month will be…

£18,000 - £4,000 - £4,000 - £1,000 + £10,000 = £19,000

Definition or formula

[Cash in bank, previous period] + Sum of [Net cash income] - Sum of [Total costs], for period

Typical data sources

» Tracking spreadsheet
» Accounting software

Cash in bank

Ref: F1.4.0.1
Gold Star KPI

To: Manage assets

Description
There's not too much explanation required for this one. It's simply the total amount of available (cleared) cash in your bank, PayPal or wherever else you store your money. Simple though it is, this is the most important measure for your business, along with net profit.

Without cash, you can't function as a business. Enough said?

Example from Woeful Widget Warehouse
Will logs into his online company bank account and sees the cleared company funds are £24,500. The company also has an overdraft of £2,000 in another account, so...

Net total 'Cash in bank' is £24,500 - £2,000 = £22,500

Definition or formula
Sum of [Cash in bank] for all company bank accounts

Typical data sources
» Bank records (don't forget to include payment services like Stripe and PayPal, if they can hold cash)

Total assets

Ref: F1.4.0.2
Silver Star KPI

To: Manage assets

Description
An asset is something that you own that has value. So your 'Total assets' are the sum total of all the things your business has that have financial value.

Example from Chaos Coffee Shop
Charlie has the following assets....

- Inventory: £3,000
- Equipment: £8,000 (net value)
- Cash: £10,000
- Equity in his coffee shop property £115,000 (the difference between its market value - £300,000 and the amount he owes on the mortgage - £185,000).

So, Charlie's total assets are:

£3,000 + £8,000 + £10,000 + £115,000 = £136,000

Definition or formula
Sum of [Value of assets] for the company - [Depreciation]

Typical data sources
» Inventory control system
» Receipts, bank records (statements or transactions download
» Invoices
» Accounting software/spreadsheets
» Asset register/log

345

Working capital ratio

Ref: F1.4.0.3
Gold Star KPI

To: Manage assets

Description

The working capital ratio shows the ratio of assets to liabilities. This gives a strong indication of whether the business can pay its bills.

A ratio of 2.0 (or 2:1, if you prefer) is generally a good place to be for short term liquidity (cash or things you can rapidly turn into cash).

The inverse of this measure is called the Debt Ratio.

Example from Chaos Coffee Shop

Charlie's assets are £136,000, his liabilities are £200,000 (see F1.5.0.1 on page 349 for where this figure came from), so his working capital ratio is £136,000 / £200,000 = 0.68.

This is a weak position to be in. Much of his assets and liabilities revolve around his mortgage on the coffee shop. If I were Charlie, I'd want this to be nearer 2.0.

Definition or formula

[Total assets] / [Total debt]

Typical data sources

» Inventory control system
» Receipts, bank records (statements or transactions download)
» Invoices
» Accounting software/spreadsheets
» Asset register/log

Cost of inventory

Ref: F1.4.1.1
Silver Star KPI

Drives: Manage inventory (stock)
To: Manage assets

Description

The value of inventory (stock) that your business owns. This is an important figure: too low a value of inventory and you may have problems meeting customer demand promptly; too much inventory and you may have valuable cash tied up in inventory, adversely affecting your cash flow.

Example from Woeful Widget Warehouse

Will has...

- £500 of 'Widget Spinners'
- £4,000 of 'amusing cat mouse mats'
- £43,000 of 'water soluble coffee cups'

His total value of inventory is £500 + £4,000 + £43,000 = £47,500

Will has had problems shifting the 'water soluble coffee cups'. Do you think he can fully recover £43,000? What are his options here when it comes to valuing the cups?

Definition or formula

Sum of [Value of inventory]

Typical data sources

» Inventory control system
» Inventory/stock check

Common problems and mistakes

It is not uncommon for businesses to have significant amounts of "inventory" that is in fact unsellable. It's an easy trap to fall into where you value the inventory at its nominal sales value, ignoring the fact that it is in fact impossible to sell. In terms of understanding what's really happening in your business it's a seriously bad move. Accounting policy is to always value at the lower end of cost or net realisable value.

Inventory turnover ratio

Ref: F1.4.1.2
Silver Star KPI

Drives: Manage inventory (stock)
To: Manage assets

Description

The inventory turnover ratio is the 'cost of goods sold' for a given period divided by the 'average inventory' for that period. This is another way of looking at whether you're carrying the right level of inventory or not. Low turnover ratio suggests that you have weak sales and/or are carrying too much inventory. A high turnover ratio implies strong sales and/or inventory may be very low.

It is a way of expressing how long your average stock level is likely to last.

Example from Chaos Coffee Shop

Charlie spends £300 per week on coffee beans - £15,000 per year including holidays. On average, he has 60kg - £600 worth of beans - in stock. So...

Inventory turnover ratio is £15,000 / £600 = 25

In other words two weeks of stock.

Definition or formula

[Cost of goods sold] / [Value of average inventory]

Typical data sources

» Inventory control system, 'inventory/stock check'
» Accounting software/spreadsheets

Working capital

Ref: F1.4.0.4
Silver Star KPI

To: Manage assets

Description

This is what's left when you take away what you owe (liabilities) from your current assets. It's an important measure of whether you're about to go bankrupt or not, so keep a close eye on this one!

Example from Dangerous Developers

Daniella has £18,000 in the company bank account. This month she needs to pay £1,000 for some office furniture they bought last month and she owes £3,000 to freelance user-interface designers.

Her working capital:

£18,000 - £1,000 - £3,000 = £14,000

Definition or formula

[Current assets] - [Current liabilities]

Typical data sources

» Inventory control system
» Loan, credit and overdraft records
» Receipts, bank records (statements or transactions download)
» Invoices
» Accounting software/spreadsheets
» Asset register/log

Common problems and mistakes

You should not include property or fixed assets as assets for the purposes of this calculation. Working capital is all about the money you can 'get your hands on' rather than locked away in property.

Total accounts receivable

Ref: F1.4.2.1
Gold Star KPI

Drives: Minimise the amount owed to me
To: Manage assets

Description

'Total accounts receivable' is the money owed to your business from others (called 'debtors') for services or goods already delivered. Knowing this figure is an important part of staying solvent, to put it simply we need it to know whether or not we're about to go bust. So after 'cash in the bank' and 'net profit' this is definitely one to keep a close eye on.

It may take the form of credit you offer to a customer, a supplier or employee.

Example from Dangerous Developers

Daniella has submitted £10,000 of invoices to clients, which have not yet been paid. So...

Total accounts receivable: £10,000

Definition or formula

Sum of [Money owed to your business]

Typical data sources

» Tracking spreadsheet
» Accounting software
» Manual comparison of invoices to payments into bank account

Common problems and mistakes

Letting accounts receivable get out of control, for example overdue unpaid invoices, can lead to bad debt - debts that may never be fully repaid. These bad debts can quickly erode profit and cash flow.

Average debtor days

Ref: F1.4.2.3
Silver Star KPI

Drives: Minimise the amount owed to me
To: Manage assets

Description

Debtor days give you an indication of how quickly cash is being collected from people that owe it to your business. The longer it takes to collect the greater the number of debtor days.

Example from Woeful Widget Warehouse

Will sells lots of his products to small shops. His average monthly sales are £18,000. At the end of this month he is owed £24,000.

*His Debtor days are: (24,000 / 18,000) * 30 = 40 days*

Definition or formula

365 days * [Trade receivables (what you are owed)] / [Annual credit sales (total amount you sell on credit)]

For a shorter period, use the number of days in that period, rather than 365 - for example 30 days for a month - and you would use the credits sales for that shorter period, rather than a year

Typical data sources

» Tracking spreadsheet
» Accounting software
» Manual review of invoice age and whether they have been paid or not

Total liabilities

Ref: F1.5.0.1
Silver Star KPI

To: Manage liabilities

Description
This is how much we would be called to pay back if repayment were demanded on all of the things we owe.

Example from Chaos Coffee Shop
Charlie has an outstanding mortgage of £185,000, an outstanding company vehicle loan of £10,000 and unpaid tax of £5,000 from last year.

Total liabilities are: £185,000 + £10,000 + £5,000 = £200,000

Definition or formula
Sum of [Liabilities]

Typical data sources
» Tracking spreadsheet
» Accounting software
» Loan, credit and overdraft records

Total accounts payable

Ref: F1.5.1.1
Gold Star KPI

Drives: Manage the amount I owe
To: Manage liabilities

Description
'Total accounts payable' is the amount of money borrowed by your business from another party. This will include money you owe to vendors and suppliers for purchases of goods and services made using credit. Knowing this figure is an important part of staying solvent, to put it simply we need it to know whether or not we're about to go bust. So after 'cash in the bank' and 'net profit' this is another one to keep a close eye on.

Example from Dangerous Developers
Daniella needs to pay £1,000 for some office furniture they bought last month and she owes £3,000 to freelance user-interface designers.

Total accounts payable are £1,000 + £3,000 = £4,000

Definition or formula
Sum of [Accounts payable]

Typical data sources
» Outstanding supplier invoices
» Unpaid credit card bills
» Loan agreements
» Overdrafts

Tax owed

Ref: F1.5.2.2
Gold Star KPI

Drives: Manage owed and due tax
To: Manage liabilities

Description

You find out the tax on profits owed by your company at the end of your financial year, once you have processed your company accounts . This amount isn't normally payable for a number of months, but you will now know what it is. It's important not to be surprised by that payment so planning in when you have to pay can help you manage your cash flow effectively. Different businesses in different countries pay different types of tax, but it's common to have to find fairly substantial sums of money at regular intervals, so looking ahead helps you manage this. The same applies to other forms of tax, such as sales tax. Putting them on a spreadsheet and tracking against your cash will help you form a simple cash forecast.

Example from Woeful Widget Warehouse

Woeful Widgets' tax year ends on the 31st of December. Will has his accounts done by the end of May, and must pay any outstanding profit taxes by the end of October. He has five months from knowing the exact figure to paying the outstanding amount. Sales taxes are due each quarter, and must be paid within six weeks of the amount being due.

Will likes to use tax estimates in his cash forecast and update those estimates when he knows each tax figure exactly, to improve the accuracy of the forecast.

Definition or formula

Sum of [Unpaid taxes owed for previous tax period]

Typical data sources

» Notifications from your accountant
» Notifications from the tax office

Health & Safety

Number of accidents

Ref: H1.1.1.1
Gold Star KPI

Drives: We keep accurate accident records
To: Understand how we are performing with health & safety

Description

Where there are accidents we will normally need to record these accidents in a log. This KPI is simply the total of recorded accidents in the period. Look at 'Lost days' to get some indication of severity. Keeping a close eye on this figure is a useful, if lagging, indicator of our safety performance.

Example from Mayhem Manufacturing

In the Mayhem Manufacturing workshop they use an accident log book. That log book shows…

Number of accidents (past year): 3

..of which 1 was a 'lost time accident' meaning someone took some time off as a result of the accident.

Definition or formula

Count of [Reported accidents]

Typical data sources

» Accident log book
» H&S management software

Setting targets

Don't under any circumstances target individuals or teams for a reduction in these. Doing so will almost always 'work' but normally does so by people simply not reporting accidents. The key is to focus on the **root cause**, not the reporting of near misses.

Common problems and mistakes

It is important to build a culture of 'it's good to record accidents, whatever the cause' to prevent under-reporting.

A potential engagement issue may occur when there are long periods between accidents. There will be many periods with nothing to report. This a great outcome, but not a very engaging figure to report. It might be better to focus on 'days since last accident' - just be careful this doesn't become a disincentive to report accidents.

Number of near misses

Ref: H1.1.1.2
Gold Star KPI

Drives: We keep accurate accident records
To: Understand how we are performing with health & safety

Description

Near misses are events that could have ended in an accident, but which by good fortune did not. Recording these is a crucial part of any safety improvement activity.

Near misses are important as they are strongly correlated with accidents. Taking action on the causes of near misses may well help you prevent accidents.

Example from Mayhem Manufacturing

In the Mayhem Manufacturing workshop they use an accident log book. That log book shows…

Number of near misses (past year): 12

Definition or formula

Count of [Reported near misses]

Typical data sources

» Accident log book
» H&S management software

Setting targets

As for accident reporting, don't under any circumstances target individuals or teams for a reduction in reported numbers. Doing so will almost always 'work' but normally does so by people simply not reporting near misses. The key is to focus on the **root cause**, not the reporting of near misses.

Lost days due to work-related ill-health

Ref: H1.1.1.3
Gold Star KPI

Drives: We keep accurate accident records
To: Understand how we are performing with health & safety

Description

Where one of your team needs to take time off due to injury, this tally shows how much time was taken. It's an indicator of more serious injuries.

Example from Mayhem Manufacturing

One accident in the past year resulted in an employee taking time off - 3 days for a back muscle injury.

Lost days due to work-related ill-health: 3

Definition or formula

Count of [Days lost to work-related health and safety incidents]

Typical data sources

» Accident log book
» H&S management software
» Time and attendance records

Number of reported safety process breaches

Ref: H1.1.1.4
Gold Star KPI

Drives: We keep accurate accident records
To: Understand how we are performing with health & safety

Description

Breaching safety procedures is a common cause of near misses and lost time accidents. Recording the count of breaches is the first step in addressing them.

Recording process safety breaches is a key part of the 'safety improvement cycle' in which problems are addressed. When safety procedures are breached it is worth understanding why they were breached. Sometimes it is slack behaviour, but often it is impractical procedures or inadequate training - both of which will need to be addressed.

Example from Mayhem Manufacturing

Mohammed likes to have a wander round the workshop as often as possible. He notes down any safety issues he spots, and picks up the problems with the team right there and then. Most of the issues he spots are related to not wearing proper 'personal protective equipment' like goggles and gloves.

Number of reported safety process breaches: 14 last month

Definition or formula

Count of [Identified health and safety breaches] in period

Typical data sources

» Accident log book
» H&S management software

External audit scores

Ref: H1.1.2.2
Gold Star KPI

Drives: We audit regularly and rigorously
To: Understand how we are performing with health & safety

Description

External audits may be from companies employed by you, organisations you have a business relationship with, or by government inspectors. Where the score is quantified (score, grade or letter outcome) record it, along with the points raised, to track your performance from inspection to inspection.

You will often want to trend the break-down of the score to see how you are doing on each element, and identify where your opportunity to improve is to be found.

Example from Mayhem Manufacturing

Mayhem use a H&S consulting firm - Sanguinous Safety - to review Mayhem's performance. They give them a rating on a scale of 1-100 (higher is better).

Mayhem's score at the last review was...

External audit score: 76

Definition or formula

[Value of external audit score]

Typical data sources

» External audit report(s)

Internal audit scores

Ref: H1.1.2.3
Silver Star KPI

Drives: We audit regularly and rigorously
To: Understand how we are performing with health & safety

Description

If you run internal audits which produce a score or grade, track them over time to see how you are trending.

You will often want to trend the break-down of the score to see how you are doing on each element, and identify where your opportunity to improve is to be found.

Example from Mayhem Manufacturing

Mayhem use a similar audit to their H&S consulting firm - to keep on top of Mayhem's H&S performance. They give themselves a rating on a scale of 1-100 (higher is better).

Mayhem's own audit score at the last review was...

Internal audit score: 82

Definition or formula

[Value of internal audit score]

Typical data sources

» Internal audit report(s)

Number of outstanding internal audit actions

Ref: H1.3.1.1
Silver Star KPI

Drives: We act quickly to resolve identified issues
To:　　We identify & fix health & safety issues swiftly & effectively

Description

Internal audits only deliver value if you act on the improvement findings and do so promptly. This figure shows the volume of outstanding actions.

Having an accident where the risk was previously identified and action was agreed but then never carried out is a very scary place to be, both morally and legally. Once you identify a safety-related action you must act on it, and do so promptly.

Example from Mayhem Manufacturing

There were 15 safety action points identified in Mayhem's last internal audit. Of those 12 have been addressed.

Number of outstanding internal audit actions: 3

There are documented reasons for the last 3 actions remaining outstanding - actions are underway to address all 3 as quickly as reasonably possible.

Definition or formula

Count of [Outstanding internal audit actions]

Typical data sources

» Audit report(s)
» Health and safety action log
» H&S management software

Average time to implement internal audit actions

Ref: H1.3.1.2
Silver Star KPI

Drives: We act quickly to resolve identified issues
To:　　We identify & fix health & safety issues swiftly & effectively

Description

Internal audits only deliver value if you act on the improvement findings and do so promptly. This figure shows how quickly you implement actions designed to reduce risks.

Taking prompt action to resolve outstanding issues helps minimise your safety risks and also legal risks that might arise from unresolved audit actions.

Example from Mayhem Manufacturing

There were 15 safety action points identified in Mayhem's last audit. Of those 12 have been addressed.

Average time to implement internal audit actions: 22 calendar days

There are 3 actions still outstanding from the same original batch, so this average time is likely to increase.

Definition or formula

Sum of [Days to implement closed internal audit actions] / Count of [Closed internal audit actions]

Typical data sources

» Audit report(s)
» Health and safety action log
» H&S management software

Number of outstanding external audit actions

Ref: H1.3.1.3
Gold Star KPI

Drives: We act quickly to resolve identified issues
To: We identify & fix health & safety issues swiftly & effectively

Description

Where you have externally identified risks and actions to mitigate risks, the pressure to close those actions is even greater. This measure will show you how many actions you still have open.

Example from Mayhem Manufacturing

There were 8 safety action points identified in the last external audit. Of those 8 have been addressed.

Number of outstanding internal audit actions: 0

Definition or formula

Count of [Outstanding external audit actions]

Typical data sources

» Audit report(s)
» Health and safety action log
» H&S management software

Average time to implement external audit actions

Ref: H1.3.1.4
Gold Star KPI

Drives: We act quickly to resolve identified issues
To: We identify & fix health & safety issues swiftly & effectively

Description

Where you have externally identified risks and actions to mitigate risks, the pressure to close those actions is even greater. This measure will show you how long it takes to close off audit actions.

Example from Mayhem Manufacturing

There were 8 safety action points identified in the last audit. All eight have been addressed.

Average time to implement internal audit actions: 12 calendar days

Definition or formula

Sum of [Days to implement closed external audit actions] / Count of [Closed external audit actions]

Typical data sources

» Audit report(s)
» Health and safety action log
» H&S management software

Number of critical issues identified by regulator inspection

Ref: H1.4.1.1
Gold Star KPI

Drives: Earn & maintain the correct health & safety certification
To: We are legally compliant with health & safety regulation

Description

Where your external inspection identifies critical issues or actions which must be corrected, this is the tally of how many issues were identified.

Example from Mayhem Manufacturing

Mayhem had a visit from the 'Health and Safety' inspector who told Mohammed there were two serious deficiencies in the design of his machine guards (there to prevent finger injuries). He was told that he must resolve these.

Number of critical issues identified during regulator inspection: 2

Definition or formula

Count of [Critical issues identified by regulator inspection]

Typical data sources

» Regulator inspection report(s)
» Health and safety action log
» H&S management software

Outstanding critical issues identified by regulator inspection

Ref: H1.4.1.2
Gold Star KPI

Drives: Earn & maintain the correct health & safety certification
To: We are legally compliant with health & safety regulation

Description

Where your external inspection identifies critical issues or actions which must be corrected, this is the tally of how many issues were identified and are still outstanding.

Example from Mayhem Manufacturing

Mayhem had a visit from the 'Health and Safety' inspector who told Mohammed there were two serious deficiencies in the design of his machine guards (there to prevent finger injuries). Mohammed's team resolved these issues within the week.

Number of critical issues outstanding from regulator inspection: 0

Definition or formula

Count of [Outstanding critical issues identified by regulator inspection]

Typical data sources

» Regulator inspection report(s)
» Health and safety action log
» H&S management software

KPI Family: HRI
Staff & Payroll

Number of delayed wage payments

Ref: HR1.1.1.1
Gold Star KPI

Drives: Payments are reliably made by expected date
To: We pay our staff on time

Description

This measure shows how many pay packets missed the target payment date.

Paying your staff on time, and correctly, is critical. Late pay generates anger and anxiety like few other problems.

Example from Roughshod Repairs

Last month the BACS payment run for the whole staff failed, and all monthly wage payments had to be fixed and run the next day.

Number of delayed wage payments last month: 25

Definition or formula

Count of [Delayed wage payments]

Typical data sources

» Payroll records
» Bank records
» Employee complaints

Number of manual wage payments

Ref: HR1.2.1.3
Gold Star KPI

Drives: We minimise mistakes
To: We pay our staff correctly

Description

When payments go wrong there's usually either a manual payment or an adjustment on the next pay packet. Manual payments, where payments are made outside of the usual standard payment process or time window, can be a useful indicator of how often payments go wrong.

If you are having regular issues with payment reliability or accuracy, you may want to look at some of the other mistakes-related measures shown here too.

Example from Roughshod Repairs

Two new joiners were completely missed off the pay run this month. They were paid manually, using a CHAPS payment in each case. Two others had their overtime missed off their payment. They were also manually paid.

Number of manual payments last month: 4

Definition or formula

Count of [Manual wage payments]

Typical data sources

» Payroll records
» Bank records
» Employee complaints

Number of benefits-related errors

Ref: HR1.2.3
Gold Star KPI

Drives: We administer benefits correct
To: We pay our staff correctly

Description

Benefits-related errors would include pension contributions, benefits in kind, healthcare, car allowance and so on. Where mistakes are made on this, this measure shows the count of those mistakes as a total.

Example from Roughshod Repairs

Two members of staff did not have the correct amount deducted from their pay packet as part of the 'cycle to work scheme'.

Number of benefits related errors: 2

Definition or formula

Count of [Benefits-related errors]

Typical data sources

- » Payroll records
- » Benefits calculations
- » Bank records
- » Employee complaints

Number of tax-related errors

Ref: HR1.2.4.1
Gold Star KPI

Drives: We administer payroll taxes correctly
To: We pay our staff correctly

Description

For many employees in many countries, the employer has a responsibility to deduct tax at source, and sometimes to credit tax too. When mistakes are made in this process, this measure shows the tally of those mistakes.

Example from Roughshod Repairs

Rebecca, the payroll admin at Roughshod, discovered that they have not been taxing healthcare benefits as 'benefits in kind'. They need to sort this out.

The error affects 11 of the team, for every month in the past financial year. There's some debate on whether to count this as 1 (fundamental error), 11 (people affected) or 132 errors (12 months x 11 errors). In the end they count it as 11 errors as there are 11 corrective actions, one per employee required.

Number of tax-related errors: 11

Definition or formula

Count of [Tax-related errors]

Typical data sources

- » Payroll records
- » Benefits calculations
- » Bank records
- » Employee complaints

Number of record-keeping issues identified

Ref: HR1.2.5.1
Silver Star KPI

Drives: We keep accurate records
To: We pay our staff correctly

Description

Where we identify problems with HR record-keeping, for example an incorrect address or old phone number, this tally will show the number of these problems in any given period.

Example from Roughshod Repairs

When Rebecca emails (and follows up repeatedly) to check all HR contact details are correct, she receives 32 corrections from the staff.

Number of record keeping issues identified: 32

Definition or formula

Count of [Record keeping issues identified]

Typical data sources

» Admin logs
» Accuracy surveys of employee details

Common problems and mistakes

We need to be careful not to punish ourselves for doing the 'right thing'. For example contacting all our staff to validate contact details is likely to increase this figure, but for all the right reasons.

Hours worked by each team member

Ref: HR1.3.1.1
Gold Star KPI

Drives: We don't burn out our team
To: We actively manage hours worked

Description

This measure simply shows the number of hours worked by each team member.

In many countries the hours an employee can work on a regular basis is legally restricted. In addition to this, sustained periods of long hours can have a drastic, negative effect on staff morale, health and family relations. Tracking and managing staff hours is both a moral and risk management 'must'.

Example from Roughshod Repairs

Roughshod keep records of all their staff hours. Here's a snippet from the records for last week...

* *Rachel - 34 hours*
* *Robert - 38 hours*
* *Raquel - 37 hours*
* *Robin - 34 hours*
* *Rafael - 35 hours*

Definition or formula

Sum of [Hours worked] per individual

Typical data sources

» Time and attendance system
» Timesheets

Staff sickness & absence rate

Ref: HR1.3.2.1
Gold Star KPI

Drives: We don't burn out our team
To: We retain our team

Description

This is the percentage of available labour days which are lost due to sickness or unauthorised absence. This can be an early warning indicator of stressed or demotivated staff, and of course represents lost resource for delivering service to customers.

Staff sickness can be a useful 'mood indicator' and is often more reliable than opinion-based tools like staff surveys.

Example from Roughshod Repairs

Last week three of the Roughshod team were off sick, taking a total of 4 days between them. There are 25 staff and they all work 5 days, normally.

Sickness and absence rate: 4 / (25 x 5) = 3.2%

Definition or formula

Sum of [Sickness and absence days] / Sum of [Total planned days work]

Typical data sources

» Time and attendance system
» Timesheets

Common problems and mistakes

It's important to be absolutely clear about what constitutes authorised and unauthorised absence to avoid confusion.

Staff turnover

Ref: HR1.3.2.2
Gold Star KPI

Drives: We don't burn out our team
To: We retain our team

Description

This measure shows the proportion of your team that leave and need to be replaced.

High staff turnover can cause problems resulting from inexperience, extra recruitment effort and team disruption. It can also be an indicator of team unhappiness. Very low staff turnover can also bring problems, such as an uneven team age profile, a lack of new ideas and unhealthy team dynamics.

Example from Roughshod Repairs

In the past year 5 of the total team of 25 at Roughshod have left and been replaced.

Staff turnover: 5 / 25 = 20%

Definition or formula

Count of [Exited staff requiring replacement] / Count of [Actual team size at start of period]

Typical data sources

» HR staff records

KPI Family: HR2
Recruitment

Number of applicants

Ref: HR2.1.1.1
Gold Star KPI

Drives: We have plenty of appropriate candidates
To: We attract the right candidates effectively

Description

For a recruitment process to work, we need a sensible volume of appropriate applicants. This metric shows how many people applied.

Example from Roughshod Repairs

Roughshod Repairs have been running a recruitment campaign for new agents. They have received 105 applications for the roles advertised.

Number of applicants: 105

Definition or formula

Count of [Applicants]

Typical data sources

» Recruitment management system
» Recruitment tracking spreadsheet
» Recruitment tracking database

Applicants rejected at application stage

Ref: HR2.1.1.2
Silver Star KPI

Drives: We have plenty of appropriate candidates
To: We attract the right candidates effectively

Description

For a recruitment process to work, we need a sensible volume of appropriate applicants. This metric shows how appropriate those applications received were.

Example from Roughshod Repairs

Of the 105 applicants, 67 were rejected at the CV sift phase as having unsuitable qualifications or experience.

Percentage of applicants rejected at application stage: 67 / 105 = 64%

Definition or formula

Count of [Rejected first-stage applicants] / Count of [Applicants]

Typical data sources

» Recruitment management system
» Recruitment tracking spreadsheet
» Recruitment tracking database

Time from first contact to first day on site

Ref: HR2.2.1.4
Gold Star KPI

Drives: Our initial selection process is swift and effective
To: We have an efficient selection process

Description

Recruitment processes can sometimes drag. When this happens applicants drop out and sometimes the business situation changes before offers are accepted. Measuring the contact-to-first-day-on-site duration gives an overview of how well the end-to-end process is working.

The cost per candidate will vary dramatically by role seniority. For junior roles the whole process may only last a week, for senior roles it may stretch into years, so it may make sense to band this metric by role type.

Example from Roughshod Repairs

The recruitment team track all applications in a recruitment database. For the last agent recruitment process...

Average time from first contact to first day on site: 6 weeks 2 days

Definition or formula

Average of [Days from first contact to first day on site]

Typical data sources

» Recruitment management system
» Recruitment tracking spreadsheet
» Recruitment tracking database

Common problems and mistakes

Be clear on whether you measure elapsed time in working days or calendar time.

Applicant to recruit ratio

Ref: HR2.2.1.5
Silver Star KPI

Drives: Our initial selection process is swift and effective
To: We have an efficient selection process

Description

How many applicants are applying for each final recruited role?

Too low a ratio suggests that we may not have had enough choice to get really good recruits. Too high a ratio may mean an overly general advertising campaign and wasted effort spent on sifting the applications.

Example from Roughshod Repairs

In the last agent recruitment round 4 agents were recruited from 127 applicants.

Applicant to recruit ratio: 127 / 4 = 32:1

Definition or formula

Count of [Applicants] / Count of [Recruits]

Typical data sources

» Recruitment management system
» Recruitment tracking spreadsheet
» Recruitment tracking database

367

Dropouts before end of process

Ref: HR2.2.3.1
Silver Star KPI

Drives: We let candidates know the outcome quickly
To: We have an efficient selection process

Description
Candidates often drop out before receiving an offer or being rejected. This measure shows what percentage of candidates drop out or stop responding.

Example from Roughshod Repairs
In the last agent recruitment process 23 applicants dropped out or failed to respond within a week of a request.

Percentage dropouts before end of process: 23 / 127 = 18%

Definition or formula
Count of [Dropouts] / Count of [Applicants]

Typical data sources
» Recruitment management system
» Recruitment tracking spreadsheet
» Recruitment tracking database

Common problems and mistakes
It may not always be clear-cut whether someone has dropped out, particularly if they just become unresponsive. You will need to set criteria for defining a drop out - for example no response within a week of a requested response.

Offers accepted

Ref: HR2.3.1.1
Silver Star KPI

Drives: Candidates find our offer acceptable
To: We have a high acceptance and retention rate

Description
When we find a candidate and make them an offer, what percentage accept?

This metric can give us a indication of how attractive our offer is to applicants. Too low and it may suggest an uncompetitive package or business perception problems.

Example from Roughshod Repairs
In the last agent recruitment process 6 offers were made, of which 4 were accepted.

Percentage of offers accepted: 4 / 6 = 67%

Definition or formula
Count of [Offers accepted] / Count of [Offers made]

Typical data sources
» Recruitment management system
» Recruitment tracking spreadsheet
» Recruitment tracking database

Average tenure

Ref: HR2.3.2.1
Silver Star KPI

Drives: Candidates stay with the organisation
To:　　We have a high acceptance and retention rate

Description

The average tenure tells us how long our staff have been with us on average.

Very short tenure can be destabilising for a business, due to lack of experience and continuity. It can also be a symptom of serious underlying issues. Excessively long tenure can also bring its own problems, with a lack of energy and new ideas. The ideal is to have a spread of experience within your business. For this reason it's often a good idea to show tenure using a histogram - so you can easily understand the profile.

Example from Roughshod Repairs

The average tenure of the call centre team: 2 years and 8 months.

Definition or formula

Sum of [Duration from recruitment date to present] / Count of [Employees]

Typical data sources

» HR records

Common problems and mistakes

Be clear on whether you are including people who have *exited* the business or just those *still in the business*. In this example we have excluded any leavers.

Total recruitment costs

Ref: HR2.5.1.1
Silver Star KPI

Drives: We understand the costs involved in recruitment
To:　　The candidates we select are good for the roles

Description

How much are we sending on recruitment? This figure shows the total spend.

Example from Roughshod Repairs

The Roughshod team estimated the recruitment cost based on two person-months of admin support, about a week of management time and about £2k worth of advertising.

Estimated cost for last recruitment round: £8,000

Definition or formula

Sum of [Recruitment spend] per period/campaign/role

Typical data sources

» Manual calculation
» Accounts system

Recruitment cost per successful candidate

Ref: HR2.5.1.2
Gold Star KPI

Drives: We understand the costs involved in recruitment
To: The candidates we select are good for the roles

Description
Recruitment cost per successful candidate is a useful measure of productivity for our recruitment process.

The cost per candidate will vary dramatically by role seniority. For junior roles the whole process may only last a week, for senior roles it may stretch into years. The costs will vary in line with the different timescales.

Example from Roughshod Repairs
The last recruitment round resulted in 4 appointments. The cost of the recruitment process was £8,000.

Recruitment cost per successful candidate: £8,000 / 4 = £2,000 per recruit

Definition or formula
Sum of [Recruitment spend] / Count of [Candidates recruited]

Typical data sources
- » Manual calculation
- » Accounts system
- » Recruitment management system
- » Recruitment tracking spreadsheet
- » Recruitment tracking database

Applications fully vetted/verified

Ref: HR2.6.1.2
Gold Star KPI

Drives: Verification of details (id, qualifications etc.)
To: We undertake background checks rigorously

Description
We need to vet candidates for the safety of the business and often to comply with legal requirements (e.g. medical or financial businesses). This figure shows what percentage of the applications were fully vetted.

Example from Roughshod Repairs
Offers accepted: 4. Candidates vetted (references, criminal record and credit check): 4

Percentage of applications fully vetted/verified: 4 / 4 = 100%

Definition or formula
Count of [Vetted recruits] / Count of [Recruits]

Typical data sources
- » Recruitment management system
- » Recruitment tracking spreadsheet
- » Recruitment tracking database

KPI Family: II
Equipment Investment

Ownership costs/original investment costs per annum

Ref: I1.1.1.1
Gold Star KPI

Drives: Net profit/loss on investment
To: We see a positive return from our investments

Description

This shows the total cost of ownership of the new equipment, excluding additional labour and energy.

Example from Chaos Coffee Shop

Charlie has decided to invest in a Gargantuo espresso machine with 4 groups (the heads that make coffee), so he can make coffees faster at peak times and sell more coffee.

* *The machine costs £6,000, which he will depreciate over 3 years (£2k per year depreciation).*
* *The machine will need to be serviced annually - £400 per service and he has decided to pay another £400 a year for rapid-response breakdown cover on the machine.*
* *Annual cost of ownership (first 3 years): £2,800 per annum, £800 a year, year 4 onwards.*

Maintenance costs/original investment costs per annum: £2,800/£6,000 = 46.7% per year (first 3 years)

Maintenance costs/original investment costs per annum: £800/£6,000 = 13.3% per year (year 4 onwards)

Definition or formula

Per annum ownership costs / Investment costs

= ([Annual depreciation] + Sum of [All running costs per year]) / Sum of [Original investment costs]

Typical data sources

» Relevant itemised maintenance costs from accounting records
» Relevant itemised costs from maintenance records
» Original investment costs
» Actual or estimated energy usage for equipment item
» Depreciation figure from accounts

Net profit/loss on investment

Ref: I1.1.1.2
Gold Star KPI

Drives: Net profit/loss on investment
To: We see a positive return from our investments

Description

Does the new equipment make you money or cost you money once you have taken into account the lease cost/purchase price/depreciation of the asset investment?

It may not always be possible to answer this question, depending on the line of business you are in, and how good your records are. It's certainly worth attempting to measure though!

Example from Chaos Coffee Shop

Charlie thinks he will sell an extra 100 cups of coffee a week through faster service. The gross margin on an average cup of coffee is £2.25.

Annual additional gross profit: 100 cups x £2.25 x 52 weeks = £11,700 gross profit on extra cups

Net profit: Extra profit from sales - annual cost of new machine

= £11,700 - £2,800 (annual running cost, first 3 years)

= £8,900 profit

So it looks like the new coffee machine makes great financial sense if it delivers the extra sales volume Charlie is expecting.

Definition or formula

Sum of [Gross profit on extra sales] - Sum of [All direct annual costs of investment]

Typical data sources

» Relevant itemised costs from accounting records
» Relevant itemised costs from maintenance records
» Actual or estimated energy usage for equipment item
» Income derived from asset
» Profit derived from asset
» Depreciation figure from accounts

Investment running costs

Ref: I1.1.1.3
Gold Star KPI

Drives: Net profit/loss on investment
To: We see a positive return from our investments

Description

Is your new equipment cost effective? Are the running costs in line with expectation? How do the costs compare with the equipment it replaced? The only way you are going to answer these questions is by tracking the running costs.

Example from Chaos Coffee Shop

After the first year of the new Gargantuo coffee machine Charlie checks the service book. The costs are mostly in line with expectation, although there was an extra £200 for a new heating coil, the cost of which was not covered by the maintenance contract.

Running costs:

* £400 servicing
* £400 callout cover
* £200 for new coil

Investment running costs = £1,000

Even with the higher than expected costs, the new machine is highly profitable.

Definition or formula

Sum of [Investment equipment running costs]

Typical data sources

» Relevant itemised costs from accounting records
» Relevant itemised costs from maintenance records
» Actual or estimated energy usage for equipment item

Additional gross investment-related profits

Ref: I1.2.1.1
Silver Star KPI

Drives: Investment supports sales
To: Our investments drive growth

Description

So your new wonder-machine is driving extra sales - what's the gross profit on those sales before you deduct the investment cost/depreciation?

By looking at the profitability of any new sales volumes being brought in, you can decide whether it was a wise purchase. Use this information to shape future purchases.

Example from Chaos Coffee Shop

At the end of the year, Charlie looks back to see whether the purchase of the new Gargantuo coffee machine actually delivered the increased sales. He finds a steadily increased volume of coffee sold over the year. It is difficult to say whether the coffee machine is the main reason for the growth, but he knows they would have struggled without it. He decides to count all growth last year in the profit calculation.

Looking back, he sold 8,000 more cups of coffee this year than the previous year. At a gross margin of £2.25 per cup this means £18,000 gross profit.

Additional sales revenue less running costs and depreciation: £18,000 - £2,800

Additional investment related profit = £15,200

It confirms that the new machine was a sound investment.

Definition or formula

Sum of [Additional sales revenue] - Sum of [Cost of goods sold - for additional sales]

Typical data sources

» Purchasing records
» Inventory control system
» EPOS system/till summary
» Receipts, bank records (statements or transactions download)
» Invoices
» Accounts software

Sales value enabled by investment

Ref: I1.2.1.2
Silver Star KPI

Drives: Investment supports sales
To: Our investments drive growth

Description

What extra sales or revenue opportunities are opened up by your new kit?

Example from Chaos Coffee Shop

Charlie thinks he will sell an extra 100 cups of coffee a week through faster service. The sale price of an average cup of coffee is £2.50.

Annual additional gross profit: 100 cups x £2.50 x 52 weeks = £13,000 additional income.

Definition or formula

Sum of [Additional sales revenue]

Typical data sources

» Relevant sales and accounts records, attributable to investment
» Accounting system
» Sales system

Property Investment

Maintenance costs/original investment costs per annum

Ref: I2.1.1.1
Gold Star KPI

Drives: Net profit/loss on investment
To: We see a positive return from our investments

Description

Properties need to be maintained to keep them pleasant to use and to protect their value. This figure shows maintenance costs as a percentage of your original investment - putting those costs into perspective.

Tracking costs is an important element in understanding the return on investment you are really seeing.

Example from Woeful Widget Warehouse

Will owns the building that Woeful Widget Warehouse uses. It's a warehouse unit with a current market value of £250k. Last year he spent £3k on roof repairs and other maintenance.

Maintenance costs/original investment costs, per annum = £3,000/£250,000 = 1.2%

Definition or formula

Sum of [Maintenance and repair costs] / [Current market value of property]

Typical data sources

» Maintenance and repair invoices and receipts
» Property valuation website or estate agent valuation

Net profit/loss on investment

Ref: I2.1.1.2
Gold Star KPI

Drives: Net profit/loss on investment
To: We see a positive return from our investments

Description

The profit on a property usually comes in two forms, rental income and increase in the value of the property.

Of course the value increase only becomes 'real' when the property is sold, but it should be possible to get a rough idea of value through estate agent valuation or using a property valuation website.

Example from Woeful Widget Warehouse

Will bought the warehouse that he uses for £200k last year. Looking at property websites it looks like it is now worth £250k, a year later. Woeful Widget Warehouses (his company) pays him (personally) rental of that warehouse of £1,000 a month. Over the year he has paid out £3,000 in maintenance.

So his cash profit is: 12x£1,000 - £3,000 = £9,000

But if you include the increase in value of the property...

Net profit: £9,000 (net cash profit) + £50,000 (property value increase) = £59,000

Definition or formula

([Current market value of property] - [Market value of property last period]) + (Sum of [Rental income]) - Sum of [Maintenance and repair costs]

Typical data sources

» Maintenance and repair invoices and receipts
» Property valuation website or estate agent valuation

Sales value, enabled by investment

Ref: I2.1.2.1
Silver Star KPI

Drives: Investment supports sales
To: We see a positive return from our investments

Description

If investing in a property was intended to grow sales or profitability, did it?

It's not always easy to isolate the sales impact of a new property investment from organic growth that was happening anyway. It can be easier if there was a capacity restraint that has now been exceeded thanks to extra space.

Example from Woeful Widget Warehouse

The move to the new warehouse enabled Woeful Widget Warehouse to nearly double its range of stocked items. Looking at those new ranges, they account for an 80% growth in sales value in the year since they moved into the new property.

Sales income this year: £1,200k

Sales income this year from new lines: £533k

Definition or formula

Sum of [Sales value enabled by new property investment]

Typical data sources

» Sales records
» Finance system

Current market value

Ref: I2.2.1.1
Silver Star KPI

Drives: Market value growth - capital growth
To: Our investments grow

Description

Properties values change over time. This figure shows the current market value - how much we should expect to get if we sold today.

Tracking this supports our investment profit calculation and may determine whether we keep or sell our investment property.

Example from Woeful Widget Warehouse

Will bought the warehouse that he uses for £200k last year. Looking at property websites it looks like it is now worth £250k, a year later.

Current market value: £250k

Definition or formula

[Current Market Value]

Typical data sources

» Internet property valuation tools
» Estate Agent (Realtor) valuation

Common problems and mistakes

There are often costs and taxes involved in selling property, don't forget to factor these in if you are counting on extracting invested cash by selling your property.

Rental income

Ref: I2.3.1.1
Gold Star KPI

Drives: Net profit/loss on investment
To:　　We see a positive return from our investments

Description

Rental income is the money that someone pays you for the use of the property.

This is one element of the investment profit equation.

Example from Woeful Widget Warehouse

Will bought the warehouse that he uses for £200k last year. Looking at property websites it looks like it is now worth £250k, a year later. Woeful Widget Warehouses (his company) pays him (personally) rental of that warehouse of £1,000 a month.

Rental income: £1,000 a month

Definition or formula

Sum of [Rental income]

Typical data sources

» Rental records
» Bank records
» Accounting system

Occupancy rate

Ref: I2.3.1.3
Silver Star KPI

Drives: Net profit/loss on investment
To:　　We see a positive return from our investments

Description

Like hotel rooms, rental property does not generate income if it's not occupied by a paying tenant. This figure show the ratio of paid occupancy to potential occupancy.

100% occupancy may not be achievable, particularly if periodic major renovation and repair is required.

Example from Pointless Prose

Patricia has a small house she has bought as investment, that she lets on a short-term basis to private individuals. In the past year she has had three tenants, On the two occasions she has changed tenants, it took three weeks each time to find, vet and sign up a new tenant.

* *Paid rental weeks last year: 46 weeks*
* *Rental weeks available: 52 weeks*

Occupancy rate: 46/52 = 88%

Definition or formula

Sum of [Actual rentable time] / [Maximum rental time available]

Typical data sources

» Rental records
» Bank records
» Accounting system
» Calendar

Average market rent

Ref: I2.3.1.4
Silver Star KPI

Drives: Net profit/loss on investment
To: We see a positive return from our investments

Description

The average market rent is the typical rent being achieved by similar properties, in terms of location, size and condition.

Positioning your rental correctly in the market is key to obtaining both the best rental income and maximising occupancy. Understanding the average market rent, and how desirable your property is compared with the market, is crucial.

Example from Pointless Prose

Patricia has used local property websites to get a feel for the 'going rate' of similar properties. She creates a simple spreadsheet and creates a list of 15 similar properties she has identified. The advertised rental rates vary from £700 per month to £825. From her list...

Average market rent: £775 per month

There is some clear variation in condition and desirability for the advertised properties. She knows there is a lot of rental demand and her property is in very good condition, so she decides to put it on the market at the higher end of the range.

Definition or formula

Average of [Rent for similar properties - size, location, condition and desirability]

Typical data sources

» Property rental websites
» Local adverts on web, print or notice boards

Rental yield percentage

Ref: I2.3.1.5
Gold Star KPI

Drives: Net profit/loss on investment
To: We see a positive return from our investments

Description

Rental yield shows you the percentage profit you make on the property you have invested in, after deducting running costs.

If you use a mortgage to buy the investment property then you need to include the mortgage payment (and associated costs, such as mandatory mortgage life insurance) in the 'Costs' part of the equation.

Example from Pointless Prose

Patricia paid £160k for her investment property a couple of years ago. She was able to buy it outright using an inheritance. Maintenance and repair costs are around £1,000 a year. She charges rent of £800 a month.

Rental yield: (£800 x 12 - £1,000) / £160,000 = 5.4%

Definition or formula

(Sum of [Rental income] - Sum of [Direct costs]) / [Initial property investment]

Typical data sources

» Rental records
» Bank records
» Maintenance and repair invoices
» Accounting system

Common problems and mistakes

Don't forget to include any taxes or bills that you as a landlord offer/are required to pick up in the 'costs' part of the equation.

Total lost rental

Ref: I2.4.1.1
Silver Star KPI

Drives: The property is available and habitable
To: We manage our investment risks

Description
There are various reasons why you might miss out on rental income. This figure shows the total loss of rental income, whatever the cause.

The most common causes of rental income loss will be vacancy, rent defaults or damage to the property.

Example from Pointless Prose
Patricia lost 6 weeks of rental income in between tenancies. She also had one tenant run off without paying two months rent. She recovered one month of that through the deposit, but it still leaves her a month short.

Total lost rental: (6 weeks empty + 4 weeks default = 10 weeks) x £184.62 weekly rental

Total lost rental: £1,846

Definition or formula
Sum of [Written off rent arrears] + Sum of [Damage reparations not covered by deposits] + Sum of [Lost income due to vacancy]

Typical data sources
» Rent records
» Bank records
» Property maintenance records
» Accounts records

Value of rent arrears

Ref: I2.4.2.1
Gold Star KPI

Drives: We manage rent arrears and defaults
To: We manage our investment risks

Description
Rent arrears is rent that is past the agreed payment date, but has not yet been 'written off' as bad debt.

Rent arrears are important for two reasons. Firstly late rent can affect cash flow. Secondly, late rent represents risk. As overdue rent becomes more late (and probably increases in value) it is increasingly likely it will never be paid.

Example from Pointless Prose
Patricia's current tenant has slipped one month into rent arrears. Whilst they are one month behind, they have started paying each month again, but have not cleared the original skipped month.

Value of rent arrears = £800

Definition or formula
Sum of [Overdue rent still owed]

Typical data sources
» Rent records
» Bank records
» Accounts records

Time Investment-
New Product
Development & Skills

Net cumulative profit/loss on time investment

Ref: I3.1.1.2
Gold Star KPI

Drives: Net profit/loss from time investment
To: We see a positive return from our time investments

Description

Developing new products or services takes time and money (where you sell your time for a living, they are the same thing). This measure is about taking the long-term view and seeing at what point (if ever) the investment starts to yield a net profit. Sometimes it's not just about the money. If you are in the 'advice business' (like a consultant), there can be major reputational and publicity benefits in writing a book, in addition to the royalties it generates.

Example from Ambiguous Associates

Austin decided to take two months away from billed consulting work to finish his book on 'Audacious Ambiguity'. During this time he misses out on 8 weeks - 40 days - of work billed at an average of £1,820 per day. The opportunity cost (missed work) is 40 x £1,820 = £72,800.

Initially, sales of his new book are slow. After year 1, he has seen £5,000 of book and eBook royalties. Net cumulative profit/loss on time investment...

*   *Year 1: £5,000 - £72,800 = -£67,800 (a loss)*
*   *Year 2: £22,000 (year 1+2 revenue) - £72,800 = -£50,800*
*   *Year 3: £52,000 (year 1+2+3 revenue) - £72,800 = -£20,800*

By year 4 Austin's book should be turning a net profit, even allowing for the notional 'loss' of him not billing whilst writing the book.

Now this may not fit with any accounting norms, but it enables Austin to see the long-term benefit of taking time away from billed work. His time investment won't turn a 'profit' for a number of years, but when it does start to turn a profit it will continue to generate income for Austin with next-to-no additional effort on his part - providing a 'passive income' whilst he gets on with other things.

Definition or formula

Sum of [Revenue, royalties and other incomes arising from investment] - Sum of [Costs, including lost billing opportunities]

Typical data sources

» Finance system
» Royalties
» Sales analysis
» Investment records - time, spend

Hours of 'Deep Work' on time investment

Ref: I3.1.1.4
Gold Star KPI

Drives: Net profit/loss from time investment
To: We see a positive return from our time investments

Description

Deep Work is a term coined by author Cal Newport, and refers to 'the ability to focus without distraction on a cognitively demanding task'. For many development tasks, be it coding, writing or just thinking, having focused time is crucial.

Keeping a track of the amount of time devoted to this type of work, along with careful targeting is a critical driver on development success.

Example from Ambiguous Associates

Austin has a young family and gets lots of phone calls and emails. He has finally figured out that if he gets up at 6am, and does not look at his phone or emails, he can sit down at his computer and get some uninterrupted writing time. He uses the Pomodoro method to put in an hour of 'deep work' on his new consulting concepts before the day really kicks off. He tracks these 'deep work' 'sprints' on a white board and tallies them up at the end of the week.

Deep work last week: 7hrs 40mins

He has set himself a weekly target of at least 7 hours deep work.

Definition or formula

Sum of [Time spent on focused, uninterrupted, development work]

Typical data sources

» Time logs
» Tracking board
» Diary

Common problems and mistakes

To really know if you have been engaged in 'deep work' you need to have attained, and be able to identify 'flow'. Flow is a particular state of mind where you become completely immersed in your current activity - often losing track of time. Read 'Deep Work' by Cal Newport to find out more - details in the Bibliography. If you find you lose track of time doing certain activities you like - for example computer games - that's a state of 'flow' and is the sort of mind state that you should aim for with 'Deep Work'.

Margin on sales enabled by time investment

Ref: I3.2.1.4
Gold Star KPI

Drives: Investment supports sales
To: Our time and skill investments drive growth

Description

Where your development work leads to additional sales and profits, this figure shows the total.

If you developed a new app, book or product, it will be easy to identify additional profit/royalties. Where you are enhancing previous products or services you may need to do some 'before and after' comparisons. If you take the 'before and after' approach, don't forget to factor in any underlying growth trend that was there already.

Example from Ambiguous Associates

Austin decided to take two months away from billed consulting work to finish his book on 'Audacious Ambiguity'.

Initially, sales of his new book are slow. After year 1, he has seen £5,000 of book and eBook royalties. Over the next three years they climb steadily:

Margin on sales enabled, by year:

*   *Year 1: £5,000*
*   *Year 2: £17,000*
*   *Year 3: £30,000*

Definition or formula

Sum of [Profit/royalties from development]

Typical data sources

» Finance system
» Royalties
» Sales analysis
» Investment records - time, spend

Business Vehicles

Fleet mileage

Ref: I4.1.1.2
Silver Star KPI

Drives: We manage depreciation
To: We manage depreciation and replacement

Description

Mileage is one of the drivers of cost, and one which we control.

Track mileage to see whether our anticipated replacement assumptions are still correct and an early indicator of cost.

Example from Mayhem Manufacturing

Mayhem Manufacturing runs two vans for deliveries and collection of materials. Mohammed tracks mileage of the vans on a monthly basis:

Fleet mileage last month: 2,500km

Definition or formula

Sum of [Miles driven by fleet vehicles]

Typical data sources

» Vehicle odometers
» Vehicle log books
» GPS tracking systems

Forecast months to replacement

Ref: I4.1.2.2
Gold Star KPI

Drives: We manage replacement
To: We manage depreciation and replacement

Description

Where vehicles are scheduled to be replaced based on age or projected mileage, this figure shows when that is expected to happen. It will generally be reported as a figure per vehicle as this is more meaningful than an average.

The importance of this measure is largely dependent on how you fund your vehicles. If you buy them outright, then keep a close eye on this as the cash required for the purchase could have a serious impact on your cash flow. If your vehicles are leased, then you may still have to find a deposit for the next lease vehicle.

Example from Mayhem Manufacturing

Mayhem's vans are getting on a bit. Mohammed likes to replace them when they get to 5 years old.

Forecast months to replacement:

* *Van 1 replacement: 18 months*
* *Van 2 replacement: 3 months*

Definition or formula

Count of [Months remaining to replacement or lease renewal] per vehicle

Typical data sources

» Vehicle tracking spreadsheet
» Company calendar

Fleet age

Ref: I4.1.2.4
Silver Star KPI

Drives: We manage replacement
To:　　We manage depreciation and replacement

Description

Fleet age shows us the average age of the vehicles in our fleet. It can give a feel for the likely cosmetic and mechanical condition of our fleet.

Example from Mayhem Manufacturing

Mayhem's fleet age:

* *Van 1: 42 months*
* *Van 2: 57 months*

Average fleet age: 49.5 months

Definition or formula

Average of [Fleet vehicle ages]

Typical data sources

» Vehicle tracking spreadsheet
» Company calendar

Common problems and mistakes

As an average, it may conceal large variations between individual vehicle ages.

Running costs

Ref: I4.2.2.2
Gold Star KPI

Drives: We make a profit on the investment
To:　　We see a positive return from our vehicle purchase/least

Description

Running company vehicles costs money. Major costs include: Fuel, AdBlue (urea additive), servicing, repairs, tax, insurance, breakdown insurance and congestion/pollution taxes. If you are leasing you may also have fees if you exceed an agreed mileage. You may also have parking fees, speeding fines and other sundries thrown in there too.

Think about whether you want to include vehicle depreciation in this cost.

Example from Mayhem Manufacturing

Mohammed tracks his vehicle costs on a monthly basis. His current costs for the two vehicles are:

Both vans

* *Fuel costs　£4,003*
* *Insurance　£1,000*
* *Servicing　£600*
* *Tax　£300*
* *Breakdown cover　£160*

Running costs: £6,063

Definition or formula

Sum of [Fleet running costs]

Typical data sources

» Finance system
» Invoices
» Fuel receipts/fuel card statement

Total number of accidents

Ref: I4.3.1.1
Silver Star KPI

Drives: We manage driver risk
To: We manage our vehicle investment risks

Description
Accidents put your, and other, drivers at risk. They are going to have a direct financial impact as insurance excesses. You also risk damage to the goods being delivered, loss of delivery capacity and organisational time and energy being taken up in the clean-up.

Minor accidents can act as an early-warning-indicator that something more serious may be on the horizon. Tracking, and acting on the causes of, minor accidents can help you avoid something more serious. There is also a reputational risk from accidents.

Example from Mayhem Manufacturing
Mohammed keeps a log of accidents and scrapes. He's noticed that one of his drivers has 8 minor bodywork scrapes and one rear-end shunt (his driver at the rear) whereas the other driver has a clean slate. He's starting to wonder if there's something going on here...

Total number of accidents: 9

Definition or formula
Count of [Accidents]

Typical data sources
» Accident log
» Periodic vehicle inspection and notes

Common problems and mistakes
Be clear on whether you are lumping every kind of accident or scrape into one category or whether you are going to measure them separately.

Average fuel consumption

Ref: I4.3.2.4
Silver Star KPI

Drives: The vehicle is available and serviceable and efficient
To: We manage our vehicle investment risks

Description
Fuel usage is a significant part of the running costs for most company vehicles, but it is also an indicator of mechanical condition.

A step change downwards in fuel efficiency can be an early-warning indicator that something may be wrong with the vehicle.

Example from Mayhem Manufacturing
Mohammed tracks his vehicle mileage and fuel use. Last month's figures were:

	km	litres of fuel used	km/l
Van 1	1,000	135	7.4
Van 2	1,500	143	10.5
Totals	2,500	278	9.0

So it looks like Van 1 has significantly lower fuel economy than Van 2. This could be down to more stop-start deliveries in town, but it would certainly be worth investigating.

Definition or formula
Sum of [Distance driven] / Sum of [Litres of fuel used]

Typical data sources
» Mileage log book
» GPS tracker
» Fuel card records, fuel receipts

Common problems and mistakes
Units vary, depending on where in the world you are based, but the calculation remains identical, but with Gallons instead of Litres, Miles instead of Km and so on.

KPI Family: LI

Service Improvement Activity

Data or data sheets collected on time

Ref: L1.1.1.1
Silver Star KPI

Drives: We collect data regularly and accurately
To: We measure, analyse & act on process losses

Description

The proportion of data collection sheets (if used) that are returned on time. Can also apply to electronic data collection sheets if email is relied upon for return.

Data is the foundation of any improvement work. If you rely on getting data sheets returned, then measuring the percentage returned on time - at least initially - is a good way of seeing if you are on track.

Example from Roughshod Repairs

Ruby's team are keeping data capture sheets, so they can keep a tally on the most common problems they deal with and how long they take to sort out. There were 10 agents working yesterday. 9 sheets were returned to the admin assistant charged with collating the data sheets.

Percentage of data/sheets collected on time: 9 / 10 = 90%

Definition or formula

Count of [Sheets actually returned on time] / Count of [Sheets that should have been returned on time]

Typical data sources

» Data collection tracker sheet

Completion of returned data collection sheets

Ref: L1.1.1.2
Silver Star KPI

Drives: We collect data regularly and accurately
To: We measure, analyse & act on process losses

Description

How many of the returned data collection forms were completed correctly (or at all)?

It's not enough just to get data collection sheets back on time. This figure shows what proportion, on average, of the sheets were completed correctly.

Example from Roughshod Repairs

Of the 9 sheets returned to Russell, the admin assistant, 2 were missing vital details.

Percentage completion of returned data collection sheets/ forms: 7 / 9 = 78%

Definition or formula

Count of [Sheets correctly and fully completed] / Count of [Sheets returned on time]

Typical data sources

» Data collection sheet analysis

Meetings held on time

Ref: L1.1.3.1
Silver Star KPI

Drives: Our decision-making process is regular
To: We measure, analyse & act on process losses

Description
What percentage of meetings were held on time, with the minimum core attendees?

Meeting discipline is an important part of any improvement activity. Holding meetings on time, with the core attendees present, is a good headline indicator of that discipline.

Example from Roughshod Repairs
Roughshod aim to have a 10-minute morning 'huddle' every day with the call team and a 1-hour weekly improvement session with the whole team.

One huddle was skipped due to call pressure.

Percentage of meetings held on time = 5 / 6 = 83%

Definition or formula
Count of [Meetings held on time] / Count of [Planned meetings]

Typical data sources
» Meeting tracker/log

Financial value of problems solved to root cause

Ref: L1.1.4.1
Silver Star KPI

Drives: Our problem solving works
To: We measure, analyse & act on process losses

Description
The total value of problems solved to root cause (i.e. permanently) by our improvement activity.

Rather than just counting how many problems we solve to root cause - which always encourages people to go after trivial-but-easy-to-solve issues, let's look at the value of problems solved to root cause.

Example from Roughshod Repairs
The team identified an over-the-phone solution that prevents around 20 product returns a week avoiding a repair cost of £50 in each case.

Financial value of problems solved to root cause: £1,000 per week

Definition or formula
Sum of [Financial value of problems solved to root cause]

Typical data sources
» Opportunity tracker and costing sheet

Efficiency loss by issue

Ref: L1.2.2.1
Gold Star KPI

Drives: We collect data on in-process efficiency losses
To: We identify losses in our process

Description
When we have a problem, how big is it as quantified in efficiency loss (percentage)?

When we understand this for most of our major problems, it makes prioritisation and resource allocation much easier and the resource debate less emotional.

Example from Roughshod Repairs
As an example, the team have discovered that 15% of calls coming through to the Roughshod Repairs call centre should be going straight to the manufacturer.

Example: Percentage efficiency loss by issue

* 15% of calls, or 8% of capacity, lost due to call misdirection.

Definition or formula
To show the proportion of total losses attributable to an individual issue...

Sum of [Efficiency loss] by issue / Sum of [Efficiency losses]

or, to show the absolute efficiency loss for an individual issue...

Sum of [Lost time] by issue / Sum of [Planned work time]

Typical data sources
» Opportunity tracker and costing sheet

Common problems and mistakes
To calculate the loss using the second formula you will need to convert waste and speed losses into equivalent lost process time.

Cost of efficiency losses by product/process/location/time/date

Ref: L1.2.2.4
Gold Star KPI

Drives: We collect data on in-process efficiency losses
To: We identify losses in our process

Description
Where problems vary by process, location, time and so on, this is a more detailed, granular, breakdown of where and when the efficiency losses are taking place - shown in monetary value of the efficiency loss for the overall process.

Example from Roughshod Repairs
Ruby's team have identified that waiting online to book field agents is causing Repair bookings team to take about 30% longer than they should. By gaining direct access to the technicians' calendars the improvement team think they can fix that problem completely.

Example: Field booking team waiting loss value £320 per week.

Definition or formula
Sum of [Cost of identified issue in time, materials and other direct costs] by issue

Typical data sources
» Opportunity tracker and costing sheet

Utilisation losses by product/process/time/date

Ref: L1.2.3.1
Gold Star KPI

Drives: We identify utilisation losses
To: We identify losses in our process

Description
Utilisation losses are those losses where the people or equipment you use to deliver your service are not busy. Utilisation is the percentage of 'time we were busy' / 'available work time'.

Example from Roughshod Repairs
The 8% capacity loss resulting from misdirected calls represents 8% of the working week, or 8% utilisation loss.

Example: Utilisation loss due to misdirected calls issue = 8%

Definition or formula
Sum of [Utilisation loss due to specific issue]

Typical data sources
» Opportunity tracker and costing sheet

Cost of utilisation losses by product/process/location/time/date

Ref: L1.2.3.2
Gold Star KPI

Drives: We identify utilisation losses
To: We identify losses in our process

Description
This set of figures is the cost version of 'utilisation', looking at lost labour time or lost sales - depending on the sales situation for the particular service we are looking at.

Where we miss out on sales because of lost utilisation, we should cost the loss in terms of lost sales. Where we are not utilised, but being busy would not have delivered more sales, we should just look at the loss as that of paid time for the people who were idle.

Example from Roughshod Repairs
The average team size answering the phones is 15 staff. The centre team are paid £10 an hour. The 8% capacity loss resulting from misdirected calls represents 8% x 8 hour day x 15 staff x 6 days a week x £10 per hour = £576 a week.

Example: Cost of misdirected calls issue = £576 a week

Definition or formula
Sum of [Cost of utilisation loss due to specific issue]

Typical data sources
» Opportunity tracker and costing sheet

Worked time without standard times associated

Ref: L1.2.3.3
Gold Star KPI

Drives: We identify utilisation losses
To:　　We identify losses in our process

Description
Where we are doing a substantial amount of 'stuff' without a clear picture of how long it should take it makes efficiency measurement very hard. To tackle this, we need to measure the amount of time spent on 'non-defined tasks' or tasks with no 'standard time' associated.

Tracking the percentage of time worked where there is no 'standard time' associated with that task helps us work out how well defined the process is and how easy it will be to measure efficiency and improve standard tasks.

Example from Roughshod Repairs
Within Roughshod's Repairs contact centre, there is a category of activity called 'Other'. Agents are under strict instructions only to use this category when absolutely necessary. Currently 'Other' activity is running at 12%. Ruby has decided to use paper sheets to record what 'Other' activity involves, with a view to setting up new system activities (along with 'standard times' for those activities).

Percentage of worked time without standard times associated: 12%

Definition or formula
Sum of [Time worked without standard time associated] / Sum of [Worked hours]

Typical data sources
» Efficiency analysis

Cost of rework and quality by product/process/location/time/date

Ref: L1.2.4.3
Gold Star KPI

Drives: We know how often and where defects occur in-process
To:　　We identify losses in our process

Description
Putting things right, when they go wrong, costs money. That cost is the 'cost of rework'.

This is sometimes called 'the cost of quality' or the 'cost of poor quality' - COPQ.

Example from Roughshod Repairs
When cases have to be re-opened, they are marked with a special flag on the system. Looking at this flag, Ruby can see that around 20% of the case handling time is being spent on previously closed cases.

She estimates...

Cost of rework: 20% x 8 hour day x 15 staff x 6 days a week x £10 per hour = £1,440 a week.

Definition or formula
Sum of [Cost of rework]

Optionally - by rework problem

Typical data sources
» Opportunity tracker and costing sheet

KPI Family: L2

Production Improvement Activity

Queue/backlogs levels by process
location and time

Ref: L2.1.1.1
Gold Star KPI

Drives: We understand delays in the production/service process
To: We identify details of losses in our process

Description

Sub-processes need two conditions to run: raw material at the input and somewhere to push the 'processed' item out to. If you see machines being starved of raw material, or shut down because of downstream congestion, this presents an opportunity for line improvement.

This measure is focused on the levels of work-in-progress at key points along your production process. You can either measure the 'accumulation' levels (how full the buffers are) or just record shutdowns, by machine, due to upstream starvation or downstream congestion.

Looking at queues and starvation in a process enables you to identify where the process bottleneck is and to manage it.

Example from Mayhem Manufacturing

The Mayhem Manufacturing team have built a new production line for vinyl figures - Mayhem Manikins - and are trying to improve its performance before it goes live.

When they run the full line at production speed, they notice that the assembly area seems to be delayed by the rotomould production speed, starving the assembly area of materials.

Lost time in assembly area due to starvation: 20 mins / hr or 33%

Definition or formula

Sum of [Lost time due to upstream material starvation] / Sum of [Planned run time]

or

Sum of [Lost time due to downstream congestion] / Sum of [Planned run time]

recorded on a per sub-process basis.

Typical data sources

» Observation
» Process logs and sheets
» Machine PLC controller records
» Downtime capture system

Common problems and mistakes

You will always have a bottleneck, so there's no point in chasing around to try to remove it, but you can focus your efforts on maximising performance at the bottleneck (which will usually result in higher efficiency and/or more output, depending on your commercial goals).

Efficiency loss by issue

Ref: L2.1.2.1
Gold Star KPI

Drives: We collect data on in-process efficiency losses
To: We identify details of losses in our process

Description

The overall efficiency figure is interesting, but it does not tell you what to fix to improve process efficiency. If you list known problems in priority order, in descending order of efficiency loss in percentage points, you will have the best possible 'to-do list' of problems to solve.

Note that efficiency can be lost through downtime, but also through quality failure and slow running. Most organisations tend to focus on downtime as it's the most obvious loss.

Example from Mayhem Manufacturing

The rotomoulders have been identified as the process speed bottleneck (important, as that's where you measure OEE from). The team have done an observational study on the rotomoulders. They have identified the following OEE losses in the process:

Efficiency loss by issue:

* 15% Mould heater tripped out
* 8%   Mould separation failure
* 4%   Mould bearing failure

So by solving these three problems to root cause, we should be able to increase efficiency by up to 27% points.

Definition or formula

Sum of [Percentage OEE loss] *by issue*.

Typical data sources

» Observation
» Process logs and sheets
» Machine PLC controller records
» Downtime capture system

Efficiency loss by process location

Ref: L2.1.2.2
Silver Star KPI

Drives: We collect data on in-process efficiency losses
To: We identify details of losses in our process

Description

Where certain parts of the end-to-end process cause downtime, it can be useful to group losses by process area.

This is especially useful for teams that need to know where to physically stand in the process to see relevant problems. With physically large lines this isn't always obvious.

Example from Mayhem Manufacturing

Looking at the line profile of Mayhem Manikin mould, build, paint and packaging, the efficiency loss at the bottleneck (rotomoulder) was caused by the following locations on the process:

Percentage efficiency loss by process location:

* Mould: 27%
* Cool: 1%
* Assemble: 3%
* Dry: 2%
* Paint: 0%
* Package: 0%

So, although the queue information shows 33% downtime in the assembly area, it was due to moulding problems upstream, so that's where the team need to focus their efforts to improve line performance.

Definition or formula

[Percentage OEE loss] *by physical process location* of stoppage cause.

Typical data sources

» Observation
» Process logs and sheets
» Machine PLC controller records
» Downtime capture system

Cost of efficiency losses by product/process/location/time/date

Ref: L2.1.2.4
Gold Star KPI

Drives: We collect data on in-process efficiency losses
To: We identify details of losses in our process

Description

There are generally three major costs associated with production losses:

- Lost sales
- Lost time (wages, energy etc.)
- Lost materials

By understanding which losses we are suffering, broken down in a logical way, we can estimate the benefit of solving that issue (and also decide how much we might want to invest in permanently solving the problem).

We need to understand whether lost output really represents lost sales or not. The question we must answer, before valuing losses, is 'Could we actually sell any extra output, or would we just end up stopping the line earlier if we improved efficiency?'.

Example from Mayhem Manufacturing

The rotomoulder is the bottleneck. The 'Mould heater tripped out' issue is costing Mayhem 15% lost production. Mohammed thinks he can sell all his output, and each figure makes a gross profit of £65. The 'optimum' output rate of the line is 7.2 figures per hour. We intend to run the line 8 hours a day, 5 days a week.

Cost of 'Mould heater tripped out' loss on manikin line: 15% x 7.2 figures per hour x 8 hours x 5 days x £65 gross profit per figure

= £2,808 per week loss

Definition or formula

Lost capacity

Where we can sell extra output...

[Gross margin per unit] x [Loss percentage] x [Production rate] x [Production period]

Where we cannot sell extra output...

[Costs per hour] x [Loss percentage] x [Production rate] x [Production period]

Remember also to value waste losses due to efficiency losses.

Typical data sources

» Observation
» Process logs and sheets
» Machine PLC controller records
» Waste logs
» Downtime capture system

Availability losses by product/process/time/date

Ref: L2.1.3.1
Silver Star KPI

Drives: We identify availability losses
To: We identify details of losses in our process

Description

Availability losses, sometimes called downtime, are production losses caused by stoppages - often breakdowns.

Example from Mayhem Manufacturing

Looking at the line profile of Mayhem Manikin the rotomoulders (the bottleneck processes) experienced 27% efficiency losses. Of this 19% (points) were availability losses.

Availability losses at rotomoulders for week: 19%

Definition or formula

Sum of [Availability loss] *by product/process/time/date* - as required.

Typical data sources

» Observation
» Process logs and sheets
» Machine PLC controller records
» Downtime capture system

Cost of utilisation losses by product/process/location/time/date

Ref: L2.1.3.2
Gold Star KPI

Drives: We identify availability losses
To: We identify details of losses in our process

Description

Where we have process overheads, but do not run the process the full planned time, we see utilisation losses. We still bear the cost of heating, perhaps manning, depreciation and so on, but are not making full use of the assets or people.

Example from Mayhem Manufacturing

Mayhem has the 'Volcano Pen Pot' line, which needs one operator to run it. Sales are a bit slow and Mohammed finds that the line has been producing its entire planned output in 4 hours when the line is planned and resourced for 8 hours.

Volcano Pen Pot line utilisation: 4 / 8 = 50%

The line costs £20 per hour to crew and heat.

Cost for 8 hour shift = 8 x £20 = £160

Cost of utilisation losses = (100% - 50%) x £160 = £80

Definition or formula

(Sum of [Actual 'idle' time] / Sum of [Paid run time]) x Sum of [Line costs for run period]

Typical data sources

» Observation
» Process logs and sheets
» Machine PLC controller records
» Downtime capture system

Quality loss by product/process location/time/date

Ref: L2.1.4.1
Silver Star KPI

Drives: We know how often & where defects occur in-process
To: We identify details of losses in our process

Description

Where the product we are making is not to specification, that's a quality loss. We have wasted process time and effort making something that we cannot sell.

There's also the cost of lost materials, that's covered under 'cost of yield losses'.

Example from Mayhem Manufacturing

6% of the Mayhem Manikins line rotomoulder losses are caused by 'mould separation failure'. When this happens an entire figure is lost.

Quality loss (at rotomoulder): 6%

Definition or formula

[Quality losses] *by product/process location/time/date*

Typical data sources

» Observation
» Process logs and sheets
» Machine PLC controller records
» Downtime capture system

Yield

Ref: L2.1.5.1
Gold Star KPI

Drives: We know how often & where yield losses occur in-process
To: We identify details of losses in our process

Description

Yield is the ratio of 'How much material we should have used' to 'How much material we did use'. It shows us how efficiently we converted raw materials into finished product.

It can get tricky where you have multiple raw materials. How do you reflect the fact that you have been more efficient at converting one (say PVC) than another material (say paint)? It can get unwieldy producing a yield figure for each raw material (particularly if there are lots of them). What works best is to calculate yield based on material costs and quantities. So the yield calculation becomes 'How much should the raw material have cost?' / 'How much did the raw material cost?'

Example from Mayhem Manufacturing

On the first week's test run for Mayhem Manikins, they produced 138 sellable manikins.

* *This many figures should have used 138 x £5 of raw materials = £690*
* *In fact, we actually used £1,876 of raw materials.*

Material yield: £690 / £1,876 = 37%

Definition or formula

(Sum of [Optimal material costs per unit x number of good units produced]) / Sum of [Actual material costs]

Typical data sources

» Material usage logs
» Material invoices
» Production output records
» Bill of materials
» Product recipes

Cost of poor quality by product/process/location/time/date

Ref: L2.1.4.3
Gold Star KPI

Drives: We know how often & where defects occur in-process
To: We identify details of losses in our process

Description

When we make something that we cannot sell, that's a quality loss. The loss falls into four loss types:

1. Unrecoverable material and processing losses (after recycling etc.)

2. Lost income from selling the finished product

3. Costs associated with repairs, replacement or reputational damage

4. Costs from extra quality measures to address problem. For example extra inspections or new quality inspection equipment

Example from Mayhem Manufacturing

As our rotomoulder is their speed bottleneck, and they can sell all of their output from this line, each lost figure (at, or after the rotomoulder) represents a loss of the full 'factory gate' sales price (£65) of the figure. Mayhem are not able to 'work extra hours' to make up for the unit loss. They are able to recycle the PVC lost in a mould failure, so they recover £0.90 of PVC costs. Last week 17 figures were lost at the Rotomoulder due to quality issues.

Rotomoulder quality loss value: 17 figures x (£65 lost revenue per figure - £0.90 recycling recovery)

= £1,089 per week.

Definition or formula

Capacity

Where we can sell extra output, the product is fully processed and there is no material recovery...

Cost of poor Quality = [Factory gate price per unit] x Count of [Unrepairable quality failed units]

Where we cannot sell extra output...

Cost of poor quality = [Unrecoverable cost of waste, labour and energy per unit] x Count of [Unrepairable quality failed units]

Prevention

Measures to address quality failures may add to costs...

Cost of poor quality = Sum of [Costs to address production quality issues]

Remediation

Where a failed unit needs to be replaced or repaired...

Cost of poor quality = Sum of [Repair and replacement costs]

Typical data sources

» Observation
» Process logs and sheets
» Machine PLC controller records
» Waste logs
» Downtime capture system

Common problems and mistakes

Where we can sell everything we can produce, one tricky problem is answering the question 'At what point does waste go from 'just material loss' to 'lost finished product'? The answer is 'Before the speed bottleneck, it's wasted raw materials' but ' After the speed bottleneck it's wasted finished product - you can't catch up and remake it'.

It is also common to have costs resulting from multiple aspects of 'Cost of poor quality' - for example finished units that fail may need a refund, replacement and the process may require additional inspections to prevent issues reaching customer in future.

Cost of yield losses by product/process/location/time/date

Ref: L2.1.5.3
Gold Star KPI

Drives: We know how often & where yield losses occur in-process
To: We identify details of losses in our process

Description

Yield losses can happen at a variety of places in most processes. This measure shows where, when and on what products the losses happen.

Example from Mayhem Manufacturing

Looking at the yield losses, the Mayhem team break them down by the stage of the process at which they happen, so they can focus their efforts.

* *Mould: 50%*
* *Cool: 0%*
* *Assemble: 5%*
* *Dry: 0%*
* *Paint: 5%*
* *Package: 3%*

Note these losses are expressed as % points yield loss, so should add up to 100% - yield = 63%

Definition or formula

Sum of [Yield loss] by product/process/location/time/date

Typical data sources

» Material usage logs
» Material invoices
» Production output records
» Bill of materials
» Product recipes

Common problems and mistakes

Be careful to attribute the yield loss to where it *occurred*, not where it was *detected*.

Speed loss by product/process location/time/date

Ref: L2.1.6.1
Silver Star KPI

Drives: We know how often & where speed losses occur in-process
To: We identify details of losses in our process

Description

Speed losses (output at a slower-than-optimal rate) most often have meaningful impact at the speed bottleneck of the process (the sub-process which, when all sub-processes are run flat out at 100% with no downtime, would struggle the most). Speed losses often vary by product and sometimes by shift, time and date.

Example from Mayhem Manufacturing

The bottleneck process of the Mayhem Manikin line is the rotomoulding area. Due to the over-filling of the moulds with PVC resin, and the resulting delay in cooling times, the team discover that the effective output rate is just 4.54 figures per hour, not the optimum of 7.20 figures per hour.

Speed ('production rate') at the rotomoulders: 63% or, put the other way...

Speed *loss* at rotomoulders: 37%

So the rotomoulders are running at less than two thirds of their optimum output rate.

Definition or formula

([Optimum bottleneck speed] - [Actual bottleneck speed]) / [Optimum bottleneck speed]

Typical data sources

» Observation - including speed and cycle timings
» Process logs and sheets
» Machine PLC controller records
» Settings sheets

Common problems and mistakes

It's quite common to end up with a *negative* speed loss. This happens when the actual speed is greater than the 'optimum bottleneck speed'. This *can* mean the machine is running too fast, but more usually it means the 'optimum bottleneck speed' is too cautious or just plain wrong.

Giveaway

Ref: L2.1.5.2
Gold Star KPI

Drives: We know how often & where yield losses occur in-process
To: We identify details of losses in our process

Description

The most obvious yield losses are where material ends up in the bin. There is also a less visible yield loss - giveaway. This is where we put too much raw material into the finished product. It's so important that it has its own separate measure, but 'giveaway' is a part of yield losses.

In most countries there are legal requirements not to 'short change' consumers on products sold by weight. It is often a combination of nervousness about breaking those laws, combined with poor process control that lead to companies 'giving away' too much product.

Example from Mayhem Manufacturing

After the first week test-run making Mayhem Manikin figures, the team are puzzled why they used so much PVC. They decide to weigh the figures. The target PVC weight is 300g. When they weigh the figures they discover that they actually weigh over 450g on average. A very small part of that weight will be paint, but they assume it's PVC for the sake of simplicity.

Giveaway = 0.150kg excess material (average) x 138 figures x £2.40 /kg cost of PVC

= £50 PVC giveaway

Although it's not a massive amount of money, the giveaway has two additional impacts. Firstly, the extra material means the mouldings are slower to cool down than expected, lowering the output rate. Secondly, the materials ordering is based on 300g PVC per figure, plus a small wastage allowance. The extra usage caused an outage during the test week whilst they waited for new PVC resin to arrive.

Definition or formula

Where there is just one material in finished product...

(Average of [Actual quantity of material in finished product] - Average of [Optimal quantity of material in finished product]) x [Cost of materials per kg/m/lb etc.] x Count of [Units affected]

Where the finished product is a mixture of materials it is easiest to do the calculation based on *costs*...

[Optimal quantity of material in the finished product] becomes...
[Optimal cost of materials in the finished product]

[Actual quantity of material in the finished product] becomes... [Actual cost of materials in the finished product]

Typical data sources

» Material usage logs
» Material invoices
» Production output records
» Bill of materials
» Product recipes
» Weights of finished product

Common problems and mistakes

Note the giveaway formula looks very similar to yield, but it only applies to finished, saleable, product.

It is possible to have a *negative* giveaway figure. If this happens you need to check your product is still legal and has the required performance.

Cost of speed losses by product/process/location/time/date

Ref: L2.1.6.2
Gold Star KPI

Drives: We know how often & where speed losses occur in-process
To: We reduce process losses

Description

Where we run too slowly, it can help us prioritise our improvement efforts to look at the financial impact of those speed losses. This might allow us to focus on a particular, in-demand, product. Maybe we are best spending our time on a higher margin product?

Example from Mayhem Manufacturing

If the rotomoulding area had run at optimum speed, and availability and quality rates remained the same, they should have expected 100% / 63% greater output (i.e. 159%). They produced 138 figures during the test week, running at the lower speed.

Optimal speed output at rotomoulders = 138 x (100% / 63%) = 219 figures

So a potential extra 81 figures were lost due to slow running at the rotomoulders. At a gross profit of £65 per figure:

Cost of speed loss = £65 x 81 = £5,265

Definition or formula

Where you can sell extra product at full price...

Count of [Lost units due to speed losses] x [Unit gross profit]

Typical data sources

» Observation - including speed and cycle timings
» Process logs and sheets
» Machine PLC controller records
» Settings sheets
» Product gross profit figures

Common problems and mistakes

You need to be careful that you fully understand the optimal speed for each sub-process. It may be that by increasing the output rate of the rotomoulders, the speed bottleneck actually moves, so you never see the increased output you expected.

Data/sheets collected on time

Ref: L2.2.1.1
Silver Star KPI

Drives: We collect data regularly and accurately
To: We are good at measuring & acting on process losses

Description

Process performance data is the raw material of improvement. If you have issues with collecting that data, you might want to consider focusing your first efforts on improving data collection compliance. Measuring data collection is a first step to improving that collection.

Example from Mayhem Manufacturing

The Mayhem team are collecting production sheets with records of output, speed, downtime and so on. They ask each of the sub-process teams to fill a sheet in and collect it at the end of the day.

Sheets expected: 5 (days) x 6 (sub-processes) = 30 Sheets

Sheets collected: 28

Percentage of data/sheets collected on time: 28 / 30 = 93%

Definition or formula

Count of [Sheets collected] / Count of [Sheets expected]

Typical data sources

» Tally of data collection sheets returned in period

Common problems and mistakes

This is a measure you would normally only choose if you have a specific issue with getting all your data sheets in on time and completed.

Meetings held on time with right attendees

Ref: L2.2.3.1
Silver Star KPI

Drives: Our decision-making process is regular
To: We are good at measuring & acting on process losses

Description

Meetings, whether formal improvement meetings or
5-minute 'standing huddles', are critical to improvement.
Where you struggle to get the meetings happening, or the
right attendees there, use this measure to highlight the
impact this is having on the meetings schedule.

Missing meetings can sometimes be a side effect of long,
badly-run or ineffective meetings. If there's valid criticism of
the meetings be sure to fix those problems too.

Example from Mayhem Manufacturing

The Mayhem team should hold two 10-minute production
huddles a day and a weekly one-hour improvement session.

This week one of the huddles was skipped, the rest of the
meetings took place as planned. All the meetings that took
place had the right people in them.

* Meetings expected: 11
* Meetings that took place: 10

Percentage of meetings held on time with right attendees:
10 / 11 = 91%

Definition or formula

Count of [Meetings that took place] / Count of [Meetings
expected]

Typical data sources

» Meeting action logs/minutes

Common problems and mistakes

This is a measure you would normally only choose if you
have a specific issue with meetings being held as planned,
and the right people coming.

Production Improvement Activity

Contact Centre Improvement Activity

Cases with hand-offs due to misdirection

Ref: L3.1.2.1
Gold Star KPI

Drives: We minimise contact misdirection
To: We drive down unnecessary contact volumes

Description

Where customers end up with the wrong agent, time and effort is wasted redirecting that customer, usually irritating the customer in the process. This figure shows the frequency with which that happens.

Example from Roughshod Repairs

Looking at contacts that were appropriate for the Roughshod Repairs contact centre, but ended up with the wrong team, Ruby calculates that around 10% of contacts are handed off to another team within Roughshod.

Percentage of calls with hand-offs due to misdirection: 10%

Definition or formula

Count of [Misdirected contacts / Count of [Contacts handled]

Typical data sources

» Contact centre system
» Data capture sheets

Cases with codes related to failure demand

Ref: L3.1.2.3
Silver Star KPI

Drives: We minimise contact misdirection
To: We drive down unnecessary contact volumes

Description

Where cases are reopened that are the result of some kind of failure to handle them properly previously, we have 'failure demand' or 'rework'. This figure is the percentage of contact centre cases with 'failure demand flags'.

This kind of workload is a rich hunting ground for improvement, so is well worth dedicating a specific measure to.

Example from Roughshod Repairs

When cases have to be re-opened, they are marked with a special flag on the system. Looking at this flag, Ruby can see that around...

20% of the case handling time being spent is used on previously closed cases.

She is interested in costs and estimates...

Cost of cases with codes related to 'failure demand': 20% x 8 hour day x 15 staff x 6 days a week x £10 per hour = £1,440 a week.

Definition or formula

Count of [Closed cases reopened] / Count of [Closed cases]

for same period

Typical data sources

» Opportunity tracker and costing sheet

Common problems and mistakes

If a closed case can potentially reopen at any point, it is important to set time boundaries on this calculation and to make sure you are comparing reopened cases with the right closure period.

KPI Family: MI
Public Reviews

Customers leaving feedback

Ref: M1.1.1.2
Silver Star KPI

Drives: We ask our customers to leave reviews and feedback
To: We nurture positive feedback

Description

If we want positive feedback we need two things to happen. Firstly our customers need to rate our service, secondly they need to actually leave feedback. This measures how many of them leave feedback.

By tracking this figure, you can try various ways to increase the percentage of feedback given. Typical strategies include bribery (discounts if you 'like' us on Facebook), gentle nagging and running competitions.

Example from Chaos Coffee Shop

Chaos Coffee has about 1,600 customers a week and sees about 16 reviews.

Percentage of customers leaving feedback: 16 / 1,600 = 1%

Definition or formula

Count of [Feedback on all platforms] / Count of [Unique customers]

If identification of 'unique' customers is not possible then just use 'customers'.

Typical data sources

» Online platforms (Google, Facebook, Twitter, TripAdvisor etc.)

Positive to negative feedback comments

Ref: M1.2.1.3
Silver Star KPI

Drives: We respond to negative feedback
To: We manage negative feedback effectively

Description

You will see always see positive and negative feedback. What is critical is the ratio of this feedback - does positive feedback dwarf the negative comments or the other way round?

Note this measure is shown as a ratio because percentages get quite unwieldy when they are several hundred percent (when positive comments substantially outweigh negative comments).

Example from Chaos Coffee Shop

Of the 16 reviews left last week 12 were positive, 2 were neutral and 2 were negative.

Ratio of positive to negative reviews: 12 : 2 = 6 : 1

Definition or formula

Count of [Positive reviews] : Count of [Negative reviews]

Neutral reviews excluded.

Typical data sources

» Online platforms (Google, Facebook, Twitter, TripAdvisor etc.)

Common problems and mistakes

Neutral feedback is usually excluded.

Negative feedback issues addressed to root cause

Ref: M1.2.2.2
Gold Star KPI

Drives: We tackle the problems identified in negative feedback
To: We manage negative feedback effectively

Description

When you have negative feedback the most important thing is to try and act on the root cause of the issue. This measure shows the percentage of negative feedback points you have taken action to fix.

When you get negative feedback it can be upsetting. But it can be really useful if it is specific enough to take action on. If you take effective action you can reasonably expect negative feedback on that issue to reduce in future.

Example from Chaos Coffee Shop

Charlie picked up from one of the negative reviews that there was a problem with the baby change platform in the washroom, which he wasn't aware of. He had that fixed immediately. The other negative review was so vague that it wasn't clear what could be done to make the customer happier.

Percentage of negative feedback issues addressed to root cause: 50%

Definition or formula

Count of [Negative feedback issues solved to root cause] / Count of [Negative feedback issues]

Typical data sources

» Negative feedback collected from online platforms and email
» Action log for improvement activity

Online review site scores - average

Ref: M1.3.1.1
Gold Star KPI

Drives: We track online feedback
To: We know how we are reviewed

Description

Many ratings and review sites give a star rating, or score, for overall feedback. Online review scores can be critical for generating a steady stream of new customers for many new businesses.

A summary of the scores, particularly when trended, can show you how your business is being perceived by its customers.

Drilling down into the reasons given for particular scores can also be very valuable.

Example from Chaos Coffee Shop

Charlie looks at TripAdvisor and Google.

The average scores for each are 4.5 and 4.7

Online review site scores - average: 4.6

Definition or formula

Average of [Online review scores]

Typical data sources

» Online review stats for each platform

Common problems and mistakes

Anyone can leave a review, so staff (and family) could leave positive reviews if it affected their pay. Competitors can leave bad reviews to drive customers to them, if they wanted to.

Existing-customer survey scores

Ref: M1.3.1.2
Gold Star KPI

Drives: We track online feedback
To: We know how we are reviewed

Description
Asking specific questions in a survey can give you targeted feedback that you might not get through organic reviews and feedback.

People are bombarded with surveys, so it's best to keep them short and offer a modest incentive to complete them.

Example from Chaos Coffee Shop
Charlie had some business cards printed up with just three questions and a comment box.

The three questions, with average scores...

* *How much have you enjoyed your visit? :*   *8.2*
* *How likely are you to recommend us?:*   *9.1*
* *Name one thing we can do better:*   *Free text answer*

Definition or formula
Average of [Survey scores]

Typical data sources
» Spreadsheet
» Online survey software analytics
» Social media polls

Unpaid 'Likes', '+Is' etc.

Ref: M1.3.1.3
Gold Star KPI

Drives: We track online feedback
To: We know how we are reviewed

Description
Many social platforms have 'likes', or similar. Counting these in a given period can give an indication of the 'buzz' around your product or service.

Example from Chaos Coffee Shop
Charlie looks at Facebook and sees 40 'likes' from last month. He also sees 7 '+1's on Google.

Unpaid 'likes' and '+1s': 47

Definition or formula
Count of [Unpaid 'likes', '+1's etc.]

Typical data sources
» Social media analytics

KPI Family: M2
Footfall

Number of visits per day

Ref: M2.1.1.2
Gold Star KPI

Drives: Know the number of customers coming through the door
To: We maximise visits from potential customers

Description

For many businesses, sales are linked directly to the number of people coming through the door on a daily basis.

Knowing how many visits we get on a daily basis helps us monitor and manage one of our primary sales drivers.

This figure shows the raw count of visitors. If you have a method for doing so, it's also useful to measure unique visitors too.

Example from Chaos Coffee Shop

Using a 'beam break' sensor on the door, Charlie knows how many people enter and leave his store. By dividing that total figure by two, he can get a rough estimate for the number of visitors. Here are the visits, by day of the week, for last week:

Number of visits per day:

* Mon: 390
* Tues: 400
* Weds: 550
* Thurs: 480
* Fri: 340
* Sat: 790

Number of visits (week): 2,950

Definition or formula

Count of [Visitors per day]

Typical data sources

» "Beam break" door sensor (figure divided by two)

Common problems and mistakes

If you are using your till system, you will probably have difficulty in precisely identifying visits - for example a customer who pops back to the till to buy a couple more things will show up as another visit. If you are measuring visits just to figure out how many staff to have on, this probably won't be a problem.

Timing of visits

Ref: M2.1.1.3
Gold Star KPI

Drives: Know the number of customers coming through the door
To: We maximise visits from potential customers

Description

When do customers typically arrive? The daily volume figures tell part of the story, but if the majority of your daily visitors arrive in a burst over a couple of hours you could be overwhelmed for part of the day and over-staffed for the rest of the day.

This figure, normally shown as a bar chart, gives you a typical profile of customer arrival times.

Knowing the profile of customer arrival times allows you to phase staff start and finish time, lunch times and non-customer facing activities (like training).

Example from Chaos Coffee Shop

Timing of visits is best shown as a chart. Here's what the profile looks like for Chaos Coffee, after the radio advertising campaign for last Monday...

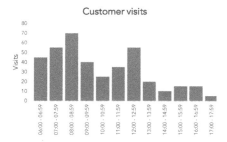

Customer visits

Definition or formula

Count of [Visitors] by time slots

Typical data sources

» "Beam break" door sensor (figure divided by two)
» If you don't have a 'beam break' sensor, you can use sales data, but that will only show 'converted' visitors

Forecast number of sales

Ref: M2.1.2.2
Silver Star KPI

Drives: We forecast the expected footfall
To: We maximise visits from potential customers

Description
If we know how many customers we are expecting, we have a chance to make sure we have the right amount of staff and stock (especially if that stock is short-shelf life, perishable, stock).

Example from Chaos Coffee Shop
Using sales data from the till system [EPOS] Charlie decides to forecast visits by day of the week. He uses this to decide on his pastry order quantities for each day. Here's his forecast:

Forecast number of sales

* Mon: 240
* Tues: 280
* Weds: 350
* Thurs: 220
* Fri: 170
* Sat: 365

Forecast number of sales (week): 1,625

Definition or formula
Average of [Sales volume] for appropriate historic period (day of week, week of month, month of year, etc.)

You may also add a correction factor, for a public holiday, weather etc.

Typical data sources
» Till/EPOS historic sales data

Common problems and mistakes
Forecasts are always inaccurate, so don't give up if you don't get it exactly right all the time. The main thing is that forecasts just need to be better than 'no forecasting at all' to justify their worth.

Traffic volumes by source

Ref: M2.1.3.2
Silver Star KPI

Drives: We find out why people visit us & how they heard about us
To: We maximise visits from potential customers

Description
If we have a number of different promotional activities we may want to identify the volumes of traffic by source - for example passing trade, web advert, radio advert etc.

Understanding your source of traffic will help you make the right marketing and advertising decisions in future, and make the most of your budget. You can use this as a day-to-day tool, to try out new ideas, or as a long-term tool to see how you are converting overall.

Example from Chaos Coffee Shop
Charlie is interested in where his customers heard about Chaos Coffee. He does a small survey, asking randomly chosen customers over a few days how they heard about Chaos Coffee. Here are the results:

Traffic volumes by source:

* Regular customers: 43%
* With a friend: 25%
* Passing trade: 14%
* Radio advert: 10%
* Local billboards: 4%
* Other: 4%

Definition or formula
Count of [Visitors] by source

Typical data sources
» Asking the customer
» Channel specific coupons or discount codes

Conversion rate

Ref: M2.2.1.1
Gold Star KPI

Drives: We convert visitors
To: We turn visitors into customers

Description

The conversion rate is the ratio of sales to the number of people who visited your shop. It is a measure of how effective we are at taking a visitor and turning them into a customer.

Example from Chaos Coffee Shop

Charlie has quite detailed data from his till (EPOS) system. He can break it down by day of week, date and so on.

* *On an average day, Chaos Coffee sees 271 sales.*

Using a 'beam break' sensor on the door, Charlie knows how many people enter and leave his store. By dividing that total figure by two, he can get a rough estimate for the number of visitors. Here are the visits, by day of the week, for last week:

* *Average number of visits per day = 492*

Average conversion rate: 271 / 492 = 55%

Charlie thinks this figure is so low as many of his customers come in groups of 2 or 3 people, with one person actually placing the order. He's not too worried about the actual figure, he's just focused on increasing it.

Definition or formula

Count of [Sales] / Count of [Visitors]

Typical data sources

» "Beam break" door sensor (figure divided by two)
» Till/EPOS historic sales data

KPI Family: M3
Web Marketing

Number of unique website visitors
per day

Ref: M3.1.1.1
Gold Star KPI

Drives: We attract website traffic
To: We maximise visits from potential customers

Description
Without traffic, nothing else is possible. What you do with that traffic is up to you, but you must attract visitors, so this is a critical measure for your site.

Example from Mayhem Manufacturing
Mohammed runs a website for Mayhem Manufacturing. Its purpose is to build a fan base for their products and to enable direct sales to anyone.

He uses a WordPress site and gets his average number of unique visitors.

Last week...

Average 'Number of unique visitors per day' = 145

Definition or formula
Average of [Unique website visitors per day]

Typical data sources
» Website admin/stats page

Average spend per 1,000 visitors

Ref: M3.1.1.3
Silver Star KPI

Drives: We attract website traffic
To: We maximise visits from potential customers

Description
The average customer spend on your website per 1,000 of visitors.

This is an easy rough guide to how good your site is at making money. It's easy to calculate and covers the start-to-finish of selling on your website.

Example from Mayhem Manufacturing
Mohammed looked at his online sales for last month, excluding delivery, and his unique visitor count and divides sales by visits...

Sales last month: £1,075 (excluding delivery)

Unique visitors: 4 thousand

Average spend per 1,000 visitors: £1,075 / 4 = £268.75

Definition or formula
Sum of [Sales] / [Thousands of unique visitors]

Typical data sources
» Website admin/stats page
» Ecommerce plugin stats
» Ecommerce software service stats

Common problems and mistakes
You should reasonably expect sales to go up in line with the number of visitors, but this will not be the case if:

1. You change the focus of material on your website to win traffic, but that new topic is not related to what you are selling.
2. You drive traffic to your site by badly designed advertising or other 'quick' ways of generating traffic that are unqualified leads.

Site uptime

Ref: M3.1.2.1
Gold Star KPI

Drives: Our website is reliable and accessible
To: We maximise visits from potential customers

Description

The site uptime percentage comes from 'site uptime' and total 'available running time' - usually 24 x 365.

To get traffic our website has to be up and running (well). Downtime will put off visitors and will probably see your site downgraded by search engines.

Example from Mayhem Manufacturing

Mohammed's website host has uptime data. They had a nasty 2 hour outage last month, but ran uninterrupted for the rest of the month.

Site uptime percentage: (31 x 24 - 2) / (31 x 24) = 99.7%

Definition or formula

(Sum of [Planned run time] - Sum of [Downtime]) / (Sum of [Planned run time]

or

Sum of [Uptime] / Sum of [Planned runtime]

Typical data sources

» Host admin page/stats

Common problems and mistakes

Make sure you use the correct number of days for a particular month in the calculation.

Total subscriber signups

Ref: M3.2.1.1
Gold Star KPI

Drives: We convert visitors to newsletter subscribers
To: We convert visits to engagement

Description

The total number of subscribers signing up for a free download, newsletter etc.

For many small businesses, getting visitors to share their details with a signup for something is one of their key goals. Keep tabs on your signup volume to see how well you are doing at this critical objective.

Example from Mayhem Manufacturing

Mohammed offers a free room-design guide to get visitors to sign up for his newsletter.

Total subscriber signups (last month): 35

This figure is for subscribers who have clicked on the confirmation (double opt-in) email link.

Definition or formula

Count of [Confirmed subscribers]

Typical data sources

» Website admin/stats page
» Website email plugin stats
» Mail service admin/stats pages

Common problems and mistakes

Be clear on whether these are confirmed (double opt-in) or just unconfirmed signups. Generally it's best to use confirmed signups here.

Total website sales value

Ref: M3.2.2.1
Gold Star KPI

Drives: We sell to our visitors
To: We convert visits to engagement

Description

The total value of sales from your website in the period.

If you intend to sell using your website, how much did you sell? Simple but important.

Example from Mayhem Manufacturing

Mohammed gets his online sales for last month from his WordPress ecommerce plugin. Excluding delivery…

Sales last month: £1,075 (excluding delivery)

Definition or formula

Sum of [Website sales value]

Typical data sources

» Website admin/stats page
» Ecommerce plugin stats
» Ecommerce software service stats

Common problems and mistakes

Be clear on whether you are including delivery, sales tax etc. in these figures.

Web sales volume

Ref: M3.2.2.2
Silver Star KPI

Drives: We sell to our visitors
To: We convert visits to engagement

Description

The number of sales transactions through our site is useful in itself, but is also needed so we can calculate other useful measures such as average basket spend.

If you sell items or services that vary widely in value, it's going to be important to keep an eye on both total value and the volume of sales. A shift in the profile of what is being bought can conceal changes in volume, or vice versa.

Example from Mayhem Manufacturing

The sales last month were made up of three transactions.

Web sales volume: 3

Definition or formula

Count of [Sales transactions]

Typical data sources

» Website admin/stats page
» Ecommerce plugin stats
» Ecommerce software service stats

Cart abandon rate

Ref: M3.2.2.4
Silver Star KPI

Drives: We sell to our visitors
To: We convert visits to engagement

Description

The cart abandon rate is the ratio of the number of abandoned shopping carts to the number of initiated transactions.

Example from Mayhem Manufacturing

When Mohammed looks through his ecommerce records, he sees that 7 sales were abandoned midway, with just 3 completed. So 10 transactions were initiated.

Cart abandon rate: 7 / 10 = 70%

Definition or formula

Count of [Abandoned carts] / Count of [Initiated transactions]

Typical data sources

» Website admin/stats page
» Ecommerce plugin stats
» Ecommerce software service stats

Setting targets

A typical online retail abandon rate is 70%.

Common problems and mistakes

Sometimes you see this defined as abandoned/completed. I don't like this measure as a zero completion rate messes the arithmetic up (you end up dividing by zero).

Visits by page

Ref: M3.3.1.1
Gold Star KPI

Drives: We know which pages and posts perform
To: Our content is engaging and popular

Description

This metric shows how many visits each page received. This, along with page visit duration, gives a strong indication of page popularity, ranking and content strength.

Example from Mayhem Manufacturing

Most modern websites allow you to see your most popular pages, ranked by number of visits.

Mohammed looks at his over the past month and finds the following are his top performers:

* *Middle Earth interior design guide: 2,300 page hits*
* *Home page: 700 hits*
* *Volcano Pen Pot landing page: 430 page hits*
* *Turtle Table landing page: 275 page hits*

Definition or formula

Count of [Visits] by page

Typical data sources

» Website admin/stats page

Average visit duration

Ref: M3.3.2.1
Silver Star KPI

Drives: We maximise site visit length
To: Our content is engaging and popular

Description
How long did someone stay on your site once they arrived?

Normally, the longer a visitor stays the richer and more engaging your content is. It's also a sign that the search term they used to arrive here was a good fit with your content - a good thing if you want to sell them stuff!

Example from Mayhem Manufacturing
Using Google Analytics, Mohammed finds that for the last week:

Average visit duration: 1min 47seconds

Definition or formula
Average of [Visit duration]

Or, more fully...

Sum of [Visit durations] / Count of [Visits]

Typical data sources
» Website admin/stats page

Total number of shares

Ref: M3.3.3.1
Silver Star KPI

Drives: People share our content
To: Our content is engaging and popular

Description
How many times did your visitors share some of your content on social media? This count shows how popular your content is. If you nail this you might even get your content to go viral, where the share rate is so high that it propagates - even more people share it onwards once it has been shared with them.

This is another strong indicator of content quality. If someone decides (without being bribed or encouraged) to share your content, then you are doing something right. This may also help your search engine rankings, as it's an indicator of content quality that the search giants use.

There are a number of ways to see how and where your material was shared. The easiest is to include share buttons on your website and look at the stats harvested by those buttons. You can also set up search engine alerts, or look on each social network analytics page to see how often your material has been shared.

Example from Mayhem Manufacturing
Mohammed uses a sharing toolbar on his WordPress website which tells him how many times each post has been shared. Looking at his best performing page, he can easily find the following:

Post: Middle Earth interior design guide:

Total number of shares:

* *415 shares*
* *218 Facebook*
* *196 LinkedIn*
* *1 Pinterest*

Definition or formula
Count of [Social shares] by page and by social network

Typical data sources
» Website admin/stats page
» Social plugin stats

Ranking by keyword or phrase

Ref: M3.4.1.1
Gold Star KPI

Drives: We appear high in search engine rankings
To: My keywords rank well

Description

This shows the approximate position of your website page on a search engine results page when a particular term is submitted to that search engine.

Ranking well on keywords and phrases is a great free way of getting a steady stream of web traffic. It's one of the best, as your material has the authority (and credibility) of being an 'organic' result - not an advert. It also usually takes time, effort and excellent quality material to achieve results - so be patient.

Example from Mayhem Manufacturing

Mohammed has certain phrases that he wants to rank highly on search engines. These include his product names. He searches for each, then notes the search engine page he ranks on and the search listing position...

Ranking:

* *Volcano Pen Pots:*   *Page 1, 1st result*
* *Turtle Table:*   *Page 1, 3rd result*
* *Hobbit Chairs:*   *Page 2, 12th result*

Definition or formula

[Ranking of search result for given term]

Typical data sources

» Search engine tests
» Ranking reporting service

Common problems and mistakes

It can be tempting to go straight for an obvious keyword like 'florist' but in reality that is likely to be insanely competitive and you are unlikely to rank on the first page of results for this term. If you have a local business, it makes much more sense (and is much easier) to rank highly for 'florist + nameofyourtown'. If you search to find your ranking, make sure you are logged out of your Google/Bing/Yahoo accounts, as being logged in can skew the results that are presented to you.

Double opt-in rate

Ref: M3.5.1.1
Gold Star KPI

Drives: We have a growing and valid subscriber list
To: We use newsletters to drive sales and traffic

Description

If you are a responsible email marketer, you will ask subscribers to confirm their subscription by clicking on an email you send to them - confirming their subscription. This is a 'double opt-in' and is the last stage before they become a subscriber. The 'Double opt-in rate' is the ratio of 'confirmed email opt-ins' to the 'number of initial signups' - the latter usually done through a web form.

Double opt-in will always yield fewer subscribers than single opt-in but has two major benefits. Firstly, you are much less likely to be flagged as a spammer and secondly you know that the email addresses given are 'deliverable' as the subscriber has received and responded to emails sent to their subscription address.

Example from Mayhem Manufacturing

Mohammed offers a free room-design guide to get visitors to sign up for his newsletter. He had 62 people fill in the newsletter signup form last month. Of those, 35 subscribers clicked on the confirmation (double opt-in) email link.

Double opt-in rate: 35 / 62 = 56%

Definition or formula

Count of [Double opt-in confirmed subscribers] / Count of [Initial, unconfirmed, subscribers]

Typical data sources

» Website email plugin stats
» Mail service admin/stats pages

423

Unsubscribe rate

Ref: M3.5.1.3
Silver Star KPI

Drives: We have a growing and valid subscriber list
To: We use newsletters to drive sales and traffic

Description

When someone no longer wants to receive your emails they will often unsubscribe from your email list. The 'unsubscribes' divided by the 'subscribers emailed' gives you the 'unsubscribe rate'.

Whilst it's always a pity to lose subscribers, learn from unsubscribes - particularly if you see a significant increase or decrease compared with the usual rate. Did you change the frequency of emails? Was there a particular topic or tone you used that was different?

Example from Mayhem Manufacturing

So far this month, Mayhem has sent out one email newsletter to all of their subscribers. 10 people unsubscribed out of a live subscriber list of 1,140.

Unsubscribe rate: 10 / 1,140 = 0.88%

Definition or formula

Count of [Unsubscribes] / Count of [Subscribers emailed]

Typical data sources

» Website email plugin stats
» Mail service admin/stats pages

Email newsletter frequency

Ref: M3.5.2.1
Silver Star KPI

Drives: We regularly communicate with our subscribers
To: We use newsletters to drive sales and traffic

Description

How often do you send out newsletters? Daily, weekly or monthly. The average frequency gives you this figure.

There's a fine line to be trodden between keeping subscribers warm and engaged and overloading them with unread emails. Look at your 'Unsubscribe rate' and 'Email click-through rate' to gauge whether you are getting it right.

Example from Mayhem Manufacturing

Mohammed sent out 3 email newsletters last month.

Email newsletter frequency: 3 per month

Definition or formula

Count of [Newsletters] per period

Typical data sources

» Website email plugin stats
» Mail service admin/stats pages

Email click-through rate

Ref: M3.5.3.1
Gold Star KPI

Drives: Our newsletters drive sales and traffic
To: We use newsletters to drive sales and traffic

Description

When you send out an email newsletter with links embedded in it, you usually want the reader to click on those links. This measure shows the percentage of emails that had one, or more, links clicked.

Most newsletter systems use unique links to allow you to track unique link clicks within email newsletters on a per-email basis.

Example from Mayhem Manufacturing

Of the 3,420 emails sent out last month, 100 had one, or more, links clicked by the recipient.

Email click-through rate: 100 / 3,420 = 2.9%

Definition or formula

Count of [Emails with one, or more, link clicks]

Typical data sources

» Website email plugin stats
» Mail service admin/stats pages

Setting targets

This varies by sector, and quality content of course, but typically click-through rates are in the 2-3% range for most sectors.

Common problems and mistakes

Don't forget, if you have more than one link in an email you need to think about how to handle several clicks from one reader. This measure definition focusses on the percentage of emails clicked on (some may have several clicks on one email), but you may also be interested in multiple clicks. Measure what makes logical sense for your campaign.

Email open rate

Ref: M3.5.3.2
Gold Star KPI

Drives: Our newsletters drive sales and traffic
To: We use newsletters to drive sales and traffic

Description

How many of your emails are actually opened? Use this measure to find out how engaging and compelling your emails are to your audience.

Most newsletter systems use unique links to allow you to track unique opens.

Example from Mayhem Manufacturing

Of the 3,420 emails sent out last month, 850 were opened by the recipient.

Email open rate: 850 / 3,420 = 24.8%

Definition or formula

Count of [Email opens] / Count of [Emails sent]

Typical data sources

» Website email plugin stats
» Mail service admin/stats pages

Setting targets

This varies by sector, and quality content of course, but typically click-through rates are in the 20-25% range for most sectors.

Efficiency - Widget Production

Staff utilisation

Ref: O1.1.1.1
Gold Star KPI

Drives: We manage process resourcing levels
To: We make best use of process time available

Description

This shows the ratio of how many hours were used productively to the number of hours that were available for productive work. It's a measure of how productively busy our workforce are.

You are almost never going to get anywhere near to, or want to get anywhere close to, 100% utilisation. Don't worry about your actual figure being much, much lower. Just try not to fall into the trap of thinking 100% is the target then starting to take out activities that must happen but aren't productive - like meetings. If you do this then you start to lose sight of the things that rob everyone of their productivity. Focus instead on getting rid of pointless time wasting activities.

Example from Mayhem Manufacturing

Mayhem runs a small workshop to make all of its bigger products. Michael, the shift supervisor at Mayhem Manufacturing, knows that he pays for four staff to build furniture during the working day. Looking at the production logs, and watching what is going on, he knows that this week his team are only busy on production in the morning. They spend the afternoon tidying, talking and having lengthy debates about their favourite football player. So for last week...

* *Productive hours: 4 staff x 4 hours x 5 days = 80 hours*
* *Available hours: 4 staff x 8 hour day x 5 day week = 160 hours*

Staff utilisation = 80 / 160 = 50%

Definition or formula

Sum of [Productive hours] / Sum of [Available hours]

Typical data sources

» Production records, time and attendance records
» Observational studies
» Personal time record sheets (tally sheets)

Common problems and mistakes

Being utilised does not guarantee that you are being productive, or that the product you are making is of good quality or something that a customer actually wants to buy.

Labour efficiency

Ref: O1.1.1.2
Gold Star KPI

Drives: We manage process resourcing levels
To: We make best use of process time available

Description

Labour efficiency is the measure of 'actual output'/'optimum output' to produce a given amount of 'good' product', where your optimum output rate is primarily determined by resource level.

Put simply, if you put two people on the job, should your production rate double? If the answer is 'yes' then use labour efficiency. If the answer is 'no' then use OEE (see 'OEE' on page 433).

This KPI is a measure of how well we use our labour to produce output, versus the *ideal* resource requirement.

It can be a useful measure in situations where, for example, you have an under-resourced production process - you know you will get less output, but you want to work out whether you have taken more or less of an efficiency hit than expected by reducing the workforce.

Example from Mayhem Manufacturing

Last week the Mayhem workshop devoted the full working week to producing Hobbit chairs. With a full crew (which they had) they should produce 0.625 Hobbit Chairs per hour, per person. Their output at the end of the week was 80 chairs.

* *Actual output: 80 chairs*
* *Optimum output = Available work hours x crew size x optimum build rate: 8 hour day x 5 day week x 4 staff x 0.625 chairs per hour = 100 chairs*

Labour efficiency = Actual output / Optimum output

= 80/100

= 80%

Definition or formula

Sum of [Actual output] / Sum of [Optimum output]

Note: Optimum output is determined by per-person output rate x number of staff on process.

Typical data sources

» Production records
» Time and attendance records
» Observational studies

Common problems and mistakes

Labour efficiency sounds similar to Staff Utilisation, but it's measured as how much was produced in a period compared with the 'ideal' output for that amount of labour time. The focus here is on output rather than how 'occupied' your team is.

Producing something is not the same as selling it. Be wary of having an efficient and productive workforce filling a warehouse with product that no-one wants to buy.

Orders - in hours work

Ref: O1.1.2.1
Silver Star KPI

Drives: We manage equipment utilisation
To: We make best use of process time available

Description
This gives an estimated production hours requirement to clear your current order levels. This figure can be very useful for capacity, delivery and resource forecasting.

For this to be a useful guide you need to have some decent estimates for how long each type of production takes. If you don't have this your forecasts could be way off.

Example from Mayhem Manufacturing
Mayhem have the following orders waiting to be built for next week:

*   Hobbit chairs   20
*   Volcano pen pots   40
*   Turtle tables   4

The person-hours per product type is:

*   Hobbit chairs   2.5
*   Volcano pen pot   0.1
*   Turtle tables   20

So the person-hours for the current order book is the sum of:

*   Hobbit chairs 2.5 x 20 = 50 person-hours
*   Volcano pen pot 0.1 x 40 = 4 person-hours
*   Turtle tables 20 x 4 = 80 person-hours

= 134 person-hours (that's about 3.4 full time equivalent staff)

Definition or formula
Sum of [Model volume x standard build time (person hours)]

Typical data sources
» Production records and standards (for standard times)
» Order book

Unit cost

Ref: O1.2.0.1
Silver Star KPI

To: We run our process efficiently

Description
The unit cost of a product is how much it costs to produce. It usually includes material, energy, labour and packaging costs, but can include lots of other things too.

Unit cost is a key part of working out your gross profit per unit. When you work out Net Profit per item you will need to include the overheads (rent, heating, admin costs etc.) and 'allocate' (divide amongst everything you make) to each item.

Example from Mayhem Manufacturing
For a Turtle table, Mohammed has the following data:

*   Person-hours build cost: 20 hours x £10 per hour = £200
*   Materials: = £40
*   Packaging: = £10
Unit cost for this item = £250

Definition or formula
Sum of [Labour, material, energy and packaging costs directly attributable to production of that item]

Typical data sources
» Production standards for hours effort
» Payroll for labour costs
» Invoices and process details for energy costs per unit
» Packaging invoices for packaging costs etc.

Common problems and mistakes
Be clear on whether you are just including controllable (direct) costs such as materials, production energy and line labour costs, or whether you are including non-controllable costs such as buildings rent, insurance etc. Also be clear on whether transportation beyond the factory gate is included.

Production downtime

Ref: O1.2.1.1
Gold Star KPI

Drives: We minimise downtime
To: We run our process efficiently

Description

Where you have a production process, one of the most visible losses of productivity is where the machines are stopped because of process problems, mechanical failure or staff shortages. Every minute lost to downtime is a minute of output lost.

It's a little more complicated than minute of downtime=lost production minute. It depends on whether the broken machine is the 'bottleneck' of the process. If it's not then you might be able to catch up, but it's by no means guaranteed.

Example from Mayhem Manufacturing

Production of the Volcano pen pots relies on an injection moulding machine. This machine was unable to run when it should have for 3 hours last week.

Production downtime (Volcano line) = 3 hours

Definition or formula

Sum of [Process bottleneck lost time]

Typical data sources

» Downtime logs at bottleneck (either manual or automatic - for some machinery)

Common problems and mistakes

If you think you have a downtime issue with a process that is not the bottleneck, then by all means measure downtime at that point, but the 'lost production hours' should always be measured at the bottleneck to see what output impact the downtime is having.

Availability

Ref: O1.2.1.2
Silver Star KPI

Drives: We minimise downtime
To: We run our process efficiently

Description

How much of the available time were we running for?

If we planned to run a machine for 10 hours, but it was only working for 5 hours, then our Availability would be 50%. This measure might show stoppages caused by problems, lack of materials or process problems.

Availability is the mirror image of downtime. If you have a non-stop production run, then your availability will be 100% and your downtime will be 0%.

Strictly speaking you need to measure availability at the bottleneck of the process. That's generally the process that has a queue of material in front of it and machines downstream waiting for material from time-to-time.

Example from Mayhem Manufacturing

The Volcano pen pot line was scheduled to run for 5 hours last week, but was down for 3.

Availability: (5-3) / 5 = 40%

As it was a short production run anyway, Mayhem were able to extend the production run to compensate (although they still wasted 3 hours of labour time). As you head towards 'flat out' working it becomes harder to do this, and you risk lost sales.

Definition or formula

(Sum of [Total production hours] - Sum of [Bottleneck downtime]) / Sum of [Total production hours]

Typical data sources

» Downtime logs at bottleneck (either manual or automatic - for some machinery)

Performance rate

Ref: O1.2.2.1
Silver Star KPI

Drives: We run production at the right speed
To: We run our process efficiently

Description
Performance rate shows the output rate a machine or line actually ran at, compared with what it should have run at (ideal speed). Speed losses are often invisible. People like running processes slower and downtime losses often reduce, but normally not by enough to compensate for the loss of output from the speed reduction.

You can "lose" output by machines or lines running slower than they should. So a machine set to make 100 widgets a minute that was set to only run at 70 widgets per minute would be running at 70% speed/rate/performance (sorry, all these names are used – it's a bit confusing). This measure would show us problems that caused lost output but were not serious enough to completely stop production.

Example from Mayhem Manufacturing
When the Volcano injection moulder is working, it should produce a volcano every 2 mins - a 30 unit per hour production rate. The operators have problems with the polymer granule feed when they run at this speed, so they have slowed the machine down to a 3 minute cycle - or 20 units per hour.

Performance rate = 20/30 = 67%

Definition or formula
Performance Rate = (Actual bottleneck speed / Ideal bottleneck speed)

Typical data sources
» Machine/production logs and records
» Observation
» Process set-up sheets

Common problems and mistakes
Performance rate (speed) problems are often much less visible when you slow down a machine, so operators and managers often do this rather than solving the actual problem. Where you are getting lower output rates you should speed the machine up (under close supervision, and having risk-assessed doing so) and use a structured problem-solving approach to eliminate the speed/rate-related problems permanently.

OEE

Ref: O1.2.2.3
Gold Star KPI

Drives: We run production at the right speed
To: We run our process efficiently

Description

OEE stands for 'Overall Equipment Effectiveness'. It is a commonly used efficiency measure. What do we mean by efficiency? Put simply, it is 'How much we made, compared with how much we *could* have made.'

To work out OEE we multiply together the three numbers..

- Quality rate
- Performance rate
- Availability

There is an alternative (quick) way to get the OEE. It doesn't show you what type of losses you have, but does give you a very useful 'Sanity check' on the OEE figure. The alternative method is...

Optimum hours to produce actual output / Actual hours run

The optimum hours is just [Good output] / [Optimum bottleneck speed]

Example from Mayhem Manufacturing

The OEE for Volcano pen pots is the Quality Rate x Performance Rate x Availability (these values are from O1.2.3.2, O1.2.2.1 and O1.2.1.2).

= 87.5% x 66.7% x 40%

= 23%

Definition or formula

OEE = [Quality Rate] x [Performance Rate] x [Availability]

Typical data sources

» Production records
» Quality records

Common problems and mistakes

If you get an OEE of more than 100% do not be delighted, be critical. It normally means that your Performance Rate is based on too low an output rate. If this happens, it's time to recalculate using a more realistic performance rate (don't forget to go back and recalculate your historic performance).

Producing something is not the same as selling it. Be wary of having an efficient and productive workforce filling a warehouse with product that no-one wants to buy.

Quality rate

Ref: O1.2.3.2
Silver Star KPI

Drives: We minimise waste
To: We run our process efficiently

Description

We may manage to make some product that is not good enough to sell. The percentage of output which is 'good' is called the 'quality rate'. If we make 350 widgets, but only 280 of them are good enough to sell then our quality rate would be 80%.

Losses through poor quality can be some of the most expensive kind of waste, as raw material and effort is wasted as well as production time.

Example from Mayhem Manufacturing

When the team examined the Volcano pen pots they had produced, they found that 5 of the 40 produced had defects in the moulding, meaning they had to be scrapped.

= (40-5) / 40

Quality rate = 87.5%

Definition or formula

Quality Rate = ([Actual output] – [Scrapped output]) / [Actual output]

Typical data sources

» Quality records

Common problems and mistakes

Make sure you understand whether poor quality can be fixed or whether you have to scrap the product. This has a big impact on the 'cost of poor quality'.

Waste

Ref: O1.3.1.3
Gold Star KPI

Drives: We measure conversion efficiency
To: We make best use of our raw materials

Description

Throwing material or product in the bin is an obvious and expensive loss. Recording waste, why it happened and when, is a first step towards tackling and reducing process waste.

Don't forget, when you throw an item in the bin that has been part, or all, of the way through your process, it's not just the cost of the raw materials you are throwing away. All the energy and labour that has been invested in that product also ends up in the bin.

Example from Mayhem Manufacturing

The Mayhem team threw away 5 Volcano pen pots, or 500g of polymer, when these pots did not meet their quality requirements.

Waste: 500g of polymer

Definition or formula

Sum of [Weight of lost material]

or

Sum of [Value of lost goods or material]

or

Count of [Finished goods scrapped]

Typical data sources

» Production records
» Quality records

Common problems and mistakes

As it is very hard to compare 'apples' with 'pears' it can be useful to convert different waste figures into financial values. Just be careful about whether your value was on the cost of materials or the lost profit from sales. You can only value waste on the lost profit of a sale if you weren't able to make a replacement for the scrapped one and sell it - i.e. you are running flat out and are unable/barely able to meet customer demand.

Material Yield

Ref: O1.3.1.2
Gold Star KPI

Drives: We measure conversion efficiency
To: We make best use of our raw materials

Description

Material yield is the percentage of how much material we should have used *out of* how much material we did use. It shows us how well we converted our raw material into good quality finished product. It's tempting to think that yield is just another way of representing scrap or waste product, but it also includes things such as 'giveaway'. Giveaway would include things such as putting 13 biscuits in a 12-biscuit pack, including excess product in a pack or overfilling a can of paint. These barely-visible losses tend to be systematic (happen on lots of your output) and can have a serious impact on your profitability if not spotted and fixed.

Example from Mayhem Manufacturing

Each Volcano pen pot should use 100g of material. By the end of production, we had 35 saleable pen pots, so in an ideal world we should have used 3.5kg of polymer. We actually used 4.2kg of polymer granules.

Yield= 3.5/4.2 = 83%

We know that around 500g of material was wasted when we had to throw away five defective pen pots. The remaining 200g might be worth investigating if the material is expensive or we start to produce a lot of them.

For more complex yield examples, see Production Improvement 'KPI Family: L2' on page 395.

Definition or formula

Yield = [Optimum quantity of material for good finished products] / [Actual quantity of material for finished goods]

Typical data sources

» Production records
» Quality records

Common problems and mistakes

Yield can get a bit tricky if you have multiple raw materials involved in a product. Knowing the 'bill of materials' (BoM, or 'ingredients list') can make the calculation a lot easier. The hardest yield calculations are where you have complex groupings of ingredients or components and losses part way through the process (i.e. you don't lose a 'whole' finished product, rather part of it).

KPI Family: 02
Efficiency - Hours

Orders - Hours work

Ref: O2.1.1.1
Gold Star KPI

Drives: We have a pipeline of work
To: We make best use of time available

Description

Knowing how many hours you have booked can enable you to plan your work (and, if necessary, marketing and sales activity).

This is a leading indicator of income and needs to be closely watched - especially if you are in a business with little 'spontaneous' activity - business that turns up expectedly.

Example from Pointless Prose

Patricia does some online coaching for writers. She charges based on an hourly rate. Next week she has 4 hours of work which, based on her terms and conditions, are non-refundable and are now considered booked.

Order hours: 4 (for next week)

Definition or formula

Sum of [Booked hours work]

Typical data sources

Sales notes, contracts, sales pipeline spreadsheet or sales software

Utilisation

Ref: O2.1.2.2
Gold Star KPI

Drives: We manage staff utilisation
To: We make best use of time available

Description

Utilisation shows how many hours you did bill compared with how many hours you could have billed. It's a measure of how **productively** busy you are.

You are almost never going to get anywhere near to, or want to get anywhere close to, 100% utilisation. Don't worry about your actual figure being much, much lower. Just try not to fall into the trap of thinking 100% is the target then starting to take out activities that must happen but aren't productive - like meetings. If you do this then you start to lose sight of the things that rob everyone of their productivity. Focus instead on getting rid of pointless time wasting activities.

Example from Pointless Prose

Patricia plans to do 10 hours of hourly-billed work a week. Last week she did 6 billed hours.

Utilisation: 6/10 = 60%

Definition or formula

[Billed hours] / [Available billable hours]

Typical data sources

» Time and attendance records
» Activity logs, task records
» Timesheets
» Contract hours
» Overtime logs

Hours billed

Ref: O2.1.2.3
Gold Star KPI

Drives: We manage staff utilisation
To: We make best use of time available

Description

The life-blood of any hourly-billed business is the number of hours billed. Most businesses don't need much reminding to keep a close eye on this. No billed hours = no income.

Keep notes of what you were doing, not just the hours you did, and consider supplying that log when you invoice. This may head off any challenges about why things took the time they did.

Example from Pointless Prose

Last week Patricia delivered and invoiced 6 hours of work…

Hours billed = 6

Definition or formula

Sum of [Time billed]

Typical data sources

» Time logging software
» Time sheets
» Invoices

If you bill at an hourly rate, but do fractions of an hour be sure to keep accurate records for billing.

Common problems and mistakes

Be careful about under-billing. Many freelancers will throw extra time into work and then not bill for it. Whilst this can build customer satisfaction it can also set a dangerous precedent and could displace other paid work, if you are busy and in demand.

Efficiency - Hours

Efficiency - Per Word Billing

Writing productivity

Ref: O3.1.1.1
Silver Star KPI

Drives: We are productive writers
To: We make best use of time available

Description
Productivity is simply 'at what rate did we do our work?'. For writing our measure is Output (words) / Time (hours).

Many word processors, including Microsoft Word, record total editing time and word count, making it easy to calculate this.

Example from Pointless Prose
Patricia wrote a series of stories and articles for 'Out of your Shell', the world-renowned tortoise-horror magazine. She is paid by the word and it took her 9 hours to write three articles totally 2,500 words.

Writing productivity: 2,500/9 = 278 words per hour

Definition or formula
Sum of [Sold or saleable words] / Sum of [Writing time]

Typical data sources
» Personal writing logs - for time
» Software timers - word processors
» Sales and invoice records for number of words sold

Common problems and mistakes
If you do use your word processor's editing timer just make sure you don't clone and edit an existing document as it will screw up the editing time.

Make sure you are consistent in units. Don't mix hours with minutes or word counts in 1,000s and 1s.

Paid words written

Ref: O3.1.1.3
Gold Star KPI

Drives: We are productive writers
To: We make best use of time available

Description
The life-blood of any per-word-billed business is the number of words billed. Most businesses don't need much reminding to keep a close eye on this. No billed words = no income.

Example from Pointless Prose
Patricia's three published articles this week contained..

Paid written words: 2,500 words

Definition or formula
Sum of [Paid words written]

Typical data sources
» Sales invoices
» Sales records

Booked work

Ref: O3.1.2.1
Gold Star KPI

Drives: We have a pipeline of work
To: We make best use of time available

Description

Knowing how many words you have booked can enable you to plan your work (and, if necessary, marketing and sales activity).

This is a leading indicator of income and needs to be closely watched - especially if you are in a business with little 'spontaneous' activity - business that turns up expectedly.

Example from Pointless Prose

Patricia has been asked by 'Out of Your Shell' magazine to produce 2,000 words a week for the next 3 months. So her booked work is…

Booked work: 2,000 words for each of the next 12 weeks

Definition or formula

Sum of [Booked words] per period

Typical data sources

» Contracts
» Emails showing agreement
» Booking records

Common problems and mistakes

Just be clear on what you mean by booked. Do you mean 'verbally agreed' or 'contractually agreed'. Whatever you choose, be consistent.

Writing utilisation

Ref: O3.1.3.2
Silver Star KPI

Drives: We manage staff utilisation
To: We make best use of time available

Description

Even though you are selling words, it is **time** that enables you to write. Utilisation shows how many words you *did bill* compared with how many words you *could have billed* if you had written at the *optimum writing rate* for all the time available. You are almost never going to get anywhere near to, or want to get anywhere close to, 100% utilisation. Don't worry about your actual figure being much, much lower. Just try not to fall into the trap of thinking 100% is the target then starting to take out activities that must happen but aren't productive - like meetings. If you do this then you start to lose sight of the things that rob everyone of their productivity. Focus instead on getting rid of pointless time wasting activities or interruptions that drop your effective writing rate.

Example from Pointless Prose

Patricia plans to do 10 hours of word-billed work a week. Her optimum writing rate is 300 words per hour. She actually wrote for 9 hours last week and wrote 2,500 words. So, if we divide her output by her ideal writing rate -

2,500/300 = optimal writing equivalent = 8.3 hours

Utilisation: 8.3/10 = 83%

Definition or formula

([Sold words] / [Optimal writing rate]) / [Available billable hours]

Typical data sources

» Sales invoices
» Work hours log
» Billed words
» Optimal writing rate (you will need to figure this out)

Common problems and mistakes

This measure is almost an efficiency measure, as we use the 'How long should it have taken to write those words' in our calculation. The reason for doing this is that when we are not very busy we tend to lower our output rate (productivity) to fill the time, which can skew the utilisation measure.

Average billing rate per 1,000 words

Ref: O3.2.1.1
Gold Star KPI

Drives: We bill at the optimum £ rate
To: We get best value from working time

Description

Your two levers of income as a writer are:

1. How many words you write

2. How much you are paid for the words you sell

By keeping your average billing rate as high as possible you maximise the reward for your effort.

There is clearly going to be a trade off between achieving the maximum billing rate and keeping a good flow of work arriving - high prices may deter some custom.

Example from Pointless Prose

Patricia is paid...

* *£350 per 1,000 words by 'Out of Your Shell' magazine*
* *£250 per 1,000 words by 'Scared Shell-less' magazine*

She sold 2,000 words to 'Out of Your Shell' and 3,000 words to 'Scared Shell-less'.

Her total income was £700+£750=£1,450 and her total word count was 5,000 words.

Average billing rate per 1,000 words = £1,450/5 (thousand) words = £290

Definition or formula

Sum of [Writing income] / Sum of [Paid words in 1,000s]

Typical data sources

» Sales invoices
» Word counts

Common problems and mistakes

Remember you are billing per 1,000 words, not per word, so divide by 5, not 5,000, if you wrote 5,000 words!

Efficiency - Contract Services

Booked days of work

Ref: O4.1.1.1
Gold Star KPI

Drives: We have a pipeline of work
To: We make best use of time available

Description

This shows us how many confirmed days of billed work we have ahead of us. This is firm work, that we should count on turning into revenue, barring any unexpected mishaps.

You need to put this into context, depending on the type of work you do. Some types of work are booked on the morning of delivery, other types, like a wedding photographer, may be booked months or even years ahead. Based on knowledge of your business you can decide how critical this is to your success and income.

Example from Ambiguous Associates

Austin is the only consultant at AA at the moment and he has 10 days of booked work for the month ahead.

Booked days of work for next period: 10 days

Definition or formula

Count of [Days booked work] for period

Typical data sources

» Sales pipeline spreadsheet
» Sales software

Days available

Ref: O4.1.2.1
Silver Star KPI

Drives: We manage staff utilisation
To: We make best use of time available

Description

This shows how many days are available for billed work. We would arrive at this figure by starting with the total nominal available working days in the year, then deducting holidays, training days and any other anticipated non-working days - such as legally required lost days (e.g. legally mandated certification or inspection). We will need this figure to work out 'Utilisation'.

Example from Ambiguous Associates

Austin works weekdays, but keeps one day a month free for non-billable work such as admin.

Days available for billable work in next period: 19

Definition or formula

[Working days in period] - [Planned non-working days in period]

Typical data sources

» Resource planning spreadsheet
» Wall holiday planner

Utilisation

Ref: O4.1.2.2
Silver Star KPI

Drives: We manage staff utilisation
To: We make best use of time available

Description

Utilisation shows what proportion of the days we could have billed that we actually billed. This is a kind of efficiency measure for selling-your-time types of businesses.

Example from Ambiguous Associates

Last month Austin had 20 days available for billable work. He actually billed 19 days.

Utilisation: 19/20 = 95%

Definition or formula

Count of [Billed days] / ([Working days in period] - [Planned non-working days in period])

Typical data sources

» Calendar notes
» Written records
» Invoices
» Time logging software
» Time sheets

Days billed

Ref: O4.1.2.3
Gold Star KPI

Drives: We manage staff utilisation
To: We make best use of time available

Description

Billed days is simply the number of days of work which were billed to clients. This is the other figure required to calculate utilisation.

Example from Ambiguous Associates

Austin worked 19 days last month.

Days billed: 19

Definition or formula

Count of [Billed days]

Typical data sources

» Calendar notes
» Written records
» Invoices

Unit delivery cost

Ref: O4.3.0.1
Silver Star KPI

To: We get best value from billing days

Description
This is the cost associated with delivery, for instance hotel costs (if not paid by client) or travel to and from the client site.

The cost of delivering a project can eat into your margin substantially if you don't have an agreement to charge the client expenses, especially if you have an obligation to be in a certain place at a certain time. Last minute flights and hotel rooms in booked-out capital cities can be eye-wateringly expensive.

Example from Ambiguous Associates
Austin's recent work involved his company, AA, covering all expenses. His expenses for 19 days work were £3,800.

£3,800/19 = £200 per day

Unit (day) delivery costs: £200 per day.

Definition or formula
Sum of [Delivery expenses and costs] / Count of [Billed days]

Typical data sources
» Calendar notes
» Written records
» Invoices
» Accounting records
» Expense records

Common problems and mistakes
Be clear whether this figure is inclusive or exclusive of sales tax

Average billing rate per day

Ref: O4.3.1.1
Gold Star KPI

Drives: We bill at the optimum day rate
To: We get best value from billing days

Description
It can be tempting to win business by reducing your day rate. Keeping an eye on this measure can help you understand whether you are still price-competitive, over or under-priced.

Example from Ambiguous Associates
Austin has two clients, the Careless Corporation and Ghouls Global. He charges Careless Corporation £1,550 a day and Ghouls Global £2,100 a day for his time. He worked for Ghouls for 9 days and Careless for 10 days.

* *Total revenue: 9 x £2,100 + 10 x £1,550 = £34,400*
* *Days worked: 19*

Average billing rate per day: £34,400/19 = £1,811

Definition or formula
Sum of [Invoiced day rate income] / Count of [Billed days]

Typical data sources
» Calendar notes
» Written records
» Invoices
» Accounting records

Common problems and mistakes
It can get a little confusing if you mix expensed work with non-expensed work. One solution is to knock off your expenses from non-expensed day rates and use that Net figure, instead of the headline rate.

Efficiency - Service Delivery

System availability

Ref: O5.2.1.2
Gold Star KPI

Drives: We minimise system downtime
To: We run our process efficiently

Description

For some businesses it's impossible to work without certain critical systems. Having these systems available, and knowing when they are down, is important.

If your systems are provided by a third party then having reliable data on outages (data you need to calculate availability) puts you in a much stronger negotiating position.

Example from Roughshod Repairs

Roughshod rely on their case handling and telephony systems in order to handle calls and process claims. They had a major outage last month, taking the call system down for 2 hours. Their planned opening hours are 70 hours a week - 280 hours last month.

System availability = (280-2)/280 = 99.3% availability

Definition or formula

(Sum of [Total intended up time] - Sum of [Lost time due to outage]) / Sum of [Total intended up time]

Typical data sources

» System logs
» Manual data capture

Common problems and mistakes

Although system logs look nice and accurate, it's always good to have a manual log as well - manual logs can have much richer information on the reason for the outage - making problem solving much simpler.

'Right first time' services delivered

Ref: O5.2.2.1
Gold Star KPI

Drives: We minimise mistakes and rework (waste)
To: We run our process efficiently

Description

Getting things right first time keeps customers happy, costs low and staff in a good mood.

Right first time can be a leading indicator of complaints too.

Example from Roughshod Repairs

Ruby insists that any problems, meaning something was done again, with Roughshod Repair's processes are recorded. The staff do this on a shared spreadsheet. Ruby then looks at the overall number of tasks and calculates the 'Right first time figure'.

* *RMA instructions issued:*   12,000 Done,   400 Redone
* *Technician visit arranged:*   8,000 Done,   1,200 Redone
* *Repaired:*   7,000 Done,   1,000 Redone
* *Case closed:*   11,900 Done,   300 Redone

Total activities: 38,900

Total activities redone: 2,900

Right first time rate: (38,900-2,900)/38,900 = 93%

Definition or formula

(Count of [Activities] - Count of [Activities redone]) / Count of [Activities]

Typical data sources

» Ticket system
» Manual logs

Common problems and mistakes

If rework activities vary dramatically in duration and seriousness you may decide not to consolidate them. One way you could create a consolidated figure is to do it on the basis of correction cost or labour hours. To make this work you need to have fairly robust data on the standard timings and process costs.

Procurement & Supply

Market price comparator by product - percentage deviation

Ref: O6.1.1.1
Gold Star KPI

Drives: The prices we agree are competitive
To: We obtain goods and services at the optimal cost

Description

This comparator allows us to see what percentage above or below competitors' prices we are paying. You may choose to make the comparison against the market average, or against a selection of specific suppliers.

Despite the slightly long-winded title, this is about comparing the prices we are paying for goods and services with alternative suppliers. Whilst we may consciously choose a premium product or service, it's always useful to be aware of the 'going rate' and how much we pay above or below that average.

Example from Chaos Coffee Shop

Charlie likes to buy raw premium Arabica beans from a specific estate in Costa Rica. These beans are hand-selected by Capuchin monkeys bred just for that task and are processed under the full moon using a secret family process. He pays £10 per kg for his special green beans. His research shows an average market price of £8.25 for similar beans, so...

Market price comparator: (£10-£8.25)/£8.25 = +21%

So Charlie is paying around 21% above the current average market price for green Arabica beans from Costa Rica. He's going to ask if the monkeys can work a little harder.

Definition or formula

([Price we pay] - [Comparator price]) / [Comparator price}

Note: You may decide to use a market average as your comparator.

Typical data sources

» Internet research
» Trade body figures
» Trade journals
» Supplier research and quotations

Weighted market price comparator by product - percentage deviation

Ref: O6.1.1.2
Silver Star KPI

Drives: The prices we agree are competitive
To: We obtain goods and services at the optimal cost

Description

Where you need a selection of goods or services it can sometimes be useful to put together a 'basket' of supplies and/or services required for your product. This 'basket' can then be costed and you see the impact on the 'cost of goods sold' for specific products/services you are making/ delivering.

Example from Chaos Coffee Shop

To make a basic cup of coffee, we need a cup, coffee, milk and sugar. About half of the medium Americanos that Charlie sells have milk in them. Based on current costs, Charlie's cup costs are made up like this...

		Current	*Price comparator*
*	Coffee:	£0.10	£0.08
*	Paper cup and lid:	£0.09	£0.09
*	Milk (50%):	£0.02	£0.02
*	Sleeve:	£0.02	£0.02
*	Sugar:	£0.02	£0.01
*	**Cup of coffee**	**£0.25**	**£0.22**

Weighted market price comparator: (0.25 - 0.22) / 0.22 = +13.6%

So compared with the average market price, Charlie could potentially shave 3p a cup off his costs by going for the average market price.

Definition or formula

(Sum of [Price we pay for each item in basket] - Sum of [Comparator price for each item in basket]) / Sum of [Comparator price for each item in basket]

Note: You may decide to use a market average as your comparator.

Typical data sources

» Internet research
» Trade body figures
» Trade journals
» Supplier research and quotations

Audit fail percentage

Ref: O6.2.1.3
Silver Star KPI

Drives: Products/services comply with legal & safety rules
To: We manage procurement risk

Description

Where we rely on supplier certification, we must audit that certification occasionally to check that it is valid. This measure is a count of the number of audit fails on supplier certificated goods or services.

An audit fail can signal very major issues, especially if it uncovers issues that have reached the market, that have been going on for a long time and have significant safety or warranty implications.

Example from Chaos Coffee Shop

Charlie's beans come with a guaranteed moisture content of no more than 12%. Each batch has a certificate showing the actual value. More than this and they can start rotting, and of course you are paying for water rather than coffee beans.

Charlie has randomly checked the sacks of green beans with his calibrated hand-held moisture meter. He finds that three out of the ten he tested are above 12% moisture. He's not happy!

* *Audit tests run: 10*
* *Audit tests failed: 3*

Audit test failure rate: 3/10 = 30%

Definition or formula

Count of [Audit tests failed] / Count of [Audit tests taken]

Typical data sources

» Quality audit records

Total cost of supplier quality issues

Ref: O6.2.2.4
Silver Star KPI

Drives: Products/services comply with internal requirements
To: We manage procurement risk

Description

Keeping an eye on the cost impact of supplier issues enables us to minimise process disruption caused by suppliers and to quantify the impact of those issues - crucial for review and negotiation of contracts in future.

Example from Chaos Coffee Shop

Charlie tracks any refunds and replacements he makes when there are coffee quality issues.

Charlie's team have had a steady stream of complaints showing in the customer service log book, complaining about a lack of aroma and bitter taste in his Charming Charlie blend of coffee. Charlie has been offering a refund, a free replacement with his 'Astounding Arabica' coffee, and a voucher for a free cup of coffee to calm these customers down in the short term.

Looking at the log book, he sees 20 complaints from last month. Each complaint will represent three cups of coffee costs (the original coffee, a replacement cup with a different blend and a voucher for another). The cost of a cup of coffee is £0.25, so 20 complaints...

Total cost of supplier quality issues: 20 complaints x 3 cups cost x £0.25 = £15

Of course the more serious issue may be the people who don't bother complaining but start going to a competitor for their daily coffee instead.

Definition or formula

Sum of [Additional costs associated with identified quality issues]

Typical data sources

» Quality records

Inbound deliveries on time and in full percentage (OTIF)

Ref: O6.3.1.1
Gold Star KPI

Drives: Supplies are delivered on time and in full
To: Our suppliers offer acceptable operational performance

Description

To keep our operation running smoothly we need to have what we ordered delivered on time and in full (i.e. the delivery is complete).

Example from Chaos Coffee Shop

Late deliveries can stop business. When the milk delivery didn't turn up last week it crippled sales for an hour until one of the staff could nip to the local supermarket.

* *Chaos Coffee had 78 deliveries scheduled last month. One was late.*
* *Also, of those 78 deliveries scheduled last month, three were incomplete, missing Danish Whirls in those deliveries.*
* *Late or incomplete deliveries - 4*

On time in full deliveries = (78-4)/78 = 94.9%

Definition or formula

(Count of [Inbound deliveries] - Count of [Late and/or incomplete deliveries]) / Count of [Inbound deliveries]

Typical data sources

» Delivery notes
» Order records
» Stock management system

Number of quality issues identified in deliveries

Ref: O6.3.1.3
Gold Star KPI

Drives: Supplies are delivered on time and in full
To: Our suppliers offer acceptable operational performance

Description

Quality issues from suppliers can affect us and our customers in multiple negative ways. The first step in addressing these problems is identifying (and recording) them as early as possible. If you aren't clear exactly what the 'delivery time' *is* (perhaps goods go to an internal warehouse then out to production sites), use 'the earliest point we can realistically identify quality issues' as a guide.

Supplier quality issues can have a bad effect on us in many ways, including:

* Delayed production runs
* Excess process downtime
* Product returns
* Warranty claims
* Reputational damage
* Workforce frustration

Example from Chaos Coffee Shop

Charlie identified three sacks of coffee beans with excessive moisture. His team also found that some of the donuts were leaking jam - on three separate occasions.

Number of quality issues in month: 6

Definition or formula

Count of [Quality issues identified]

Typical data sources

» Quality records

Value of past-terms payments withheld

Ref: O6.4.2.1
Silver Star KPI

Drives: We treat our suppliers decently
To: We manage a contracts and suppliers effectively

Description

Some organisations systematically withhold payment to suppliers. In other situations payments may be withheld whilst genuine supply issues are sorted out. This figure shows you the value of outstanding payments to suppliers that are now 'past agreed terms'.

Withholding payments is a short-term cash flow tactic that can damage suppliers and your relationship with them. If you are going to do this, then at least knowing the value of these withheld payments and managing them closely should prevent it going out of control.

Example from Chaos Coffee Shop

Charlie is withholding payment for the sacks of coffee beans that he found to be over their certified maximum moisture. The value of these beans is £200.

Value of past-terms payments withheld: £200

Definition or formula

Sum of [Value of payments past agreed days]

Typical data sources

» Invoices, accounting system
» Work records
» Accounting software

Average days payment deviation from the agreed terms

Ref: O6.4.3.1
Silver Star KPI

Drives: We manage supplier payment fairly and promptly
To: We manage a contracts and suppliers effectively

Description

Some organisations systematically withhold payment to suppliers. In other situations payments may be withheld whilst genuine supply issues are sorted out. This figure shows you the average number of days 'past agreed terms' of outstanding payments to suppliers.

Withholding payments is a short-term cash flow tactic that can damage suppliers and your relationship with them. If you are going to do this, then at least knowing how many days past 'agreed payment terms' these payments are and managing them closely should prevent it going out of control.

Example from Chaos Coffee Shop

The payments Charlie is withholding due to excess moisture in beans are 10 days past payment terms. As he deals with a single supplier and there has been one month's invoice affected so far, the average days past payment terms is also 10 days.

Average days payment deviation from the agreed terms: 10

Definition or formula

Average of [Days payments past agreed days]

Typical data sources

» Invoices
» Accounting system
» Work records
» Accounting software

455

Total procurement admin cost

Ref: O6.5.1.1
Silver Star KPI

Drives: Cost of running the procurement function
To: We manage the cost of procurement

Description

It costs money to administer procurement. If it's a figure of interest to you, then you might decide to track it.

You may decide to recharge particular elements, especially around non-conformances, to your supplier. To do this accurately, a cost breakdown of your procurement admin costs is very useful. You may also want to include any additional operational costs or losses arising from those supply issues in the cost.

Example from Chaos Coffee Shop

Charlie looks at his, and the team's, time spent administering suppliers and deliveries. When he multiplies that by his and the team's hourly rate he estimates it costs him about £70 a week.

Total procurement admin cost: £70 per week

Definition or formula

Sum of [Administrative costs]

Typical data sources

» Hourly labour costs
» Estimated effort
» Time logs

Fulfilment - Product & Services

Sales lost or cancelled due to supply issues

Ref: O7.1.1.3
Gold Star KPI

Drives: We have orders in stock
To: We deliver the right products/services at the agreed time

Description

The percentage of orders where we are unable to supply a customer and they cancel the order.

Each cancelled order is a loss to your business, but it's also the 'tip of the iceberg' when it comes to delivery time dissatisfaction. You can be sure that for every person who cancels a late order there are many, many, more who are unhappy. You will also have an uphill struggle persuading someone who cancelled to come back to you again.

Example from Mayhem Manufacturing

After production problems with the Volcano pen pots, which were on back order for several weeks, 5 customers cancelled their orders out of a queue of 280 orders that month.

Sales lost or cancelled due to supply issues: 5/280 = 1.8%

Definition or formula

Count of [Orders cancelled due to supply issues] / Count of [Orders]

Typical data sources

» Sales system
» Order management system

Common problems and mistakes

It may not always be possible to identify why a customer cancelled an order. If that's the case, then asking in a polite, non-confrontational, way is a good start.

Delivered on time

Ref: O7.1.3.1
Silver Star KPI

Drives: We deliver on time
To: We deliver the right products/services at the agreed time

Description

Dispatching the parcel is only part of the service. The carrier still needs to get it there on time. This figure will show if they are delivering on their promises.

Most delivery systems, be it parcels, emails or messages, have a confirmation of delivery. We can use this confirmation and time of delivery to compile this information.

Example from Mayhem Manufacturing

Mayhem send many of their products by parcel delivery service. Last month, out of the 265 parcels sent on time, 252 were delivered (or attempted) on time.

Delivered on time percentage: = 252/265 = 95.1%

Definition or formula

Count of [Delivery attempted on time] / Count of [Orders dispatched]

Typical data sources

» Sales system
» Order management system
» Courier/postal reports or online portal

Common problems and mistakes

Be clear on whether you are only counting parcels that were dispatched on time, or including all parcels - even ones that were sent late.

Also be clear on whether you count an attempted delivery as 'On time'. Generally you would count this, as it's often not in the courier's control whether the customer is available to receive delivery or not.

On time in full (OTIF) - outbound

Ref: O7.1.3.4
Gold Star KPI

Drives: We deliver on time
To: We deliver the right products/services at the agreed time

Description

A measure of 'Did we complete orders on time?' shown as a percentage of all the orders sent.

The OTIF figure gives a useful 'at a glance' indicator of the overall health of your fulfilment operation. Lots of things can derail OTIF, so you may have to look deeper if it starts to trend the wrong way.

Example from Mayhem Manufacturing

Of the 275 orders that Mayhem needed to dispatch last month, 265 were sent on time and in full.

On time in full (OTIF) % - outbound: 265/275 = 96.4%

Definition or formula

Count of [Orders dispatched on-time and in full] / Count of [Orders dispatched]

Typical data sources

» Sales system
» Order management system

Common problems and mistakes

You may send partial orders, where agreed with the customer. If it has been agreed then you should count this as OTIF. If it has not been agreed in advance with the customer then it is not OTIF.

Delivery contents complaints

Ref: O7.2.1.1
Silver Star KPI

To: We make it simple and easy for customers to order

Description

Was the right item delivered? Was it in good condition? When customers complain about the content of the delivery, this is the figure that shows the percentage of orders with complaints.

Like any kind of complaint, each actual complaint may well represent many more unhappy customers who didn't get round to complaining. Understanding the root cause of the issue can help you head-off future complaints.

Example from Mayhem Manufacturing

Out of 275 orders sent last month, one customer complained about their volcanoes being a different colour from the web photo and two complained of damaged products.

Delivery contents complaints %: 3/275 = 1.1%

Definition or formula

Count of [Order contents complaints] / Count of [Orders dispatched]

Typical data sources

» Sales system
» Order management system

Common problems and mistakes

It may be worth classifying content complaints, as there are lots of different types of complaints, from condition, design through to colour.

Returns rate as percentage of orders

Ref: O7.3.1.1
Silver Star KPI

Drives: We manage our returns rate
To: We make it easy to sort out fulfilment problems

Description

How many orders were sent back using your returns process, as a percentage?

Returns, whilst an essential part of most businesses, have a cost associated and may also be an early indicator of other underlying issues. Keep an eye on this figure and investigate if it starts moving.

Example from Mayhem Manufacturing

Five orders were returned out of the 275 sent last month.

Returns rate as % of orders: 5/275 = 1.8%

Definition or formula

Count of [Orders returns] / Count of [Orders dispatched]

Typical data sources

» Sales system
» Order management system

Common problems and mistakes

If some returns are much more costly than others, consider also tracking returns costs (possibly as a % of sales).

Average return to refund/replace days

Ref: O7.3.2.1
Silver Star KPI

Drives: We manage our returns process
To: We make it easy to sort out fulfilment problems

Description

Customers want swift, hassle-free, returns and refunds. Measuring this average duration will help you monitor your refund/replace process.

Example from Mayhem Manufacturing

From receipt of a return, Mayhem's team turn around and refund on the same day. Depending on where you start and stop the clock:

From receipt to issuing the refund: 1 working day
From postage to cleared funds: 4 working days

Clearly the second measure is a better measure of customer experience, but is affected by factors such as the country the customer is in, the speed of courier used by the customer for the return and the speed at which the customer's bank clears funds.

Definition or formula

[Payment receipt time for customer] - [Return dispatch time, from customer]

or

[Payment authorisation time by supplier] - [Return receipt time, at supplier]

Typical data sources

» Sales system
» Order management system
» Courier/postal reports or online portal
» Bank account payment records

Common problems and mistakes

Be clear on whether you:

• Include just business days, or calendar days?
• Start the clock from when the customer sends the parcel (good, but trickier to measure) or when you receive the return?
• Count a refund from when it was *issued* or when the customer has cleared funds in their account?

Call, Email & Webchat Handling

Average speed of answer

Ref: O8.1.1.1
Gold Star KPI

Drives: We answer calls rapidly
To: We deal well with customer calls

Description
How quickly did our team answer a call, on average?

Clearly faster is better here, unless you have some unhealthy drivers around wanting to make it harder to access real humans as a cunning plan to herd people towards your self-service online offering - driving down cost (and driving up customer irritation).

Example from Roughshod Repairs
Ruby interrogates her contact centre software and finds that the

Average speed of answer (for yesterday): 12 seconds

Next she decided to look at the call abandon rate to see whether that figure supported the rosy picture painted by the 'Average speed to answer' figure.

Definition or formula
Average of [Time from first connection to answer by human]

Typical data sources
» Contact centre software

Common problems and mistakes
The average speed of answer only tells part of the story. It could be that we had terrible performance for a small part of the day. Look at the call duration histogram, or distribution, to get the full picture. Also look at the 'speed of answer' across the full day and week.

Call abandon rate

Ref: O8.1.1.2
Gold Star KPI

Drives: We answer calls rapidly
To: We deal well with customer calls

Description
When customers get really fed up with waiting to have their calls answered they will hang up. This figure shows the percentage of calls that were abandoned by the customer.

Call abandonment is a much better measure than arbitrary measures (for example 80:20, aiming to have 80% of calls answered in 20 seconds - who says that is 'good'?). Remember though, an abandoned call is just the tip of the 'dissatisfaction' iceberg. For every person who gets fed up and hangs up, there will be more who are very irritated but hang on in hope of their call being answered - so don't take a low figure for abandonment on face value.

Example from Roughshod Repairs
Out of 554 inbound calls received yesterday there were 28 abandoned calls.

Call abandon rate: 28/554 = 5%

Looking closely at the time-line of abandonments, Ruby notices they are entirely clustered around lunch time, with none happening outside of a 12:00 to 14:00 window.

Definition or formula
Count of [Calls abandoned] / Count of [Calls received]

Typical data sources
» Contact centre software

Total calls handled

Ref: O8.1.2.1
Gold Star KPI

Drives: We handle calls efficiently
To: We deal well with customer calls

Description

Total calls handled shows you how busy your centre has been.

Remember to add in abandonment figures if you want to get a demand figure.

Example from Roughshod Repairs

Ruby uses the contact centre software to pull up the 'calls handled count' for yesterday. The system reports...

Calls handled: 526

Definition or formula

Count of [Calls received]

Typical data sources

» Contact centre software

Calls handled per agent per active hour

Ref: O8.1.2.2
Gold Star KPI

Drives: We handle calls efficiently
To: We deal well with customer calls

Description

This figure shows agent productivity.

Having a very high, or low, figure can be an indicator of problems, particularly when associated with specific agents. Too high may indicate rushed or incomplete calls. Too low may indicate skills issues or a chatterbox. You can't diagnose issues from this data, but it does tell you where to look.

Example from Roughshod Repairs

There were 15 agents on duty yesterday, putting in a total of 90 active agent hours. During that day the team handled 526 calls.

Calls handled per agent per active hour: 526/90 = 5.8 calls per agent hour

Definition or formula

Count of [Calls handled] / Sum of [Active agent hours]

Typical data sources

» Contact centre software

Volume of calls by reason code

Ref: O8.1.2.3
Silver Star KPI

Drives: We handle calls efficiently
To: We deal well with customer calls

Description

Breaking down calls by reason code means we can start to understand why people are contacting us.

Understanding the reasons people contact us enables us to:

- Identify high importance problems and issues
- Adjust our product and service based on issues identified
- Create self-service channels to reduce handling costs - e.g. specific redirects to a dedicated web page
- Use recorded message for specific issues, for queuing customers
- Focus and improve our agent training to be able to handle most common issues

Example from Roughshod Repairs

Of the calls handled, analysis showed the following:

* *Warranty claims: 300 calls*
* *Technical question: 100 calls*
* *Missed appointments: 60 calls*
* *Failed repair: 40 calls*
* *Change of appointment: 26 calls*

As the team are not there to handle technical queries, and failed repairs are something we should not have in an ideal world, the Roughshod Repairs improvement team decide to focus on these for their next improvement project.

Definition or formula

Count of [Calls received] by reason code

Typical data sources

» Contact centre software

Common problems and mistakes

Misclassification can completely ruin this type of analysis. Regular agent training and engagement, along with feedback on misclassification, is essential to get accurate and reliable classification of call reasons.

Average cost per call resolved

Ref: O8.1.2.7
Silver Star KPI

Drives: We handle calls efficiently
To: We deal well with customer calls

Description

The average cost per call resolved gives you a useful yard-stick, based on outcomes (call is resolved) rather than activity (we handle calls).

This metric will encourage the team to focus on managing resources to the right level and resolving customer cases.

Example from Roughshod Repairs

Ruby takes the agent cost per hour (£10) and the number of agent hours (working hours) from yesterday (90) and divides it by the number of calls resolved (490):

Average cost per call resolved: 90 x 10/490= £1.84 per call

Definition or formula

Sum of [Active agent hours] x [Average agent cost per hour] / Count of [Calls resolved]

Typical data sources

» Contact centre software
» Payroll

Call handler utilisation

Ref: O8.1.2.10
Silver Star KPI

Drives: We handle calls efficiently
To: We deal well with customer calls

Description

Utilisation is a measure of how occupied our team is. Being occupied does not automatically mean they are being productive, but it can be a useful indicator of a big mismatch between resource and demand. If your utilisation goes too high it will often lead to extended/degraded waiting times for customers contacting you.

There is a fine balancing act between having reasonably high utilisation (keeping costs under control) and having agents available to handle the inevitable surges in contact centre demand. Forecasting, often using the Erlang C formula, can help you tread this fine line.

Example from Roughshod Repairs

Interrogating the call centre software, Ruby finds that her agents were active on calls for 70 of the 90 active agent hours.

Call handler utilisation: 70 / 90 = 78%

Definition or formula

Sum of [Call handler active hours] / Sum of [Available agent hours]

Typical data sources

» Contact centre software
» Time and attendance system

First touch resolution

Ref: O8.1.2.11
Gold Star KPI

Drives: We handle calls efficiently
To: We deal well with customer calls

Description

When a customer contacts us, the ideal is to resolve their issue or problem in the first call, email or webchat. This measure shows the percentage of inbound contacts that get fully resolved in that first contact.

First touch resolution, though not always possible, has many benefits. It reduces hand-offs, which are a common source of additional cost and often generate errors and mis-understandings. Customers generally only have to explain themselves once, only have one agent to deal with and tend to get sorted more quickly - leading to higher levels of customer satisfaction.

Example from Roughshod Repairs

Looking at call+email+webchat summaries for closed cases Ruby sees that...

* *Cases handled last month: 14,400*
* *Cases resolved at first touch: 6,800*

First touch resolution percentage for last month: 47%

Definition or formula

Count of [Cases resolved on first touch] / Count of [Cases closed]

Typical data sources

» Contact centre software

465

Post-call feedback scores

Ref: O8.1.3.1
Gold Star KPI

Drives: We handle the calls interaction well
To: We deal well with customer calls

Description
The score given by a customer at the end of a call, typically rating the service they received, whether their issue was resolved and if they would recommend the service to others.

These scores can sometimes be actively manipulated by agents during the call preceding the survey. Some agents might say things such as 'Have I done everything I need to, to receive a 5 star rating from you today?'

Example from Roughshod Repairs
At the end of a call, callers are invited to punch a score into their handset, rating the call on a scale of 1-5.

Average 'Post-call feedback score' for calls to the Roughshod call centre last month was 4.3

Definition or formula
Average of [Customer feedback score for call]

Typical data sources
» Contact centre software

Call listening audit score

Ref: O8.1.3.2
Gold Star KPI

Drives: We handle the calls interaction well
To: We deal well with customer calls

Description
A call audit score is normally the outcome of a supervisor or trainer listening in on a sample of calls and rating the call on certain criteria.

The criteria for rating calls would often include:

- Greeting
- Correct verification
- Contact information verification
- Problem solving abilities
- Compliance with protocol
- Call handling skills
- Customer service quality (use of caller's name through call etc.)
- Script compliance
- Closure
- Follow up

The result of all of these elements would be a call score.

Example from Roughshod Repairs
Roughshod's head of quality, Rachael, listens in to at least two calls per agent per week. She completes a tracker in a spreadsheet and trends the scores over time. She uses a 100 point scale for the scores and is particularly interested in agents who are consistently above or below the average.

The current centre average call score is 73%

Definition or formula
Average of [Call listening audit score]

Typical data sources
» Audit tracker sheet or software

Incoming call volume

Ref: O8.1.4.1
Gold Star KPI

Drives: Right number of agents available to handle calls
To: We deal well with customer calls

Description
How many calls we received - a close proxy to the level of demand.

It's a proxy, not an exact indicator, of the amount of call-based work coming to us as calls can contain different numbers and complexities of issues.

Example from Roughshod Repairs
The call centre software tracks incoming call volumes and shows that for yesterday the volume was:

Incoming call volume: 554

Definition or formula
Count of [Incoming call volume]

Typical data sources
» Contact centre software

Volume - FTE forecast accuracy

Ref: O8.1.4.2
Silver Star KPI

Drives: Right number of agents available to handle calls
To: We deal well with customer calls

Description
This a measure of how many call handling staff we forecast that we would need versus how many we really should have had on the day (based on volume and patterns of demand)

The more accurate this figure is, the better chance we have to organise the right number of agents, delivering that oh-so-tricky balance of good agent utilisation and rapid response times.

Example from Roughshod Repairs
Looking at the volumes for yesterday...

* *The system predicted we would need 15 agents, with phased starts.*
* *In fact we needed 12 to deliver our target call wait time.*

Volume-FTE forecast accuracy: 12/15 = 80%

Definition or formula
Sum of [Actual required FTE] / Sum of [Forecast FTE]

Typical data sources
» Contact centre software or forecasting model, if separate

Average speed of email response

Ref: O8.2.1.1
Gold Star KPI

Drives: We answer emails rapidly
To: We deal well with customer emails

Description

How fast did we respond to the email?

An autoresponder (a machine generated email saying 'We have received your email and a human will respond to it at some point') is not really a response, just a reassurance that your email was delivered. With this measure we are talking about a real response.

Example from Roughshod Repairs

Ruby interrogates her contact centre software and finds that the

Average speed of response for emails yesterday: 3 minutes 10 seconds

Definition or formula

Average of [Speed of email response]

Typical data sources

» Contact centre software

Customer-chased emails

Ref: O8.2.1.2
Silver Star KPI

Drives: We answer emails rapidly
To: We deal well with customer emails

Description

When customers get fed up with waiting, they start chasing. This is the volume of emails generated through chasing.

These chasers are important for two reasons. Firstly, it shows that your customer service is falling below the customer/client's expectations. Secondly, this extra traffic will further worsen the backlog problems that caused you to be delayed in answering the original query - putting your contact centre into a death-spiral of demand outstripping capacity if you aren't careful.

To be able to analyse this information you will need your agents to classify or tag chaser emails as such, perhaps using a dedicated reason code.

Example from Roughshod Repairs

Rachael has set up a special reason code for chaser emails and finds that of the 55 emails received yesterday, 7 were chaser emails.

Percentage of customer-chased emails= 7 / 55 = 13%

Definition or formula

Count of [Chasing emails] / Count of [Emails received]

Typical data sources

» Contact centre software - requires allocated reason codes in reviewed emails

Common problems and mistakes

Sometimes 'chasers' come through a different channel from the original contact. If your CRM/ticket system allows, match all chasers with all tickets, regardless of channel, to get a full picture of what is going on.

Number of emails handled per agent per active hour

Ref: O8.2.2.1
Silver Star KPI

Drives: We handle emails efficiently
To: We deal well with customer emails

Description
This figure shows agent productivity.

Having a very high, or low, figure can be an indicator of problems, particularly when associated with specific agents. Too high may indicate rushed or incomplete emails. Too low may indicate skills issues. You can't diagnose issues from this data, but it does tell you where to look.

Example from Roughshod Repairs
There were 2 agents on email duty yesterday, putting in a total of 12 active agent hours. During that day the team handled 55 emails.

Emails handled per agent per active hour = 55/12 = 4.6 per agent hour

Definition or formula
Count of [Emails handled] / Sum of [Active agent hours]

Typical data sources
» Contact centre software

Average cost per email resolved

Ref: O8.2.2.5
Silver Star KPI

Drives: We handle emails efficiently
To: We deal well with customer emails

Description
The average cost per email resolved gives you a useful yard-stick, based on outcomes (issue is resolved) rather than activity (we handle emails).

This metric will encourage the team to focus on managing resources to the right level and resolving customer cases.

Example from Roughshod Repairs
Ruby takes the agent cost per hour (£10) and the number of email handling agent hours (working hours) from yesterday (12) and divides it by the number of emails resolved (55):

Average cost per email resolved = 12x10 / 55= £2.18 per email

Definition or formula
Sum of [Active agent hours] x [Average agent cost per hour] / Count of [Emails resolved]

Typical data sources
» Contact centre software
» Payroll

Volume of emails by reason code

Ref: O8.2.2.6
Silver Star KPI

Drives: We handle emails efficiently
To: We deal well with customer emails

Description
Breaking down emails by reason code means we can start to understand why people are contacting us.

Understanding the reasons people contact us enables us to:

- Identify high importance problems and issues
- Adjust our product and service based on issues identified
- Focus and improve our agent training to be able to handle most common issues

Example from Roughshod Repairs
Of the emails handled yesterday, analysis showed the following:

* *Warranty claims: 30 emails*
* *Technical question: 10 emails*
* *Chaser emails: 7*
* *Missed appointments: 4 emails*
* *Failed repair: 2 emails*
* *Change of appointment: 2 emails*

Definition or formula
Count of [Emails received] by reason code

Typical data sources
» Contact centre software

Total emails handled

Ref: O8.2.2.7
Gold Star KPI

Drives: We handle emails efficiently
To: We deal well with customer emails

Description
Total emails handled shows you how busy your centre has been.

It's a proxy, not an exact indicator, of the amount of email-based work coming to us as emails can raise different numbers and complexities of issues.

Example from Roughshod Repairs
Ruby uses the contact centre software to pull up the 'Emails handled count' for yesterday. The system reports...

Total emails handled = 55

Definition or formula
Count of [Emails received]

Typical data sources
» Contact centre software

Email handler utilisation

Ref: O8.2.2.8
Silver Star KPI

Drives: We handle emails efficiently
To: We deal well with customer emails

Description

Utilisation is a measure of how occupied our team is. Being occupied does not automatically mean they are being productive, but it can be a useful indicator of a big mismatch between resource and demand. If your utilisation goes too high it will often lead to extended/degraded waiting times for customers contacting you.

There is a fine balancing act between having reasonably high utilisation (keeping costs under control) and having agents available to handle the inevitable surges in contact centre demand. Forecasting, often using the Erlang C formula, can help you tread this fine line.

You may also need to consider follow-up work after the email. In our case study we are assuming there's no follow-up work, but your situation may be different.

Example from Roughshod Repairs

Interrogating the call centre software, Ruby finds that her agents were working on emails for 1.53 of the 12 active agent hours.

Email handler utilisation: 1.53 / 12 = 13%

Ruby is a little alarmed by this and is wondering whether to 'pool' call and email staff to relieve some of the pressure on the busy call handling staff.

Definition or formula

Sum of [Email handler active hours] / Sum of [Available email agent hours]

Typical data sources

» Contact centre software
» Time and attendance system

Post-response email feedback scores

Ref: O8.2.3.1
Gold Star KPI

Drives: We handle email interactions well
To: We deal well with customer emails

Description

The score given by a customer at the end of a case, typically rating the service they received, whether their issue was resolved and if they would recommend the service to others.

These scores can sometimes be actively manipulated by agents during the email preceding the survey. Some agents might write things such as 'Have I done everything I need to, to receive a 5 star rating from you today?'

Example from Roughshod Repairs

After the closure of their case emailers are sent a link inviting them to rate their experience on a scale of 1-5.

Average 'Post-resolution feedback score' for emails in the Roughshod call centre last month was 4.0

Definition or formula

Average of [Customer feedback score for email]

Typical data sources

» Contact centre software

Email response audit score

Ref: O8.2.3.2
Gold Star KPI

Drives: We handle email interactions well
To: We deal well with customer emails

Description

An email audit score is normally the outcome of a supervisor or trainer reviewing and scoring a sample of emails based on certain criteria.

The criteria for rating calls would often include:

- Greeting
- Problem solving abilities
- Compliance with protocol
- Email composition skills
- Customer service quality (tone, grammar, accuracy and so on)
- Standard response compliance (where appropriate)
- Closure
- Follow up

The result of all of these elements would be an email score.

Example from Roughshod Repairs

Roughshod's head of quality, Rachael, reviews at least two response emails per agent per week. She completes a tracker in a spreadsheet and trends the scores over time. She uses a 100 point scale for the scores and is particularly interested in agents who are consistently above or below the average.

The current centre average email response score is 79%

Definition or formula

Average of [Email response score]

Typical data sources

» Audit tracker sheet or software

Incoming email volume

Ref: O8.2.4.1
Gold Star KPI

Drives: Right number of agents available to handle emails well
To: We deal well with customer emails

Description

How many emails we received - a close proxy to the level of demand.

It's a proxy, not an exact indicator, of the amount of email-based work coming to us as an email can contain wildly different numbers and complexities of issues.

Example from Roughshod Repairs

The call centre software tracks incoming email volumes and shows that the volume for yesterday the volume was:

Incoming email volume: 55

Definition or formula

Count of [Incoming email volume]

Typical data sources

» Contact centre software

Volume - FTE forecast accuracy

Ref: O8.2.4.2
Silver Star KPI

Drives: Right number of agents available to handle emails well
To: We deal well with customer emails

Description

This a measure of how many email staff we forecast that we would need versus how many we really should have had on the day (based on volume and patterns of demand).

The more accurate this figure is, the better chance we have to organise the right number of agents, delivering that oh-so-tricky balance of good agent utilisation and rapid response times.

With emails there's a slower speed of response expectation from customers, but if you take too long to respond customers will often call, to chase the email, leading to failure-induced increases in demand.

Example from Roughshod Repairs

Looking at the volumes for yesterday...

* *The system predicted we would need 1 agent.*
* *In fact we needed 0.25 to turn around all of the emails within the day.*

Volume-FTE forecast accuracy: 0.25 / 1 = 25%

This, coupled with the poor utilisation figure for the email team, worries Ruby, the manager.

Definition or formula

Sum of [Actual required FTE] / Sum of [Forecast FTE]

Typical data sources

» Contact centre software or forecasting model, if separate

Average speed of webchat first response

Ref: O8.3.1.1
Gold Star KPI

Drives: We answer webchats rapidly
To: We handle webchats well

Description

How quickly did our team answer the webchat, on average?

Clearly faster is better here, unless you have some unhealthy drivers around wanting to make it harder to access real humans as a cunning plan to herd people towards your self-service online offering - driving down cost (and driving up customer irritation).

Example from Roughshod Repairs

Ruby interrogates her contact centre software and finds:

Average speed of first response for webchats for yesterday: 8 seconds.

Next she decided to look at the 'webchat abandonment rate' to see whether that figure supported the rosy picture painted by the 'Average speed of first response' figure.

Definition or formula

Average of [Time from first connection to answer by human]

Typical data sources

» Contact centre software

Webchat abandonment rate

Ref: O8.3.1.2
Silver Star KPI

Drives: We answer webchats rapidly
To: We handle webchats well

Description

When customers get really fed up with waiting to have their webchat answered they will give up. This figure shows the percentage of webchats that were abandoned by the customer.

An abandoned webchat may just be the tip of the 'dissatisfaction' iceberg. For every person who gets fed up and gives up, there will be more who are very irritated but put up with slow response rates - so don't take a low figure for abandonment on face value.

On modern computer desktops there are plenty of distractions for the customer and webchat windows can easily get covered up and forgotten about. For this reason webchat abandon rates can be quite high.

Example from Roughshod Repairs
* *Out of 100 inbound chats received yesterday there were 30 abandoned chats.*

Webchat abandon rate: 30/100 = 30%

Definition or formula
Count of [Webchats abandoned] / Count of [Webchats received]

Typical data sources
» Contact centre software

Number of webchats handled per agent per active hour

Ref: O8.3.2.1
Silver Star KPI

Drives: We handle webchats efficiently
To: We handle webchats well

Description

This figure shows agent productivity.

Having a very high, or low, figure can be an indicator of problems, particularly when associated with specific agents. Too high may indicate rushed or incomplete webchats or attempting to run too many chats concurrently. Too low may indicate skills issues or a chatterbox. You can't diagnose issues from this data, but it does tell you where to look.

Example from Roughshod Repairs
Using the contact centre software, Ruby can see...

* *Active agent hours: 12*
* *Chats handled: 100*

Number of webchats per agent per active hour: 100/12 = 8.3

Definition or formula
Count of [Chats handled] / Sum of [Active agent hours]

Typical data sources
» Contact centre software
» Time and attendance system

Average cost per webchat resolved

Ref: O8.3.2.4
Silver Star KPI

Drives: We handle webchats efficiently
To: We handle webchats well

Description

The average cost per webchat resolved gives you a useful yard-stick, based on outcomes (issue is resolved) rather than activity (we handle webchats).

This metric will encourage the team to focus on managing resources to the right level and resolving customer cases.

Example from Roughshod Repairs

Ruby takes the agent cost per hour (£10) and the number of webchat handling agent hours (working hours) from yesterday (12) and divides it by the number of webchats resolved (65):

Average cost per webchat resolved: 12x10 / 65= £1.85 per email

Definition or formula

Sum of [Active agent hours] x [Average agent cost per hour] / Count of [Webchats resolved]

Typical data sources

» Contact centre software
» Payroll

Average chat concurrency

Ref: O8.3.2.5
Silver Star KPI

Drives: We handle webchats efficiently
To: We handle webchats well

Description

Customers take time to think, type and respond. Rather than just sitting and waiting for a response, agents can handle more than one webchat at a time. The number of chats handled at the same time is called 'concurrency'.

Whilst concurrency can be a great way of getting the most from your agents' time, taking it too far can backfire. If your concurrency goes too high you will see:

• Customers abandoning webchats due to slow responses
• Agents getting confused and making mistakes
• Agents becoming overloaded and stressed

Example from Roughshod Repairs

The contact system calculates concurrency for the user in Roughshod Repairs contact centre.

Average web chat concurrency: 1.5

Definition or formula

Average of [Concurrent webchats]

Typical data sources

» Contact centre software

Total webchats handled

Ref: O8.3.2.6
Gold Star KPI

Drives: We handle webchats efficiently
To: We handle webchats well

Description

How many webchats we received - a close proxy to the level of demand.

It's a proxy, not an exact indicator, of the amount of webchat-based work coming to us as webchats can include different numbers and complexities of issues.

Example from Roughshod Repairs

Ruby uses the contact centre software to pull up the 'Webchats handled count' for yesterday. The system reports...

Total webchats handled = 100

Definition or formula

Count of [Webchats received]

Typical data sources

» Contact centre software

Webchat handler utilisation

Ref: O8.3.2.7
Silver Star KPI

Drives: We handle webchats efficiently
To: We handle webchats well

Description

Utilisation is a measure of how occupied our team is. Being occupied does not automatically mean they are being productive, but it can be a useful indicator of a big mismatch between resource and demand. If your utilisation goes too high it will often lead to extended/degraded waiting times for customers contacting you.

There is a fine balancing act between having reasonably high utilisation (keeping costs under control) and having agents available to handle the inevitable surges in contact centre demand. Forecasting, often using the Erlang C formula, can help you tread this fine line.

Example from Roughshod Repairs

Interrogating the call centre software, Ruby finds that her agents were working on webchats for 8.3 of the 12 active agent hours.

Webchat handler utilisation: 8.3 / 12 = 69%

Definition or formula

Sum of [Webchat handler active hours] / Sum of [Available webchat agent hours]

Typical data sources

» Contact centre software
» Time and attendance system

Volume of webchats by reason code

Ref: O8.3.2.9
Silver Star KPI

Drives: We handle webchats efficiently
To: We handle webchats well

Description

Breaking down webchats by reason code means we can start to understand why people are contacting us.

Understanding the reasons people contact us enables us to:

- Identify high importance problems and issues
- Adjust our product and service based on issues identified
- Create self-service channels to reduce handling costs - e.g. specific redirects to dedicated help pages
- Focus and improve our agent training to be able to handle most common issues

Example from Roughshod Repairs

Of the webchats handled yesterday, analysis showed the following:

* *Warranty claims: 50 webchats*
* *Technical question: 30 webchats*
* *Chasers: 10 webchats*
* *Missed appointments: 6 webchats*
* *Failed repair: 3 webchats*
* *Change of appointment: 1 webchat*

Definition or formula

Count of [Webchats received] by reason code

Typical data sources

» Contact centre software

Post-webchat feedback scores

Ref: O8.3.3.1
Gold Star KPI

Drives: We handle webchat interactions well
To: We handle webchats well

Description

The score given by a customer at the end of a webchat typically rating the service they received, whether their issue was resolved and if they would recommend the service to others.

These scores can sometimes be actively manipulated by agents during the webchat preceding the survey. Some agents might say things such as 'Have I done everything I need to, to receive a 5 star rating from you today?'

Example from Roughshod Repairs

After the closure of their case customers are asked to rate their experience on a scale of 1-5.

Average post-webchat feedback score: 4.7

Definition or formula

Average of [Customer feedback score for webchat]

Typical data sources

» Contact centre software

Webchat response audit score

Ref: O8.3.3.2
Gold Star KPI

Drives: We handle webchat interactions well
To: We handle webchats well

Description

A webchat audit score is normally the outcome of a supervisor or trainer reviewing and scoring a sample of webchats based on certain criteria.

The criteria for rating calls would often include:

- Greeting
- Problem solving abilities
- Compliance with protocol
- Response composition skills
- Customer service quality (tone, grammar, accuracy and so on)
- Standard response compliance (where appropriate)
- Closure
- Follow up

The result of all of these elements would be a webchat audit score.

Example from Roughshod Repairs

Roughshod's head of quality, Rachael, reviews at least two response webchats per agent per week. She completes a tracker in a spreadsheet and trends the scores over time. She uses a 100 point scale for the scores and is particularly interested in agents who are consistently above or below the average.

Current average webchat response score: 85%

Definition or formula

Average of [Webchat interaction response score]

Typical data sources

» Audit tracker sheet or software

Volume - FTE forecast accuracy

Ref: O8.3.4.1
Silver Star KPI

Drives: Right number of agents available to handle webchats well
To: We handle webchats well

Description

This a measure of how many webchat staff we forecast that we would need versus how many we really should have had on the day (based on volume and patterns of demand).

The more accurate this figure is, the better chance we have to organise the right number of agents, delivering that oh-so-tricky balance of good agent utilisation and rapid response times.

Example from Roughshod Repairs

Looking at the volumes for yesterday…

The system predicted we would need 2 agents.

In fact we needed 1.39 (so two dedicated staff, or one sharing responsibilities with another area) to turn around all of the webchats.

Volume-FTE forecast accuracy: 1.39 / 2 = 70%

Given that, as run currently, Ruby likes staff dedicated to one channel - webchat in this case - they had the right number of staff on duty to handle the volume. You will need a little 'slack' to allow for forecasting errors - unanticipated short term spikes in demand.

Definition or formula

Sum of [Actual required FTE] / Sum of [Forecast FTE]

Typical data sources

» Contact centre software or forecasting model, if separate

KPI Family: 09
Equipment Maintenance

Unplanned equipment downtime due to failure

Ref: O9.1.1.1
Gold Star KPI

Drives: The equipment is reliable
To: We manage the reliability of our equipment

Description

Equipment downtime due to failure tells you for how long each piece of equipment was not available.

This may be down to maintenance issues, although there are many other non-maintenance reasons (utilities failure, flood, fire, earthquake, theft etc.). Classifying downtime by reason enables you to makes sense of the data.

Understanding equipment downtime, even when it did not stop production, enables you to 'head off' potential problems. Most processes, even if they are not the bottleneck process, will stop production if they are down for long enough.

Often manual recording of downtime is best, as the operator can record details of why the equipment was down, not just time and duration.

Example from Mayhem Manufacturing

Mohammed has had lots of problems with his injection moulder. Last week the moulder was scheduled to run for five hours, but was down for three of those with a mould heating fault.

Unplanned equipment downtime due to failure: 3 hrs

Definition or formula

Sum of [Unplanned equipment downtime due to failure]

Typical data sources

» Downtime logs (either manually recorded by operator or automatic for some machinery)

Total equipment downtime

Ref: O9.1.1.5
Gold Star KPI

Drives: The equipment is reliable
To: We manage the reliability of our equipment

Description

'Total equipment downtime' tells you for how long your production equipment was not available. This includes planned maintenance and unplanned outages. Whilst non-bottleneck outages may not necessarily stop production, a low total equipment downtime is likely to be closely linked to good production availability.

The ultimate goal of maintenance is to keep your production process running smoothly when it needs to. Although a lagging measure, the availability of your production process is a key outcome of maintenance effectiveness. Reviewing 'Total equipment downtime' rather than just 'Unplanned downtime' prevents the temptation to 'hide' downtime by reclassifying it.

Example from Mayhem Manufacturing

Because of reliability problems, Mohammed had organised a pre-flight check on the injection moulder, which took 30 mins. This meant the total downtime was...

* *Unplanned maintenance: 3 hrs*
* *Planned maintenance: 0.5 hrs*

Total equipment downtime: 3.5 hrs

Definition or formula

Sum of [All equipment downtime]

Typical data sources

» Downtime logs (either manually recorded by operator or automatic for some machinery)

Total cost of maintenance

Ref: O9.2.1.2
Gold Star KPI

Drives: Maintenance is cost-effective
To: We maintain our own equipment

Description
Understanding your total cost of maintenance alongside your equipment reliability and process efficiency (OEE) allows you to assess the value-for-money from your current maintenance process.

Example from Mayhem Manufacturing
Mohammed has one dedicated technician - Matt - who spends a quarter of his time on maintenance. A quarter of Matt's time is £8k per year. They spend about £8k a year in spare parts, tools and maintenance consumables. There is also a third party contract to maintain several of the more complex machines, this costs £5k a year.

Total cost of maintenance = £8k + £8k + £5k = £21k

Definition or formula
Sum of [All maintenance related costs]

Typical data sources
» Purchasing records and invoices
» Payroll
» Third party maintenance contracts

Work orders performed when first scheduled

Ref: O9.2.2.1
Silver Star KPI

Drives: We stay on schedule with maintenance
To: We maintain our own equipment

Description
Work orders performed when first scheduled is a useful indicator of the discipline and capacity of your maintenance department. Skipped maintenance tends to lead to equipment failure and overtime bills further down the line.

Example from Mayhem Manufacturing
Matt, the maintenance tech, picks up maintenance tickets first thing in the morning. Last month he had 60 tickets. Of these, five needed parts to be ordered before he could action them and he forgot to look at them in advance.

* *Tickets issued: 60*
* *Tickets resolved on scheduled day: 55*

Works orders performed when first scheduled: 55/60 = 92%

Definition or formula
Count of [Tickets actioned on scheduled day] / Count of [Tickets to be actioned on day]

Typical data sources
» Maintenance management system
» Maintenance ticket/job logs

Maintenance costs per asset

Ref: O9.2.2.2
Silver Star KPI

Drives: We stay on schedule with maintenance
To: We maintain our own equipment

Description
Some equipment can become a 'black hole' for time, effort and spare parts. Having this figure enables you to make an informed decision about when it is time to replace an asset with a new and (hopefully) more reliable piece of kit.

Example from Mayhem Manufacturing
Matt and Mohammed are concerned about the costs the injection moulder is clocking up. Looking at the past month, the injection moulder took half of Matt's maintenance time and nearly three quarters of the parts spend:

Injection moulder maintenance costs:

* Time: £333 /month
* Parts: £500 / month

Total monthly cost of moulder: £833 / month

Definition or formula
Sum of [Parts costs, labour costs and service costs] per machine/piece of equipment

Typical data sources
» Maintenance management system
» Maintenance ticket/job logs
» Supplier invoices
» Payroll and timesheets

Work order backlog by priority and equipment criticality

Ref: O9.2.2.4
Gold Star KPI

Drives: We stay on schedule with maintenance
To: We maintain our own equipment

Description
When you start skipping scheduled maintenance or get a backlog of repair tasks, that's a sign of trouble ahead. Keep an eye on this to make sure you don't end up in an impossible-to-recover situation.

Show a particular interest in outstanding job tickets for safety-related work or tasks where a catastrophic failure may cause serious additional damage and losses.

Example from Mayhem Manufacturing
One maintenance task needing attention is a safety interlock switch. Matt is struggling to source the correct part, but without it the operator risks losing her fingers. Mohammed decides to shut the machine down and focus on finding an alternative part as quickly as possible.

Work order backlog tasks: 1

Criticality: Severe health and safety risk

Definition or formula
Count of [Backlog maintenance tasks] grouped by assigned criticality/risk rating.

Typical data sources
» Maintenance management system
» Maintenance ticket/job logs

Service level agreement compliance

Ref: O9.3.1.1
Gold Star KPI

Drives: The 3rd party maintenance service meets our requirements
To: Others maintain our equipment for us

Description

When we sub-contract or outsource our maintenance, did the supplier do what they promised?

Assuming the contract is well written, we should be looking for our maintenance contractor to meet their service-level obligations and to demonstrate this transparently.

Example from Mayhem Manufacturing

FaffFree Service Contractors look after Mayhem's planing machine, drilling machine and paint oven. They commit to sending a technician round within 4 hours of a fault being reported and servicing the machines every 6 months.

So far there have been 5 outages, all responded to within 4 hours and they have serviced the machines as scheduled.

Service Level Agreement compliance: 100%

Definition or formula

As agreed with supplier, usually a percentage or pass/fail threshold.

Typical data sources

» Often your supplier - but important to keep your own records for validation, even if not agreed in the contract

Total maintenance contract costs

Ref: O9.3.1.2
Gold Star KPI

Drives: The 3rd party maintenance service meets our requirements
To: Others maintain our equipment for us

Description

Is our outsourced maintenance contract good value for money? You will need this figure, amongst others, to make that judgement.

You are most likely to want to keep a close eye on this where the cost of maintenance is not 'all inclusive' but is driven by incidents, requests or something else that is not pre-determined. If your contractor can maximise their income by making the most of any contractual 'grey areas', you need to assume they will.

Example from Mayhem Manufacturing

Mayhem spend £8k a year on the services of FaffFree. There were an additional £1k of out-of-contract maintenance costs with FaffFree (which were put under 'parts' spend).

Maintenance contract costs: £8k + £1k = £9k

Definition or formula

Sum of [Total maintenance contract costs]

Typical data sources

» Maintenance logs
» Invoices and receipts from contractor

Out-of-contract contract costs

Ref: O9.3.1.3
Silver Star KPI

Drives: The 3rd party maintenance service meets our requirements
To: Others maintain our equipment for us

Description

Some contracts allow for 'extras'. Tracking these amounts and reviewing alongside your 'standard' maintenance costs will give you the whole picture.

Example from Mayhem Manufacturing

The agreement with FaffFree, the maintenance contractors, is that any modifications to the machines made after the contract is agreed will not be covered by the all-inclusive parts and labour repair agreement.

Nearly £1k of repairs have fallen into this category so far - and put under the 'parts' spend.

Additional out-of-contract contract costs: £1k

So far this hasn't been an issue, but it could get expensive if these parts break, so Mohammed is thinking about re-negotiating this contract.

Definition or formula

Sum of [Out-of-contract contract costs]

Typical data sources

» Maintenance logs
» Invoices and receipts from contractor

Complaints & Incident Handling

Volume of outstanding complaints

Ref: O10.1.1.2
Gold Star KPI

Drives: We track and respond promptly to complaints
To: We manage the processing of complaints

Description

The volume of outstanding complaints shows how many complaints you have in your system that are yet to be resolved.

If you know your 'Complaint closure rate' (per day etc.) you can quickly see how long it will take to clear the outstanding complaints at that rate. If your 'Outstanding complaints' graph is trending up then you may well have an operational problem - either too little complaint handling capacity, growing demand or stalled complaint resolutions.

Example from Roughshod Repairs

Roughshod Repairs get quite a few complaints. Of the 30 in the past month, 10 are still outstanding.

Volume of outstanding complaints: 10 complaints

Definition or formula

Count of [Outstanding complaints]

Typical data sources

» Complaints ticket system
» Contact centre software
» Complaints log

Average time to complaint resolution

Ref: O10.1.1.3
Gold Star KPI

Drives: We track and respond promptly to complaints
To: We manage the processing of complaints

Description

The average time to complaint resolution is the average time it takes to close a complaint.

Typically we use the median, as this is less likely to be skewed by the very extremes of the resolution rate curve (e.g. a few very old complaints that may be hanging around for valid reasons - e.g. legal action).

Example from Roughshod Repairs

Using their contact centre software, Ruby finds:

Average time to complaint resolution: 12 days

Definition or formula

Average of [Elapsed time to resolve or close complaint]

Typical data sources

» Complaints ticket system
» Contact centre software
» Complaints log

Common problems and mistakes

Be clear on whether you are going to measure *calendar* days or *working* days. Calendar days are a better picture of the wait that the customer experiences, but it does mean that you get pessimistic picture of performance when a problem arrives late on a Friday but the team doesn't start working on it until Monday morning.

Whichever approach you use, be clear on the choice and make sure everyone understands the logic behind the decision.

Overall complaint processing costs

Ref: O10.1.2.1
Gold Star KPI

Drives: We manage the costs of resolution
To: We manage the processing of complaints

Description

Where complaints are a significant part of your operation, knowing the cost involved in processing them is essential.

If complaints also require spend by other parts of the organisation - for example a production investigation - be sure to include these if you can.

Example from Roughshod Repairs

Ruby checked the complaints system to see the total agent time spent handling complaints and the operational costs of any actions taken for complaints last month...

Overall complaint processing costs: £1,500

Definition or formula

Sum of [Direct and indirect costs of handling, resolving or closing complaint]

Typical data sources

» Complaints ticket system
» Contact centre software
» Complaints log

Per-complaint average processing cost

Ref: O10.1.2.2
Silver Star KPI

Drives: We manage the costs of resolution
To: We manage the processing of complaints

Description

By dividing the 'Overall complaint processing costs' by the number of cases handled (closed) we can arrive at an approximate per-complaint cost.

Per-complaint costs can be useful in decision-making, especially when looking at investments designed to reduce complaints. Don't forget that there is also a much harder-to-measure aspect of complaints - loss of customer goodwill and brand prestige.

Example from Roughshod Repairs

The complaints team typically used two hours of agent time to handle the complaint, at £10 per hour, and incurred a £30 operational cost to actually fix the problem.

Per-complaint process average cost: £50

Definition or formula

Sum of [Direct and indirect costs of handling, resolving or closing complaint] / Count of [Complaints resolved or closed]

Typical data sources

» Complaints ticket system
» Contact centre software
» Complaints log

Value of complaints by root cause

Ref: O10.2.1.1
Silver Star KPI

Drives: We understand the reasons behind complaints
To: We work to avoid future complaints

Description

Most organisations have recurring problems and complaint issues. This is the total cost to your organisation of resolving complaints, grouped by the root cause or problem type. By working out the value of these complaints, by root cause, we can support improvement work and decision-making.

Example from Roughshod Repairs

Ruby doesn't have the time or energy to work out the exact cost of resolving problems, by problem type, but she does have the volume of problems by root cause (for last month) and the average cost to resolve a problem (£50). Volumes of complaints last month...

* *Warranty Declined:15*
* *Device fault not fixed: 12*
* *Additional customer charge: 3*

Approximate 'Value of complaints by root cause'....

* *Warranty Declined:£750*
* *Device fault not fixed: £600*
* *Additional customer charge: £150*

Definition or formula

Sum of [Direct and indirect costs of handling, resolving or closing complaint] by root cause

or

Count of [Complaint - by root cause] x Average of [Per-complaint process average cost]

Typical data sources

» Complaints ticket system
» Contact centre software
» Complaints log

Common problems and mistakes

If the root cause of the problem isn't understood at this stage, you should devise a meaningful categorisation method - ideally capturing some descriptive detail to enable categorisation further down the line.

Post-complaint resolution average feedback score

Ref: O10.3.1.1
Gold Star KPI

Drives: Customers are happy with how complaints are resolved
To: We sort out our complaints properly

Description

When we ask for customer feedback, after a complaint is closed, this is the average score. When we deal with a complaint, our end outcome is not really a fixed product or service, but a fixed customer. This score tells you how well we did at that objective.

Example from Roughshod Repairs

When a complaint is closed, a feedback form is sent out. The average score (on a scale of 1-5) is then compiled along with any additional comments, into a one page complaints report:

Post-complaint resolution average feedback score: 3.4

From the comments, it seems that people who were denied repairs under warranty terms and conditions significantly dragged the score down.

Definition or formula

Average of [post-complaint resolution feedback score]

Possibly broken down by complaint type, if useful.

Typical data sources

» Complaints ticket system
» Contact centre software
» Complaints log
» Online survey software
» Email/SMS survey responses

Common problems and mistakes

People responding to a feedback request is a biased (or self-selecting) group. I know that I have skipped feedback where service has been terrible but I liked the person I was dealing with, or felt sorry for them. Another source of bias is the complaint type. There are some complaints, where the customer or client is in the wrong, where they will still not be happy with the outcome - even if they have been dealt with promptly, correctly and courteously. It can be useful to create extra stats which include and exclude these categories.

Professional Qualification & Membership

Percentage of staff requiring certification with certification

Ref: P1.1.1.1
Gold Star KPI

Drives: We are qualified to the correct level
To: Our team are professionally qualified

Description

Some roles require professional membership and/or certification. This measure will show both staff that have never qualified/been certified and those who have let their qualification/certification lapse.

In some situations it is mandatory, in others it may increase your billed rate or help you win business more easily.

There may also be legal and insurance implications to lapsed qualifications/certification.

This is a slow-moving measure that you would only look to review at 6 or 12 month intervals. (If you are recruiting heavily then you may need to review this more often.)

Example from Ambiguous Associates

Austin is a 'Certified Ambiguous Advisor'. Of the four consultants in his team, three have CAA certification, the fourth must always have one of the other three sign off his work.

Percentage of staff requiring certification who have certification... 3/4 = 75%

Definition or formula

Count of [Team members with valid certification] / Count of [Team members requiring (or benefitting from) valid certification]

Typical data sources

» Professional body membership records
» Professional body certification records

Spend on professional qualifications and memberships

Ref: P1.2.1.3
Silver Star KPI

Drives: Our qualifications and subs are renewed and valid
To: Team are members of the appropriate professional body

Description

Some memberships to professional bodies and professional exams can be pretty costly.

Track this figure to understand the level of spend and the benefit you are gaining from that membership/certification. This is particularly relevant where membership/certification is not a legal or regulatory requirement.

Example from Ambiguous Associates

Renewing your 'Certified Ambiguous Advisor' certification costs £400 a year. In addition, Adam the trainee pays £1,500 a year for his Ambiguous training materials on his monitored professional development scheme.

Spend on professional qualifications and memberships: £2,700

Definition or formula

Sum of [Membership, certification, professional training or association fees]

Typical data sources

» Professional body payments and membership dues receipts

Service Quality

Percentage of orders with customer-reported problems

Ref: Q1.1.1.1
Gold Star KPI

Drives: We serve our customers accurately
To: Our customers are happier than competitors' customers

Description

The number of orders with (one or more) problems that are picked up by the customer.

This is about as bad as it gets for reputation and cost. Not only do you have the cost of retrieving the incorrect order and re-delivering the correct order, you also have an annoyed or angry customer. Understanding why the error happened and fixing the issue to root cause is a must.

Example from Woeful Widget Warehouse

Will has had several angry phone calls from customers who received the wrong colour of Fearsome Face paint. He had 12 order complaints out of 275 shipped last month.

% Orders with customer reported problems: 12 / 275 = 4.4%

Definition or formula

Count of [Orders with customer reported problems] / Count of [Orders fulfilled]

Typical data sources

» Complaint handling system/records
» Order management system/records

Common problems and mistakes

As this is an 'orders with detected problem(s)' measure, be careful that you don't accidentally count orders with two (or more) problems as multiple orders.

Percentage re-opened cases

Ref: Q1.1.2.1
Gold Star KPI

Drives: We sort out problems well and quickly
To: Our customers are happier than competitors' customers

Description

Re-opened cases happen when we think an issue has been sorted, but it hasn't.

This can be a customer service disaster, as you have missed the chance to fix the problem, probably aggravating an already angry customer. Understanding the reason for a re-opened case, and fixing the issue to root cause should be a very high priority for any organisation.

Example from Roughshod Repairs

Ruby has noticed that some agents seem to be closing cases that weren't properly resolved. Her ticket handling stats back this up…

* Cases handled last month: 14,400
* Cases re-opened: 2,016

% re-opened cases: 2,016 / 14,400 = 14%

Definition or formula

Count of [Re-opened cases] / Count of [Cases closed]

Typical data sources

» Ticket management system
» Complaint handling system
» Tracking sheets or records

Common problems and mistakes

Targetting the 're-opened cases' figure can easily drive the wrong behaviours. The key is not to target a reduction in recorded 're-opened cases' *directly* but to target the number of 'problems solved to root cause' that *underly* the reported re-opened cases. When you successfully solve the root causes behind re-opened cases, the re-opened cases figure should naturally reduce.

Problem resolution time (median)

Ref: Q1.1.2.2
Silver Star KPI

Drives: We sort out problems well and quickly
To: Our customers are happier than competitors' customers

Description

This shows the 'middle' - or median - time taken to resolve a problem.

Fixing problems swiftly is critical, but using mean (the most common type of average) can be skewed by a few very old cases. Using the median lessens the impact of a few very fast or very slow resolutions. It is always worth looking at a profile plot showing case age and frequency, as a single figure does not tell the whole story.

Example from Roughshod Repairs

Roughshod Repairs have a wide variety of cases open at any given time. Their ticket handling system produces stats on resolution times and shows that for last month…

Problem resolution time (median): 14 working days.

Definition or formula

Median value [Age of closed cases]

or, for more insight

Chart profile of [Age of closed cases]

Typical data sources

» Ticket management system
» Complaint handling system
» Tracking sheets or records

Common problems and mistakes

Look to 'restart' the clock on cases that re-open, rather than 'resetting' the clock. Doing this will discourage agents from rapidly closing cases inappropriately to hit targets or look good.

Median live complaint age

Ref: Q1.1.2.3
Silver Star KPI

Drives: We sort out problems well and quickly
To: Our customers are happier than competitors' customers

Description

This shows the 'middle' - or median - age of complaints that are still live (have not yet been closed).

This is a closely related measure to 'Problem resolution time' but this refers to current live cases, so can be an early indication of case handling right **now**. Including historic closure rates can hide or delay noticing current operational problems.

Example from Roughshod Repairs

Ruby's contact centre operation has had a run of ill staff members and technical issues with their PCs. She has noticed that the median live case age is increasing by a day, every couple of days, a real sign of the operation not coping with existing cases and new volume.

Current median complaint age: 8 days

Definition or formula

Median value [Age of live cases]

or, for more insight

Chart profile of [Age of live cases]

Typical data sources

» Ticket management system
» Complaint handling system
» Tracking sheets or records

Common problems and mistakes

Be clear on whether you are dealing with calendar or working days. If you aren't sure, ask yourself the question 'What does the customer care about?'.

Expressions of dissatisfaction percentage

Ref: Q1.1.2.6
Gold Star KPI

Drives: We sort out problems well and quickly
To: Our customers are happier than competitors' customers

Description

Sometimes people are unhappy, but don't actually complain. These can be called 'Expressions of dissatisfaction' - grumbles, if you like - and are well worth tracking. They may not be as serious as a full-blown complaint, but they give you an indication that something is not right.

Example from Chaos Coffee Shop

Charlie looks through his TripAdvisor reviews and noticed five comments over the last month that concerned him

1. Two comments that the toilets were not up to scratch

2. Three comments that there were no proper baby change facilities.

He logs these as...

Expressions of dissatisfaction: 5

...and resolves to sort out the underlying issues.

Definition or formula

Count of [Expressions of dissatisfaction or grumbles]

Typical data sources

» Online reviews
» Listening to customer conversations
» Social media
» Feedback forms

Common problems and mistakes

What is a grumble and what are just 'suggestions' can be a hard line to draw. If you struggle, set the boundary using examples that people can refer to, this will help them categorise things correctly.

Internal quality audit scores

Ref: Q1.2.1.1
Silver Star KPI

Drives: We manage our service delivery quality
To: Our service is problem free

Description

Many businesses audit their processes and procedures. Tracking the results of internal quality audit scores can be used to trend overall quality performance, identify issues and fix them before they affect the customer.

In an ideal world, we don't have quality problems. But if we do, finding quality problems before your customer, or regulator, does is a much better option. Performing an internal audit and closely examining and reacting to the score will help you stay on the 'front foot', dealing with problems before they become complaints or regulatory breaches.

Example from Chaos Coffee Shop

Charlie's head barista, Colin, does an 'observational' quality audit of each of his team at least once a week. He watches to see that they follow procedure, make coffee in the correct way, keep the work area clean, have a good attitude and sell in the right way. Each of these is scored and recorded.

Average internal quality audit score: 83%

Definition or formula

Sum of [Individual quality assessment scores within audit]

or, where there are multiple audits...

Average of [Individual quality assessment scores within audit]

Typical data sources

» Quality audit records, either paper or electronic

Common problems and mistakes

It is important to have clear guidelines on any parts of the audit that may seem to be down to judgement (subjective). Often, practical examples of a high, medium and low score can help those running the audit make sure they stick to a similar scoring system.

Customer survey scores

Ref: Q1.3.1.1
Gold Star KPI

Drives: We measure and improve our customer happiness
To:　　We know how happy our customers are

Description

If your business asks your customers to rate your service, then this is the summary of those scores. These scores can be very valuable as they will help flag actual, and potential, issues before they become full-blown complaints.

Example from Chaos Coffee Shop

Charlie offers entry into a monthly free prize draw to anyone who fills in a 3-question customer satisfaction card, with a comments box on it at the bottom.

He has noticed the score for 'Is our coffee better than any other coffee shop you use?' has been steadily dropping over the past three months. This is a big worry and he's started to investigate what the problem is.

Definition or formula

Average of [Customer survey scores]

or, for more insight

Chart profile of [Customer survey scores]

Typical data sources

» Paper-based customer survey responses, online survey tools (e.g. SurveyMonkey)
» End-of-call surveys

Common problems and mistakes

Comments are super-important here, scores without supporting commentary or other data (e.g. complaints information) can be frustrating as it can be hard to know what to do to improve things.

Be a little careful about the difference between public feedback and private feedback. Agents are increasingly using phrases like 'Have I done everything I need to do to get a five star rating in our call today?'. This a way of 'gaming' the scoring system and can cover up real opportunities to improve service, as some customers are nice and give five stars when there's still room for improvement.

Net Promoter Score

Ref: Q1.3.1.2
Silver Star KPI

Drives: We measure and improve our customer happiness
To:　　We know how happy our customers are

Description

Net Promoter Score is based on the question 'How likely is it that you would recommend our company/product/service to a friend or colleague?' and is scored on a scale of 0 (detractors) to 10 (promoters). Net Promoter Score is a fairly simple measure to implement and understand.

Example from Woeful Widget Warehouse

Will decides to run a 'Net Promoter Score' Survey with his customers every six months. His first NPS survey showed the following….

* Promoters = 52%
* Passives = 18%
* Detractors = 30%

NPS = [Percentage 'Promoters'] - [Percentage 'Detractors']

= 52% - 30% = 22%

He's not quite sure what to make of the score, so sensibly decides to look at the trend over time, rather than worrying too much about whether it's a good score or not.

Definition or formula

Responses are categorised based on 0-6=detractor, 7-8=passives and 9-10 are promoters.

NPS = [Percentage 'Promoters'] - [Percentage 'Detractors']

The net score can vary from -100 (everyone is a detractor) to +100 (everyone is a promoter).

Typical data sources

» Net Promoter Score surveys - paper, online or phone response

Common problems and mistakes

Although it is widely used in corporations there is research that questions whether it is any better at predicting loyalty behaviours than the answer to other simple questions such as 'Overall satisfaction?' or 'Likelihood to purchase again?'.

Customer retention rate

Ref: Q1.3.1.3
Gold Star KPI

Drives: We measure and improve our customer happiness
To: We know how happy our customers are

Description
The percentage of customers you have retained over a given period. Holding on to your existing customers is the foundation of growth. Every customer you retain, is one fewer new customer you need to find to grow. Defining 'current' custom for some businesses can be tricky, you may need to come up with a 'cut-off time' where you assume they are no longer buying from you. It's also a requirement that you can identify your customers as individuals through some method - e.g. House number + postcode, loyalty card number, date of birth and first name etc.

Example from Woeful Widget Warehouse
Will finds that most of his customers order every month. He runs a list of all those who have ordered in the last month and compares that with last month's purchases and his list of credit-account holders. If someone drops off the 'active customer' list, he will give them a call to check that everything is OK. Will measures retention rate from month to month...

* *Last month Woeful Widget Warehouse had 23 customers*
* *Last month he recognised 8 customers from the previous month*

Customer retention rate (month to month) = 8 / 23 = 35%

Definition or formula
Count of [Customers recognised from previous period] / Count of [Customers from this period]

Typical data sources
» Sales records/sales systems

Common problems and mistakes
Defining 'current', 'live' or 'repeat' custom for some businesses can be tricky. You may need to come up with a 'cut-off time' where you assume they are no longer buying from you. It's also a requirement that you can identify your customers as individuals through some method - e.g. House number + postcode, loyalty card number, date of birth and first name etc.

Average customer live relationship duration

Ref: Q1.3.1.4
Silver Star KPI

Drives: We measure and improve our customer happiness
To: We know how happy our customers are

Description
Where you have measurable repeat business, this shows the average (calendar) duration to the current time.

Example from Woeful Widget Warehouse
Looking at the 8 customers Will recognises as repeat business last month from previous months, he identifies the following customers with unbroken records of purchasing every month...

* *Awful Accessories = 15 months of orders*
* *Better Boxes = 2 months of orders*
* *Crafty Capers = 12 months of orders*
* *Difficult Doohickies = 13 months of orders*
* *Elegant Escapades = 3 months of orders*
* *Funny Fiddlers = 21 months of orders*
* *Gross Gizmos = 18 months of orders*
* *Hilarious Hats = 5 months of orders*

The average of these is...

(15 + 2 + 12 + 13 + 3 + 21 + 18 + 5) / 8 = 11.13

Average customer live relationship: 11 months

Definition or formula
Sum of [Number of continuous periods repeat business from same customer] / Count of repeat customers]

Typical data sources
» Sales records/sales systems

Common problems and mistakes
Defining 'current', 'live' or 'repeat' custom for some businesses can be tricky. You may need to come up with a 'cut-off time' where you assume they are no longer buying from you. It's also a requirement that you can identify your customers as individuals through some method - e.g. House number + postcode, loyalty card number, date of birth and first name etc.

Volume of new complaints

Ref: Q1.3.2.1
Gold Star KPI

Drives: Minimal complaints
To: We know how happy our customers are

Description

A complaint is a description of a problem that a customer (or prospective customer) has with your products or services. Although it is a lagging indicator (complaints usually show up after something has gone wrong), it is still an incredibly important measure to monitor and react to. This measure shows the volume of complaints.

The complaint volume figure can be useful for operational purposes - such as planning complaint handling resources.

Example from Chaos Coffee Shop

Charlie's team have had a steady stream of complaints showing in the customer service log book, complaining about a lack of aroma and bitter taste in his Charming Charlie blend of coffee. He's anxious about the quality issue. After carefully analysing the product, he's discovered the beans for his Charming Charlie have not been roasted correctly - he suspects excessively moist Vietnamese Robusta beans from the end of the season - and he's pursuing this with his supplier.

Definition or formula

Count of [Complaints]   (See also 'Service Improvement Activity' on page 389)

Typical data sources

» Complaints log
» Feedback comments on website
» Complaints on social media

Setting targets

Complaints is one area, like health and safety 'near misses', where you really don't want to set a target that you incentivise people to achieve. If, for example, you incentivise a team to reduce complaints, this will often be achieved in the worst possible way and without solving the underlying dissatisfaction.

Common problems and mistakes

You may decide to grade complaints by severity, but this can be risky as some people feel very passionately about things that you may think are trivial.

The comments and commentary that come with complaints are extremely important. These comments allow you to start investigating in the right place and can save you huge amounts of wasted effort.

Percentage of sales with complaints

Ref: Q1.3.2.2
Gold Star KPI

Drives: Minimal complaints
To: We know how happy our customers are

Description

This measure shows complaints as a percentage of products or services sold - clearly you should expect a higher count of complaints when you sell 10m of something compared with 10.

Many people are reluctant to complain. It requires effort and sometimes emotional conflict, so when your customers do complain it's a sign that something really has to be done. Resolving complaints splits into (1) Fixing the customer and immediate problem, (2) Making sure the problem never happens again.

If you consistently perform these two steps well, and don't go bust whilst doing it, you will most likely end up with a very successful business.

Example from Mayhem Manufacturing

Mohammed reviews his complaints for anything produced in January. His production volumes were...

* *Hobbit chairs: 65*
* *Volcano pen pots: 218*
* *Turtle desks: 13*

His complaints, for products made in January, were...

* *Hobbit chairs: 2*
* *Volcano pen pots: 5*
* *Turtle desks: 0*

So complaint percentages, for January production, are...

* *Hobbit chairs: 3.1%*
* *Volcano pen pots: 2.3%*
* *Turtle desks: 0.0%*

Definition or formula

Count of [Complaints] / Count of [Sales]

Typical data sources

» Complaints log, feedback comments on website, complaints on social media etc.
» Sales volume records from sales tracking system or EPOS.

Setting targets

Complaints is one area, like health and safety 'near misses', where you really don't want to set a target that you incentivise people to achieve. If, for example, you incentivise a team to reduce complaints, this will often be achieved in the worst possible way and without solving the underlying dissatisfaction.

Common problems and mistakes

A major challenge with this measure is that there may be a delay between a product or service being delivered and a complaint arising. To be accurate you must assign the complaint to the correct period, so you have to be able to track specific sales and also accept that the percentage complaints for historic periods may continue to rise for an unknown period after the sales are made.

Depending on your situation, it may make more sense to assign complaints to the manufacturing period (for manufacturing defect complaints) or the sales period (for sales service-related complaints).

Number of positive feedback letters and emails

Ref: Q1.4.1.1
Gold Star KPI

Drives: Our customers tell us they are happy
To: Our customers are happy

Description

A count of the number of items of positive written feedback received.

You may decide to include written reviews from Google and TripAdvisor. Just be consistent and make sure you understand the legal implications if you are thinking of using those reviews in publicity materials.

Positive feedback, particularly in writing, is special for any business. Most people don't take the trouble to do it, so when you get this kind of feedback, it's great. It also gives you fantastic material for your marketing and promotions. If you can use the name of the person giving feedback (with their permission) that's even better, as it gives the feedback real authenticity.

Example from Roughshod Repairs

Ruby's team have been delighted to received a steady stream of 'thank you' letters and emails. They keep a tally and a folder with the letters themselves. This month…

Number of positive feedback letters and emails: 22

Definition or formula

Count of [Written positive feedback items]

Typical data sources

» Email inbox
» Physical letters
» Review sites (if included)

Common problems and mistakes

What to do if you get a mixture of positive and negative feedback? I'd be tempted to be harsh and categorise it as negative feedback - looking to fix as many of the problems flagged up in the feedback as possible.

KPI Family: Q2
Product Quality

In-process rework percentage

Ref: Q2.1.1.1
Gold Star KPI

Drives: Minimise the cost & frequency of rework problems
To: We minimise production problem rectification

Description

Where problems are detected and fixed during production, this is called in-process rework.

This kind of rework normally happens because of mis-specification or quality issues. This type of waste can end up being expensive and difficult to detect (particularly when stuff doesn't end up in a bin, just takes up workforce time to fix) as people tend not to want to own up to messing things up.

Example from Mayhem Manufacturing

Michael, the shift supervisor at Mayhem Manufacturing, has just discovered that 5 of 20 Hobbit chairs produced last month were painted the wrong colour. All five needed repainting.

The in-process rework rate for chairs is 5/20: 25% for last month.

Definition or formula

Count of [Items reworked] / Count of [Items manufactured]

Typical data sources

» Production records/rework logs

Common problems and mistakes

Things can get a little misleading if you produce a wide range of items with wildly different complexity. If that is the case then think about measuring rework by product type or some kind of cost-based or time-based rework measure. For cost-based rework you look at the cost of rework as a percentage of the ideal manufacturing cost.

Rework percentage by reason

Ref: Q2.1.1.5
Silver Star KPI

Drives: Minimise the cost & frequency of rework problems
To: We minimise production problem rectification

Description

When we have rework, breaking down the reasons behind that rework is an essential first step of improvement. This measure shows the percentage of internal rework by reason.

The key is to group rework activities into meaningful categories. If you are struggling to do this, then grouping by the place in the process that the problem originates from (rather than is detected) is a good start, as it will steer you to the right location to watch the process and find out more.

Example from Mayhem Manufacturing

Michael has looked at the rework data from last month and sees the following hours spent on rework...

	Hours	Percentage
Cutting team	3 hours rework	25.%
Painting	6 hours rework	50.0%
Assembly	2 hours rework	16.7%
Packing & dispatch	1 hour rework	8.3%

He decides that the painting area seems to be the most urgent one to tackle, based on the % lost hours to rework.

Definition or formula

Sum of [Cost of rework] by reason

or

Sum of [Hours of rework] by reason

Typical data sources

» Production records/rework logs

Field failure claims rate within warranty

Ref: Q2.2.1.1
Gold Star KPI

Drives: Our product does not fail with the customer
To: Our product is fit for purpose

Description

When a product fails and a customer makes a legitimate claim on the warranty, several bad things have already happened. The product has failed to meeting its purpose, the customer has lost the use of that product and the customer is sufficiently irritated to claim on the warranty and your organisation bears the cost of fixing the product and the customer.

Keeping a close eye on failure rates can help you understand your product performance and spot looming customer satisfaction problems. Big warranty issues can turn into public-relations issues too.

Example from Woeful Widget Warehouse

Will has had a number of complaints about his comedy mouse mats becoming soft and gooey, clogging up customers' mice and making a mess. He has sold 300 in the past year and has had 50 claims for products sold in the past year.

* *Failure volume in warranty = 50*
* *Mouse mats sold and still in warranty period = 300*

Field failure rate within warranty = 50/300 = 17%

Definition or formula

Count of [Valid warranty claims] / Count of [Sales still within warranty period]

Typical data sources

» Sales records
» Warranty claim records

Refund requests

Ref: Q2.5.2.8
Silver Star KPI

Drives: We sort out problems well and quickly
To: Our customers are happier than competitors' customers

Description

This is the count of situations where a refund has been requested.

There may be a number of different reasons for a refund request, including….

1. Late delivery
2. Change of mind
3. The product does not perform as it should
4. The product is faulty and within a refund period

Example from Mayhem Manufacturing

Mohammed offers a money-back guarantee. He has had one Hobbit Chair returned in the last month. He took note of the reason for the refund - wrong size - and is looking into better size information on his website.

Number of refund requests: 1

Definition or formula

Count of [Refund requests]

Typical data sources

» Sales records
» Order system
» Accounting records

Common problems and mistakes

You need to be clear about whether you are talking about the number of requests, or items refunded. Requests will normally be higher than items refunded. Measure whichever makes most sense for your business.

Product Quality

KPI Family: Q3
Guarantee & Warranty

Percentage of fraudulent claims

Ref: Q3.1.1.1
Silver Star KPI

Drives: We track warranty abuse
To: Our warranty is not abused

Description

Sometimes warranty claims fall outside of the terms set by manufacturers - perhaps timescale, usage (professional use, where warranty only covers domestic) or abuse.

The relevance of this will depend very significantly on your sector, typically making up 3-15% of warranty costs.

Example from Roughshod Repairs

Roughshod Repairs have discovered, through serial number review, that a percentage of Nintbox4 consoles they have been asked to repair are 'grey imports' - consoles imported from Japan and not covered by warranty. These are not covered by their contract with Nintbox and should be declined.

A review of all Nintbox4 repairs showed:

*   37 repairs of which 3 were 'grey imports'.

Percentage of fraudulent warranty claims: 3/37 = 8%

Definition or formula

Count of [Fraudulent warranty claims] / Count of [Warranty claims]

Typical data sources

» Warranty and repair records
» Sales database
» Serial number records
» Warranty registration records

Common problems and mistakes

Poor record keeping, of both warranty information and serial numbers makes fraud detection much harder or even impossible.

Percentage of sales with warranty claims

Ref: Q3.2.1.5
Gold Star KPI

Drives: We process claims cost efficiently
To: We manage our warranty claims efficiently

Description

The percentage of sales with a warranty claim can give us a warning of reliability or design issues.

Watching this trend can enable you to 'get the jump' on looming reliability problems, potentially saving you cash and reputational damage.

Example from Roughshod Repairs

Roughshod Repairs repair Nintbox4 consoles for gaming company Nintbox, a niche retro console manufacturer.

A review of all Nintbox4 repairs showed:

*   37 repairs for the period in which Nintbox sold 5,000 consoles

The percentage of sales with warranty claims was 37/5,000 = 0.74%

Definition or formula

Count of [Warranty claims] / Count of [Sales for period]

Typical data sources

» Sales records/software
» Warranty records/warranty tracking system

Common problems and mistakes

This can only show warranty claims to date, so the figure is likely to continue rising until the end of the warranty period for the products.

Average claims-to-resolution time for valid claims

Ref: Q3.2.2.1
Gold Star KPI

Drives: We process valid claims swiftly
To: We manage our warranty claims efficiently

Description

This is the time period experienced by the customer between submitting their warranty and a repaired item being returned, or their claim being declined.

As this is a customer-centric measure, you should measure the days the customer has been waiting, whether or not your organisation works 7 days a week.

Example from Roughshod Repairs

Looking at their repair records, Nintbox4 repairs take an average of 10 calendar days to be delivered back to the customer, from the initial warranty-claim being received.

Average claims-to-resolution time for valid claims: 10 days

Note: Roughshod handle lots of different types of claims. They do look at the overall average, but also break that down into product types and brands. This is also relevant as they have specific SLAs with each manufacturing warranty customer that they service.

Definition or formula

Sum of ([Time at end of claim] - [Time at start of claim]) / Count of [Claims]

Typical data sources

» Warranty records/warranty tracking system
» Ticket management system

Common problems and mistakes

If the repair end-to-end time has customer actions in it - for instance packaging the item and returning it via post - this can lead to process delay and variability that is not directly in your control. You may decide to separate out this part of the end-to-end time to show which parts you can, and cannot, control. You may also decide to make an assumption that the customer receives the fixed item 1 day after it is dispatched (if you are using next day delivery). Just make sure this assumption is accurate if you are going to use it.

Percentage customer disputed decisions

Ref: Q3.3.1.1
Silver Star KPI

Drives: We assess the validity correctly
To: We process claims correctly

Description

Sometimes warranty claims are declined. This may be because the claim falls outside of the warranty, the product has been abused or your warranty team have messed up the claim. Customers will sometimes complain when their warranty claim is declined.

Track this figure to identify issues with customer expectation of the product warranty or to identify processing accuracy issues with your warranty team/function.

Example from Roughshod Repairs

The customer who had a 'grey import' warranty claim turned down wrote an angry email disputing the decision. For Nintbox4…

Percentage customer disputed decisions: 1/37 = 2.7%

Definition or formula

Count of [Customer-disputed warranty decisions] / Count of [Warranty claims]

Typical data sources

» Warranty records/warranty tracking system
» Ticket management system
» Warranty disputes records

Volumes of claims by root cause

Ref: Q3.4.1.1
Gold Star KPI

Drives: We have the data to improve our products and fix issues
To: We understand reasons behind warranty claims

Description

We can normally break down warranty claims by the type of problem they are solving.

Doing this gives us insight into underlying design or usage problems, allows us to feed into new product design and plan resource and spare part levels for future claims.

Example from Roughshod Repairs

Looking the 37 Nintbox4 repairs, Ruby groups them as follows:

* DVD drives scratching optical disks: 22
* Power supply failure: 8
* Broken USB ports: 4
* Logic board failure: 3

Definition or formula

Count of [Warranty reason] by reason type

Typical data sources

» Warranty records/warranty tracking system
» Ticket management system.

Common problems and mistakes

Be careful about misallocating reason codes. Sometimes a failure may have a more subtle root cause, for example an overheated processor might be the symptom of dust-clogged fan design issue.

Cost of claims by root cause

Ref: Q3.4.1.2
Gold Star KPI

Drives: We have the data to improve our products and fix issues
To: We understand reasons behind warranty claims

Description

Knowing how cost breaks down by root cause (or reason for warranty repair/replacement) can help us put a value to specific problems and make the right decisions about resource management.

Claims vary in terms of the cost of fixing them. Looking at this measure, in addition to the raw number of claims, will help you keep an eye on the impact of warranty claims.

Example from Roughshod Repairs

Roughshod's Nintbox4 repairs cost the following (total cost by claim type):

* DVD drives scratching optical disks: £660
* Power supply failure: £240
* Broken USB ports: £100
* Logic board failure: £240

You may also choose to include the 'Per repair' cost for each repair reason.

Definition or formula

Sum of [Cost of claims] by reason

Typical data sources

» Warranty records/warranty tracking system
» Ticket management system
» Production records for repair department

Total cost of claims

Ref: Q3.5.3.2
Gold Star KPI

Drives: We manage the cost of our claims
To: Our warranty is competitive

Description

Understanding the overall cost of warranty claims is an important part of managing costs, and profitability, of your organisation.

A spike in total cost of claims can be an early warning indicator of problems ahead.

Example from Roughshod Repairs

Roughshod repair lots of different product lines. Roughshod's Nintbox4 repairs cost the following (total cost by claim type):

* DVD drives scratching optical disks: £660
* Power supply failure: £240
* Broken USB ports: £100
* Logic board failure: £240

Total cost of Nintbox4 claims £1,240.

They would work out their total warranty repair costs in the same way, including all of their repair lines.

Definition or formula

Sum of [Warranty repair and replacement costs]

Typical data sources

» Warranty records/warranty tracking system
» Ticket management system
» Production records for repair department

Common problems and mistakes

This is a lagging indicator of problems. It's wise not to focus too hard on managing the cost of warranty claims (unless fraudulent) but to focus on the root causes of warranty claims. This won't be quick, but is the most effective way of driving down warranty costs whilst protecting your reputation in the long term.

Post-claim customer survey average score

Ref: Q3.6.1.1
Silver Star KPI

Drives: Customers tell us how happy they are
To: Customers are happy with how we handle warranty claims

Description

A key element of warranty work is maintaining a good reputation and making sure your relationship with the customer remains as good as it can possibly be. Getting the customer to complete a 'post warranty claim' questionnaire is a good way to do this.

It may be a simple 'Would you recommend our company?' question or a more detailed online form, but asking how the warranty claim went should give you vital clues about how the customer felt at the end of the experience.

Example from Roughshod Repairs

Roughshod Repairs use three simple questions, scored 1-5, to find out how content their customers are with the way the warranty claim went. Those scores are:

A. On an overall basis, how satisfied are you with our performance?

B. How satisfied are you with the ease of doing business with us?

C. Would you recommend us to a friend?

The average score to these three questions, for the last period, was 3.7. So...

Post-claim customer survey average score = 3.7 or 74%

Definition or formula

Average of [Post-claim customer survey average score]

Typical data sources

» Warranty records/warranty tracking system
» Ticket management system
» Production records for repair department

Common problems and mistakes

Turning down a warranty claim is likely to have a serious adverse effect on this score. You may choose to have a way to look at the score including and excluding that group of customers, to see how much of an impact their opinions have.

Guarantee & Warranty

KPI Family: RI
Creative Effort

Hours planned for 'Deep Work'

Ref: R1.2.1.1
Gold Star KPI

Drives: Progress versus plan
To:　　We make progress against our milestones

Description

Deep work is the intensely focused state that enables us to make strides in our thinking and productivity. This state does not generally happen by accident, as it is very easily broken by minor interruptions and distractions.

Planning, and tracking, deep work is critical to achieve your targeted hours in this state - and ultimately your creative objectives.

Example from Ambiguous Associates

Austin is working on his next book. He knows that he can only really focus properly in short bursts. He uses the Pomodoro method, working intensely for 20 minute stretches, with short breaks in between. He plans to do 60 of these 'sprints' a week, clocking up 20 hours of 'Deep Work' each week. Every time he does a sprint, he puts a green magnetic marker on a white board. At the end of the week he totals up the 20 minute markers and logs the 'Deep Work' in a spreadsheet.

Deep work last week: 20 hours 40 minutes

Hours planned for deep work: 20 hours

Definition or formula

Sum of (Time spent in 'Deep Work' state]

Typical data sources

» Time logs
» Tracking board
» Diary

Common problems and mistakes

To really know if you have been engaged in 'deep work' you need to have attained, and be able to identify 'flow'. Flow is a particular state of mind where you become completely immersed in your current activity - often losing track of time. Read 'Deep Work' by Cal Newport to find out more - details in the Bibliography. If you find you lose track of time doing certain activities you like - for example computer games - that's a state of 'flow' and is the sort of mind state that you should aim for with 'Deep Work'.

Technical Research & Development

Number of patents applied for

Ref: R2.4.0.1
Silver Star KPI

Drives: Our patents are genuinely novel
To: We have a steady stream of new and effective patents

Description

Having something that is potentially patentable may be some indication that you have a novel idea. Measuring the number of patents applied for may be an indication of the number of novel ideas being produced.

Example from Car Crevice Cleaners

Last year Colin applied for 6 patents. Two were rejected, two granted and two applications are still pending.

Number of patents applied for: 6

Definition or formula

Count of [Unique patent application submissions]

Typical data sources

» Unique patent application documents

Note, you may submit the same idea to more than one geographic patent office. This is still just one patent application for the sake of this measure.

Setting targets

Targeting patent applications can be a very risky thing to do. As there are few quality checks before a patent is applied for, it could be very easy for your team to stick in flaky patents just to boost numbers.

Common problems and mistakes

What this figure does not show is whether the idea/design you patented:

1. Will work

2. Is a good idea

3. Is relevant to your business or sector

4. Will make money

Number of patents granted

Ref: R2.4.0.2
Gold Star KPI

Drives: Our patents are genuinely novel
To: We have a steady stream of new and effective patents

Description

To have a patent granted there must be some provable level of novelty (although the level of evidence required varies by country). Patents granted may be an indicator of genuinely novel ideas.

Example from Car Crevice Cleaners

Colin had two patents granted last year.

Number of patents granted (last year): 2

Definition or formula

Count of [Unique patents granted]

Typical data sources

» Patent office patents officially granted

Note, you may be granted a patent for an idea in more than one geographic patent office. This is still just one patent for the sake of this measure.

Setting targets

Targeting patents can be a very risky thing to do. It could be very easy for your team to successfully apply for mad/useless patents just to boost numbers. The patent application process can also be expensive, so you could quickly waste money on useless patents.

Common problems and mistakes

What this figure does not show is whether the idea/design you patented:

1. Will work

2. Is a good idea

3. Is relevant to your business or sector

4. Will make money

Profitable patents age profile

Ref: R2.4.1.1
Gold Star KPI

Drives: We have a spread of patent ages providing income
To: We have a steady stream of new and effective patents

Description

Patents have a fixed life span. This measure shows where in that life span your patents are.

Tracking patent life spans will enable you to identify risk that comes with major revenue streams depending on live patents. When those patents expire, the profitability of products can plummet, particularly if your brand is weak or your product is commoditised.

Example from Car Crevice Cleaners

Colin invented the 'crevice-cleaner' 18 years ago and 'roof rake' 10 years ago. Products covered by these two patents account for nearly 80% of his profit. In the US patents usually expire 20 years after the earliest filing date.

Remaining US patent time:
* Crevice cleaner: 2 years (US)
* Roof rake: 10 years (US)

Definition or formula

Count of [Years remaining on patent] by patent

Typical data sources

» Patent filing documents
» Patent office portal/database

Value of sales by patent

Ref: R2.5.3.1
Gold Star KPI

Drives: We generate sales, revenue & profit from patents
To: We use patents effectively

Description

Some patents may be key to being able to sell and profit from certain products. Other patents may never make you a penny.

Tracking value of sales by patent allows you to identify your 'star' patents and to focus your efforts on maximising income, licensing and protecting those income generators.

Example from Car Crevice Cleaners

Colin keeps a record of sales by patent type.

Value of sales by patent:

* *Crevice Cleaner: £150k in sales and licences last year*
* *Roof Rake: £30k in sales and licence fees last year*

Definition or formula

Sum of [Sales and other income] related to specific products covered by a patent

Typical data sources

» Sales system
» Finance system

Return on product R&D investment

Ref: R2.6.1.1
Gold Star KPI

Drives: Market share increases as a result of concept/improvement
To: Our innovations add value and generate revenue

Description

For a growing business, research and development is all about making money at some point. This measure looks at the payback ratio of cash invested and profit delivered by research and development.

Return on R&D is about identifying which investments (of time, effort and money) converted into income and profits.

Example from Car Crevice Cleaners

Colin has been fooling about with a special alloy wheel cleaner that will clean all the nooks and crannies in one go.

- He spent £10k on prototypes and testing.
- He patented the design 12 months ago at a cost of £500.
- He brought it to market last year making a profit of £8k on WonderWheelsWasherWiper in year 1 then £25k profit in year 2.

Showing this cumulatively...

* R&D return in year 1: (£8k - £10.5k) / (£10.5k) = -24%
* R&D return in year 2: ((£8k + £25k - £10.5k) / £10.5k = +214%

Definition or formula

(Sum of [Profit arising from sales enabled by R&D] - Sum of [R&D costs]) / Sum of [R&D costs]

Typical data sources

» Profit figures, by product types
» Profit figures over time
» Profit split by those products affected by R&D and those not

Common problems and mistakes

It can be hard to track the impact of R&D, particularly where there are multiple innovations introduced at once (which ones worked?) or there's a long delay between the research and the benefits.

Look for differences which may give you some rough-cut idea. Did the innovation only affect certain product lines? If so, you can compare the growth rates for both and reasonably assume the difference may be because of your research and development work.

Market share increase attributable to innovation

Ref: R2.6.1.2
Silver Star KPI

Drives: Market share increases as a result of concept/improvement
To: Our innovations add value and generate revenue

Description

Some research and development work may not lead directly to profitability, but might help you enter markets (or increase share in markets) that were previously inaccessible.

Market share is often a key goal for rapidly growing businesses. In the electric car business Tesla is making a hefty loss on its cars, but it aggressively targeted the 'everyday' car market and had to innovate on many fronts to get into this (as yet) unprofitable market segment.

Example from Car Crevice Cleaners

Before the invention of the Crevice Cleaner, Colin's company had no sales share in that market. Through some web research and sensible estimates, he arrives at the following figures...

* Competing devices market share 1 million sold per annum.
* Crevice cleaners sold in UK to date: 1.5 million

Market share attributable (estimated) to Crevice Cleaner patent: 1.5 / 2.5 = 60%

So 'Market share increase attributable to innovation' = 60%

Definition or formula

Sum of (Sales derived directly from innovation] / Sum of [Estimated market size]

Typical data sources

» Industry surveys, demographic data
» Sensible estimates (using Fermi decomposition, for example)
» Internal sales figures

Time from idea to product on sale

Ref: R2.9.0.2
Gold Star KPI

To: Ideas are swiftly prototyped

Description

Innovation and development can take time, especially if it gets pushed to the background when pressing operational issues pop up. Tracking the time from start to finish enables you to make sensible decisions about resources and focus.

If you take too long to develop or innovate, the market moves on. Fast development and innovation are key to success.

Example from Car Crevice Cleaners

It took 13 months for Colin to take his WonderWheelsWashWiper from a sketched concept to a marketable product…

Time from idea to product on sales: 13 months.

Where you have more than 1 product just average the development time.

Definition or formula

Date [Product on sale] - Date [Development started]

Typical data sources

» 'Ideas and development log' where new ideas are noted and tracked

I use Evernote, so ideas are automatically time-stamped when you create a new note in that 'Ideas' notebook.

Common problems and mistakes

Being clear when an R&D piece of work 'starts' can be tricky, especially when you are a small business with lots of ideas flying around. Keeping an 'ideas and development log' with ideas, dates and updated notes can help this process.

Where development takes more than one period (year, for example) you need to think carefully in which year you report costs, development effort and so on.

Service Research & Development

Total additional profit from new services

Ref: R3.2.1.2
Gold Star KPI

Drives: New services are profitable
To: New services contribute financially

Description

This is a lagging indicator, as even successful new services may take time to generate profit, but ultimately a major yardstick of success.

Create a place holder on your dashboard or weekly report for this KPI and it will be a constant jab-in-the-ribs to get on and earn some income from new services!

Example from Dangerous Developers

Daniella is looking at new cloud-based services that she can charge clients a subscription for.

Her team have developed a patch-management cloud service for small businesses. So far they have sold 20 single-seat licences. The licences are £20 a month gross profit.

Total additional profit from new service 20 x £20 = £400 a month profit.

Definition or formula

Sum of [Gross profit from new services]

Typical data sources

» New Service Development log
» Finance system

Number of new service improvement ideas

Ref: R3.4.1.1
Silver Star KPI

Drives: We have a steady supply of new ideas to try
To: Improve an existing service

Description

Not all service ideas are revolutionary, many of them just build on existing services in small ways. Keep a tally of these to see how you are (or aren't) innovating on existing services.

This type of innovation is less glamorous than 'new' ideas, but can often deliver major payback and be implemented quicker than completely new services.

Example from Dangerous Developers

Dangerous Developers decided to increase their app development fees, but at the same time added a 'self service' update portal - allowing clients to view development effort and progress any time they like.

Number of new service improvement ideas: 1

Definition or formula

Count of [Service improvement ideas]

Typical data sources

» New Service Development log

Setting targets

It's generally best not to specifically target a certain number of new ideas, as it's very easy to come up with a large number of poor quality ideas if you need to. Best instead to review the figure, but focus on the quality and thought processes leading up to the figure.

Number of new improved service ideas tested

Ref: R3.4.2.1
Gold Star KPI

Drives: We test our improved service ideas for performance
To: Improve an existing service

Description

It is important to continue to innovate in your 'core' services, even if you have great hopes for your completely 'new' services. Keeping a tally of how many tests you have run for 'improvement' of existing services makes sure you keep your eye on the ball.

Not all ideas need to be massive or even particularly clever, but continuously improving your service offer will keep you competitive and profitable, if done properly.

Example from Dangerous Developers

The 'customer self-service project portal' was one of five service improvement ideas Dangerous Developers tested.

New service ideas tested: 5

Definition or formula

Count of [Tested service improvement ideas]

Typical data sources

» New Service Development log

Common problems and mistakes

Don't test terrible ideas just to increase this figure, be honest with yourself about whether an idea is really worth testing.

Number of new service ideas

Ref: R3.5.1.1
Silver Star KPI

Drives: We have a steady supply of new ideas to try
To: Develop new services

Description

If you don't come up with any new ideas, you are unlikely to innovate or improve your offer. Keeping track of this figure will give you some indication of the focus on generating new ideas.

Whilst the number of new ideas is no measure of quality, a very low figure may be grounds for concern. Many smaller businesses are totally engrossed in survival, so this number should focus the mind on the longer term, less urgent, task of developing new service ideas.

Example from Dangerous Developers

The cloud-based patch management service was one of three ideas that underwent initial build and testing. Just one has delivered any revenue so far.

Number of service ideas: 3

Definition or formula

Count of [New service ideas]

Typical data sources

» New Service Development log

Setting targets

It's generally best not to specifically target a certain number of new ideas, as it's very easy to come up with a large number of poor quality ideas if you need to. Best instead to review the figure, but focus on the quality and thought processes leading up to the figure.

Number of new service ideas tested

Ref: R3.5.2.1
Gold Star KPI

Drives: We test our new ideas for performance promptly
To: Develop new services

Description

Testing ideas is a key part of the 'new service ideas' pipeline. Keeping a tally of how many tests you have run gives you some guide to progress.

Testing can take all sorts of forms. Often something as simple as a test AdWords campaign will tell you if your product is going to be a hit or not.

Example from Dangerous Developers

Dangerous Developers did initial test builds of three ideas, but they also tested three other ideas by running Google AdWords campaigns and seeing how many people clicked on the ads (not many did).

New service ideas tested: 6

Definition or formula

Count of [New service ideas tested]

Typical data sources

» New Service Development log

Common problems and mistakes

Don't test terrible ideas just to increase this figure, be honest with yourself about whether an idea is really worth testing.

Intellectual Property Protection (Patents & Copyright)

Value of royalties received

Ref: R4.1.1.1
Gold Star KPI

Drives: We manage payment of due royalties
To: We manage royalties/franchise payments

Description

This is the income you receive for book, video or music royalties.

The royalties you receive from legitimate sales enable you to value the lost royalties from piracy.

Example from Ambiguous Associates

Austin's new book is selling really well by year three of its publication. He sells 6,000 copies across eBook and paperback sales, with an average royalty of £5 per copy.

Value of total royalties received: £30,000

Definition or formula

Sum of [Royalties and commissions paid]

Typical data sources

» Online sales portals (e.g. Amazon)
» Downloaded royalty spreadsheets
» Bank account royalty receipts

Number of infringements identified

Ref: R4.2.1.3
Silver Star KPI

Drives: We identify intellectual property infringements
To: We manage licensing

Description

Keeping a simple tally of the number of infringements tells you if you have any kind of a piracy problem.

Value of royalties evaded would be a better measure, but is really hard to measure/unknowable.

Example from Ambiguous Associates

Using Google Alerts, Austin has identified a notorious commercial document sharing site that has a copy of his first book on it. He sees that his book has been shared 1,200 times from that site, with no royalties being paid.

Number of infringements identified: 1,200

Definition or formula

Count of [Number of infringements identified]

Typical data sources

» Search engine alerts (e.g. Google Alerts)
» Online searches of document sharing sites
» Newsgroups and Bit Torrent trackers etc.

Common problems and mistakes

In the example from Ambiguous Associates, a single 'infringement' - the document sharing site - led to 1,200 pirated copies being downloaded. I would count this as 1,200 infringements, even though there is only one initial 'share' as this represents a loss of royalty income on (up to) 1,200 books. I say 'up to' as you have to ask yourself the question 'Would the 1,200 have actually 'bought' your book if it weren't free?'

Web alerts received

Ref: R4.2.1.4
Silver Star KPI

Drives: We identify intellectual property infringements
To: We manage licensing

Description
One of the first steps towards detecting copyright infringement is a web alert for relevant trade marks or keywords.

One of the simplest ways to do this is to set up a Google alert for the relevant term, then set the frequency with which you would like to receive updates.

Example from Ambiguous Associates
Austin uses Google Alerts to alert him on a daily basis of certain keywords that have appeared on the web. Because his search terms are directly related to his trademarked terms, the alerts give him a pretty good idea of any new (and unauthorised) links on the web.

Yesterday he had 12 alerts, eleven were benign mentions of his last book, but one showed a document sharing site was now listing an ePub edition of his book - without permission.

Web alerts received: 12

Definition or formula
Count of [Web alerts received]

Typical data sources
» Web alert service
» Web alert emails

Value of damages recovered

Ref: R4.2.2.4
Silver Star KPI

Drives: We enforce what is owed to us
To: We manage licensing

Description
If you are seeking any kind of copyright infringement compensation, keep track of how much has been recovered using this figure.

Prevention is better than cure when it comes to infringement. Any recovery action, beyond a sternly-worded letter, is likely to eat up any cash benefit of the recovered amounts - plus it may well consume your valuable time too.

Example from Ambiguous Associates
Austin has just decided to issue a 'DMCA takedown request' on the electronic copies of his book he found online, rather than bothering with legal action.

Value of damages recovered: £0

Definition or formula
Sum of [Value of damages recovered]

Typical data sources
» Legal documents and agreements
» Finance system
» Finance records

Sales Value, Activity & Results

Average order value by customer

Ref: S1.1.1.2
Gold Star KPI

Drives: We cross-sell to existing customers
To: We maximise sales to existing customers

Description

Shows the average order value by customer. Trended over time this will show how effective we are at maximising the value of each sale, through upselling or cross-selling. Depending on the environment, there are a number of different sales activities that can influence this. Selling accessories, upgrades or extra services are classic 'cross-sells'. Encouraging the customer to opt for a higher specification product or service is an 'upsell'. Either of these, done right, will nudge this KPI in the right direction.

Example from Chaos Coffee Shop

Charlie wants to increase the value of each sale. Now he makes sure he and his staff offer a £1 donut with every coffee served. This KPI shows him how successful they are at this.

Average order value: £5.17 per till transaction last week.

During the promotion, this figure moved up to £5.78.

Definition or formula

Sum of [All order values] / Count of [Customers]

Typical data sources

» Sales management system
» Sales spreadsheet or database, accounts/finance system
» Invoice records
» Till receipts

Common problems and mistakes

This value will vary from period-to-period whether or not you are changing your sales process. It is important to look at the 'natural' variability in the value before you get too excited (or despondent) about whether your clever new sales approach is working. Also, make sure you are clear what 'by customer' means. In some situations it's really clear, in other businesses it may not be so easy to establish - for example a 'self service' group holiday booking for several families. Don't get bogged down in trying to stick to the exact KPI definition shown here, do what makes sense.

Average spend per sale to existing customers

Ref: S1.1.2.1
Gold Star KPI

Drives: We sell more to existing customers
To: We maximise sales to existing customers

Description

'Average spend per existing customer' is closely related to 'Average order value by customer', but relates to customers that we have dealt with before. Unlike the 'Average order value per customer' we can look at the profile of spending for existing customers, answering questions like 'Do they spend more or less in Year 2 of being our customer?'. For this to work properly you need some sort of customer identifier. This will usually be a discount card, address or membership.

Example from Chaos Coffee Shop

Charlie has a loyalty card scheme. He has noticed that since Dire Donuts opened a few doors down from Chaos Coffee,

Average spend per existing customer (with a loyalty card): £3.40

This has dipped from £3.80 the previous week. He can pretty much figure out which customers have defected to Dire Donuts and target them with special promotions.

Definition or formula

Sum of [All order values: previous customers only] / Count of [Customers: previous customers only]

Typical data sources

» Sales management system
» Sales spreadsheet or database
» Accounts/finance system
» Invoice records
» Till receipts
» Customer loyalty records

Common problems and mistakes

As with 'Average order value by customer' this value will vary from period-to-period whether or not you are changing your sales process. It is important to look at the 'natural' variability in the value before you decide if your clever new sales approach is working.

Total lifetime spend by customer

Ref: S1.1.2.2
Gold Star KPI

Drives: We sell more to existing customers
To: We maximise sales to existing customers

Description

This shows the total amount a customer has spent with your business, since their first purchase. Some customers may be particularly loyal or important to your business. Looking at your top spenders enables you to target these customers with offers or premium service to make sure they stay with your business and spend up to their potential. To measure this you must have a unique customer identifier, such as a name and address, loyalty or membership number.

Example from Dangerous Developers

Daniella has around 50 previous clients, but when she looks at the sales by customer since they started, she realises that 70% of her income has come from just one customer. This is important for two reasons, firstly she needs to be thinking hard about how to keep this customer loyal and happy with their service. Secondly she needs to think about what will happen if they lose that customer (or they stop paying their bills).

Definition or formula

Sum of [All order values: previous customers only] by customer

Typical data sources

» Sales management system
» Sales spreadsheet or database
» Accounts/finance system
» Invoice records
» Till receipts
» Customer loyalty records

Common problems and mistakes

Identifying when a customer is no longer a customer can be hard. A high value customer who has stopped spending with you may be possible to save, but the sooner you identify that they have gone to a rival, the better the chance you have to recover them. It varies hugely between customers, but focus on the observable behaviours/outcomes that might give you some indication that they have strayed - e.g. have they stopped opening the email newsletters?

Lead conversion rate

Ref: S1.2.1.1
Gold Star KPI

Drives: Leads are converted
To: Effective lead conversion

Description

A sales lead is where a potential customer has shown some interest. This measure shows how good we are at turning those 'expressions of interest' into sales. Measuring lead conversion rate helps avoid 'lead stuffing' where we are tempted to include 'leads' that really have no hope of converting into sales.

Example from Dangerous Developers

Daniella keeps a spreadsheet of leads, showing when the lead was logged, what the lead was regarding and the outcome. Looking at her leads for last month....

- Leads - 15
- Sales - 2

So the lead conversion rate is 2 / 15 = 13%

Now 9 of those leads are dead, but 4 are neither sales nor dead. See the 'Common Problems' section below for how to deal with these.

Definition or formula

Count of [Sales] / Count of [Leads]

Typical data sources

» Sales management system/CRM system
» Sales spreadsheet or database

Common problems and mistakes

One of the challenges with tracking lead conversions is that the lead time can be very long and not have a definite end point. There are two ways to tackle this.

1. Revisit historic 'conversion rates' and update them with any late sales. If you do this, you need to accept that recent periods may not be the final view.

2. You have a 'hard stop' i.e. a certain period after a lead comes in (typically at the end of period, or certain number of periods after the lead arrives). This will under-call your lead conversion, but will allow you to do a firm comparison between more recent periods.

Segmented value of sales

Ref: S1.4.1.1
Silver Star KPI

Drives: Sales value
To: We sell in line with our plan

Description
This shows the breakdown of sales by **type**. This may be product families, models or particular types of service. Although technically this is just a breakdown of 'Total value of sales', it is such a common and important breakdown it justifies its own entry.

Example from Chaos Coffee Shop
Charlie likes to break down sales into food and drinks categories. Here's his breakdown from last week...

Segmented value of sales:
- Hot drinks: £3,700
- Food: £1,800

Definition or formula
Sum of [Sales revenue] by segment or category

Typical data sources
» EPOS/Till records
» Sales system

Total value of sales

Ref: S1.4.1.2
Gold Star KPI

Drives: Sales value
To: We sell in line with our plan

Description
This shows the total value of all sales for a given period

We need to be clear when a 'sale' is made. Is it when a contract is signed, the product is delivered or the cash is in the bank?

Example from Chaos Coffee Shop
Charlie's total value of sales last week was £5,500. So...

Total value of sales = £5,500

Definition or formula
Sum of [Sales value] for period

Typical data sources
» Sales management system
» Sales spreadsheet or database
» Accounts/finance system
» Invoice records
» EPOS/Till records

Setting targets
Excessive focus on this can lead to very significant operational risks. It's not unknown for sales people to book work that isn't yet signed off to hit period sales targets or to book sales then cancel them in the next period to hit targets.

Common problems and mistakes
You need to be clear whether this includes or excludes sales taxes etc.

The definition of a sale varies a bit depending on the type of business. For a coffee shop it's pretty easy, for a high value service business we need to be clear whether it's 'one request of service', 'signing a new contract' or something else.

Average value per sale

Ref: S1.4.1.3
Silver Star KPI

Drives: Sales value
To: We sell in line with our plan

Description

This is identical to 'Average order value by customer' (S1.1.1.2), except you calculate the average value based on per **transaction**, not per **customer**, making it easier in most situations. It's up to you which you measure. Does it make more sense to measure by customer sale or order? It depends on your business, and it generally makes sense to measure just one or the other.

Volume of sales words/hours/widgets

Ref: S1.4.2.1
Gold Star KPI

Drives: Sales volume
To: We sell in line with our plan

Description

Almost all businesses have some kind of 'unit of production', the thing which you sell. This is usually a physical product (and quantity), a number of hours service delivery or a service outcome. This measure is the total of those units.

Example from Dangerous Developers

Daniella's team charges their customer based on hours worked, in line with the agreed contract and contract variations.

Last week they invoiced 82 hours - that's their sales volume.

Definition or formula

Sum of [Volume sold] by variant (if appropriate)

Typical data sources

» Sales management system
» CRM system
» Sales spreadsheet or database

Common problems and mistakes

You may have a variety of products or services that cannot simply be added up to one figure. In this situation it's best to deal with volumes by product/service type/variant.

531

Targeted sales value

Ref: S1.5.0.1
Silver Star KPI

To: Booked revenue meets or exceeds target

Description

This isn't really a KPI, but it's such a common target that it deserves a special entry of its own. This is the value of sales that you would like your team/business to hit in a given period.

Deciding on the value to use is a fine balancing act. Setting the value too high can destroy morale and undermine the credibility of the target. Setting it too low can lead to missed opportunity and excessive incentive payments.

Example from Roughshod Repairs

Ruby has a sales manager, Robert, who is targeted with winning new contracts with electronics firms.

Robert has been targeted with bringing in an extra £500k of new client sales each year.

Ruby takes the total sales from last year, adds £500k to it and that is the sales target for this year.

Definition or formula

[Targeted sales value]

Typical data sources

Manager with sales responsibility, will usually also include wider management team due to criticality of this figure.

Setting targets

Excessive focus on this can lead to very significant operational risks. It's not unknown for sales people to book work that isn't yet signed off to hit period sales targets or to book sales then cancel them in the next period to hit targets.

Booked sales value

Ref: S1.5.0.2
Gold Star KPI

To: Booked revenue meets or exceeds target

Description

This measure shows how much work or product you have already sold but have yet to deliver. This is a particularly important measure where you have capacity that you want to use - for example, a physiotherapist who wants a full diary for the week, a hotel that wants their rooms booked up or a manufacturing firm that wants to keep its machines and people busy making goods that will be sold. Too much booked work can also be a bad thing, leading to poorer customer service on new orders.

Whilst this is a very important measure, keep an eye on profitability (especially Gross profit per unit product/service/item). It can be tempting to fill the order book at all costs and end up working for a loss.

Example from Dangerous Developers

Daniella and Dave have 4 apps under development for clients. They know the quoted hours and delivery dates for each. Putting these on a spreadsheet they can see that the next 4 weeks are completely booked with work, so Daniella needs to focus on sales and delivery dates later than that pipeline of work.

Definition or formula

Sum of [Booked sales value] for period

Typical data sources

» Sales management system
» CRM system
» Sales spreadsheet or database

Common problems and mistakes

It's important to keep an eye on the amount of booked work/time. It's great to feel secure and have plenty in the pipeline, but too much booked business can lead to poor service for new customers. A very large amount of booked work suggests you should look at extra capacity or putting your prices up!

New qualified leads each month

Ref: S1.6.1.1
Gold Star KPI

Drives: We win new accounts
To: Plenty of good quality leads

Description

This is the number of leads each month, where a few simple questions have been asked to make sure this is a serious lead (lead qualification).

Qualifying a lead varies hugely depending on the type of sale, but it will usually involve establishing:

- The customer need, and whether it is something that we as a business can provide.
- Are our prices in line with the customer expectation?
- If the person we are dealing with is a decision maker?
- If the customer has the funds to make the purchase?
- If the required delivery is time realistic?

Example from Dangerous Developers

Daniella keeps a spreadsheet for tracking leads, showing when the lead was logged, what the lead was regarding and the outcome. To qualify a lead she makes sure that the prospect has been asked a few simple questions. Those that pass are flagged as 'qualified' on her spreadsheet.

Looking at her leads for last month she can identify the number of new, qualified, leads...

New qualified leads last month = 15

Definition or formula

Count of [Qualified leads] in period

Typical data sources

- » Sales management system
- » CRM system
- » Sales spreadsheet or database

Common problems and mistakes

This a measure for order-based businesses and isn't applicable to businesses that rely on 'passing' trade, like shops and restaurants.

Number of new accounts or customers

Ref: S1.6.1.2
Silver Star KPI

Drives: We win new accounts
To: Plenty of good quality leads

Description

This shows how successful we are at attracting new customers. You would typically use this in an environment where we are trying to expand our customer base.

Example from Woeful Widget Warehouse

Will is trying to add new shops to his customer list. He's running a number of marketing efforts and wants to see if that's turning into new accounts and customers.

In the past month he has had 4 new shops open accounts with Woeful Widget Warehouse...

Number of new accounts (last month): 4

He's looking at this measure, in conjunction with 'Total lifetime spend by customer' (for the new customers), to see whether the new customers are turning into regular business.

Definition or formula

Count of [New accounts opened or New customers]

Typical data sources

- » Order management system
- » CRM system
- » Customer account spreadsheet or database

Common problems and mistakes

Depending on your type of business there may be a big difference between opening an account and using it (i.e. being a customer). Be clear on what you are trying to achieve with this measure and the nature of your business before deciding whether account opening qualifies as a 'new customer'.

Sales - Hourly Billing

Average billing rate per hour

Ref: S2.1.1.1
Gold Star KPI

Drives: We bill at the optimum hourly rate
To: We get well paid for our sold billing hours

Description

This shows the average rate you charged for your billed time. For an hourly paid individual/company, there are only two drivers on income, the hours worked and the price you charge for those hours. Keeping your average billing rate per hour high gets you the most benefit from your hard work.

Example from Dangerous Developers

Last week Daniella and Dave did 82 hours of client work (between them) and invoiced £3,100 (before sales tax).

Average hourly rate that week was £3,100 / 82 = £37.80 per hour.

Definition or formula

Sum of [billed amount] / Sum of [Actual hours worked]

Typical data sources

» Receipts
» Bank records (statements or transactions download)
» Supplier invoices
» Accounting software
» Time logs/spreadsheet

Common problems and mistakes

You need to be crystal clear on whether you really bill per hour, or just put in the required hours to deliver on a quote. If you quoted £100 based on 10 hours, but in reality it took you 20 hours, your nominal hourly rate is £10 per hour but in reality it is only £5 per hour. Other pitfalls include whether or not you include travelling time in your 'worked hours'. I do, and I charge for them, as you can't do much else with that time - in particular you can't sell that time to any other clients.

Also be clear on whether you include sales tax in the figure. It doesn't really matter whether you do or don't (I don't, in my view it's not real 'income') as long as you are consistent and know which figure is used.

Market rate ratio

Ref: S2.1.1.2
Silver Star KPI

Drives: We bill at the optimum hourly rate
To: We get well paid for our sold billing hours

Description

The market ratio is a comparator between the average hourly rate you charge and the average for your sector. It helps you understand if you are 'cheap' or 'expensive' for the sector you are in.

Being 'cheap' or 'expensive' for your sector is not necessarily a good or bad thing. It is important to be clear on where you want to position your service and make sure you sit in the price bracket you intend to be in. Want to be a premium provider? You will want to have a ratio substantially above 1. Want to be 'bargain basement' then keep below a ratio of 1.

Example from Dangerous Developers

Dangerous Developers charge an actual average hourly billing rate of £37.80 per hour. From their research it looks as though the market rate, for UK developers, in their sector is nearer £80 per hour.

Their ratio is £37.80 / £80.00 = 0.47 (or 47%, if you prefer). They are cheap, really cheap.

They are seriously below the market rate, which may explain why they are turning work away at the moment.

Definition or formula

[Average billing rate per hour] / [Average market rate for same country and sector]

Typical data sources

» Average billing rate per hour and market research data - start by searching the web. You can buy this data, but it's not normally necessary.

Common problems and mistakes

When you compare yourself with the market rate be careful about the quality of the figure you are comparing yourself with. If you can, be clear on whether the 'hours' figure they are using is the 'nominal' one or whether they use the hours really consumed in delivering the service. It can make a big difference.

Original contract hours sold

Ref: S2.2.1.1
Gold Star KPI

Drives: We extend existing clients
To: Grow existing customers and contract hours

Description

This is the total of the contract hours included in agreed contracts.

These are the initial quoted hours. Extensions would be used in the calculation below to give the 'Contract extension ratio' ('Contract extension ratio' on page 544).

Example from Dangerous Developers

Dangerous Developers agreed to contracts with a total quoted effort of 2,800 hours last year.

Original contract hours sold: 2,800

Definition or formula

Sum of [Hours agreed in contracts]

Typical data sources

» Contract records and time logs/spreadsheet
» Invoiced hours

Sales - Words

Contract extension ratio

Ref: S3.2.1.2
Silver Star KPI

Drives: We extend existing client contracts
To:　　Grow existing contracts

Description

This is the ratio of actual hours billed to the original hours agreed. The more this number is above 1.00 the more 'extra' hours have been sold on top of the original agreement.

A high ratio can be a good thing, a delighted client asking for more work, or it can be a sign of problems, a project that is over-running and a client who feels they have no choice but to pour more money into it as they are committed and need the finished product. Either way, it's a number that is useful to keep an eye on and analyse if things go too far away from the norm.

Example from Dangerous Developers

Analysing last year's projects, Dangerous Developers identified that they developed 8 apps and that took 3,280 hours. The contracts for those 8 apps were initially based on 2,800 hours, and the agreed extensions came to 480 hours. The contract extension ratio is:

3,280 / 2,800 = 1.17 or 17% extension rate

Definition or formula

Sum of [Hours agreed in contracts] / (Sum of [Hours agreed in contract] + Sum of [Extra hours agreed with client])

Typical data sources

» Contract records and time logs/spreadsheet

Common problems and mistakes

We need to be really clear on billed vs. unbilled hours. This figure is focused on billed extensions. If unbilled hours are an issue you may consider a similar measure but focused on unbilled hours over-runs.

Average fee per 1,000 words

Ref: S3.1.1.1
Gold Star KPI

Drives: The rate we are paid for our work
To:　　We are well paid for our words

Description

This shows the average rate you charge for your writing per 1,000 words sold.

How fast you write is also a major lever on your income. This is covered separately in 'O3 - Efficiency - Words'.

Example from Pointless Prose

Patricia writes a 2,000 word piece for the tortoise-horror magazine 'Scared Shell-less'. She is paid £500 for the piece.

Average fee per 1,000 words is:

= £500 / 2 (thousand)

= £250 per thousand words

Definition or formula

Sum of [Billed amount] / Count of [Sold words written in 1,000s]

Typical data sources

» Receipts
» Bank records (statements or transactions download)
» Supplier invoices
» Accounting software
» Writing software word count

Market rate ratio

Ref: S3.1.1.2
Silver Star KPI

Drives: The rate we are paid for our work
To: We are well paid for our words

Description

The market ratio is a comparator between the average 1,000 word rate you charge and the average for your sector. It helps you understand if you are 'cheap' or 'expensive' for the sector you are in.

Being 'cheap' or 'expensive' for your sector is not necessarily a good or bad thing. It is important to be clear on where you want to position your service and make sure you sit in the quartile of pricing. Want to be a premium provider? You will want to have a ratio substantially above 1. Want to be 'bargain basement' then keep below a ratio of 1.

Example from Pointless Prose

The going rate, according to the trade website, for that kind of work is £200 per 1,000 words, so...

Market rate ratio is:

£250 / £200 = 1.25

Patricia is significantly above the 'going rate' for her kind of work.

Definition or formula

[Average billing rate per 1,000 words] / [Average market rate for same country and sector]

Typical data sources

» Web research
» Purchasing market data (but it's not normally necessary)

Common problems and mistakes

Rates can be quite variable, as can access to reliable and up-to-date data.

Be clear on what your income per 1,000 words does and does not include. Do you include sales tax or not? Whatever you decide, note it down in your KPI definitions and be consistent.

Sales - Contract Services

Original contract days sold

Ref: S4.2.1.1
Gold Star KPI

Drives: We extend existing client contracts
To: Grow existing contracts

Description

This is the total of the contract days included in agreed contracts.

These are the initial quoted days. Extensions would be used in the calculation below to give the 'Contract extension ratio'.

Example from Pointless Prose

Patricia originally agreed to do 1 day a week for 40 weeks a year.

Original contract days sold: 40

Definition or formula

Count of [Days agreed in contracts]

Typical data sources

» Contract records
» Time logs/spreadsheet

Contract extension ratio

Ref: S4.2.1.2
Silver Star KPI

Drives: We extend existing client contracts
To: Grow existing contracts

Description

This is the ratio of actual hours billed to the original days agreed. The more this number is above 1.00 the more 'extra' days have been sold on top of the original agreement.

A high ratio can be a good thing, a delighted client asking for more work, or it can be a sign of problems, a project that is over-running and a client who feels they have no choice but to pour more money into it as they are committed and need the finished product. Either way, it's a number that is useful to keep an eye on and analyse if things go too far away from the norm.

Example from Pointless Prose

Tortoise World proved to be an unexpected hit online. They asked Patricia to do 2 days a week, up from the the original contract of 1 day a week, so her...

Contract extension ratio is: 80 / 40 = 2.0 extension ratio

...or 100% extension rate (40 extra days / 40 original days).

Definition or formula

(Count of [Days agreed in contract] + Count of [Extra days agreed with client]) / Count of [Days agreed in contracts]

or

Count of [Extra days agreed with client]) / Count of [Days agreed in contracts]

Typical data sources

» Contract records and time logs/spreadsheet

Common problems and mistakes

We need to be really clear on billed vs. unbilled hours. This figure is focused on billed extensions. If unbilled hours are an issue you may consider a similar measure but focused on unbilled hours over-runs.

KPI Family: S5
Sales - Pricing

Product basket price comparison

Ref: S5.2.1.1
Silver Star KPI

Drives: We offer price and service that are competitive
To: Competitive pricing

Description

As well as comparing individual prices, you can look at a typical selection of products and services that might be bought together. The total cost of this basket of products can then be compared with your competitors. Using the 'basket of goods' approach can be a powerful way of managing promotions, enabling you to promote individual lines but adjust other prices up to keep the typical set of lines bought together at roughly the same level.

Example from Chaos Coffee Shop

Charlie has noticed that customers often buy breakfast from Chaos Coffee, a coffee, bacon roll and pastry. He has calculated the basket price like this...

* Coffee - £2.50
* Bacon roll - £2.00
* Danish pastry - £1.75

Total basket price: £6.25

Comparing this with Bubble Beverages, he notices that their basket price is £6.40. Comparing Chaos Coffee and Bubble Beverages baskets...

Price basket comparison: £6.25 / £6.40 = 97.6%

So Chaos Coffee's basket is about 2.5% cheaper than Bubble Beverages.

Definition or formula

Sum of [Price of each item in our basket] / Sum of [Price of each item in competitor's version of basket]

Typical data sources

» Pricing system
» Competitor survey (visit their premises, website or ask existing customers to find out their prices)

Common problems and mistakes

Make sure you are actually comparing like with like, in terms of quality, quantity and delivery format.

Average competitor selling price

Ref: S5.3.1.2
Gold Star KPI

Drives: Be competitive
To: Minimise discounts

Description

One of the 'big levers' for sales in most environments is price competitiveness. How expensive a product is, compared with your competition, will determine whether you have queues out the door of your shop or a pile of out-of-date stock.

Of course price is only one of the drivers on sales, perceived service, quality, brand prestige and availability all play their part.

Example from Woeful Widget Warehouse

One of Woeful Widget's big sellers is the pack of 100 latex modelling balloons. Will keeps a close eye on competitors to make sure he stays competitive on these, even if he's not the cheapest. He knows this is one of the items where his customers are quite aware of the price and they are quick to notice if they seem expensive.

Will charges £5.50 for a pack. His competitors charge between £5.40 and £6.50 with an average price of £6.10 for the ten firms he identifies as his primary competitors. Will knows that his delivery charges are highly competitive, so he is happy with the price point he has at the moment.

Definition or formula

Average of [Item price at identified competitors]

Typical data sources

» Web search
» Customer feedback
» Mailshot promotions or any other kind of competitor product advertising.

Average selling price

Ref: S5.4.1.1
Gold Star KPI

Drives: Maximise price
To: Optimise revenue

Description

Where price is by negotiation, then you will want to keep a close eye on the price you achieve at the end of those negotiations.

A good understanding of cost of the product or service being sold will help you put the average price in context.

Example from Dangerous Developers

Daniella handles negotiations with clients. Each app contract is different, so Daniella has decided to compare the £/hour she achieves during the contract negotiations. So for her latest app, Choco Connoisseur, she estimates 800 hours of development effort and has quoted £40,000 to the client. The client has signed off on the contract and Daniella calculates the hourly rate to be:

Average selling price: £40,000 / 800 = £50 per hour

So long as the project doesn't take more hours than expected, this is significantly above their historic hourly rate, so looks like a step in the right direction.

Definition or formula

Average of [Sale price achieved] for products of similar type

Typical data sources

» Sales pipeline spreadsheet
» Sales software

Total value of discounts

Ref: S5.4.2.1
Silver Star KPI

Drives: Maximise individual product/service profit margins (F1)
To: Optimise revenue

Description

If your sales team have the final say on price, or you have a price-match policy, an early warning indicator of price problems may be having to give frequent discounts to win business.

Example from Woeful Widget Warehouse

Will runs a 'price match' promise. If a customer finds a product cheaper then Woeful Widget Warehouse will beat that price by 10%. He has noticed that last month this price match was used 5 times by customers buying Walrus Wailer Whistles.

* *Woeful Widget Warehouse price: £10.00*
* *Competitor price match price: £9.00*
* *Beat it by 10% price: £8.10*
* *Discount per item: £1.90*

Total value of discounts: 5 x £1.90 = £9.50

Definition or formula

Sum of [Discount given to customer from usual price]

Typical data sources

» Internal pricing list
» Evidence of competitor pricing from customer, discount voucher or notes from sales staff

Common problems and mistakes

Frequent discounting may be a sign of poor price competitiveness, but it could also be the sign of a poorly structured sales incentive scheme. Where sales staff are targeted on sales value, rather than profit, and have the discretion to offer discounts, they will often make full use of those discounts to hit their bonus targets.

Sales - Advertising, Pay Per Click & Organic Traffic

Click-through rate

Ref: S6.1.1.1
Silver Star KPI

Drives: Inline advert performance
To: We use inline and pay per click advertising effectively

Description
This measure shows what proportion of people clicked on an advert when it was displayed. This usually refers to web browser inline adverts, but may apply to inline adverts in any application, for instance a messenger app that supports inline adverts.

This tells you more than 'Impressions' as there must be some glimmer of interest from your reader to want to click on the advert.

Example from Mayhem Manufacturing
Mohammed has decided to advertise his mini-volcano pen holders on the web. His advert is displayed 1,000 times. 10 people click on the advert.

Click-through rate is: 10 / 1,000 = 1%

Definition or formula
Count of [Ad click-throughs] / Count of [Impressions]

Typical data sources
» Online advertising platform admin view

Common problems and mistakes
Make sure you don't create an advert that is designed purely to drive clicks, but isn't strictly related to your product or service. An indicator of relevance will be your sales conversion rate for those clicks.

Impressions per ad

Ref: S6.1.1.2
Silver Star KPI

Drives: Inline advert performance
To: We use inline and pay per click advertising effectively

Description
This tells us how many times our advert has been shown/displayed. The advertising platform is paid regardless of whether the advert is clicked on.

The number of times an advert is displayed is almost entirely controlled by the advertising platform.

Example from Roughshod Repairs
Roughshod Repairs paid to run one particular advert on electronics industry news websites in Europe and the US. Their advert was displayed 25,000 times.

Impressions per advert = 25,000

Definition or formula
Count of [Impressions]

Typical data sources
» Online advertising platform admin view

Common problems and mistakes
If the advertising platform are paid per click, then they will normally optimise the impressions to maximise click-through. If they are paid per impression you need to exercise healthy caution about how and where they are displayed. Clearly the advertising platform doesn't have any particular interest in the effectiveness of your ads.

Facebook frequency

Ref: S6.1.1.3
Silver Star KPI

Drives: Inline advert performance
To: We use inline and pay per click advertising effectively

Description

Facebook frequency shows the average number of times each individual has seen your ad. It is Impressions divided by Reach (see 'Total reach' on page 554).

Managing this figure means you can be sure you're not over-saturating your audience with your ads. Aim to keep your Frequency under 4 for ads being shown in the News Feed and under 8 for ads shown in the Right Sidebar.

Example from Mayhem Manufacturing

Mohammed ran a Facebook advertising campaign for his pen holders.

The current average frequency is 12.

Mohammed is probably over-exposing his target market (and really annoying them in the process). He is thinking about increasing the reach of the adverts (spending his money on a wider audience) or trimming back his budget.

Definition or formula

Count of [Facebook Frequency]

Typical data sources

» Facebook analytics for advertisers

Setting targets

Aim to keep your Frequency under 4 for ads being shown in the News Feed and under 8 for ads shown in the Right Sidebar.

Common problems and mistakes

Over exposing an individual to Facebook banner ads can lead to "banner blindness". The symptom of this is decreased click-through rates and a resulting increase in cost per click and cost per sale.

Cost per click by channel

Ref: S6.1.1.4
Gold Star KPI

Drives: Inline advert performance
To: We use inline and pay per click advertising effectively

Description

Shows the advertising costs per sale, broken down by channel (online, radio, print and TV, for example).

This gives you a sanity check. If you are spending anywhere near your per-sale profit margin on click acquisition, then you know that you are heading for trouble, no matter how good your conversion rate is.

Example from Mayhem Manufacturing

Mohammed paid £400 for 1,000 clicks using keyword advertising.

The cost per click, for search adverts is £400 / 1,000

= £0.40 per click

Definition or formula

Sum of [Advertising costs for channel] / Count of [Clicks generated for channel]

Typical data sources

» Analytics from advertising provider

Common problems and mistakes

Whilst this is a useful measure, it can't be used in isolation. Poor conversion rates once you have a click, can still make good click costs wasted expenditure. It should be used in partnership with Cost per sale and Return on Investment to give a proper picture.

In-page ad click rate

Ref: S6.3.1.1
Silver Star KPI

Drives: We attract people to our website
To: We gain sales through organic web traffic

Description

Where we have a website that is designed to attract organic traffic we may place our own adverts on pages around our website. This measure tells us how many of these internal adverts are clicked on.

This can also be a useful proxy for how engaged your readers are with your offer. Perhaps think about running 'split tests', where you run similar ads with subtle differences, to see what works best.

Example from Dangerous Developers

Dangerous Developers give away a free white paper on app design on their website. They position the ads on most of their website pages and require interested visitors to sign up using their contact details if they want to download the paper.

Last month the in-page ads were clicked 73 times, so the In-page ad click rate is 73 click per month, for that month.

Definition or formula

Count of [In-page ad clicks] / Sum [Time periods covered]

Typical data sources

» The backend software for your website (e.g. WordPress, Drupal etc.) or plugin used to serve the ads

Common problems and mistakes

Don't trick people into clicking by using misleading claims. They will find out they have been tricked and be annoyed.

Confirmed newsletter signups

Ref: S6.3.1.2
Gold Star KPI

Drives: We attract people to our website
To: We gain sales through organic web traffic

Description

For many growing businesses the newsletter is one of their primary marketing tools. The number of signups to your newsletter gives you a good indication of interest and engagement in your product.

It's important to use confirmed opt-in for newsletter signups to avoid being marked as a spammer. When you use opt-in emails a number of factors affect deliverability, so look very carefully at the spam rating of your confirmation emails to make sure that they don't languish in the junk email folder of your enthusiastic newsletter recruit.

Example from Dangerous Developers

Dangerous Developers use a newsletter signup popover on their website. Like all good marketers, Daniella's system sends out a confirmation email.

Last month Daniella's newsletter signup system sent out 100 confirmation emails. Of these 60 were confirmed.

The confirmed newsletter signups were 60 for last month.

Definition or formula

Count of [Confirmed newsletter signups]

Typical data sources

» Email marketing software
» WordPress plug-in that is used to manage your email marketing campaign

Common problems and mistakes

This signup rate is very strongly affected by the quality of any 'freebie' that you are offering and the type of signup form you are using. It's not uncommon for your signup rate to go up by a factor of 10 when you move from simple, passive, inline forms to more assertive "popover forms".

Facebook follower growth

Ref: S6.3.2.1
Silver Star KPI

Drives: We attract people through Facebook
To: We gain sales through organic web traffic

Description

Rather than counting page hits or page likes this measure refers to the number of unique people who are taking an interest in your business.

You should be looking to consistently grow your following through interesting content and engaging with your audience.

Example from Chaos Coffee Shop

Charlie has seen a steady growth in Chaos Coffee's Facebook following. Last month he added 50 followers to his base of 2,000.

Follower growth = 50 / 2,000 = 2.5%

Definition or formula

[Additional followers in period] / [Total followers for previous period]

Typical data sources

» Facebook Insights

Facebook page engagement

Ref: S6.3.2.3
Silver Star KPI

Drives: We attract people through Facebook
To: We gain sales through organic web traffic

Description

Total number of unique people who engaged with your Page, as well as different engagement types. An 'engagement' is a 'like', 'comment' or 'share'.

Engagement also contributes towards reach. When users engage, your post will appear in their timeline, increasing visibility to their friends. Engagement is also a factor in Facebooks EdgeRank algorithm - if you rank well on this you will appear in more News Feeds.

Example from Chaos Coffee Shop

Charlie's Chaos Coffee logs into the Facebook insights and finds...

Page engagement: 3,000

The engagement figure is not good or bad in itself, the key insight is from the **trend**. Is it showing a meaningful trend up or down and can that trend be linked to marketing/advertising activity?

Definition or formula

Count of [Comments + Likes + Shares + Mentions] / [Post Reach]

Typical data sources

» Facebook Insights

Total reach

Ref: S6.3.2.4
Gold Star KPI

Drives: We attract people through Facebook
To: We gain sales through organic web traffic

Description

The number of unique people who were served any activity from your Page.

You can drive reach organically (not driven by paid adverts), using payments, or virally (people share your content). Reach shows your effective audience and is a better measure of audience than Fans, who may not have seen your post, and it may well have reached people who are not Fans.

Example from Chaos Coffee Shop

Charlie shared a picture of a donut that looked a lot like his Pug dog. Of course he didn't pay to promote this picture - it doesn't really say a lot about the quality of his donuts. His post went a bit crazy and his Facebook stats showed the following:

Organic reach: 80k

Viral reach: 1.2m

Definition or formula

[Total Reach] as reported by your advertising platform

Typical data sources

» Facebook Insights

Common problems and mistakes

As with all things Facebook, or social media, being popular doesn't automatically translate into better business. Important though it is, don't obsess just on Reach.

Twitter engagements

Ref: S6.3.3.1
Gold Star KPI

Drives: We attract people through Twitter
To: We gain sales through organic web traffic

Description

Total number of times a user interacted with a Tweet. Clicks anywhere on the Tweet, including Retweets, replies, follows, likes, links, cards, hashtags, embedded media, username, profile photo, or Tweet expansion. Twitter offers both Engagement Rate (a percentage) and Engagements (a count of Engagements) going back over the past 28 days.

Engagement rate can tell you whether you are increasing your web activity, ROI (return on investment) or brand awareness.

Example from Mayhem Manufacturing

Mohammed has started sharing pictures of his new product lines on Twitter. He looks at the Engagements with each post and is seriously thinking about doing this BEFORE he launches a new product. Here's the results from his last 4 posts….

* *Armoured gauntlet wireless mouse: 2k engagements*
* *Gollum 'Precious' sunblock: 1.2k engagements*
* *Hobbit Hole Dog Kennel: 35k engagements*
* *Orc facial cleanser: 400 engagements*

Clearly there's a lot more interest in the Hobbit Dog Kennel than the other lines.

Definition or formula

Count of [Engagements] for period. Broken down by Tweet if required.

Typical data sources

» Twitter analytics

Twitter followers

Ref: S6.3.3.2
Silver Star KPI

Drives: We attract people through Twitter
To:　　We gain sales through organic web traffic

Description

The count of your business account followers, subscribing to your Tweets, on Twitter.

Whilst a healthy following can be the sign of good content and engagement, it's probably best to focus on Twitter Engagements directly. Having lots of followers can rapidly become an ego trip, and it's best not to obsess on this.

Example from Chaos Coffee Shop

Charlie tweets discount coupons for use on quiet days of the week. These seem popular and he now has 2,100 followers and rising.

Twitter Followers: 2,100

Definition or formula

Count of [Twitter followers]

Typical data sources

» Tweets from user admin page on twitter.com

Common problems and mistakes

Just because you have a large following, don't assume that anyone notices or reads your tweets. There are lots of ways to grow your following, including 'buying' followers through third parties. Don't even think about doing this, as the followers you buy (if they even exist) are not following you because they are genuinely interested, so no good will come of it.

Tweets

Ref: S6.3.3.3
Silver Star KPI

Drives: We attract people through Twitter
To:　　We gain sales through organic web traffic

Description

This is simply the number of times you have tweeted in the period being measured.

To build engagement you need to tweet. You are unlikely to get meaningful engagement unless you tweet reasonably frequently. Keep an eye on this to make sure you are out there and giving followers a chance to engage and share.

Example from Dangerous Developers

Daniella knows that Twitter is 'important' but always seems to get side-tracked. She looked at her Twitter stats for the last 28 days and sees this…

Tweets: 1 last month

She resolves to do better next month.

Definition or formula

Count of [Tweets] per period

Typical data sources

» Tweets from user admin page on twitter.com

Common problems and mistakes

Quantity does not mean quality. Regular tweets keep you fresh in the mind of your followers, but too many may lead to people **unfollowing** you.

555

Retweets

Ref: S6.3.3.4
Silver Star KPI

Drives: We attract people through Twitter
To: We gain sales through organic web traffic

Description
Number of times users retweeted the tweet.

Retweets are where Twitter users share a tweet in their Twitter feed with those who follow them. A retweet indicates that content is regarded as important and people feel the urge to share it with people who follow them.

Retweets give rapid feedback on the quality of your tweets. Lots of retweets mean people like and value what you are tweeting. No retweets shows indifference.

Example from Chaos Coffee Shop
Charlie uses a third party website to check to see how many of his tweets have been retweeted. He finds that for his posts this month…

Retweets: 2

Definition or formula
Count of [Retweets]

Typical data sources
» Third party Twitter analytics websites

Common problems and mistakes
Retweets can indicate outrage or shock, so remember to look at the context of a spike of retweets, not just the figure.

Before-and-after traffic and sales

Ref: S6.4.1.1
Silver Star KPI

Drives: Lots of people see our advert
To: We use TV/radio advertising effectively

Description
Unless we use a discount voucher or some other kind of tracking code it can be difficult to identify cause-and-effect with TV and radio advertising. To work around this we can simply look at the raw volume of sales traffic before and after the advertising campaign. Many things can affect sales volume and customer visits. Make sure you understand what the drivers are before you get too excited or depressed about the success/failure of your campaign.

Example from Chaos Coffee Shop
Charlie ran a radio advertising campaign on the local radio station. He tracked sales and customer numbers in the week before and the week after.

Week before radio campaign: £5,500 revenue, 1,100 customers

Week of the radio campaign: £6,500 revenue, 1,625 customers

Definition or formula
Count of [Revenue during promotion] / Count of [Revenue before promotion]

or

Count of [Traffic during promotion] / Count of [Traffic before promotion]

Typical data sources
» Various, depending on channel

Common problems and mistakes
Sales volumes can vary regardless of whether you're running an advertising campaign or not. Try to separate natural sales variation from any increase generated through an advertising campaign. Look and see if there are days-of-the-week, week-of the-month or month-of-the year underlying trends that you need to be aware of before you jump to any conclusions about how successful your advertising is.

Marketing Return on Investment
(ROI)

Ref: S6.4.2.1
Gold Star KPI

Drives: Our TV/Radio adverts deliver leads and sales
To: We use TV/radio advertising effectively

Description

Return on investment tells you how much profit you get back for your spend on advertising. If you get more than £1 profit back for every £1 spent on advertising then it is a good investment and if it's *less* than £1 return for every £1 spent on advertising then it is a poor investment.

Some campaigns will have an enduring effect for some time after it is run (still have that advert's theme tune for chocolate rattling round your head 20 years later, anyone?) so use judgement when you decide on the period over which you measure the impact of your adverts.

Example from Chaos Coffee Shop

Charlie's Radio advertising campaign cost him £1,000 and delivered an extra £5,000 in sales over the next 3 months. The gross profit on those extra sales was £4,381, so...

Charlie's ROI: 3,381 / 1,000 = 3.4:1

So it looks like those radio ads were a pretty good investment. Of course he may have some additional benefit after this four week period, pushing the ROI even higher.

Definition or formula

Sum of [Additional gross profit from advertising - Advertising spend] / Sum of [Advertising spend]

Typical data sources

» Sales records and advertising invoices

Common problems and mistakes

We use additional gross profit for this calculation on the assumption that overheads and fixed costs have already been covered by your 'base sales' so every extra item sold yields the 'gross profit' - the sale price of the item less any direct costs. If your sales actually dipped during a campaign this assumption would no longer be valid.

Sales revenue generated by channel

Ref: S6.5.1.1
Gold Star KPI

Drives: Our promotional spend is cost effective
To: We manage our advertising spend effectively

Description

Shows the amount of revenue generated by channel, for example inline adverts, Facebook or Twitter. This is fairly straightforward to do where your channels have traceability. It can become harder where you have non-traceable campaigns running (like TV, Radio or newspaper campaigns with no traceable code or coupon).

Example from Mayhem Manufacturing

Mohammed can see where his sales come from each month and has collected the following data:

- Facebook £750, Twitter £400, Google AdWords £2,000 and organic web £675

He can also show this as a percentage split, by dividing each by the total revenue for that period (£3,825)...

* *Facebook £750 / £3,825 = 20%*
* *Twitter £400 / £3,825 = 10%*
* *Google AdWords £2,000 / £3,825 = 52%*
* *Organic web £675 / £3,825 = 18%*

Definition or formula

Sum of [Sales value by channel] for period

Typical data sources

» Sales tracking software
» Facebook dashboard
» Twitter analytics
» Web shop analytics

Common problems and mistakes

It may take some care and attention to separate out organic web traffic from sales that originate elsewhere. Remember some of your 'organic' web sales may originate from social media. You can normally figure out the source of traffic from your website admin page, but it may take some digging.

Promotional cost per lead by channel

Ref: S6.5.1.2
Silver Star KPI

Drives: Our promotional spend is cost effective
To: We manage our advertising spend effectively

Description
For Facebook we might define a 'lead' as a link click. If we know the 'Cost per click' for Facebook, then it will give us the cost per lead for that particular channel.

Example from Mayhem Manufacturing
Mohammed ran a Google AdWords campaign on AdWords. He counts each AdWords click as a lead. The price per click on AdWords is £0.40, so that is his 'Promotional cost per lead'.

Definition or formula
[Cost per lead]

or

Sum of [total campaign cost] / [number of leads generated]

Typical data sources
» Landing page
» Phone and email records (for leads)
» Advertising invoices for costs

Common problems and mistakes
This measure can help you figure out where there are problems in your sales pipeline. If you have a low 'cost per lead' but a high 'cost per sale' then you are almost certainly pulling in poor 'qualified' leads - leads which are unlikely to buy from you for any number of reasons (inappropriate product, wrong area, too expensive etc).

Promotional cost per sale by channel

Ref: S6.5.1.3
Gold Star KPI

Drives: Our promotional spend is cost effective
To: We manage our advertising spend effectively

Description
This measure is the promotional cost per sale, by channel. It enables us to decide which channel is giving us best value for our sales budget.

Example from Mayhem Manufacturing
The AdWords campaign delivered 1,000 leads at a cost of £0.40 each. These led to 5 sales. So the cost per sale was….

[Cost of campaign] / [Number of sales resulting from campaign]

Promotional cost per sale: £400 / 5 = £80

Ouch! Each sale, with a gross profit of £10, is costing £80. Mohammed needs to have a serious look at his AdWords campaign.

Definition or formula
[Cost per sale] by channel

or

Sum of [total campaign cost] / Count of [Sales generated]

Typical data sources
» Sales records and advertising invoices

Common problems and mistakes
Just because one particular sales channel seems to be cheaper per lead than another don't automatically discard the more expensive channel. It may be the most cost-effective channel is saturated so reallocating budget may not give you the increase in sales expected. Also additional sales through less "cost-effective" channels may still be profitable, so think carefully before pulling the plug on a profitable campaign even if it's not as attractive as your superstar channel.

Revenue generated per ad

Ref: S6.5.1.4
Silver Star KPI

Drives: Our promotional spend is cost effective
To: We manage our advertising spend effectively

Description

Revenue generated per ad shows you the gross amount of extra income brought in as a result of advertising.

The ease of measuring this varies substantially depending on the channel. For online it is extremely easy to get this figure: more often than not it is provided by your online advertising platform. For print, TV and radio it is more challenging. In that situation you might be better off looking at 'before-and-after traffic and sales'.

Example from Mayhem Manufacturing

For Mohammed's AdWords campaign he only ran one advert. This advert generated £75 in sales.

Revenue generated per ad: £75

Definition or formula

Sum of [Additional sales revenue resulting from advertising] per advert

Typical data sources

» Sales records, advertising invoices and ad analytics

Common problems and mistakes

Remember this is nothing to do with profitability, simply revenue. Shifting extra unprofitable units will result in revenue generated from an ad but ultimately losses to the business even before you factor in the cost of advertising. So it's critical that you understand the net profit on any product you decide to promote and don't get carried away just because an advert is generating revenue.

Total advertising spend

Ref: S6.5.1.5
Gold Star KPI

Drives: Our promotional spend is cost effective
To: We manage our advertising spend effectively

Description

The total amount spent on advertising in the period being measured.

Keeping a handle on what you're spending on advertising, like any business cost control, is crucial. If you're making a net profit on your advertising then great, but make sure you KNOW this and aren't just guessing.

Example from Chaos Coffee Shop

Charlie spent £1,000 on radio adverts and £200 on targeted local AdWords in the last month.

Total advertising spend: £1,000 + £200 = £1,200

Definition or formula

Sum of [Advertising spend for all channels]

Typical data sources

» Advertiser invoices

Common problems and mistakes

Even if you're running a successful and profitable advertising campaign, just make sure you keep an eye on cash flow. A big step up in sales is great in theory but it can put considerable stress on your cash flow if you don't keep an eye on things.

Sales per visit by channel

Ref: S6.5.1.6
Silver Star KPI

Drives: Our promotional spend is cost effective
To:　　We manage our advertising spend effectively

Description
The average value of sales, per transaction, by channel.

Example from Mayhem Manufacturing
Analysing sales records, Mohammed finds...

Average sales value by channel per sale:

* *Facebook adverts: £25*
* *Google adverts: £36*
* *Twitter: £12*
* *Newsletter: £175*

Digging into the numbers, he finds that newsletter customers are much more likely to buy his high-value Turtle Table, whereas social media customers are much more likely to buy his low-cost Volcano pen pot.

Definition or formula
Average of [Sales transaction value] by advertising channel

Typical data sources
» Sales records
» Advertising invoices
» Ad analytics

Common problems and mistakes
Be clear whether you are including postage, packaging and sales tax in the raw figures used to calculate this KPI.

This measure relies on our ability to identify the source channel of a sale. This is generally easier with electronic promotional channels. For channels like radio and TV the use of channel-specific promotion codes may make it easier to identify the sales source.

Promotion generated leads volume by channel

Ref: S6.5.2.1
Gold Star KPI

Drives: Our promotions perform well
To:　　We manage our advertising spend effectively

Description
The number of sales leads that are created by your marketing activity, split by channel (online adverts, Facebook, Twitter etc.)

Segmenting your promotional campaigns by channel enables you to focus in on the channels that are delivering best for you. This measure simply looks at the number of leads by channel to give you that focus.

Example from Dangerous Developers
Daniella used trade press adverts and a stand at 'AppyDayz trade show' to generate new leads. She saw the following:

* *25 leads from the trade show*

* *3 leads referencing the advert in trade press*

This shows the leads volumes by promotional channel.

Definition or formula
Count of [Promotion generated leads] by promotion type

Typical data sources
» Landing page
» Phone and email records etc.

Common problems and mistakes
It can be tricky to identify where a lead comes from for some promotions - e.g. press adverts. Best ask the lead, or offer a discount code that enables you to identify the origin of the lead.

Lead landing page conversion rate

Ref: S6.5.2.2
Gold Star KPI

Drives: Our promotions perform well
To: We manage our advertising spend effectively

Description

The ratio of people visiting the page to the number taking intended action (for example, buying something).

Often campaigns have a landing page intended to "seal the deal" and make a sale when someone visits that page. Looking at the ratio of visitors to sales can give you a good indication of how well your page is designed and is performing.

Example from Mayhem Manufacturing

Mohammed has a dedicated landing page to promote his high-end Turtle Tables. His WordPress dashboard shows that of 100 visitors to that lead landing page, 1 bought a Turtle Table…

Lead landing page conversion rate = 1 / 100 = 1%

Definition or formula

Count of [Number of conversions] / Count of [Landing page leads]

Typical data sources

» Web site records
» Google analytics
» Web shop analytics

Common problems and mistakes

Particularly for higher value items, people may not buy on the first visit. It may make sense to put some 'baby steps' into the conversion process. For example, you may measure brochure downloads or quotation requests as an 'expression of interest' and a step towards an eventual purchase of an item.

KPI Family: S7
Sales Referrals

Paid referral conversion rate

Ref: S7.1.2.1
Silver Star KPI

Drives: Referral volumes
To: People recommend us for reward

Description
This figure shows the percentage of referrals which we paid for that turned into sales.

If we pay for leads, rather than sales commission, it's important to keep an eye on this figure as you could end up paying for leads that do not convert into sales.

Example from Dangerous Developers
Daniella has a number of network contacts that she has offered sales commission to, if they pass on sales leads that convert. Daniella has had 5 leads in the past year, two of which turned into contracts.

Paid referral conversion rate: 2 / 5 = 40%

Definition or formula
Count of [Referrals converted into sales] / Count of [Sales lead referrals provided]

Typical data sources
» Sales records/sales system

Common problems and mistakes
For big-ticket sales, with low numbers of referrals and conversions, this number can jump around a lot. In this example just one more or fewer sales would take us to 60% or 20% at a stroke.

Number of paid referrals received

Ref: S7.1.2.2
Silver Star KPI

Drives: Referral volumes
To: People recommend us for reward

Description
This measure shows us how many referrals we receive from paid third-parties.

Remember to keep an eye on the quality of these referrals (Inbound paid-for referrals return on investment) and, if you are paying a finder's fee, whether they convert or not.

Example from Dangerous Developers
Daniella had 5 leads passed to her last year by network contacts working on commission.

Number of paid referrals received is 5

Definition or formula
Sum of [Number of inbound paid referrals]

Typical data sources
» Sales records/sales system

Common problems and mistakes
Just be clear you are counting all referrals not just ones that you converted to sales.

Inbound paid-for referrals return on investment (ROI)

Ref: S7.1.3.1
Gold Star KPI

Drives: Quality of referrals
To: People recommend us for reward

Description

Shows the ratio of profit to the cost of paid-for inbound referrals.

This is the acid-test for our inbound referral activity, did the profit from the paid-for referrals more than cover the cost of those paid referrals?

Example from Dangerous Developers

Daniella's leads turned into two contracts worth £80k profit. Her 'Cost of inbound referrals' was £11k.

Inbound paid-for referrals ROI = (£80k - £11k) / £11k = 6.3

That's a lot more than 1, and is a healthy positive return on investment.

Definition or formula

(Sum of [Additional profit] - Sum of [Cost of promotion]) / Sum of [Cost of promotion]

Typical data sources

» Sales records/sales system

Common problems and mistakes

If you are working on commission referrals then you should always have a positive ROI, as long as you understand each product's profitability and negotiate a sensible commission that ensures you still make a profit.

Cost of paid inbound referrals

Ref: S7.1.4.1
Silver Star KPI

Drives: Referral Commissions
To: People recommend us for reward

Description

Total cost of all paid-for referrals, both paid leads and commissions.

This is one of the elements you need in order to work out your ROI for inbound referrals.

Example from Dangerous Developers

Daniella pays 10% commission for leads that convert and a £1k finders fee for leads that don't convert. Of the five leads last year, the two that converted attracted £8k of commission in total, the three that did not convert attracted a total of £3k finders fee.

Total cost of inbound referrals = £11k

Definition or formula

Sum of [Cost of paid inbound referrals] including commissions and finders' fees

Typical data sources

» Sales records/sales system

Unpaid inbound referral conversion rate

Ref: S7.2.1.1
Silver Star KPI

Drives: Asking for referrals
To: People recommend us because they like us

Description

This shows you how well you are turning organic referral leads into sales.

Any big changes in this may invite you to look at your pricing, competition or sales techniques.

Example from Pointless Prose

Patricia gets much of her work by word-of-mouth referrals from previous clients. Last month she had 12 people approach her about work based on recommendations. Of these, 8 turned into paying work.

Unpaid referral conversion rate: 8 / 12 = 67%

Definition or formula

Count of [Unpaid inbound referrals converting into sales] / Count of [Unpaid inbound referrals]

Typical data sources

» Sales records/sales system

Number of inbound unpaid referrals

Ref: S7.2.1.4
Gold Star KPI

Drives: Asking for referrals
To: People recommend us because they like us

Description

Unpaid referrals are where people recommend us for no specific reward. This measure is a simple count of those referrals.

Most of us make frequent unpaid referrals. We do it when we recommend a good decorator, lawyer or car mechanic. These referrals tend to have high conversion rates because of the credibility of a friend recommending a business or service. The number of unpaid referrals shows us the state of our business reputation and perceived quality of our work. Unpaid referrals are the foundation of any highly successful business, so the bigger this number the better.

Example from Pointless Prose

Patricia gets much of her work by word-of-mouth referrals from previous clients. Last month she had 12 people approach her about work based on recommendations.

Number of inbound unpaid referrals: 12

Definition or formula

Count of [Unpaid inbound referrals]

Typical data sources

» Sales records/sales system

Common problems and mistakes

With a large number of referrals comes risk. If you aren't able to service all the business that comes to you, you risk reputational damage. If this happens you may need to focus on increasing your delivery capacity or put your prices up.

Total value of converted outbound referrals

Ref: S7.3.3.1
Gold Star KPI

Drives: Financial value of referrals
To: We recommend other products for profit

Description

This shows the sales value generated for affiliates through providing outbound leads, in the form of referrals.

If chosen well, these referrals can enhance your reputation with your customer and offer an useful extra stream of income.

Example from Dangerous Developers

Daniella also passes sales leads to other contacts, on a commission basis, when Dangerous Developers can't meet the technical requirements of the customer. She passed on business to other organisations that resulted in £200k of sales for those organisations.

Total value of converted outbound referrals: £200k

Definition or formula

Sum of [Converted outbound referrals value]

Typical data sources

» Sales records/sales system

Common problems and mistakes

The quality and integrity of the service you refer to is a reflection on you and your reputation. If you make a poor choice in referral partners, you can seriously damage your reputation. Choose carefully and keep an eye on the quality of the product or service you are recommending.

Outbound referrals bonuses/commissions

Ref: S7.3.3.4
Gold Star KPI

Drives: Financial value of referrals
To: We recommend other products for profit

Description

Many referral relationships work on the basis of sales commission, with the referrer receiving a percentage of the sales value. This measure shows the total of that commission for a given period.

One of the good things about outbound referrals is typically it's mostly profit, as there's no cost of fulfilment - you are just passing the lead to another company to deliver. So even modest figures can contribute significantly to profitability.

Example from Dangerous Developers

Daniella passed on business to other organisations that resulted in £200k of sales for those organisations. She gets a 10% commission on referred sales which convert. So...

Outbound referrals bonuses/commissions: £20k

Definition or formula

Sum of [Outbound referrals bonuses/commissions]

Typical data sources

» Sales records/sales system

Common problems and mistakes

This measure requires either: (1) a trusting relationship between you and your commission payer or (2) transparency/access to sales figures. The amount you are paid depends on sales data held by another business, so if they are not completely honest, it will be easy for them to defraud you when it comes to commission payments.

Sales Referrals

Sales - Proposals & Contracts

Percentage of proposals accepted

Ref: S8.1.1.1
Gold Star KPI

Drives: The proposals convert into work
To: We write successful proposals

Description

The proportion of proposals that are progressed to the contract stage.

This measures our judgement on when to submit proposals, the quality of our proposals and the competitiveness of our offer. It can often be hard to isolate why a proposal succeeds or fails, so you may have to look at other measures, such as pricing indicators to build a clearer picture.

Example from Roughshod Repairs

Roughshod Repairs submitted 6 proposals to electronics firms, to handle their warranty claims. Of these 2 progressed to contract stage…

Percentage of proposals accepted: 2 / 6 = 33%

Definition or formula

Count of [Proposals accepted] / Count of [Proposals submitted]

Typical data sources

» Sales pipeline spreadsheet or sales software

Common problems and mistakes

You will need to make a decision about whether you simply count the proposals submitted and accepted in a period - and accept you may have a situation where more proposals are accepted than submitted, or you allocate acceptances to the month in which they are submitted. If you go for the second solution you will have to accept that this percentage may change for several months after a monthly figure is calculated. Do what makes sense for your business.

Number of proposals submitted

Ref: S8.1.1.2
Gold Star KPI

Drives: The proposals convert into work
To: We write successful proposals

Description

The number of proposals submitted. For many businesses it's not possible to win work without submitting proposals.

Good quality proposals take time, effort and resources. There's a line to be trodden between keeping a good pipeline of work under way and wasting time and money on hopeless tendering processes.

Example from Roughshod Repairs

Roughshod Repairs submitted 6 proposals to electronics firms last month, to handle their warranty claims.

Number of proposals submitted: 6

Definition or formula

Count of [Proposals submitted]

Typical data sources

» Sales pipeline spreadsheet or sales software

Average proposal request-to-delivery production time

Ref: S8.1.2.1
Gold Star KPI

Drives: Proposal process is swift
To: We write successful proposals

Description

The average time taken, from request through to delivery to client, to produce a proposal.

The prospective client doesn't really care how your internal process works, all they normally care about is when they will get the proposal. This measure shows you how long that process takes.

Example from Roughshod Repairs

Roughshod Repairs submitted 6 proposals last month, they varied from 3 to 30 working days effort to produce them.

Average proposal request-to-delivery production time: 15 working days

Definition or formula

Average of [Elapsed working days from proposal request to delivery]

Typical data sources

» Simple sales production log, noting start dates, finish dates, effort and queries
» Software used to generate your proposals

Common problems and mistakes

If your proposal production process is too slow then you risk looking unprofessional and even missing the submission deadline.

Remember to be clear on whether you are measuring this in working days or calendar days (including weekends and bank holidays). There are arguments for both, depending on your business and market, but be clear on which you are using and be consistent.

Average person hours per proposal

Ref: S8.1.3.1
Silver Star KPI

Drives: Proposal process is efficient
To: We write successful proposals

Description

Average hours of in-house (or paid external) effort required to produce proposals.

Proposals take time and effort. Often they tie up your most skilled and experienced resource. There are direct and indirect costs to the business in producing proposals. This figure gives you some visibility of that cost - in hours.

Example from Roughshod Repairs

Each proposal that Ruby's team prepares involves a full-time owner and many specialist contributors. Through keeping tally sheets on a few proposals, they have found….

Average person hours per proposal: 30 person-hours

Definition or formula

Sum of [Person hours per completed proposal] / Count of [Proposals completed]

Typical data sources

» Simple sales production log, noting start dates, finish dates, effort and queries
» Software used to generate your proposals

Common problems and mistakes

Gathering this information can be tricky. Some organisations are very geared up to measuring effort, sometimes down to 10 minute slots, for others recording effort can be a massive culture shock.

Think about whether you write big proposals that span periods, or whether most proposals are completed 'in-period'. Depending on the nature of the proposals you write, you may decide to track this figure for proposals that are still being written, or only for completed proposals.

Be careful that this, as with any time allocation category, doesn't become a dumping ground for any time that people cannot allocate to other work.

Number of contract-related legal disputes in progress

Ref: S8.2.1.1
Silver Star KPI

Drives: Minimal disputes and legal action
To: Our contracts are clear and effective

Description

The number of legal disputes, at any stage, in flight during that period.

Where litigation is common, and potentially expensive, a business might want to track the number of disputes. If this applies to your business, you will probably want to measure cost, resource commitment and risk too.

Example from Roughshod Repairs

One of Roughshod's electronics customers is claiming that Roughshod performed unnecessary repairs on TVs they were contracted to manage warranty repairs for.

Number of contract-related legal disputes in progress: 1

Definition or formula

Count of [Active contract-related legal disputes]

Typical data sources

» Simple sales production log, noting start dates, finish dates, effort, costs and queries

Average contract request-to-delivery time

Ref: S8.2.2.1
Gold Star KPI

Drives: Contract process is swift
To: Our contracts are clear and effective

Description

The average time taken, from request through to delivery to client, to produce final contracts.

Once a proposal has been accepted you don't want to let that client go 'off the boil' so keeping the contract production time as short as possible is crucial to getting things signed off.

Example from Roughshod Repairs

From request to being dispatched by guaranteed-next-day-delivery the Roughshod Contracts team take on average 17 working days. Adding one day on for actual delivery...

Average contract request-to-delivery time : 18 days

Definition or formula

Average of [Elapsed working days from contract request to delivery]

Typical data sources

» Simple sales production log, noting start dates, finish dates, effort and queries
» Software used to generate your proposals

Common problems and mistakes

The contract delivery process may well include time for negotiations and client queries that may have a delayed response, so a longer-than-ideal time may not be easily fixed in-house. Even if that is the case, it's worth breaking down the contract production process to see where things could be improved.

Average person hours per contract

Ref: S8.2.3.1
Silver Star KPI

Drives: Contract process is efficient
To: Our contracts are clear and effective

Description

The average time taken, from request through to delivery to client, to produce a contract.

Contracts take time and effort. Often senior resource is involved in producing contracts. There are direct and indirect costs to the business in producing proposals. This figure gives you some visibility of that cost - in hours.

Example from Roughshod Repairs

Each contract that Ruby's team prepares involves a full-time owner and some specialist contributors. Through keeping tally sheets they have found…

Average person hours per contract = 13 person-hours

Definition or formula

Sum of [Person hours per completed contact] / Count of [Contracts completed]

Typical data sources

» Sales production log, noting start dates, finish dates, effort and queries
» Software used to generate your proposals, use this to keep track of dates, effort etc.

Common problems and mistakes

Be careful that this, as with any time allocation category, doesn't become a dumping ground for any time that people cannot allocate to other work.

Number of new contracts issued

Ref: S8.2.3.3
Silver Star KPI

Drives: Contract process is efficient
To: Our contracts are clear and effective

Description

The number of new contracts issued in the period.

Signed contracts are the lifeblood of many businesses. Getting contracts issued (and signed) is vital. This figure shows you how you are trending and if there's trouble ahead.

Example from Roughshod Repairs

Ruby's team issued 2 new contracts last month.

Number of new contracts issued: 2

Definition or formula

Count of [New contracts issued] in period

Typical data sources

» Sales production log, noting start dates, finish dates, effort and queries
» Software used to generate your proposals, use this to keep track of dates, effort etc.

Number of new contracts signed off

Ref: S8.2.3.4
Gold Star KPI

Drives: Contract process is efficient
To: Our contracts are clear and effective

Description

The count of the number of contracts agreed and signed off by clients.

Without a signed contract there is no sale. This is a milestone that represents a successful sale and is probably one figure that all businesses keep a very close eye on, whether they have read a book on KPIs or not.

Example from Roughshod Repairs

Of the live contracts out with clients to sign off, one was actually signed:

Number of new contracts signed off: 1

Definition or formula

Count of [New contracts signed] in period

Typical data sources

» Sales production log, noting start dates, finish dates, effort and queries
» Software used to generate your proposals, use this to keep track of dates, effort etc.

Common problems and mistakes

For many organisations, this may be a small figure, even zero for some periods, so be careful about targeting a specific figure if you are involved in lower-frequency 'big-ticket' sales.

KPI Family: TI
Business Premises

Maintenance tasks identified

Ref: T1.1.1.1
Silver Star KPI

Drives: The structure and roof are maintained
To: Our premises are well maintained

Description

A key part of staying on top of maintenance is identifying a steady stream of appropriate maintenance tasks on the properties we use. This figure shows the simple tally of tasks identified.

Example from Roughshod Repairs

Roughshod's office is a free-standing 60 year-old building with some exterior cladding and remodelled interior to make it feel a little more modern.

Robin, one of the team, looks after building maintenance. She keeps a list of maintenance tasks that she either fixes herself or gets subcontractors in to deal with as-and-when required.

Based on her current list...

Number of maintenance tasks identified: 23

Definition or formula

Count of [Maintenance tasks identified]

Typical data sources

» Maintenance log
» Maintenance management system

Maintenance tasks completed

Ref: T1.1.1.2
Silver Star KPI

Drives: The structure and roof are maintained
To: Our premises are well maintained

Description

Maintenance tasks need to be completed to be of any benefit. This figure shows the proportion of those tasks completed.

Example from Roughshod Repairs

Of the tasks identified, Robin has a one-month goal for completing those tasks (unless it's urgent, e.g. leaking roof, or safety-related). Of the 23 tasks identified last month, 17 have been completed.

Percentage maintenance tasks completed: 17 / 23 = 74%

Definition or formula

Count of [Maintenance tasks completed] / Count of [Maintenance tasks identified]

Typical data sources

» Maintenance log
» Maintenance management system

Maintenance spend - premises

Ref: T1.1.1.3
Gold Star KPI

Drives: The structure and roof are maintained
To: Our premises are well maintained

Description

The overall cost of maintenance on the properties we use.

Example from Roughshod Repairs

Roughshod spent £2,472 on repairs and maintenance of their premises last month.

Maintenance spend: £2,472 (last month)

Definition or formula

Sum of [Costs related to property repair and maintenance]

Typical data sources

» Maintenance log
» Maintenance management system
» Finance records
» Finance system

Cosmetic tasks completed

Ref: T1.1.2.2
Silver Star KPI

Drives: The cosmetic appearance of the building is maintained
To: Our premises are well maintained

Description

When we decide to sort a cosmetic issue, it's normally because it needs improving.

Cosmetic tasks often slip down the agenda compared with urgent (e.g. leaky roof) or safety-related (e.g. loose stair carpet) tasks. Whilst that's quite understandable, as humans we tend to stop noticing cosmetic issues, but customers and visitors do notice.

We need to make sure we actually do the task. This percentage shows how good we are at following through on this.

Example from Roughshod Repairs

Of the 23 maintenance tasks identified last month, 7 of them were 'Cosmetic' tasks. Six cosmetic tasks remain outstanding over a month later.

Percentage of cosmetic tasks completed: 1 / 7 = 14%

Definition or formula

Count of [Cosmetic maintenance tasks completed] / Count of [Cosmetic maintenance tasks identified]

Typical data sources

» Maintenance log
» Maintenance management system

Decoration spend

Ref: T1.1.2.3
Silver Star KPI

Drives: The cosmetic appearance of the building is maintained
To: Our premises are well maintained

Description

Keeping the property looking presentable is important for most businesses. This is a simple total of the spend on decorative costs.

This figure enables us to keep an eye on the cosmetic property spend to make sure we aren't neglecting or overspending on property appearance.

Example from Roughshod Repairs

Last month Roughshod spent £1,120 on painting and decorating projects.

Decoration spend: £1,120

Definition or formula

Sum of [Spend on premises decoration and cosmetic appearance]

Typical data sources

» Maintenance log
» Maintenance management system
» Finance records
» Finance system

Planned utility testing activities completed on time - percentage

Ref: T1.2.1.1
Silver Star KPI

Drives: All other utilities have been tested to required standard
To: Our premises are safe

Description

Law dictates that a number of utilities and electrical devices need to be tested each year.

Track compliance with this requirement to head off safety and legal problems later on.

Example from Roughshod Repairs

Last month an appliance safety check and gas safety check was due at the Roughshod Repairs premises. Both checks took place, as intended.

* *Number of checks planned: 2*
* *Number of checks performed: 2*

Percentage of planned utility testing activities completed on time: 100%

Definition or formula

Count of [Utility and mandatory check tasks completed] / Count of [Utility and mandatory check tasks scheduled]

Typical data sources

» Maintenance log
» Maintenance management system
» Diary records of required testing

Planned risk assessments completed

Ref: T1.2.2.2
Gold Star KPI

Drives: We have undertaken risk assessments where appropriate
To: Our premises are safe

Description

Risk assessments are an important part of health and safety for many businesses. Assessing (and recording outcomes of) property related risks is essential and this figure will show you whether you are implementing your plan.

This assumes you have a plan in place. If you haven't, get your skates on and sort one out. People can get hurt if you don't do this stuff.

Example from Roughshod Repairs

The team at Roughshod Repairs think they have risk assessed most of their 'business as usual' risks, but have a schedule of reviewing risks to make sure the assessments remain relevant to the activities as they are performed currently.

* *Last month 6 risk assessment reviews were due*
* *Last month 6 scheduled risk assessments were performed*

Percentage of planned risk assessments completed: 100%

Definition or formula

Count of [Risk assessment tasks completed] / Count of [Risk assessment tasks scheduled]

Typical data sources

» Maintenance log
» Maintenance management system
» Diary records of required risk assessments

Number of outstanding safety-related actions

Ref: T1.2.2.3
Gold Star KPI

Drives: We have undertaken risk assessments where appropriate
To: Our premises are safe

Description

If you identify safety-related actions - things that need to be fixed on the property because they are risky - you need to make sure you fix them. This number shows how many actions are still outstanding.

Identifying an issue then not fixing it leaves you hugely exposed if an accident then happens. Decide on a reasonable time frame to take action and track anything that slips past this time frame as 'outstanding'.

Example from Roughshod Repairs

Of the 23 maintenance tasks identified last month, 2 of them were 'Safety' tasks. No safety tasks remain outstanding over a month later.

Number of outstanding safety related actions: 0

Definition or formula

Count of [Outstanding safety related actions]

Typical data sources

» Maintenance log
» Maintenance management system
» Safety incident log

KPI Family: T2
Stock

Mislabelled units

Ref: T2.1.1.1
Silver Star KPI

Drives: We know what we have
To: We stock the correct items

Description

Mislabelled units could result in the need to re-label stock items, customer complaints or potential fatalities (mislabelled food products have the potential to kill customers with allergies). This percentage shows how much of an issue you have. Mislabelled stock can also lead to stock-outs and customer frustration.

Tracking **mislabelled** units helps us identify systematic (or sporadic) labelling issues, preventing rework costs, out of date or permanently lost stock items.

Example from Woeful Widget Warehouse

Of 100 SKUs (stock keeping units, or 'types' of product), one pallet was incorrectly labelled.

Percentage mislabelled units: 1 / 100 = 1%

Definition or formula

Count of [Units discovered mislabelled] / Count of [Unit put away]

Typical data sources

» Stock management system
» Stock tracking spreadsheet

Common problems and mistakes

Of course, many of the mislabelling issues may not be discovered until a full stock take - leading to significant lag in this measure.

Misplaced units

Ref: T2.1.1.2
Silver Star KPI

Drives: We know what we have
To: We stock the correct items

Description

At best, misplaced units result in re-locating a stock item. At worst it means losing that item forever. This percentage shows how much of an issue you have.

The percentage of **misplaced** units helps us identify systematic (or sporadic) put-away issues, preventing rework costs, out of date, or permanently lost stock items.

Misplaced stock can also lead to stock-outs and customer frustration.

Example from Woeful Widget Warehouse

Of 100 SKUs (stock keeping units, or 'types' of product), two were later discovered to have been incorrectly located and/or the location was incorrectly added to the stock keeping system.

Percentage misplaced units: 2 / 100 = 2%

Definition or formula

Count of [Units discovered misplaced / Count of [Unit put away]

Typical data sources

» Stock management system
» Stock tracking spreadsheet

Common problems and mistakes

Many of the located stock issues may not be discovered until a full stock take - leading to significant lag in this measure.

Stock-outs

Ref: T2.2.1.3
Gold Star KPI

Drives: We stock the correct items
To: We optimise the amount of stock we hold

Description

When an item that a customer orders is out of stock - that's a stock-out.

If it's an unintended stock-out - something we would normally intend to have in stock, but isn't - that's bad. Tracking unintended stock-outs and fixing them to root cause is the best way to prevent them in future.

Example from Woeful Widget Warehouse

On 23 occasions in the past month, Woeful Widget Warehouse has been out of stock on 'core' items that customers have ordered.

Stock-outs: 23

Definition or formula

Count of [Stock-outs]

Typical data sources

» Stock management system
» Stock tracking spreadsheet
» Order system

Total stock value

Ref: T2.2.2.1
Gold Star KPI

Drives: We manage working capital
To: We optimise the amount of stock we hold

Description

Stock can represent a significant amount of tied up cash (working capital).

Having too much stock can starve your business of cash. Having too little stock can lead to stock-outs and longer lead times. There's a balance to be had, and keeping an eye on this measure, Inventory Turnover Ratio (page 347) and the Stock-outs (definition opposite) measure should give you an indication of how you are doing.

Example from Woeful Widget Warehouse

Based on the current stock in the system…

Total stock value: £400k

Definition or formula

Sum of (Cost price of sellable stock]

Typical data sources

» Stock management system
» Stock tracking spreadsheet
» Order system

Common problems and mistakes

If we have reliable and consistent figures on theft and damage, it makes sense to estimate the levels of both losses since the last stock take and factor these into our stock value figure as an estimate.

Note, damaged, out of date or unsellable stock should be written down/off as appropriate.

Total theft value

Ref: T2.3.1.2
Gold Star KPI

Drives: Our stock is safe and secure
To: We minimise waste and losses

Description
Things get stolen, particularly in retail environments. Tracking and managing this figure is essential to protect our margins, particularly in tight-margin businesses.

Example from Woeful Widget Warehouse
Woeful Widget's theft figure is very low, thanks to a stable and long-term workforce, but a few items (£250 in the past month) seem to have gone missing between the supplier and the stock put-away.

Total theft value = £250

Definition or formula
Sum of [Losses due to theft]

Typical data sources
» Stock management system
» Stock tracking spreadsheet
» Order system
» Stock taking reconciliation

Common problems and mistakes
It may be hard to distinguish between theft, mislabelling and misplacing stock, at least until a full stock take. Keeping all three under control gives us the best chance of identifying and tackling specific issues when they pop up.

Warehouse On-Time-In-Full

Ref: T2.4.1.3
Gold Star KPI

Drives: We manage operational performance well
To: We can access the right items swiftly, accurately and easily

Description
The warehouse exists to fulfil complete orders at the right time. The on-time-in-full (OTIF) measure shows how often we achieve this goal.

The reasons behind the OTIF percentage will lie with the other measures here, but OTIF gives a great headline figure to start with.

Example from Woeful Widget Warehouse
The warehouse keeps a record of 'problems' with orders. A problem is either the wrong product, missing order item or late shipment. All the problems last month were around incorrect or missing items in dispatched orders. 52 of 275 orders had problems:

Warehouse OTIF: (275-52) / (275) = 81%

Definition or formula
(Count of [Orders shipped] - Count of [Incorrect and/or late shipping]) / Count of [Orders shipped]

Typical data sources
» Stock management system
» Stock tracking spreadsheet
» Order system

Total holding costs

Ref: T2.4.2.3
Silver Star KPI

Drives: We manage operational costs well
To: We can access the right items swiftly, accurately and easily

Description
Holding stock involves cost. These costs include building maintenance, heating, fork lift truck costs, labour, parts etc. This figure is the total of all stock associated costs.

Example from Woeful Widget Warehouse
Will goes through his financial records and identifies the following costs related to holding stock:

* *Warehouse staff (3) £60,000*
* *Warehouse building upkeep £3,000*
* *Forklift truck costs £10,000*
* *Packaging £15,000*
* *Energy £4,000*
* *New racking £12,000*
* *Other costs £8,000*

Total holding costs: £112,000

Definition or formula
Sum of [Warehousing related costs and expenses]

Typical data sources
» Stock management system
» Stock tracking spreadsheet
» Finance records
» Finance system

Common problems and mistakes
You will need to decide whether you include the cost of cash tied up in physical stock (working capital) in this costs calculation.

Stock

Fraud & Theft

Cashing-up discrepancies

Ref: U1.1.1.4
Gold Star KPI

Drives: We spot incidents of theft
To: We spot and record incidents of fraud and theft

Description

A common method of employee theft from retail businesses is till theft. This figure shows the difference between the cash in the till (less initial 'float') and the value of sales recorded by the till.

Example from Chaos Coffee Shop

Charlie had some issues in the past with a dishonest employee. He noticed that the till was consistently short of around £30 a day when the till was 'cashed up' at the end of the day.

Cashing-up discrepancies from a day that was short:

*   Till roll sales recorded: £916.67
*   Cash (minus float): £886.67
*   Cashing-up discrepancy: £30

Definition or formula

Sum of [Cash sales recorded on till roll] - Sum of [Cash in till minus float]

Typical data sources

» Till roll
» Electronic till records
» Manual count of cash in till
» Cashing up records

Cash register 'no sales'

Ref: U1.1.1.5
Silver Star KPI

Drives: We spot incidents of theft
To: We spot and record incidents of fraud and theft

Description

Sales rung into the till system as 'no sales', with the staff then pocketing the cash from the transaction, is a common method of till fraud.

An excessive number of 'no sales' on the till roll may be an indication that staff theft is taking place from the till. Typically there may be other indicators, such as an deliberately placed obstruction in front of the customer-side till display.

Example from Chaos Coffee Shop

Looking at the till roll, Charlie sees 35 'No sales' on the till roll from a certain date, when he suspected one of the staff may be stealing from the till.

'No sales' = 35

This seems suspicious, as Charlie knows that there were typically no more that 10 'no sales' in the past.

Definition or formula

Count of ['No sales']

Typical data sources

» Till roll
» Electronic till records

Total value of fraud

Ref: U1.1.2.1
Gold Star KPI

Drives: We spot incidents of fraud
To: We spot and record incidents of fraud and theft

Description
The value of fraud committed.

Example from Roughshod Repairs
The Roughshod team have uncovered a fraud where customers would demand repair or replacement of foreign-bought broken games consoles they bought on internet auction sites, sold for parts only. This fraud was successful in 5 cases last month.

Total value of fraud last month: £550

Definition or formula
Sum of [Value of fraud]

Typical data sources
» Fraud log, once fraud is detected

Total value of theft recovered

Ref: U1.2.1.1
Silver Star KPI

Drives: We recover theft items
To: We recover fraud and theft losses wherever possible

Description
Where stolen goods are recovered, this is the value of the recovered goods.

If the goods are not in original condition it may be necessary to reduce the value recorded in line with the reduced resale value.

Example from Chaos Coffee Shop
Charlie wasn't able to get any of his Compost Cakes back.

Total value of theft recovered: £0.00

Definition or formula
Sum of [Value of theft recovered]

Typical data sources
» Recovery log

Total value of fraud recovered

Ref: U1.2.2.1
Silver Star KPI

Drives: We recover fraudulent transactions
To: We recover fraud and theft losses wherever possible

Description
Where fraud has taken place and is discovered, this is the amount recovered.

Example from Roughshod Repairs
The Roughshod team managed to take the fraudsters to the 'Small Claims Court' and have so far recovered £175 of their fraud-related costs.

Total value of fraud recovered: £175

Definition or formula
Sum of [Value of fraud recovered]

Typical data sources

» Recovery log

Total cost of fraud and theft prevention measures

Ref: U1.4.1.1
Silver Star KPI

Drives: We manage the cost of fraud and theft prevention
To: We manage our fraud and theft processes effectively

Description
Where investment has been made to reduce or deter theft or fraud, this is the total amount of investment.

This may be extra security staff, technology investment such as RF tags or closed-circuit cameras.

Example from Roughshod Repairs
The Roughshod team have introduced a new serial number lookup database, written by one of their support team, using serial numbers provided by the console manufacturers. They can identify foreign imports straight from the case form and reject them immediately. The system cost around £700 in development time and effort.

Total cost of fraud and theft prevention measures: £700

Definition or formula
Sum of [Theft or fraud prevention improvements cost]

Typical data sources

» Finance records - identified prevention spends

Ratio of recovered costs to prevention costs

Ref: U1.4.1.3
Gold Star KPI

Drives: We manage the cost of fraud and theft prevention
To: We manage our fraud and theft processes effectively

Description

When we spend money on fraud or theft prevention we want to know it was money well spent. Look at the ratio of benefit to cost (typically in the first year) to decide if it was a sensible investment.

It's hard to measure the deterrence element, unless you have previous data to use as a baseline.

Example from Roughshod Repairs

Based on the monthly cost of the fraud uncovered…

* *Estimated annual cost of import fraud: £550 x 12 months = £6,600*
* *Cost of fraud reduction solution: £700*

Ratio of benefit to cost: £6,600 : £700 = 9.4:1 in first year

Definition or formula

Sum of [Value of fraud recovered] / Sum of [Theft or fraud prevention improvements cost]

Typical data sources

» Finance records - identified prevention spends
» Recovery log

Bibliography

How to Make an IMPACT: Influence, Inform and Impress with Your Reports, Presentations and Business Documents

Financial Times Series

Author	Jon Moon
Publisher	Financial Times/ Prentice Hall
ISBN	0273713329, 9780273713326

Jon Moon's book is a highly readable and practical book on how to present text, tables and diagrams. An absolute must if you want to free yourself from the tyranny of bullet points and template-sameness.

Information Dashboard Design: The Effective Visual Communication of Data

Author	Stephen Few
Publisher	O'Reilly Media Incorporated
ISBN	0596100167, 9780596100162

Many of the ideas I use in my 'BlinkReporting' approach come from Stephen Few's book. It's more of a source book than a bedtime read, but it is a very useful source of ideas and examples.

KPI Checklists

Author	Bernie Smith
Publisher	Metric Press
ISBN	978-1-910047-00-2

The first book on the ROKS™ approach. A high level overview of what's now called the ROKS Enterprise™ approach.

The Visual Display of Quantitative Information

Author	Edward R. Tufte
Publisher	Graphics Press USA
ISBN	0961392142, 9780961392147

This is a classic from the father of Sparklines. If I'm honest, it's the book I read least as it has a fairly dense academic feel to it. However, you cannot fault Tufte's ideas or influence. Worth owning just for the fabulous quality of the physical book!

The Checklist Manifesto: How to Get Things Right

Author	Atul Gawande
Publisher	Profile Books
ISBN	1846683149, 9781846683145

This is probably the most 'un-put-downable' of the books on this list. It is a very compelling argument in favour of using checklists in most complex professional environments (yes, MI department, I'm looking at you!)

Bibliography

HBR's 10 Must Reads On Strategy

Author | Harvard Business Review

Publisher | Harvard Business School Press

ISBN | 9781422157985, 1422157989

This is a clear, simple and really well-written set of articles on the fundamentals of strategy. A classic (and readable) text.

Deep Work

Author | Cal Newport

Publisher | Piatkus (5 Jan. 2016)

ISBN | 0349411905, 978-0349411903

This book is here because I refer to Newport's concept of 'deep work'. It is also well worth a read as a potentially life-changing way of understanding what you are doing and the impact of work quality on your productivity.

Understanding Variation. The Key to Managing Chaos

Author | Donald J Wheeler

Publisher | Longman Higher Education (31 Dec. 1993)

ISBN | 0945320353, 978-0945320357

An old book, but very readable with a crystal-clear explanations of how control charts, specifically XmR charts, work and can be used. Don't be fooled into thinking this just applies to manufacturing businesses!

This is Lean: Resolving the Efficiency Paradox

Author | Niklas Modig and Par Ahlstrom

Publisher | Rheologica Publishing (1 Nov. 2012)

ISBN | 9789198039306

A very clear explanation of Lean that focuses on the *ideas* behind Lean, *not* the toolkit.

The Goal: A Process of Ongoing Improvement

Author | Eliyahu M Goldratt

Publisher | Routledge; 3 edition (17 Nov. 2004)

ISBN | 0566086654, 978-0566086656

A highly readable explanation of the 'theory of constraints' (how production output is determined) written as a thriller.

Thinking, Fast and Slow

Author | Daniel Kahneman

Publisher | Penguin

ISBN | 0141033576, 978-0141033570

A fascinating book on the way in which we make mistakes in our conscious and unconscious thinking. This is where you need to go if you want to find out more about cognitive bias.

Index

Index